A Treasury of Judaism

A Treasury of Judaism

COMPILED AND EDITED BY

Philip Birnbaum

HEBREW PUBLISHING COMPANY · NEW YORK

Acknowledgments

Deep appreciation is hereby expressed to publishers and authors for permission to include in this volume selections from the books listed below.

Samuel Rosenblatt, *Saadyah Gaon—The Book of Beliefs and Opinions,* Yale University Press, 1948.

Stephen S. Wise, *Gabirol's Improvement of the Moral Qualities,* Columbia University Press, 1902.

Moses Hyamson, *Bahya—Duties of the Heart,* Bloch Publishing Company, 1942.

Abraham S. Halkin, *Maimonides' Epistle to Yemen,* translated from the Arabic by Boaz Cohen, New York, 1952.

Samuel Rosenblatt, *Abraham Maimonides' High Ways to Perfection,* The Johns Hopkins Press, 1938.

H. G. Enelow, *Ibn Al-Nakawa's Menorath Hamaor,* Bloch Publishing Company, 1930.

Israel Abrahams, *Hebrew Ethical Wills,* Jewish Publication Society of America, 1926.

Mordecai M. Kaplan, *Luzzatto's Mesillath Yesharim,* Jewish Publication Society of America, 1936.

Louis Ginzberg, *The Legends of the Jews,* Jewish Publication Society of America, 1942.

Jacob R. Marcus, *The Jew in the Medieval World,* Commission on Jewish Education, Cincinnati, 1938.

Louis I. Newman, *The Hasidic Anthology,* Bloch Publishing Company, 1944.

Solomon Schechter, *Studies in Judaism,* Jewish Publication Society of America, 1915.

Abraham E. Millgram, *Anthology of Medieval Hebrew Literature,* Philadelphia, 1935.

ACKNOWLEDGMENTS

Samson Raphael Hirsch, *The Nineteen Letters of Ben Uziel,* Funk and Wagnalls Company, 1899.

Jacob Breuer, *Fundamentals of Judaism,* Philipp Feldheim, New York, 1949.

Louis Ginzberg, *Students, Scholars and Saints,* Jewish Publication Society of America, 1945.

Nahum N. Glatzer, *In Time and Eternity,* Schocken Books, 1946.

Marvin Lowenthal, *The Memoirs of Glueckel of Hameln,* Harper and Brothers (Behrman Book House), 1932.

Menahem G. Glenn, *Israel Salanter,* Dropsie College, 1953.

Irving Fineman, *Hear Ye Sons,* Longmans, Green and Company, 1933.

Jacob B. Agus, *Banner of Jerusalem,* Bloch Publishing Company, 1946.

Herbert Weiner, *From the Teachings of Rav Kook,* Commentary, May 1954.

Contents

CONTENTS

CONTENTS

CONTENTS

My son, make your books your companions. Let your shelves be your treasure grounds and gardens. If you are weary, change from garden to garden. Your desire will renew itself, and your soul will be filled with delight.

—*Rabbi Judah ibn Tibbon*

Foreword

This *Treasury of Judaism* is designed to acquaint the average reader with the ethical teachings of some seventy Jewish classics covering a period of thirty centuries. It contains meaningful selections from the entire Hebrew Bible, the Apocrypha, the Talmud, and a rich variety of works by the best known Jewish teachers and philosophers.

Much of Judaism's great wealth of literature is practically unknown to a vast majority of men and women. In troubled times, however, many of them feel a great and genuine need for an acquaintance with the wisdom of the prophets and their direct successors. It is when the hearts of men are oppressed that they turn for guidance to the precepts of ancient, medieval and contemporary teachers like Moses, Isaiah, Rabbi Akiba, Maimonides and Luzzatto.

Although Judaism is the least known religion, it has had a profound influence on the pattern of universal culture. And this is quite in keeping with a talmudic statement that God gave the Law to Moses in the desert, in a no-man's land, so that the people of Israel might not claim exclusive possession of it. Indeed, it is the Law of Moses that governs huge sections of humanity in the world today.

One of the ancient Rabbis declared that, as all mankind traces its ancestry to Adam, all men are brothers, the children of one parentage. All men, therefore, are equally capable of achieving the zenith of moral and ethical behavior. According to Rabbi Judah of Regensburg, who lived in the twelfth century, the main purpose of Judaism is to promote mutual understanding and peace among all people.

Judaism lays great stress on reverence for parents, respect for the aged, and charity toward the infirm and the weak. In all dealings with men, honesty and truthfulness are absolutely required. Stealing, flattery, falsehood and

13

oppression—even the withholding of a man's wages so much as overnight—are forbidden. Talebearing, gossip and unkind insinuation are prohibited, as is hatred of one's neighbor in one's heart. The dumb animal has claims upon the kindly help of man, even though it belongs to one's enemy.

Justice, truthfulness, care for the weak, regard for the rights of others, love for fellow man and mercy for the beast are the virtues taught by Judaism. "Learn to be good" is the keynote of the prophetic appeal. The tone of Judaism is optimistic. The world is good and life is precious, for both are the creation of God who is the source and ideal of all goodness and morality. As God is merciful and gracious, so should man be. Man, as a child of God, has duties toward himself as well as toward his fellow man. According to a statement in the Talmud, he who subjects himself to needless fasting, or even denies himself the enjoyment of wine, is a sinner. Man is in duty bound to preserve his health. The philosophy of Judaism is best expressed in the familiar maxim: "The world is based on three principles: justice, truth, and peace."

Leo Tolstoy answered the question "What is a Jew?" in these terms: He is the religious fountain out of which all the rest of the peoples have drawn their beliefs and their religions. He is the pioneer of liberty and the pioneer of civilization. "Ignorance was condemned in olden Palestine more even than it is today in civilized Europe." He is the emblem of civil and religious toleration. "Love the stranger and the sojourner," Moses commands, "because you have been strangers in the land of Egypt."

Every civilized person, no matter what his religious belief, cannot help but be interested in the universal aspects of Jewish thought. Here is an attempt to present in one volume a comprehensive picture of Jewish ethical teachings as they developed during several thousand years. Whoever uses this treasury consistently will gain an inspiring conception of the abiding ideals and ideas envisioned by a galaxy of unforgettable prophets and sages. Many will be surprised to learn how much of the thinking which has come down to us through the ages still has a direct bearing on our present-day lives.

Since this book is intended for readers of all ages, it is written throughout in a non-technical and simple style. The editor has chosen to follow the wise counsel of Moses Maimonides who, in a letter to Samuel ibn Tibbon, translator of his famous *Guide for the Perplexed* from Arabic into Hebrew, wrote: "Whoever wishes to translate each word literally, and at the same time adheres slavishly to the order of the words and sentences in the original, will meet with much difficulty. The translator should first try to grasp thoroughly the sense of the subject, and then state the theme with perfect clarity. This, however, cannot be done without changing the order of the words, substituting many words for one word, or one word for many words, so that the subject is perfectly intelligible in the language into which it is translated."

It has been the editor's aim to include in this volume a variety of material to suit everyone's taste in terms of enlightenment, guidance and interesting reading, and make it all intelligible to the ordinary reader without the aid of footnotes and commentaries. Books like Job and Ecclesiastes, which are scarcely read by reason of the many obscure and difficult passages, have been made accessible and instructive to the average person by eliminating whatever is unclear and of doubtful meaning, so that the reader is able to concentrate on that which captures the imagination and stirs the heart.

The ethical teachings in a book like *The Testaments of the Twelve Patriarchs* become even more transparent as a result of condensation. This Jewish document, written in Hebrew more than a century before the common era, has close parallels to passages in the New Testament. According to Dr. R. H. Charles, editor of the Apocrypha in English, "the Sermon on the Mount reflects the spirit and even reproduces the very phrases of our text. Many passages of the Gospels exhibit traces of the same, and St. Paul seems to have used the book as a vade mecum . . ."

Emphasis has been laid on the unity of Jewish teachings

15

which testify to the age-old struggle for peace and brother-hood. As its literature indicates, Judaism has made its influence felt in the moral, social and religious behavior patterns of millions of people throughout the world, and its precepts are practised daily, even though the source of the code is unknown to many.

Unfortunately, many medieval Jewish literary master-pieces suffered in translation and proved unduly difficult to readers unfamiliar with Arabic, for the Hebrew translators rigidly adhered to the syntax and forms of expression characteristic of the Arabic rather than the Hebrew. The same is true of the English translation of the Bible, known as "Bible English," which abounds with puzzling sentences such as: "He redeemeth him from the hand of him that is stronger than he" (Jeremiah 31:11), meaning: *He saves him from a stronger power.* For the sake of clarity, numerous passages have been retranslated here into an English that everybody understands. The pronouns *thou* and *thee* have been used only where they are addressed to God, since they convey a more reverent feeling than the common *you.* As in the English Bibles, no pronouns have been capitalized in the middle of a sentence, since the too frequent use of capitals makes for confusion.

For purposes of simplification, no abbreviations have been used in this book. Phrases like *before the common era* and *in the common era* have not been abbreviated to the usual B.C.E. and C.E. It is sufficient to know that all the historical dates regarding the biblical and the apocryphal books refer to the period preceding the common era (B.C.); otherwise they refer to the common era (C.E.).

It is sincerely hoped that many people will find in this *Treasury of Judaism* much to awaken their interest and stimulate their thinking. They may well be induced to delve further into the classic works condensed herein, and take to heart their message. May this book enlighten the minds of all those who strive to make this world a better place to live in; may it be an inspiration to those who seek knowledge and truth.

PHILIP BIRNBAUM

16

The Bible

It has been said that a knowledge of the Bible without a college education is better than a college education without a knowledge of the Bible. One can learn more about human nature by reading the Bible than by living in the largest city. The Bible has been translated into more than a thousand tongues. It has been, and continues to be, the foremost and best guide toward the ideal moral life. The Bible contains more complete and accurate descriptions of good and evil than any other book extant, and no other book has done so much to influence mankind.

The Bible consists of twenty-four books which are divided into three parts: the Torah, the Prophets and the Writings. The second part—the Prophets—is subdivided into the writings of the Former Prophets and Latter Prophets. The Former Prophets comprise four historical books: Joshua, Judges, Samuel and Kings. The Latter Prophets are also made up of four books: Isaiah, Jeremiah, Ezekiel and the Twelve Minor Prophets. Grouped in one volume, the Twelve Minor Prophets are Hosea, Joel, Amos, Obadiah, Jonah, Micah, Nahum, Habakkuk, Zephaniah, Haggai, Zechariah, and Malachi. They are termed *Minor Prophets* because each of the twelve books is comparatively short. The book of Obadiah, for example, has only one chapter. On the other hand, Isaiah, Jeremiah and Ezekiel are called Major Prophets because the books are long. The book of Isaiah, for example, has sixty-six chapters.

The third part of the Bible, known as Hagiographa or Sacred Writings, consists of the remaining eleven books: Psalms, Proverbs, Job, Song of Songs, Ruth, Lamentations, Ecclesiastes, Esther, Daniel, Ezra-Nehemiah and Chronicles.

The five biblical books which are known as the Five Scrolls are recited in the synagogue, as part of the liturgy, on the following special occasions: *Song of Songs* on Passover; *Ruth* on Shavuoth; *Lamentations* on Tish'ah b'Av, the fast day commemorating the destruction of Jerusalem; *Ecclesiastes* on Sukkoth, the autumn festival; and *Esther* on Purim. The Five Scrolls form a class by themselves, and are arranged in the Hebrew Bible according to the sequence of the said occasions.

The first part of the Bible, from the creation of the world to the death of Moses, is variously referred to by as many as five titles: Torah, Law, Pentateuch, the Five Books of Moses and the Five Fifths (Hummashim). The five books of the Torah are: Genesis, Exodus, Leviticus, Numbers and Deuteronomy. These names are descriptive of the contents of the books: *Genesis* (origin) begins with the story of creation; *Exodus* (going out) tells of the going out from Egypt; *Leviticus* (pertaining to Levites) contains laws which relate to the priests, members of the tribe of Levi; *Numbers* derives its title from the census of the Israelites in the wilderness; *Deuteronomy* (repetition of the law) contains a restatement of the Mosaic laws.

The study of Torah has always been the highest ideal of the Jewish people. The Talmud and the Midrash are rich in quotations from the Torah. The unquenchable thirst for knowledge and education among Jewish people stems from their traditional veneration of the Torah. "The study of Torah excels all things" is an ancient talmudic statement incorporated in the daily prayerbook. According to the Talmud, a single day devoted to the Torah outweighs a thousand offerings; a non-Jew who studies the Torah is as great as the high priest.

One of the sages is quoted in the *Ethics of the Fathers* to the effect that one should study the Torah over and again, for everything is contained in it, and there is nothing more excellent than it. We turn to the Torah again and again, always to discover in it fresh meanings, new approaches to reality. The Torah speaks to us as it has spoken through the centuries to men of all generations.

Genesis

Genesis contains the early history of mankind, describes the lives of the forefathers of Israel, and ends with the death of Joseph. Its records, covering a period of more than two thousand years from the creation, go back to remote antiquity. The narratives in Genesis were handed down, through many generations, by word of mouth before they were ever written down; and these stories became the vehicle for countless ethical and spiritual lessons.

Throughout the book there is a noble conception of man, what he was created to be and what he has the power to become. The statement that man was made in the image of God strikes the keynote of all that follows. The moral grandeur and depth of meaning, as well as the simplicity and sublimity of the story of creation, are universally recognized. All men are descended from Adam and Eve, all men are related; hence the unity of all mankind. This is said to be the most fundamental teaching in the entire Bible: *all* men are created in the image of God.

Israel's ancestors are represented here in their family relations: as husband and wife, parent and child, brother and sister. Here are illustrations of truthfulness, grace and loveliness, with a wealth of instructive example.

Great moral truths are woven into the texture of the narratives of Genesis. Indeed, there is no more impressive book in the Bible than Genesis. Its charm and power are inherent in the personal portraits of Abraham, Jacob and Joseph, breathing and alive in the freshness of the world's dawn.

Like the rest of the Torah, Genesis is primarily a book of instruction; it conveys the idea that the Creator of the universe forever guides those who trust in him. Its language is adapted to the understanding of young and old alike. Children can grasp the outline of its story, while erudite scholars continue to discover fresh meanings in it.

When God first created the heavens and the earth, the world was waste and void; darkness lay over the deep; and the spirit of God moved above the waters.

God said: "Let there be light," and there was light. God saw that the light was good, and he separated the light from the darkness. God called the light Day, and the darkness he called Night. There was evening and there was morning, the first day.

God said: "Let there be an expanse between the waters." And so God made the expanse, and called it Heaven. There was evening and there was morning, the second day.

God said: "Let the waters under the heaven be gathered into one place, and let the dry land appear." And so it was. God called the dry land Earth, and the gathered waters he called Seas. God saw that it was good. Then God said: "Let the earth bring forth plants yielding seed and trees bearing fruits of every kind." And so it was. God saw that it was good. There was evening and there was morning, the third day.

God said: "Let there be lights in the sky, to separate day from night and to mark days and years." And so it was. God made the two great lights, the greater light to rule the day and the lesser light to rule the night, and the stars. God saw that it was good. There was evening and there was morning, the fourth day.

God said: "Let the waters abound in life, and let birds fly above the earth across the sky." And so God created the great sea-monsters and every kind of living creature and every kind of winged bird. God saw that it was good. God blessed them, saying: "Be fruitful, multiply, and fill the waters of the seas; and let the birds multiply on the earth." There was evening and there was morning, the fifth day.

God said: "Let the earth bring forth every kind of living creature, cattle, reptiles, and wild beasts." And so it was. God saw that it was good. Then God said: "Let us make man in our image, after our likeness; let him have dominion over the fish in the sea, the birds of the air, the cattle, every wild beast of the earth, and every reptile that crawls on the earth." So God created man in his own image; male and female he formed them. God blessed them and said: "Be fruitful, multiply, fill the earth and subdue it; have dominion over the fish in the sea, the birds of the air and every living thing that moves upon the earth."

Thus the heavens and the earth were finished, and all their host. By the seventh day God had completed the work which he had made, and he rested on the seventh day from all his work. Then God blessed the seventh day and hallowed it, because on it he rested from all the work which he had done.

The Lord God formed man from the dust of the ground and breathed into his nostrils the breath of life. He planted a garden in Eden, where he put the man to till it and look after it. And the Lord God commanded him, saying: "You are free to eat from any tree in the garden, but you shall not eat from the tree of knowledge, for you shall die the day you eat from it."

Then the Lord God said: "It is not good for man to be alone; I will make a helpmate for him." So the Lord God caused a deep sleep to fall upon the man; he took one of his ribs, shaped it into a woman and brought her to the man. The man said: "This, at last, is bone of my bones and flesh of my flesh; she shall be called woman because she was taken from man."

Now the serpent said to the woman: "Did God say that you must not eat fruit from any tree in the garden?"

The woman replied: "We may eat fruit from the trees of the garden; but, as to the tree in the middle of the garden, God said: 'You shall not eat from it, you shall not touch it, lest you die.'"

"No," said the serpent, "you shall not die; God knows that on the day you eat from it your eyes will be opened and you will be like gods knowing good and evil."

The woman saw that the tree was good for food; she took some of its fruit and ate it; she also gave some to her husband, and he ate. Then the eyes of both were opened and they realized that they were naked, so they hid themselves among the trees of the garden.

The Lord God called to the man: "Where are you?" And he said: "I heard thy voice in the garden and I was afraid, because I was naked, so I hid myself." God said: "Who told you that you were naked? Have you eaten from the tree of which I forbade you to eat?" The man said: "The woman thou gavest me as a companion, she gave me some fruit of the tree, and I ate." Then the Lord God said to the woman: "What is this that you have done?" The woman said: "The serpent misled me, and I ate."

The Lord God said to the serpent: "Because you have done this, cursed are you above all cattle; dust you shall eat all the days of your life." To the woman he said: "In pain you shall bear children, yet your desire shall be for your husband." To the man he said: "Because you have listened to your wife, in the sweat of your brow you shall eat bread till you return to the ground from which you were taken; you are dust, and to dust you shall return."

The man called the name of his wife Eve (Life), because she was the mother of all living beings. Eve bore Cain, and later she bore his brother Abel. Abel was a shepherd, while Cain was a farmer.

In the course of time Cain brought some fruit of the ground as an offering to the Lord, while Abel brought some fat firstlings from his flock. The Lord favored Abel and his offering, but had no regard for Cain and his offering. So Cain was very angry and downcast.

"Why are you angry?" the Lord said to Cain; "why are you downcast? If you do well, you will be accepted; if you do not well, sin is lying in wait for you, eager to be at you, but you must master it."

Cain said to his brother: "Let us go into the field." When they were in the field, Cain rose up against his brother Abel and killed him. And the Lord said to Cain: "Where is your brother Abel?" He said: "I do not know; am I my brother's keeper?" And the Lord said: "What have you done? Your brother's blood cries to me from the ground! And now, cursed shall you be; you shall be a fugitive and wanderer on the earth." And the Lord put a mark on Cain to prevent anyone from killing him.

Now when men began to multiply over the earth, the Lord said: "My spirit shall not remain in man forever, for he is flesh; his days shall be one hundred and twenty years." When the Lord saw that the wickedness of man on earth was great, and that man's impulse is never anything but evil, he said: "I will blot out man from the face of the

22

earth—man and beast and reptile and bird; I am indeed sorry that I have made them."

Noah, however, was an upright man and found favor with the Lord. So God said to Noah: "I have resolved to put an end to all flesh; the earth is filled with violence on account of them; I will destroy them together with the earth. Make yourself an ark, for I am about to bring a flood upon the earth; everything that is on the earth shall perish. You shall enter the ark, you and your sons and your wife and your sons' wives along with you. You shall take into the ark two of every living creature of every kind, to keep them alive with you; they shall be male and female. Store up every sort of food for you and for them." Noah did all that God had commanded him.

After seven days the waters of the flood came upon the earth; all the fountains of the great deep burst forth, and the windows of the heavens were opened. Rain fell upon the earth forty days and forty nights. Whatever was on the dry land died; the Lord blotted every living creature from the earth; only Noah and those inside the ark were left. For a hundred and fifty days the waters swelled over the earth. Then God made a wind blow, and the waters subsided steadily till they dried off the earth.

Noah came out of the ark along with his sons and his wife and his sons' wives. God blessed Noah and his children and said to them: "Be fruitful and multiply, and fill the earth. Whoever sheds the blood of man, by man shall his own blood be shed, for God made man in his own image."

When the whole world had one language, one vocabulary, there was a migration from the east; men came upon a plain in the land of Shinar and settled there. Then they said to one another: "Come, let us make bricks; let us make a name for ourselves by building a city and a tower reaching to heaven; it will keep us from being scattered upon the face of the whole earth."

"They are one people," said the Lord, "and they have one language. Come, let us go down and confuse their language, that they may not understand one another's speech." So the Lord dispersed them over the face of all

the earth, and they gave up building the city. Hence it was
called Babylon, because there the Lord confused the language of the whole earth, and from there the Lord dispersed them over the face of the whole earth.

Abraham was the son of Terah who was a descendant of
Noah's eldest son Shem. Now the Lord said to Abraham:
"Leave your country and go to the land which I will show
you. I will make a great nation of you; all the nations of
the earth shall be blessed through you." So Abraham left
Chaldea, taking his wife Sarah and his nephew Lot with all
the property they had acquired, and reached the land of
Canaan. Then the Lord appeared to Abraham and said: "I
give this land to your descendants." He built an altar to the
Lord who had appeared to him, and he traveled on toward
the Negev.

Abraham was very rich in cattle, silver and gold; and
Lot, who went with Abraham, also had flocks and herds
and tents. The land could not support them both; their
possessions were so large that they could not dwell together. So Abraham said to Lot: "Let there be no strife
between you and me, between your herdsmen and my
herdsmen. Separate yourself from me; if you go to the left,
I will go to the right; or if you go to the right, I will go to
the left."

They parted company, and Lot moved toward Sodom.
Then the Lord said to Abraham: "Look around now from
where you are, northward and southward and eastward
and westward; all the land you see I give to you and your
descendants for all time. I will make your descendants as
numerous as the dust of the ground. Arise, walk through
the length and the breadth of the land, for I give it to you."

Now it was during the reign of Amraphel, king of Shinar,
that four kings captured all the possessions and all the provisions of Sodom and Gomorrah and went away; they also
carried off Lot and his possessions. As soon as Abraham
heard that his kinsman had been taken captive, he led
forth his trained men, three hundred and eighteen of them,
and went in pursuit as far as Dan, where he routed the
enemy. He recovered all the possessions, and also brought

24

back his kinsman Lot with his possessions, and the women and the people.

The king of Sodom went out to meet him, and the king of Salem brought out bread and wine, saying: "Blessed be Abraham by God Most High, Creator of heaven and earth; and blessed be God Most High who has delivered your enemies into your hand!"

The king of Sodom said to Abraham: "Let me have the prisoners, and take the goods for yourself." But Abraham answered the king of Sodom: "I swear to the Lord God Most High, Creator of heaven and earth, that I will not take a thread or string of yours! You will not have to say: 'I have made Abraham rich.' I will take nothing except what the young men have eaten; but let my comrades have their share of the spoil."

After this the Lord said to Abraham in a vision: "Fear not, Abraham, I will shield you; your reward shall be very great." But Abraham said: "Lord God, what canst thou give me when I continue childless, and Eliezer of Damascus, a slave, is my heir?" Then the Lord said to him: "This one shall not be your heir; your own son shall be your heir." He took him outside and said: "Look up to the sky and number the stars if you can; such shall be the number of your descendants."

Once Abraham sat at the door of his tent in the heat of the day and beheld three men. He ran to welcome them and, bowing to the ground, he said: "My lords, do not pass by your servant; wash you feet and rest under the tree till I fetch some food that you may refresh yourselves." They said: "Do as you say."

So Abraham hastened to Sarah's tent and said: "Quick, make some cakes." Then he ran to the herd and picked a tender calf, which he handed to the servant to prepare. He placed the food before them and they ate.

"Where is your wife Sarah?" they asked him. "She is inside the tent," he answered. Then one said: "I will come back to you next year, when your wife Sarah shall have a son." Sarah was listening behind the door. Now Abraham and Sarah were well advanced in years. So Sarah laughed to herself: "After I have grown old, and my husband is old, can I regain my youth?"

The Lord said to Abraham: "Why did Sarah laugh, saying: 'Shall I indeed bear a child, although I am old?' Is anything too wonderful for the Lord? At this time next year I will return to you, and Sarah shall have a son."

The men of Sodom were wicked and sinned against the Lord. So the Lord said: "Because the outcry against Sodom and Gomorrah is great, and their sin is very grave, I will go down and see whether they have indeed acted as viciously as the outcry indicates." The men—who were angels —set out toward Sodom, and Abraham went with them to see them off.

Then Abraham stood before the Lord and said: "Wilt thou destroy the righteous along with the wicked? Suppose there are fifty good men within the city; wilt thou destroy the place and not forgive it for the sake of the fifty good people in it? Far be it from thee to act like that, to make the good perish along with the bad! Shall not the Judge of all the earth act justly?" The Lord said: "If I can find fifty good persons in Sodom, I will forgive the whole place for their sake."

Then Abraham went on: "I have taken upon myself to speak to the Lord, I who am dust and ashes. Suppose five are lacking out of the fifty good people? Will you destroy the whole city for the lack of five?" He replied: "I will not destroy it if I can find forty-five in it." Again Abraham asked him: "Suppose forty are found there?" He answered: "I will spare it for the sake of the forty."

Then he said: "Oh let not the Lord be angry if I speak again. Suppose thirty are found there?" He answered: "I will not do it if I find thirty there." And he said: "I am venturing to speak to the Lord: suppose there are twenty good people in it?" He answered: "For the sake of twenty I will not destroy it." Then he said: "Oh let not the Lord be angry and I will speak just once more: if ten good men are to be found there?" He answered: "For the sake of the ten I will not destroy it." But there were not even ten good men there.

The angels seized Lot and his wife and his two daughters

by the hand, through the mercy of the Lord toward Lot, and led them forth and set them outside the city. When they brought them forth, they said: "Flee for your life; do not look back, flee to the hills, lest you perish."

Then the Lord rained sulphur and fire on Sodom and Gomorrah; he overthrew these cities and all the inhabitants. Lot's wife looked back and she was turned into a pillar of salt. In the morning when Abraham went to the place where he had stood before the Lord, he looked in the direction of Sodom and Gomorrah, and there was smoke rising from the land like smoke from a furnace.

The Lord remembered Sarah as he had promised; the Lord did for Sarah as he had spoken. Sarah bore a son at the time of which God had spoken. Abraham named his son Isaac. When Isaac was eight days old, Abraham circumcised him as God had commanded.

Abraham was a hundred years old when his son Isaac was born, and Sarah said: "God has given me a delightful surprise; all who hear of it will be amused on my account. Who could predict to Abraham that Sarah would nurse a child?" Abraham prepared a great feast on the day that Isaac was weaned.

When Sarah saw that Ishmael, whom Hagar the Egyptian had borne to Abraham, was playing with Isaac, she told Abraham: "Send away that servant and her son." This was extremely displeasing to Abraham. But God said to Abraham: "Do not resent it: listen to whatever Sarah tells you, for it is Isaac who shall be regarded as your child. As for the son of your servant, I will make a nation out of him too, because he is your child."

Abraham rose early in the morning and gave Hagar some food and a bottle of water, and sent her away. She went off and wandered about in the desert of Beersheba. When the water in the bottle was consumed, she threw the child under a bush and sat down some distance away, saying: "Let me not see the child dying." But as she sat and wept, God heard the boy's cry; then the angel of God called from heaven to Hagar, and said to her: "What ails you, Hagar? Fear not, for God has heard the cry of the boy. Come, take hold of the boy, for I will make a great nation

27

out of him." Then God opened her eyes and she saw a well of water. She went and filled the bottle with water and gave the lad a drink. God was with the boy, who grew up and lived in the desert and became an archer.

God put Abraham to the supreme test. He said to him: "Take your son, Isaac, whom you love; go to the land of Moriah and offer him there as a burnt-offering on one of the mountains that I will tell you." So Abraham rose early in the morning, saddled his donkey and took with him his two servants and his son Isaac; he cut wood for the burnt-offering and started for the place about which God had told him.

On the third day Abraham looked up and saw the place at a distance, So he said to his servants: "You stay here with the donkey while I and the boy go yonder. We will worship and come back to you." Abraham took the wood for the burnt-offering and laid it on his son Isaac, while in his hand he held the fire and the knife; and the two of them went off together.

Isaac said to Abraham: "Here are the fire and the wood, but where is the lamb for a burnt-offering?" Abraham answered: "God will provide the lamb." They came to the place of which God had spoken, and Abraham built an altar, arranged the wood on it, bound his son Isaac, and laid him on the altar.

Then Abraham raised the knife to slay his son, but the angel of the Lord called to him from the heavens: "Abraham, Abraham, do not lay your hand on the boy, do nothing to him; now I know that you revere God, seeing that you have not refused me your son." Abraham looked up and saw behind him a ram caught in the thicket by its horns. He went and took the ram, and offered it as a burnt-offering instead of his son.

When Sarah died, at the age of a hundred and twenty-seven, Abraham buried her in the cave of Machpelah at Hebron. Now Abraham was old, well advanced in years, and the Lord had blessed him in every way. "Promise me," Abraham said to his eldest servant, "that you will not marry my son to a daughter of the Canaanites; you must go to my own country and kindred and choose a wife for my son

Isaac. The Lord God, who brought me here from the land of my birth and promised to give this land to my descendants, will send his angel ahead of you and provide you with a wife for my son back there."

The servant took ten of his master's camels and started for Mesopotamia, for the city of Nahor. Outside the city he made the camels kneel beside the well at the time of evening when women came out to draw water. "O Lord," he said, "pray grant me success today and be kind to my master, Abraham. The girl who will give me a drink and offer to water my camels as well—may she be the maiden thou hast chosen for my master's son."

Before he had done speaking, out came Rebekah, a beautiful girl, carrying a pitcher on her shoulder. She went down to the spring, filled her pitcher, and came up. Then the servant ran to her and said: "Pray let me drink a little water from your pitcher."

"Drink, sir," she said; and she quickly lowered the pitcher and gave him a drink. When she had finished giving him a drink, she said: "Let me draw water for your camels also." So she quickly emptied her pitcher into the trough and ran again to the well to draw water for all the camels. The man gazed at her in silence watching to see if the Lord would make his journey successful.

When the camels had finished drinking, he gave the girl a golden ring and two golden bracelets, and asked her: "Whose daughter are you? Is there room in your father's house for us to spend the night?" "I am the daughter of Bethuel," she said. "We have plenty of straw and fodder, and there is also room to spend the night."

The man bowed his head and said: "Blessed be the Lord, who has led me straight to the house of my master's family." Then the girl ran and told her mother's household about it. Her brother, Laban, ran out to the man at the spring, and said: "Come in; why do you stand outside? I have a house ready, and a place for the camels." So the man went into the house, while Laban brought straw and fodder for the camels.

When Abraham's servant had told them about his errand, he added: "Now, tell me whether or not you will deal kindly with my master, so that I may know what to do next." Laban and Bethuel answered: "This comes from the Lord; here is Rebekah, take her and go; let her be the wife of your master's son." When Abraham's servant heard this, he gave jewels and garments to Rebekah; he also presented costly gifts to her brother and her mother. He and his men ate and drank and stayed all night.

When they rose in the morning, he said: "Do not detain me, since the Lord has prospered my way; let me go, that I may return to my master." They said: "We will call the girl, and ask her." So they called Rebekah, and asked her: "Will you go with this man?" She replied: "I will." So they sent off their sister Rebekah with her nurse, and Abraham's servant and his men, blessing Rebekah in these words: "Our sister, may you be the mother of myriads." Then Rebekah and her maids started, riding on camels, after the man. Thus the servant took Rebekah and went off.

Now, Isaac lived in the Negev. It was evening, and he had gone out to meditate in the field; as he looked up, he saw the camels coming. When Rebekah saw Isaac, she alighted from her camel and asked the servant: "Who is the man walking in the field to meet us?" The servant said: "It is my master." Then she took her veil and covered herself. Isaac took her inside the tent, and she became his wife. He loved her, and consoled himself after his mother's death.

Abraham lived a hundred and seventy-five years; he died at a good old age, after a full life. His sons Isaac and Ishmael buried him in the cave of Machpelah.

Rebekah gave birth to twins, Esau and Jacob. When they grew up, Esau became a skillful hunter, a man of the field; while Jacob was a quiet man who stayed in tents.

One day Jacob was cooking some food, when Esau came famished from the field. He said to Jacob: "Let me eat some of that red pottage, for I am famished!" Jacob said: "First sell me your birthright." Esau replied: "Here I am dying of hunger; of what use is a birthright to me?" So he sold his birthright to Jacob for a pottage of lentils. Esau ate and drank, got up and went away—so lightly did Esau value his birthright.

Isaac charged Jacob: "You shall not marry any Canaanite woman; go to the house of your mother's father, and get a wife there." So Jacob went to Paddan Aram, to Laban the brother of Rebekah. He came to a well in the field. When he saw Rachel the daughter of Laban, he removed the heavy stone that covered the well and watered her flock. He kissed her, telling her that he was Rebekah's son. As soon as Laban heard that Jacob, his sister's son, had come, he ran to meet him and took him home.

Jacob stayed a month with Laban and worked for him. Then Laban said to Jacob: "You are my kinsman, but are you to serve me for nothing? Tell me, what shall your wages be?" Jacob loved Rachel and he answered: "I will serve you seven years for your younger daughter, Rachel."

When Jacob had served seven years for Rachel, he said to Laban: "Let me have my wife; my time is completed." So Laban took his daughter Leah and brought her to Jacob in the evening. When Jacob found in the morning that it was Leah, he said to Laban: "What is this you have done to me? Did I not serve you for Rachel? Why then have you deceived me?" Laban answered: "It is not the custom in our country to marry the younger daughter before the elder. We will let you have the other in return for serving me another seven years." So Jacob served another seven years for Rachel, and Laban gave her to him in marriage.

Jacob's family increased in number; he became exceedingly rich and had large flocks, male and female servants, camels and mules. But he heard that Laban's sons were saying: "Jacob has taken away all our father's property; he has acquired all his riches from what once belonged to our father."

Jacob also saw that Laban was no longer friendly to him. He called Rachel and Leah into the field and said to them: "I see that your father is unfriendly to me. You know that I have served him with all my strength, but he has taken advantage of me. However, God did not let him harm me." Rachel and Leah replied: "What share have we in our father's house? He has treated us like strangers, for he has sold us!"

Jacob set his sons and his wives on camels, and drove off with all his cattle, which he had acquired in Paddan Aram, in order to return to his father, Isaac, in the land of Canaan. He outwitted Laban and fled with all that he had. He crossed the Euphrates and turned toward the hill country of Gilead.

Jacob had twelve sons. Those that Leah bore him were Reuben, Simeon, Levi, Judah, Issachar, and Zebulun. His sons by Rachel were Joseph and Benjamin. Bilhah, Rachel's maid, bore him Dan and Naphtali; and Leah's maid, Zilpah, was the mother of Gad and Asher.

Now Jacob loved Joseph best of all his sons because Joseph was born to him in his old age. His brothers hated Joseph and would not even speak to him. They conspired against him and sold him to a caravan of Ishmaelites, who took him down to Egypt and sold him to Potiphar, an officer of Pharaoh. But the Lord was with Joseph, and Potiphar made him his household steward and entrusted everything to him.

Years passed and Pharaoh sent for Joseph. "I have had a dream," said Pharaoh, "and there is no one to interpret it; but I have heard about you and that you can interpret dreams." Joseph replied: "God has shown to Pharaoh what he is about to do. There will come seven years of great plenty throughout the land of Egypt; after that there will arrive seven years of famine. Now therefore let Pharaoh select an intelligent man and put him in control of the land of Egypt. Let Pharaoh appoint overseers who will gather and store up the food in the good years and reserve it against the seven years of famine." Then Pharaoh said: "I hereby appoint you over all the land of Egypt. Not a man shall stir in all Egypt without your consent." Joseph was thirty years old when he entered the service of Pharaoh.

The seven years of plenty ended, and the seven years of famine began. Joseph opened all the granaries and sold grain to the Egyptians. People from other countries also came to buy grain, because the famine was severe everywhere on earth.

When Jacob learned that there was grain for sale in Egypt, he said to his sons: "I hear there is grain for sale in Egypt; go down there and buy some for us, that we may live." So ten of Joseph's brothers went down to buy grain in Egypt. Jacob did not send Benjamin for fear that harm might befall him.

When Joseph saw his brothers he recognized them but he treated them like strangers and spoke roughly to them. He asked: "Where do you come from?" They answered: "From the land of Canaan, to buy food." "You are spies," he said; "you have come to spy out the land!" "No, my lord," they replied, "your servants have come to buy food. We are honest men, we are not spies. We are twelve brothers; the youngest is with our father, and one is no more."

Joseph retorted: "You shall be tested; you shall not leave unless your youngest brother comes here also. Send one of you to bring him while the rest remain in prison. It will be a test whether you are telling the truth. Otherwise, as sure as Pharaoh lives, you are spies." So he confined them all for three days.

On the third day Joseph said to them: "Do this and you will live. If you are honest men, let one of you be held in prison, while you carry food to your starving households, but you must bring your youngest brother to me."

They said to one another: "This misfortune has befallen us because we are guilty regarding our brother, for we saw his distress and we did not heed him when he pleaded with us." They did not know that Joseph understood them, for there was an interpreter between them.

Joseph withdrew and wept. When he returned, he selected Simeon from among them and had him bound before their eyes. Then he gave orders that their baggage was to be filled with grain, that each man's money was to be replaced in his sack, and that they were to receive provisions for the journey. This was done, and they departed.

When they reached Jacob in the land of Canaan, they

told him all that had happened to them. Emptying their sacks, each one found his money. Then Jacob said: "Joseph is no more, Simeon is no more, and now you would take Benjamin." Reuben said: "Put him in my hands, and I will bring him back to you." But Jacob said: "My son shall not go with you; his brother is dead, and he is the only one left of his mother." "If you will not send our brother with us," said Judah, "we will not go. Send the lad with me, that we may live and not die. I will stand guarantee for him. If we had not delayed, we would now have returned twice."

Thereupon Jacob said: "If it must be so, then do this. Take some of the choice fruit of the land in your bags and carry it as a present to the man; take double money with you, for you must return the money that you found in your sacks; take also your brother with you."

So the men went to Egypt and presented themselves to Joseph. When Joseph saw his brother Benjamin, he said: "Is this your youngest brother of whom you spoke? God be gracious to you, my son!" He hastily retired to his chamber and wept. Having washed his face, he came out and ordered that food be served.

Joseph commanded the steward of his house: "Fill the men's sacks with food, as much as they can carry, put every man's money in his sack, and put my silver cup in the sack of the youngest man."

When the men had gone but a short distance, Joseph said to his steward: "Follow after them! Ask them: Why have you returned evil for good? Why have you stolen my lord's silver cup?" When the steward overtook them he spoke these words to them. They quickly lowered all their sacks to the ground, and the steward searched them, beginning with the eldest and going on to the youngest. The cup was found in Benjamin's sack. Rending their clothes in dismay, they went back to the city.

When Judah and his brothers came to Joseph's house, they fell before him on the ground. Judah said: "What shall we say to my lord? What shall we say? How can we clear ourselves? Now indeed we are slaves to my lord."

"Far be it from me to do that," said Joseph; "the man

in whose possession the cup was found shall be my slave, but the rest of you may go in peace to your father."

Then Judah came near to him and said: "Let your servant speak a word to my lord. You asked us, 'Have you a father or a brother?' And we told you: 'We have a father, an old man, and a young brother.' Then you said 'Bring him down that I may look at him; unless your brother comes along with you, you shall see my face no more.' Now if I go back to my father without the lad, he will surely die, for his very soul is bound up in this lad. Now therefore, let me remain instead of the lad as a slave; and let him return with his brothers. How can I return to my father without him?"

Joseph could not control himself; he called out: "Let every man leave me!" No one else was present when Joseph made himself known to his brothers. He said: "I am Joseph! Is my father still alive?" His brothers could not answer him, for they were dismayed. "Come near," he said; "I am your brother Joseph whom you sold into Egypt. Do not be distressed; it was not you but God who sent me here to preserve life. Hasten back to father and tell him that I said: God has made me lord over all Egypt; come down to me at once; you shall dwell in the land of Goshen and be near me, you, your children and grandchildren, your flocks and herds." He kissed all his brothers and wept.

Joseph gave them wagons and provisions for the journey and, as they departed, he said to them: "See that you do not quarrel on the way." So they set out from Egypt and came to their father Jacob in the land of Canaan, and told him: "Joseph is still alive, and he is ruler over all the land of Egypt!" He was stunned by the news; he did not believe them. But when they told him all that Joseph had said to them, and when he saw the wagons which Joseph had sent to convey him, his spirits revived. He said: "It is enough; Joseph my son is still alive; I will go and see him before I die."

Jacob set out with all that he had; when he arrived at Beersheba, he offered sacrifices to the God of his father Isaac. At night in a vision God said to him: "Jacob, Jacob,

I am the God of your father; do not be afraid to go down to Egypt; I will make you a great nation there. I will go down to Egypt with you, and I will also bring you back."

Jacob set out from Beersheba. The entire family of Jacob that came to Egypt numbered seventy souls. Joseph went to meet his father in Goshen. He wept as he embraced him. Jacob said: "Now that I have seen you alive I can die in peace." Joseph provided his father and the whole family with everything they needed.

Jacob lived in the land of Egypt seventeen years; his life span was a hundred and forty-seven years. When the time came for him to die, he called Joseph and said to him: "Promise me to be faithful to me; do not bury me in Egypt; let me sleep with my fathers in their burying place. Your two sons are mine; Ephraim and Manasseh are as much mine as Reuben and Simeon. I never thought I would see you, and here God has let me see even your children. May the angel who has delivered me from all evil bless the lads; may they carry on my name and the names of my fathers, Abraham and Isaac; may they grow into a multitude on earth. The people of Israel will invoke this blessing: God make you like Ephraim and like Manasseh."

Then Jacob called his sons and said: "Gather yourselves together, that I may tell you what shall befall you in days to come." He gave each a special blessing, and charged them: "Bury me beside my fathers in the cave of Machpelah. Abraham and Sarah, Isaac and Rebekah were buried there, and there I buried Leah." When Jacob finished charging his sons, he breathed his last and was gathered to his people. Joseph fell on his father's face, weeping over him and kissing him. Then he commanded the physicians to embalm his father. Forty days were required for embalming.

Joseph reported to Pharaoh, saying: "My father at the point of death made me promise on oath to bury him in the tomb which he had hewed out for himself in the land of Canaan. Now then, let me go up and bury my father, and I will return." Pharaoh replied: "Go up, and bury your father as he made you promise."

So Joseph went up to bury his father, and he was accompanied by all the courtiers of Pharaoh as well as by his brothers and his father's household. It was a very large caravan. When the Canaanites saw the mourning, they said: "This is a solemn mourning that the Egyptians are observing." Jacob's sons did for him what he had commanded them. They buried him in the cave of Machpelah, which Abraham had bought for use as a burial ground.

After burying his father, Joseph returned to Egypt along with his brothers and all who had accompanied him. Now that their father was dead, Joseph's brothers thought: "Perhaps Joseph will hate us and pay us back for all the evil we did to him." So they sent this message to Joseph: "Before he died, your father bade us to ask you to forgive the sin of your brothers and the evil they did to you." Joseph wept over their message to him.

Then his brothers came and fell down before him, saying: "We are your humble servants." But Joseph said to them: "Have no fear. Am I in the place of God? You meant to do me evil, but God meant good to come of it, so that many people should be kept alive. So do not fear; I will provide for you and your little ones." Thus he reassured them and comforted them.

Joseph remained in Egypt with all his father's family. He lived one hundred and ten years. When he was about to die, Joseph said to his brothers: "I am about to die; but God will surely remember you and bring you out of this land to the land that he promised to Abraham, Isaac and Jacob. When God will remember you, you shall carry up my bones from here." Joseph died at the age of a hundred and ten. He was embalmed and put into a coffin in Egypt.

Exodus

Exodus, the second book of the Torah, carries forward the history begun in Genesis and tells of the formation of Israel as a people. It contains the idyllic story of the birth of Moses, the divine revelation through the burning bush, and the detailed description of bitter contest between Moses and Pharaoh.

The second book of Moses is second to no other book of the Bible in its interest and religious significance. It describes the oppression and slavery in Egypt as well as the exodus and liberation, which came to the people of Israel in the hour of their greatest need and despair. The dramatic account of the giving of the Ten Commandments and the basic laws of the Torah are the most outstanding features of Exodus.

The plagues in the narrative portion of Exodus are miraculously intensified forms of the diseases or other natural occurrences to which Egypt is still liable. Frogs, gnats, flies and locusts are common pests in the country. Epidemics accompanied by a great mortality are frequently mentioned by historians. An unusual combination of natural calamities materially facilitated the exodus. The darkness that lasted three days in Egypt was, according to some scholars, the result of the hot wind called *Hamsin,* which often fills the air with thick clouds of dust and sand and forces people to stay indoors. During the annual inundation of the Nile, the water assumes a reddish color because of the red grass brought down from the Abyssinian mountains.

In its forty chapters, Exodus is replete with highly ethical concepts and laws. God's deep interest in human affairs is reflected in each of its narratives. He is represented as revealing himself to men and speaking with them intimately. The Ten Commandments, and the laws contained in the three chapters which are known as the Book of the Covenant (Exodus 20–23), are the quintessence of the remaining portion of the Torah.

These are the names of the Israelites who came to Egypt with Jacob: Reuben, Simeon, Levi, Judah, Issachar, Zebulun, Benjamin, Dan, Naphtali, Gad and Asher. When

38

Joseph and all his generation had died, a new king rose over Egypt who did not know Joseph. He said to his people: "The Israelites are too many and too mighty for us! Let us handle them shrewdly lest they multiply and fight against us." Whereupon taskmasters were set over them to crush them with heavy burdens; but the more they were oppressed the more they multiplied. Pharaoh ordered his people to throw every son born to the Hebrews into the Nile.

Now a man from the house of Levi married a daughter of Levi. She bore a son and hid him for three months. When she could hide him no longer, she put him into a basket made of bulrushes and placed it among the reeds upon the shore of the Nile. His sister stood at a distance to watch and see what might happen to him.

Now the daughter of Pharaoh came down to bathe in the river; she saw the basket among the reeds and sent her maid to fetch it. When she opened it she saw the child; it was a boy crying! She pitied him and said: "This must be a child of the Hebrews." The child's sister asked: "Shall I go and get a Hebrew woman to nurse the child?" "Go," said Pharaoh's daughter.

So the girl went for the child's mother, who took him and nursed him. When the child grew up, the mother took him to Pharaoh's daughter, who adopted him as her son. She named him Moses because she had removed him from the water.

When Moses was grown up, he went out to see his own people, and he watched them at their hard labor. He once noticed an Egyptian beating a Hebrew. Looking round, and seeing no one, he killed the Egyptian and hid him in the sand. The next day, he saw two Hebrews quarreling! Moses said to the guilty one: "Why do you strike your fellow man?" He retorted: "Who made you a prince and a judge over us? Do you mean to kill me as you killed the Egyptian?"

Fearing that Pharaoh might put him to death, Moses fled from Egypt to the land of Midian. As he was sitting beside a well, the seven daughters of Jethro came to water their flocks. Some shepherds tried to drive them from the well, so Moses went to their rescue and helped them water their flocks. When they came home, Jethro asked them: "How is it that you have returned so early today?" They answered: "An Egyptian protected us from the shepherds. He even drew water for us and watered the flock." "And where is he?" Jethro asked his daughters. "Why have you left him behind? Invite him to have bread with us."

Moses came and consented to make his home with Jethro, who gave him Zipporah, his daughter, to be his wife. She bore him a son, who was named Gershom.

One day, as Moses was tending Jethro's flock, an angel of the Lord appeared to him in a fire flaming out of a burning bush. "I will step aside," said Moses, "and behold this great sight, why the bush is in flames and yet does not burn."

God spoke out of the bush, saying: "Moses, Moses, do not come close; remove your shoes from your feet, for the place where you stand is holy ground. I am the God of your fathers Abraham, Isaac and Jacob. I have seen the affliction of my people in Egypt and heard their cry; I have come down to deliver them out of the hand of the Egyptians and bring them to a land flowing with milk and honey. I will send you to Pharaoh to bring my people out of Egypt."

Moses said: "But who am I, to go to Pharaoh and bring the people of Israel out of Egypt?" God answered: "I will be with you. Go gather the elders of Israel and tell them that the Lord has appeared to you. Then you and the elders shall go to the king and say to him: Let us go into the wilderness to worship the Lord our God."

Moses said: "My Lord, I am not a man of words, I am slow of speech."

The Lord said: "Who has made man's mouth? Who makes him speechless or deaf? Who gives him sight or makes him blind? Is it not I, the Lord? Go, then, I will teach you what to say. Aaron your brother can speak well; he shall come out to meet you. He shall speak for you to the people."

Moses then went to Jethro and said: "Pray let me return to my kinsmen in Egypt to see if they are still alive."

40

"Go in peace," said Jethro. So Moses went back to the land of Egypt. He told Aaron all that the Lord had commanded him, and Aaron told the elders of Israel what the Lord had said to Moses. And the people believed; they bowed their heads and worshiped.

Afterwards Moses and Aaron went to Pharaoh and said: "Thus says the Lord God of Israel: Let my people go." But Pharaoh said: "Who is the Lord that I should heed his voice? I do not know the Lord; I will not let Israel go!"

That very day Pharaoh commanded the taskmasters: "You shall no longer give the people straw to make bricks; let them gather straw for themselves; yet they shall make the required number of bricks." The Hebrew foremen were beaten because they could not produce the usual number of bricks. They appealed to Pharaoh: "Why do you treat us so? We are given no straw, yet we are told to make bricks." He answered: "You are lazy, lazy! That is why you say: Let us go worship the Lord."

Moses and Aaron went to Pharaoh and said: "Thus says the Lord God: How long will you refuse to humble yourself before me? Let my people go; if you refuse to let my people go, I will bring plagues upon you and your people."

Then the Lord brought ten plagues upon Egypt, namely: blood, frogs, vermin, flies, disease of cattle, boils, hail, locusts, darkness, and death of the firstborn.

It came to pass at midnight that the Lord struck down the firstborn in the land of Egypt. There was a great cry in Egypt, for there was not a house where someone was not dead.

Pharaoh sent for Moses and Aaron during the night and said: "Go, serve the Lord, as you have asked; take your flocks and your herds and be gone." The Egyptians pressed the people to hurry out of the land, crying: "We are all dead men!" So the people took their dough, unleavened as it was, and journeyed from Rameses to Sukkoth, about six hundred thousand of them on foot, besides women and children. They baked unleavened cakes of the dough which they had brought out of Egypt. They had been rushed out of Egypt and had not prepared any food for the journey.

Moses said to the people: "Remember this day in which you came out of Egypt, out of a house of slavery. You are leaving this day in the month of Aviv. And when the Lord will bring you into the land which he promised to your fathers, a land flowing with milk and honey, you shall perform this service in this month: Seven days you shall eat unleavened bread, and on the seventh day there shall be a feast in honor of the Lord. Throughout the seven days no leavened bread shall be seen in your possession. You shall tell your son on that day, saying: 'This is because of what the Lord did for me when I left Egypt.' You shall observe this precept from year to year."

When Pharaoh let the people go, God did not lead them along the shorter road through the land of the Philistines, lest the people might have regrets and return to Egypt. God led them by a roundabout road, in the direction of the wilderness and the Red Sea.

Moses took the bones of Joseph with him, for Joseph had made his people solemnly promise to do this, saying: "God will surely remember you, and you must take my bones away from here with you."

When it was reported to Pharaoh that the people of Israel had left, he and his officers changed their minds about letting them go. "What have we done!" they cried. "Why have we released the Israelites from our service?" So Pharaoh made his chariots ready and took his men with him, six hundred picked chariots and all the rest of the chariots of Egypt, manned by their captains.

The Lord hardened the heart of Pharaoh, who pursued the people of Israel. The Egyptians overtook them as they were encamped on the shore of the Red Sea. When the people of Israel looked up and saw the Egyptians marching after them, they were in great fear and cried out to the Lord.

They said to Moses: "Was it because there were no graves in Egypt that you have brought us to die in the desert? Did we not tell you in Egypt to leave us alone and let us serve the Egyptians? It would have been better for us to serve them than to die in the wilderness!"

But Moses said to them: "Have no fear, stand firm and

see the salvation of the Lord which he will perform for you today. The Egyptians you see today you shall never see again. The Lord will fight for you, and you have only to keep still."

Then Moses stretched out his hand over the sea. The waters divided, and the people of Israel went into the sea on dry ground, the waters forming a wall to right and left. The Egyptians in pursuit of them went into the sea, all of Pharaoh's horses, chariots and horsemen.

Again Moses stretched out his hand over the sea, and the sea returned to its steady flow. The Lord hurled the Egyptians right into the midst of it and not a single one of them was left.

Then Moses and the people of Israel sang this song to the Lord:

I will sing to the Lord, for he has completely triumphed; the horse and its rider he has hurled into the sea.

The Lord is my strength and song; he has come to my aid. This is my God, and I will glorify him; my father's God, and I will extol him.

Pharaoh's chariots and his army he has cast into the sea, and his choice captains are engulfed in the Red Sea. The depths cover them; they went down into the depths like a stone.

Thy right hand, O Lord, glorious in power, thy right hand, O Lord, crushes the enemy. Thou sendest forth thy wrath—it consumes them like stubble. By the blast of thy nostrils the waters piled up—the floods stood upright like a wall; the depths were congealed in the heart of the sea.

The enemy said: I will pursue them, I will overtake them, I will divide the spoil, my lust shall be glutted with them; I will draw my sword, my hand shall destroy them. Thou didst blow with thy wind—the sea covered them; they sank like lead in the mighty waters.

Who is there like thee among the mighty, O Lord? Who is like thee, glorious in holiness, awe-inspiring in renown, doing marvels? Thou didst stretch out thy right hand— the earth swallowed them.

43

*In thy grace thou hast led the people whom thou hast re-
deemed; by thy power thou hast guided them to thy
holy habitation.*

*Peoples have heard and trembled; pangs have seized the
inhabitants of Philistia. The chieftains of Edom were in
agony; trembling seized the lords of Moab; all the inhabitants of Canaan melted away.*

*Thou wilt bring them in and plant them in the highlands
of thy own, the place which thou, O Lord, hast made for
thy dwelling, the sanctuary, O Lord, which thy hands
have established. The Lord shall reign forever and ever.*

On the third month after leaving the land of Egypt, the
people of Israel entered the desert of Sinai; there Israel
encamped in front of the mountain. On the third day, in
the morning, there was thunder and lightning, a thick
cloud on the mountain, and a very loud trumpet blast; all
the people in the camp trembled. Then Moses brought
the people out of the camp, and they took their stand at
the foot of the mountain where God was. As the trumpet
blast grew louder and louder, Moses spoke and God answered him.

God spoke all these words, saying:

I am the Lord your God, who brought you out of the
land of Egypt, out of the house of slavery.

You shall have no other gods beside me. You shall not
make for yourself any idols in the shape of anything that is
in heaven above, or that is on the earth below, or that is in
the water under the earth. You shall not bow down to them
nor worship them; for I, the Lord your God, am a jealous
God, punishing children for the sins of their fathers, down
to the third or fourth generation of those who hate me, but
showing kindness to the thousandth generation of those
who love me and keep my commandments.

You shall not utter the name of the Lord your God in
vain; for the Lord will not hold guiltless anyone who
utters his name in vain.

Remember the Sabbath day to keep it holy. Six days you
shall labor and do all your work; but on the seventh day,
which is a day of rest in honor of the Lord your God, you

shall not do any work, neither you, nor your son, nor your daughter, nor your male or female servant, nor your cattle, nor the stranger who is within your gates; for in six days the Lord made the heavens, the earth, the sea, and all that they contain, and rested on the seventh day; therefore the Lord blessed the Sabbath day and hallowed it.

Honor your father and your mother, that you may live long in the land which the Lord your God is giving you.

You shall not murder.

You shall not commit adultery.

You shall not steal.

You shall not testify falsely against your neighbor.

You shall not covet your neighbor's house; you shall not covet your neighbor's wife, nor his servant, male or female, nor his ox, nor his ass, nor anything that belongs to your neighbor.

The Lord said to Moses: These are the laws which you shall present to them:

Whoever strikes a man dead shall be put to death. But if he did not intend to do it, I will designate a place to which he may flee. If a man wilfully attacks his neighbor, to kill him, you shall take that man from my very altar and put him to death.

Whoever strikes his father or his mother shall be put to death. Whoever curses his father or his mother shall be put to death. Whoever kidnaps a man shall be put to death.

When men quarrel and one strikes the other with a stone or with his fist, not fatally but enough to confine him to bed, the one who struck the blow shall go unpunished, provided that the other can get up and walk about with his staff; still, he must pay for the man's loss of time and have him thoroughly cured.

If a man digs a pit or reopens a pit and fails to cover it, and an ox or a donkey falls into it, he shall pay for the beast, and the carcass belongs to him.

If one man's ox gores to death the ox of another man, the goring ox shall be sold and the money divided between the two men; also the dead animal shall be divided between them. If the ox is known to have been in the habit of goring, and the owner has not guarded it, he shall pay ox for ox, and the dead animal shall be his.

If a man steals an ox or a sheep and either kills it or sells it, he shall pay five oxen for the ox and four sheep for the sheep.

If a thief is caught breaking into a house and is slain, there is no one punished for his death; but if this happened after sunrise, there shall be bloodguilt for him.

If a man sets fire to a field or vineyard and lets it spread to another man's field, he shall pay for it with the very best of his own field or his own vineyard.

If a man deposits money or goods with his neighbor, and it is stolen out of the man's house, the thief shall pay double if he is found. If the thief is not found, the owner of the house shall come to the judges to prove that he has not laid hands on the other man's property.

You shall not maltreat a stranger or oppress him, for you were strangers yourselves in the land of Egypt. You shall not afflict a widow or orphan; if ever you afflict them and they cry to me, I will hear their cry, and my wrath shall blaze until I slay you; and your own wives shall become widows and your own children fatherless.

If you lend money to a poor man, you must not act as a creditor, and you shall not exact interest from him. If ever you take your neighbor's garment in pledge, you shall give it back to him before the sun goes down; for that is the only covering he has. If he cries to me, I will listen to his cry, for I am compassionate.

You shall not revile the judges, nor shall you curse any of the authorities of your people.

You shall not utter a false report; you shall not join hands with a wicked man to give malicious evidence. You shall not follow a majority to do wrong; nor shall you be partial to a poor man in his lawsuit.

You shall not violate the rights of a poor man in his lawsuit. Avoid false charges. You shall never accept a bribe, for a bribe blinds the clear-sighted and perverts a just cause.

You shall not oppress a stranger; you should know the heart of a stranger, for you, too, were strangers in the land of Egypt.

The children of Israel shall keep the Sabbath, observing the Sabbath throughout their generations as an everlasting covenant. It is a sign between me and the children of Israel forever, that in six days the Lord made the heavens and the earth, and on the seventh day he ceased from work and rested.

When the Lord had finished speaking to Moses on Mount Sinai, he gave him the two tablets of the Law, the stone tablets inscribed by the finger of God.

When the people saw that Moses delayed in coming down from the mountain, they gathered around Aaron and said to him: "Come, make us a god to go in front of us. As for the man Moses who brought us out of the land of Egypt, we do not know what has happened to him." Aaron replied: "Take off the golden rings from the ears of your wives and sons and daughters and bring them to me." So all the people took off their earrings and brought them to Aaron, who made of them a molten calf. The people cried out: "This is your god, O Israel, who brought you out of the land of Egypt!"

The Lord said to Moses: "Go down at once to your people. They have made themselves a molten calf and are worshiping it." Moses came down the mountain with the two tablets of the Law in his hand, tablets written on both sides. When Joshua, who had waited for Moses at the foot of the mountain, heard the people shouting, he said to Moses: "That sounds like a battle in the camp." But Moses answered: "What I hear is the sound of people reveling." And as soon as he came near the camp, he saw the calf and the people dancing around it. Then Moses' wrath flared up; he threw down the tablets and broke them at the foot of the mountain. He took the calf they had made and fused it in the fire and ground it into powder, which he scattered on the water and then made the Israelites drink it.

On the next day Moses said to the people: "You have committed a great sin; so I will go up to the Lord; perhaps I may be able to make atonement for your sin." Then Moses went back to the Lord and said: "Alas, this people has indeed committed a great sin in making a god of gold

47

for themselves. Yet, if thou wilt not forgive their sin, then pray strike me out of the book thou hast written." The Lord answered: "Only those who have sinned against me will I strike out of my book. Now go, lead the people where I have told you; my angel shall go before you."

The Lord said to Moses: "Cut two tablets of stone like the first, and I will write upon them the words that were on the first tablets which you broke. Be ready in the morning; come up to Mount Sinai and present yourself there to me; let no man be seen throughout all the mountain." So Moses cut two tablets of stone like the first; he rose early in the morning and went up Mount Sinai, as the Lord had commanded him, taking along the two stone tablets. Then the Lord passed before him and proclaimed: "The Lord is a merciful and gracious God, slow to anger and rich in kindness and truth. He continues his kindness to a thousand generations; he forgives iniquity, transgression and sin, though he does not allow the guilty to pass unpunished; he punishes children and grandchildren, down to the third or fourth generation, for the iniquity of their fathers."

Moses at once bowed his head to the ground in worship. Then he said: "If I have found favor with thee, O Lord, be thou in our midst; this is indeed a stiff-necked people; O pardon our iniquity and sin, and make us thy very own."

When Moses came down from Mount Sinai with the two tablets of the commandments in his hands, he did not know that the skin of his face had become radiant after speaking with the Lord. Now when Aaron and all the people of Israel saw Moses and noticed how radiant the skin of his face had become, they were afraid to come near him. But Moses called to them, and Aaron and all the leaders came back to him. Moses then spoke to them. Later on, all the people of Israel came to him, and he told them all the commands that the Lord had given him on Mount Sinai.

Leviticus

Leviticus, the third book of the Torah, is primarily a book of laws, most of which concern the priests. It defines *clean* and *unclean* animals for purposes of food and contains ten chapters (17–26) commonly designated as the Holiness Code, stressing a high moral standard and containing laws of humanity and charity.

Leviticus presents a system of worship rich in symbolism and lofty in ethical standards. The desire for a visible element in worship is satisfied by numerous sacrifices, each designed to meet a particular need of the worshiper. The sacrificial system symbolized self-surrender and devotion to the will of God. The peace-offering with its communion feast conveyed the idea of fellowship. It served to keep alive the sense of dependence on God for the natural blessings of life, while it had the social value of promoting the solidarity of the nation. The daily offering symbolized Israel's pledge of unbroken service to God. The fragrant smoke of incense rising towards heaven was a natural symbol of prayer ascending to God, as in the words of the psalmist: "Let my prayer rise like incense before thee" (Psalm 141:2).

The well-known verse "You shall love your neighbor as yourself," meaning love for any human being, summarizes much of the social legislation in the book. The holiness of God requires human holiness, which includes such details as cleanliness and self-discipline. The relation between hygiene and religion is stressed in the regulations about leprosy.

Leviticus is the basis for the major part of the Jewish religion. Many Jewish virtues can be traced to the influence of this book and its ideal laws, liberating men from brutality and bestiality.

The Lord said to Moses: Speak to all the people of Israel and tell them: Be holy, for I, the Lord your God, am holy. Revere your mother and your father, every one of you, and keep my sabbaths.

You shall not steal; you shall not cheat; you shall not

speak falsely to one another. You shall not defraud or rob your neighbor; you shall not keep the wages of a hired laborer overnight. You shall not curse the deaf, or place an obstacle in front of the blind, but you shall fear your God.

You shall not act dishonestly in rendering judgment; you shall not be partial to a poor man nor favor a rich man. You shall not go about spreading slander among your people; you shall not stand by idly when your neighbor's life is at stake.

You shall not hate your brother in your heart, but you shall reason with him. Take no revenge and bear no grudge against your people; love your neighbor as yourself. Stand up in the presence of an aged man, and show respect to an old person.

When a stranger resides with you in your land, you shall not molest him. The stranger who resides with you shall be treated like a native, and you shall love him as you love yourself; for you too were once strangers in the land of Egypt. I am the Lord your God.

You shall not act dishonestly when using measures of length or weight or capacity. You shall have true scales and true weights.

Be careful to observe my commandments; I am the Lord. You shall not profane my holy name; but I must be hallowed among the people of Israel. I am the Lord who brought you out of the land of Egypt to be your God.

These are the festivals of the Lord which you shall celebrate, each in its proper season.

For six days work may be done, but the seventh day is the sabbath rest, a day for holy assembly, on which you shall do no work; it is to be kept as the Lord's Sabbath wherever you live.

The Passover falls on the fourteenth day of the first month (*Nisan*) at sunset. On the fifteenth day of this month the festival of unleavened bread begins; for seven days you shall eat unleavened bread. On the first day and on the seventh day of Passover you shall hold a holy assembly and do no hard work.

From the second day of Passover, you shall count seven

full weeks, counting fifty days to the Feast of Weeks when you shall hold a holy assembly and do no hard work.

The first day of the seventh month (*Tishri*) you shall observe as a day of rest, a day of remembrance (*Rosh Hashanah*), celebrated by trumpet blowing, when you shall do no hard work.

On the tenth day of the seventh month, the Day of Atonement, you shall hold a holy assembly; you shall fast, and do no work on that day, for it is a day on which atonement is made for you before the Lord your God. You shall observe it as a sabbath of complete rest. From the sunset of the ninth day to the sunset of the tenth day you shall keep your sabbath.

On the fifteenth day of the seventh month the seven-day feast of Tabernacles (*Sukkoth*) begins. On the first day of *Sukkoth* there shall be a holy assembly when you shall do no hard work. For seven days you shall present offerings to the Lord; on the eighth day (*Shemini Atzereth*) you shall hold a holy assembly and do no hard work. On the first day you shall take the fruit of the *Ethrog*, the branches of the palm trees and the myrtle and the water-willows (making up the *Lulav*), and rejoice before the Lord your God for seven days. These seven days you shall live in booths, that your descendants may know that I made the people of Israel to dwell in booths when I brought them out of the land of Egypt; I am the Lord your God.

The Lord said to Moses on Mount Sinai:

Tell the people of Israel: When you enter the land which I am giving you, the land shall have a sabbath in honor of the Lord. For six years you may sow your field, prune your vineyard, and gather in their produce; but during the seventh year the land shall have a complete rest, a sabbath in honor of the Lord, when you shall neither sow your field nor prune your vineyard; you shall not even reap what grows of itself after the harvest, nor shall you gather the grapes of your untrimmed vines. What grows of itself in the sabbatical year must not be enjoyed selfishly, but is to be shared with the poor and the strangers.

After counting seven times seven years, or forty-nine years, on the day of atonement, you shall sound the trumpet

51

throughout your land; you shall hallow the fiftieth year and proclaim liberty to all the inhabitants of the land; it shall be a jubilee year for you, when each of you shall return to his own property and family.

The fiftieth year shall be a jubilee year for you, when you shall neither sow nor reap what grows of itself, nor gather the grapes from the undressed vines. In this year of jubilee each of you shall return to his own property.

When you sell land to your neighbor or buy land from your neighbor, you must not defraud each other; you shall buy and sell only the number of crops till the next jubilee. If the years to the next jubilee are many, you shall increase the price; and if they are few, you shall lower the price, for it is the number of crops that is sold.

If your brother becomes poor and sells some of his property, the nearest relative shall buy it back for him. If a man has no one to buy it back for him, and afterwards becomes rich enough to buy it back himself, he shall count up the years since it was sold and refund the buyer for the rest of the years till next jubilee; in this way he will get back his own property. But if he is unable to get it back for himself, it shall remain in the hands of the purchaser only until the next jubilee; in that jubilee it shall be released, then the man can get back to his property.

If your brother becomes poor, you shall maintain him and enable him to live beside you. Take no interest from him; let your brother live beside you. You shall not ask interest on your money loans to him nor on the food which you furnish him. I am the Lord your God, who brought you out of the land of Egypt to be your God.

Numbers

Numbers, the fourth book of the Torah, contains a brief summary of the experiences of Israel in the wilderness during nearly forty years of wanderings. It records the expedition of the twelve spies into the land of Canaan, the rebellion of Korah against Moses and Aaron, the striking of the rock, and the story of Balaam. There is a clear picture of the difficulties which confronted Moses as the leader of a tired and discontented people.

Korah, the Levite, charged that the priesthood rightfully belonged to members of any Levite family, not simply the house of Aaron. Dathan and Abiram, of the tribe of Reuben, rebelled against the civil authority of Moses, charging that the leadership rightfully belonged to the descendants of Jacob's eldest son, Reuben.

Balak vainly hopes to destroy Israel by having recourse to black magic, and sends for the magician Balaam to come and curse them. But the powers of darkness could not stop the victorious march of the people of Israel. Balaam could say only what was given him to say. Therefore, he had to bless God's people.

The Lord spoke to Moses in the second year after the exodus from the land of Egypt, saying: "Take a census of all the people of Israel, family by family, all males over twenty years who are fit for active service." So Moses and Aaron, assisted by twelve men representing the twelve tribes, assembled all the people on the first day of the second month and numbered them in the wilderness of Sinai. The total number was six hundred and three thousand five hundred and fifty men able to bear arms.

The Levites were not included in the census of the Israelites. They were put in charge of the Tabernacle with all its equipment and all its belongings. Whenever the Tabernacle had to be moved, the Levites were to take it down; and whenever it had to be set up, the Levites were to set it up. The Israelites were to pitch their tents according to their companies, in military order, but the Levites were to pitch their tents around the Tabernacle.

The people of Israel complained bitterly to Moses: "Would that we had meat for food! We remember the fish we used to eat without cost in Egypt, and the cucumbers, the melons, the leeks, the onions, and the garlic. But now we are famished; we see nothing before us but this manna."

The manna was like coriander seed; the people would gather it up, grind it between millstones or pound it in a mortar, then cook it in a pot and make it into loaves which tasted like cakes made with oil. At night, when dew fell upon the camp, the manna also fell.

Moses heard the people weeping, and he said to the Lord: "Thou layest the burden of all these people upon me. I cannot carry all their burdens by myself. Where can I get meat to give to them? Pray kill me at once, and let me no longer face their distress."

Then the Lord told Moses to say to the people: "Tomorrow you shall have meat to eat; you will eat it not for one day, nor two days, nor five days, nor ten days, nor twenty days, but for a whole month, until you cannot bear the smell of it, until you loathe it. For you have spurned the Lord who is in your midst, and you have wailed: Why did we ever leave Egypt?"

So Moses went out and told the people what the Lord had said. Then there arose a wind sent by the Lord, that drove in quail from the sea and brought them down over the camp site. All that day and night, and all the next day the people gathered in the quail. As the people were devouring this food, the Lord struck them with a terrible plague. So that place was named *Graves of Greed,* because it was there that the greedy people were buried.

Miriam and Aaron spoke against Moses because he had married an Ethiopian woman. They said: "Has the Lord spoken to Moses alone? Has he not spoken to us as well?" Now the man Moses was by far the meekest man on the face of the earth. So the Lord told Moses, Aaron and Miriam to come out to the tent of meeting. The three went out, and the Lord called Aaron and Miriam to come forward. He said: "If there is a prophet among you, I shall reveal myself to him in a vision, I shall speak to him in a dream. Not so with my servant Moses, most faithful of all my household. I speak to him face to face, plainly, and not in riddles. Why then were you not afraid to speak against my servant Moses?"

The anger of the Lord was kindled against them. He departed, and behold, Miriam became leprous. Aaron cried to Moses: "My lord, let us not be punished for the sin we have foolishly committed." So Moses called to the Lord: "Heal her, O God, I beseech thee." The Lord answered: "Let her be confined for seven days outside the camp; then she can come back." So for seven days Miriam was confined outside the camp.

The Lord told Moses to send men to spy out the land of Canaan. He was to send a man from every tribe, all of them chiefs. So Moses sent spies to the land of Canaan, saying to them: "Go and see what kind of land it is; whether the people there are strong or weak, few or many; whether the cities are open or fortified; whether the land is rich or poor, and whether there is wood in it or not. Be of good courage, and bring back some fruit from there."

So they went and spied out the land. They reached the valley of Eshcol, where they cut down a branch with a single cluster of grapes on it, and two of them carried it on a pole. They also took some pomegranates and some figs. At the end of forty days they returned from spying out the land and brought back word to the people of Israel who were encamped in the wilderness at Kadesh.

Showing them the fruit, the spies said: "We came from the land to which you sent us; it flows with milk and honey, and this is its fruit. However, the people there are strong and the cities are fortified and very large; besides, we saw the Anak giants there. The Amalekites live in the Negev; the Hittites, the Jebusites and the Amorites live in the hill country; and the Canaanites dwell along the seacoast and the banks of the Jordan. We cannot attack these people; they are too strong for us. The land that we explored is a land that consumes its inhabitants; the people

55

we saw there are huge men, a race of giants; we felt like mere grasshoppers, and so we must have seemed to them."

Upon hearing this, the people of Israel raised a loud cry. They wailed and murmured against Moses and Aaron. "Would that we had died in the land of Egypt!" they cried. "Would that we were dead here in the wilderness! Why is the Lord bringing us into this land only to have us fall by the sword? Our wives and our little ones will become prey; would it not be better for us to go back to Egypt? Let us appoint a leader and go back to Egypt!"

Joshua and Caleb, who were among those who spied out the land, said to all the people of Israel: "The land is an exceedingly good land; the Lord will bring us into this land which flows with milk and honey. Only, do not rebel against the Lord; do not fear the people of the land; the Lord is with us; do not fear them." But the people threatened to stone both Joshua and Caleb.

Then the Lord appeared to Moses and said: "How long will this people refuse to believe in me, in spite of all the signs which I have performed among them? I will strike them with pestilence and wipe them out; then I will make of you a nation greater and mightier than they." But Moses prayed: "O Lord, forgive this people, as thou hast forgiven them time after time, ever since they left Egypt."

And the Lord answered: "I pardon them, as you have asked. But, as surely as I live, not one of these who has spurned me shall see the land which I promised to their fathers. I have heard their grumblings against me. Say to them: Here in the desert shall your dead bodies fall. Of all your men of twenty years and older, who grumbled against me, not one shall enter the land, except Caleb and Joshua. But your little ones I will bring in, and they shall appreciate the land which you have despised. Your children shall be wandering shepherds in the wilderness for forty years, and shall suffer for your faithlessness until the last of your dead bodies lies in the wilderness."

The Lord spoke to Moses, saying: Speak to the children of Israel and tell them to make for themselves fringes on the corners of their garments throughout their generations, and they shall put on the fringe of each corner a blue thread. When you look upon it, you will remember to keep all the commands of the Lord, and you will not follow the desires of your heart and your eyes which lead you astray. It is for you to remember and keep all my commandments, and be holy for your God. I am the Lord your God who brought you out of the land of Egypt to be your God; I am the Lord your God.

Now Korah, Dathan and Abiram, and two hundred fifty leaders of the community, combined to oppose the authority of Moses and Aaron, saying to them: "You have gone too far! What right have you to set yourselves over the Lord's people?"

Upon hearing this, Moses said to Korah and his followers: "Listen to me, you Levites! Is it not enough that God has singled you out to do service in the sanctuary and to minister to the congregation, that you want to be priests as well? It is against the Lord that you are gathered. What has Aaron done that you should grumble against him?"

Moses sent for Dathan and Abiram, but they refused to come, saying: "We will not come up! Are you not satisfied with having brought us here from a land flowing with milk and honey to kill us in the desert? Must you also play the prince over us? You have not brought us to a land abounding in milk and honey, nor have you put us in possession of fields and vineyards. Are you trying to blind the eyes of these men? No, we will not come up!"

Moses, followed by the elders of Israel, went to Dathan and Abiram. Then he warned the people, saying: "Keep away from the tents of these wicked men and do not touch anything that is theirs; otherwise you too will be swept away because of their sins." As Dathan and Abiram came out and stood at the doorways of their tents, with their wives and sons and little ones, Moses said to the people: "This is how you shall know that the Lord has sent me to do all that I have done: If these men die an ordinary death, then the Lord has not sent me. But if the Lord creates something new, and the ground opens its mouth and swallows them up, with all that belongs to them, and they go down alive into the pit, then you will know that these men have defied the Lord."

He no sooner had finished speaking than the ground beneath them split open and swallowed them up, with their families and all the men that belonged to Korah, and all their possessions. They went down alive into the pit; the earth closed over them, and they perished from the midst of the community. All the Israelites around fled at their shrieks, fearing lest the earth might swallow them also.

The Lord said to Moses: "Speak to the people of Israel, and get twelve rods from their leaders, one rod for each tribe. Write the name of each on his rod, and Aaron's name upon the rod of Levi. Then you shall deposit them in the tent of meeting, and the rod of the man whom I choose shall blossom."

Moses spoke to the people of Israel, and all their leaders gave him rods, and the rod of Aaron was among them. Moses deposited the rods before the Lord in the tent of meeting.

The next day, when he entered the tent, he found that the rod of Aaron had sprouted, put forth buds, produced blossoms and borne ripe almonds. He brought out all the rods from the presence of the Lord to the people of Israel and they looked at them; then each leader took his own rod. But the Lord said to Moses: "Put Aaron's rod back to be kept as a sign for the rebels, that you may make an end of their grumbling against me, lest they die."

Moses did as the Lord commanded him.

The people of Israel came to the wilderness of Zin and stayed at Kadesh, where Miriam died and was buried.

There was no water, so they gathered themselves against Moses and Aaron, complaining: "Would that we had died together with our brethren! Why have you brought us into this desert to die? Why did you make us leave Egypt for this evil place? It is a place with no seed, figs, vines or pomegranates; and there is no water to drink!"

Then the Lord said to Moses: "Take the staff, assemble the people, and speak to the rock in their presence, that it may yield water for them and their cattle." So Moses and

Aaron gathered the people, and Moses said to them: "Listen, you rebels! Must we bring you water from this rock?" And raising his hand, he struck the rock with his staff twice. Water gushed out abundantly, and the people and their cattle drank of it. But the Lord said to Moses and Aaron: "Because you did not have faith in me, or vindicate me in the eyes of the people of Israel, you shall not bring this people into the land that I have given them."

The people of Israel encamped opposite Jericho, on the plains of Moab, east of the Jordan. Moab was in great dread of them because of their numbers. So Balak, who was the king of Moab at that time, sent messengers to Balaam the soothsayer, summoning him with these words:

"Here is a people that has come out of Egypt; they cover the face of the earth, and are encamped opposite me. Now then, pray come and curse this people, since they are too strong for me. Perhaps this will enable me to defeat them and drive them out of the country. For I know that he whom you bless is blessed, and he whom you curse is cursed."

God appeared to Balaam at night and asked: "Who are these men with you?" Balaam answered: "Balak has sent word to me, saying: "Please come and lay a curse upon this people, that I may be able to fight against them and drive them out." But God said to Balaam: "Do not go with them and do not curse this people, for they are blessed."

Balaam rose in the morning and said to the princes of Balak: "Go back to your country, for the Lord refused to let me go with you." So the princes of Moab went back to Balak and told him that Balaam had refused to come with them.

Balak sent a larger number of princes, who came to Balaam with this message: "Let nothing stop you from coming. I will give you great honor; whatever you tell me I will do; come, I beg you, curse this people for me." But Balaam replied: "Though Balak were to give me his very house full of silver and gold, I could not transgress the command of the Lord my God. Now then, remain here overnight, that I may find out what else the Lord may have to say to me."

In the night God came to Balaam and said to him: "As
these men have come to call you, go with them; but you
shall do only what I tell you." Balaam rose in the morning,
saddled his donkey, and went with the princes of Moab.
But God was angry because he went and the angel of the
Lord stood in the road to hinder him.

Balaam was riding on the donkey, accompanied by his
two servants. When the donkey saw the angel standing on
the road with a drawn sword, the animal turned aside and
went into the field. But Balaam struck the donkey and tried
to turn her back into the road. The angel then took his
stand in a narrow lane between vineyards, with a fence on
either side. When the donkey saw the angel of the Lord,
she pressed against the wall and crushed Balaam's foot; so
he struck her again.

The angel went ahead and took his stand in a narrow
place, where there was no way to turn either to the right
or to the left. When the donkey saw the angel, she lay
down under Balaam. Balaam's anger blazed and he struck
her with his stick.

Then the Lord opened the mouth of the donkey and
she said to Balaam: "What have I done to you that you
have struck me these three times?"

"You have mocked me; if only I had a sword I would
kill you," Balaam replied.

"Am I not your own animal on which you have always
ridden? Have I ever mocked you?" the donkey complained.

The Lord opened Balaam's eyes, and he saw the angel
standing on the road with a drawn sword. Balaam bowed
his head and fell on his face.

The angel said to him: "Why have you struck your
donkey these three times? It was I who came forth to stand
in your way, because you have displeased me. The donkey
saw me and swerved from me three times. Had she not
swerved, I would certainly have slain you and spared her."

Balaam answered: "I have sinned; I did not know you
were standing on the road to stop me. Now then, if it is
displeasing to you, I will turn back."

"Go with the men," the angel said, "but you shall say

only what I tell you." So Balaam went along with the princes of Balak.

When Balak heard of Balaam's arrival, he went out to meet him. Then the Lord put a message in Balaam's mouth. Upon finding Balak together with the princes of Moab beside the burnt-offering, Balaam uttered these words:

"From Aram, Balak has brought me to lay a curse on Jacob, to denounce Israel. But how can I curse those whom God has not cursed; how can I denounce those whom the Lord has not denounced? May I die as these righteous men shall die, may my end be like theirs. God is no man to break his word, no mortal to change his mind. The Lord their God is with them! How goodly are your tents, O Jacob, your habitations, O Israel! I see them, but not as they are now; I behold them, but not as they are at present. A star has come forth from Jacob; Israel has performed valiantly."

After this, Balaam rose and went back to his place; and Balak also went his way.

The Lord told Moses and Elazar the son of Aaron to take a census of the whole Israelite community from twenty years old and upward, counting all Israelites who were fit for active service. The total number of the Israelites was six hundred and one thousand seven hundred and thirty. The total number of the Levites was twenty-three thousand, counting every male over a month old. Their number was not included in that of Israel, since they received no property in Israel. Among those numbered by Moses and Aaron in Moab, beside the Jordan opposite Jericho, there was not a man who had been in the census taken by Moses and Aaron when they counted the people of Israel in the wilderness of Sinai. Not a man of them was left, except Caleb and Joshua.

The five daughters of a man named Zelophehad appeared before Moses and the elders, pleading: "Our father died in the wilderness, though he took no part in the rising of Korah; he died for his own sin, leaving no sons. Why should our father's name be dropped from his family, just because he left no son? Give us property along with our father's kinsmen."

Moses brought their plea before the Lord, and the Lord said to Moses: "The daughters of Zelophehad are right; you shall certainly let them hold property among their kinsmen. Let a man's property always pass to his daughter, if he dies without leaving a son. If he leaves no daughter, his property shall go to his brothers; if he leaves no brothers, his property shall go to his father's brothers. If his father has left no brothers, you shall give his property to the nearest relative."

Then the Lord said to Moses: "Ascend this mountain of Abarim and see the land which I am giving to the people of Israel. When you have seen it, you shall be gathered to your people like your brother Aaron, because you disobeyed my word in the wilderness of Zin. When the people demanded water, you struck the rock instead of speaking to it in their presence."

Moses said to the Lord: "Let the Lord, God of the spirits of all flesh, appoint a leader for the community to manage all their affairs, so that the Lord's community may not be like sheep without a shepherd." So the Lord said to Moses: "Take Joshua, a man of spirit, and lay your hand upon him; have him stand before Elazar, the priest, and the whole community, and commission him in their sight. You shall invest him with some of your own authority, so that all the people of Israel may obey him."

Moses did as the Lord commanded him; he placed Joshua in front of Elazar the priest, and all the community, laid his hands upon him, and commissioned him.

Deuteronomy

Deuteronomy, the fifth book of the Torah, carries events up to the death of Moses and prepares for the succession of Joshua. The greater part of the book is taken up with the addresses of Moses to the people of Israel as they were about to cross the Jordan to the land of Canaan. In these discourses Moses reviews the events of the forty years spent in the wilderness.

There are at least three speeches. The first is a summary of the main experiences of Israel in the desert; the second reviews the Ten Commandments and includes the declaration of God's oneness; the third stresses the duty of loyalty to God.

The final chapters comprise two poems recited by Moses in the hearing of the people, and also tell the story of his death. The moving narrative describing the death of Moses reveals the final experience of the great leader. From the peak of Mount Nebo, Moses surveys the whole extent of the promised land; he dies on Mount Nebo in solitude at the age of one hundred and twenty. Deuteronomy contains a considerable number of humane laws and is one of the most beautiful and profoundly ethical books of the Bible. The long poem *Haazinu,* in the thirty-second chapter, is one of the best productions of biblical poetry.

A number of passages from Deuteronomy have been incorporated into the daily prayers, notably the *Shema,* Israel's confession of faith, which expresses the duty of loving and serving God with our whole being.

These are the words which Moses spoke to all Israel east of the Jordan. It was in the fortieth year that Moses spoke to the people of Israel concerning all the commands which he had received for them from the Lord. He said:

O Israel, give heed to the rules and regulations which I teach you, and obey them, so that you may live and possess the land which the Lord is giving you. That will prove your wisdom and your understanding in the sight of the nations, who will say: This great nation is indeed a wise and understanding people!

What great nation has laws as just as this Torah which I am setting before you this day? Only take heed lest you forget the things which your eyes have seen. Make them known to your children and to your children's children—how on the day that you stood before the Lord your God at the foot of the mountain, while the mountain burned with fire to the heart of heaven, the Lord spoke to you out of the midst of the fire. You heard the sound of words, but saw no form; there was only a voice. He declared to you his covenant, the ten commandments, and he wrote them upon two tables of stone.

The Lord took you and brought you out of the iron furnace, out of Egypt, to be a people of his own.

The Lord was angry with me, and he forbade me to enter the fine land which he is giving you as a heritage. I must die in this land instead of crossing the Jordan; but you shall go over and take possession of that good land. Take care that you do not forget the covenant of the Lord your God which he made with you; do not make an image in the form of anything which the Lord your God has forbidden you; for the Lord your God is a consuming fire, a jealous God.

Hear, O Israel, the Lord is our God, the Lord is One.

You shall love the Lord your God with all your heart, and with all your soul, and with all your might. And these words which I command you today shall be in your heart. You shall teach them diligently to your children, and you shall speak of them when you are sitting at home and when you go on a journey, when you lie down, and when you rise up. You shall bind them for a sign on your hand, and they shall be for frontlets between your eyes. You shall inscribe them on the doorposts of your house and on your gates.

And if you will carefully obey my commands which I give you today, to love the Lord your God and to serve him with all your heart and with all your soul, I will give rain for your land at the right season, the autumn rains and the spring rains, that you may gather in your grain, your wine and your oil. And I will bring forth grass in your fields for your cattle, and you will eat and be satisfied. Beware lest your heart be deceived, and you turn and serve other gods and worship them; for then the Lord's anger will blaze against you, and he will shut up the skies so that there will be no rain, and the land will yield no produce, and you will perish quickly from the good land which the Lord gives you. So you must place these words in your heart and in your soul; you must teach them to your children, that your life and the life of your children may be prolonged in the land, which the Lord promised to your fathers, for as long as the sky remains over the earth.

You are children of the Lord your God: you must not eat any detestable food. You may eat the ox, the sheep, the goat, the deer. You may eat any animal that has the hoof parted in two and also chews the cud; but you must not eat of those that chew the cud only or have the hoof parted only. You may eat anything in the waters that has fins and scales; but you must not eat anything that has not fins and scales. You may eat any clean bird; but you must not eat the vulture, the raven, the ostrich, the hawk, the stork, and the bat. All winged insects are unclean to you. You must not eat any creature that has died a natural death. You must not boil a kid in its mother's milk.

You shall appoint judges and officers to rule the people with right justice. You shall not pervert justice; you shall not be partial to anyone; you shall not take a bribe, for a bribe blinds the eyes of the wise. You shall strive for justice, and justice only, in order that you may live and possess the land given to you by the Lord your God.

A single witness shall not testify against a man in any case; only on the evidence of two or three witnesses shall a charge be sustained.

If a malicious witness testifies against a man, accusing him of wrongdoing, the two parties in the dispute shall appear before the judges, who shall make a thorough investigation. If the witness accuses his brother falsely, you shall do to him as he planned to do to his brother.

You must not be unconcerned when you see your fellow man's ox or sheep driven astray; you must surely bring them back to your fellow man. If, however, he does not live near you, or you do not know him, you shall take it home and keep it with you until he claims it. You shall do the same with everything lost by your fellow man, which you have found; you must not be unconcerned.

If you happen to come upon a bird's nest when the mother-bird is sitting on the young ones or the eggs, you must not take away the mother-bird along with her offspring; you must let the mother go, and you may take only the young, that you may prosper and live long.

When you make any vow to the Lord your God, you must pay it without delay. You shall be careful to perform any promise you have made with your lips.

When you go into your neighbor's vineyard, you may eat your fill of the grapes, but you must not put any in your bag.

When a man is newly married, he shall not go on active service with the army; he shall be free at home for one year, to be happy with the wife he has taken.

If a man kidnaps a fellow man in order to enslave or sell him, the kidnaper shall be put to death.

You shall not defraud a poor servant; you shall pay him each day's wages before sundown.

Fathers shall not be put to death for their children, nor shall children be put to death for their fathers; a man shall be put to death only for his own guilt.

You shall not violate the rights of the alien or of the orphan, or take the clothing of a widow in pledge.

When you reap the harvest in your field and overlook a sheaf there, you shall not go back to get it; let it be for the alien, the orphan or the widow. When you pick your grapes, you shall not go over the vineyard a second time; let what remains be for the alien, the orphan, and the widow.

You shall not muzzle an ox when it is treading out grain.

You shall not have weights of different sizes in your bag, one large and the other small; you shall have a true and just weight, a true and just measure. Everyone who is dishonest is an abomination to the Lord your God.

What I am commanding you today is not too difficult

and remote for you. It is not up in heaven that you should say: "Who will ascend to heaven to get it for us?" Nor is it across the sea, that you should say: "Who will cross the sea and bring it to us?" No, it is something very near to you, within your own hearts and minds.

If you obey the commandments of the Lord your God, you shall live and multiply in the land which you are now entering. But if your heart turns away to worship other gods and serve them, I declare to you this day that you shall not live long in the land which you are going to enter and possess.

I call heaven and earth to witness this day, that I have set before you life and death, the blessing and the curse. Choose life, then, that you and your descendants may live in the land which the Lord promised to your fathers Abraham, Isaac and Jacob.

Hearken, O heaven, and I will speak; let the earth hear the words of my mouth! May my message drop like the rain, my speech distill as the dew. When I proclaim the name of the Lord, give glory to our God!

He is the Creator, his work is perfect; all his ways are just. He is the faithful God, without iniquity, upright and just!

The corruption of his children has been their undoing; they are a twisted and crooked generation. Is this the way to treat the Lord, you foolish people? Is he not your Father who created you? Has he not made you and established you?

Remember the days of old, consider the ages that are past; ask your father and he will inform you, ask your elders and they will tell you. He found them in a desert land, in a howling waste of wilderness; he cared for them, and kept them as the apple of his eye.

This is the blessing which Moses, the man of God, pronounced upon the people of Israel before his death. He said:

"The Lord came from Sinai, and dawned on them from Seir; he shone forth from the mountain of Paran. The Torah which has been handed down to us is the heritage of the community of Jacob.

"May Reuben live and not die. Hear, O Lord, the cry of Judah; be thou a help against his adversaries. Levi shall teach Israel thy law; break the backs of his adversaries and foes, that they may not rise.

"There is none like God! The eternal God is your refuge. He drove the enemy out of your way. Happy are you, O Israel, a people saved by the Lord!"

Moses went up to Mount Nebo, opposite Jericho. There the Lord showed him all the land of Judah as far as the Mediterranean Sea, the Negev, and the Valley of Jericho, saying: "This is the land which I solemnly promised to give to the descendants of Abraham, Isaac and Jacob. I have let you look upon it, but you shall not enter it."

Moses died there in the land of Moab, but to this day no one knows the place of his burial. Moses was a hundred and twenty years old when he died, yet his eyes were undimmed and his vigor unabated. The people of Israel mourned over the passing of Moses for thirty days.

Joshua, the son of Nun, was filled with the spirit of wisdom; the people of Israel obeyed him, and carried out the orders given by the Lord to Moses.

Since then, no prophet has ever appeared in Israel like Moses, whom the Lord knew face to face.

Joshua

The book of Joshua continues the history of the preceding five books of Moses and narrates the conquest and settlement of the promised land, recording the completion of the great movement of which the exodus from Egypt was the beginning. It is the first of the four historical books known as Former Prophets (Joshua, Judges, Samuel, Kings) forming a continuous narrative which begins at the death of Moses and ends with the destruction of the first Temple. These writings are classed as prophetic because they were composed by divinely inspired prophets.

As successor of Moses, Joshua defeated six enemy tribes in six years and then proceeded to divide the conquered territory. The final events of his life include the distribution of the land to the tribes of Israel by lot and the appointing of the cities of refuge, which are designed to shelter anyone who might accidentally commit manslaughter. By fleeing into one of the six cities of refuge, persons pursued by avengers of blood were protected against the ancient law of life for life. Forty-two Levitical cities also served for the protection of the unintentional homicide.

Before his death at the age of one hundred and ten, Joshua delivered two addresses to the people of Israel, urging them to remain loyal to God and live according to the teachings of the Torah.

After the death of Moses, the Lord said to Joshua: "Moses my servant is dead; now arise, cross the Jordan, you and all this people, into the land which I am giving them. No man shall be able to hold his own against you all the days of your life; as I was with Moses, so I will be with you; I will never fail you nor forsake you. Be strong and brave, for you shall put this people in possession of the land which I promised to their fathers. Only observe all the law which Moses handed down to you; turn neither to the right nor to the left, that you may prosper wherever you go."

Joshua sent two spies to explore the land, especially Jericho. Upon reaching Jericho, they went into the house of a woman named Rahab. When the king of Jericho was told that some Israelites had come to spy out the land, he ordered Rahab to put them out. But the woman, who had hidden the two men on the roof, said to the king's messengers: "Yes, the men did come to me, but I do not know where they came from; at dark, they left, and I do not know where they went. You will have to pursue them immediately to overtake them."

The pursuers set out and took the road to the Jordan. Before the spies had gone to sleep, Rahab came up to them on the roof and said: "I know that the Lord has given you the land; all the inhabitants of the land are overcome with fear of you. We are disheartened; everyone is discouraged because of you. Now then, swear to me by the Lord that you will show kindness to my family and save us from death." "We pledge our lives for yours," the men answered her. "If you will not betray us, we will deal kindly and faithfully with you when the Lord gives us the land."

Then she let them down through the window with a rope, for she lived in a house built into the city wall. "Get away to the hills," she said to them, "so that the pursuers may not find you. Hide there for three days, until they have returned."

The men said to her: "When we come into the land, you shall tie this scarlet cord in the window through which you let us down; and you shall gather your father and mother, your brothers and all your family into your house. Should anyone of them pass outside the doors of your house, he will be responsible for his own death, and we shall be guiltless. But we shall be responsible if anyone in the house with you is harmed. If, however, you breathe a word about our errand, we will not be bound by the oath you have made us take."

"Let it be as you say," she replied, and she let them down by a rope through the window. When they were gone, she tied the scarlet cord in the window. They went into the hills and stayed there for three days, till the pursuers had returned. Then the two spies came down from the hills. They went to Joshua and told him all that had befallen them. They said to Joshua: "The Lord has given the entire land into our hands; the inhabitants are overcome with fear of us."

The people left their tents to cross the Jordan. They were headed by the priests, who carried the ark of the covenant. Now, as soon as the bearers of the ark reached the Jordan and their feet dipped into the water at the edge, the waters flowing down came to a stop, while the waters flowing away toward the salt sea were completely cut off. The priests carrying the ark stood still on dry ground in the middle of the Jordan, while all Israel crossed over on dry ground, opposite Jericho. When all the people had finished crossing, the priests with the ark advanced in front of the people. Then the waters of the Jordan resumed their course and overflowed their banks as before.

Twelve stones were taken out of the Jordan, and Joshua set them up at Gilgal. He said to the people of Israel: "When your children in time to come ask what these stones mean, you shall tell them that Israel crossed the Jordan here on dry ground."

The people of Israel observed the Passover when they were in camp at Gilgal. The manna ceased when they began to eat the food of the land of Canaan.

Now Jericho had shut its gates against the Israelites; no one left or entered the city. Joshua ordered the people to march around the city, with the armed men passing before the ark of the Lord and before seven priests blowing seven rams' horns. He warned the people, saying: "You must not shout, you must not say a word, until I tell you to shout; only then you shall shout."

Joshua had the ark carried around the city once; then the people returned to the camp and passed the night there. The second day they again marched around the city once and returned to the camp. This they continued to do for six days. On the seventh day, they arose at daybreak and marched around the city seven times. The seventh time, when the priests blew the horns, Joshua said to the people: "Shout, for the Lord has given you the city. Only Rahab and those who are in her house shall be spared."

The people raised a tremendous shout, and the wall collapsed; they stormed the city and captured it. Rahab and her entire family were saved and placed outside the camp of Israel because she had hidden the messengers sent by Joshua.

Joshua and all the fighting men prepared to attack Ai. He selected thirty thousand brave soldiers and sent them off by night, commanding them: "Ambush the city from the rear, at no great distance; then all of you be ready. The rest of the soldiers and I will approach the city, and when they come out against us, we will flee before them until we draw them away from it. As we run away, you shall come out of ambush and capture the city. As soon as you have captured it, you shall set it on fire."

Early the next morning, Joshua led all the people against Ai. The main army was stationed to the north of the city, with the ambush west of it. The king of Ai came out to engage Israel in battle, not knowing that there was an ambush behind the city. Joshua and all the Israelites fled, in seeming defeat, toward the desert. All the people of Ai, who pursued Joshua, were drawn away from the city which they left unprotected. Then the men in ambush rushed into the city and set it on fire, while the Israelites, who were fleeing toward the desert, turned upon their pursuers. By the time the men of Ai looked back, smoke was rising from the city! Meanwhile, the Israelites in Ai came out of the city to fight against them. They were hemmed in on either side; escape in any direction was impossible. None of them remained alive.

When the inhabitants of Gibeon heard what Joshua had done to Jericho and Ai, they acted with cunning. They went to Joshua and said: "We have come from a distant country to propose that you make a treaty with us."

"Who are you? Where do you come from?" Joshua asked. "We have come from a far off land," they replied. "Here is our bread; it was still warm the day we left home to come to you, but now it is dry and crumbled. Look at our garments and shoes; they are worn out from the very long journey."

So Joshua made a treaty with them to spare their lives.

Three days after the treaty was made, the Israelites learned that the Gibeonites were their neighbors, living in the same country. But the leaders of Israel declared: "We have sworn to them by the Lord God of Israel, and we cannot harm them; let them live!"

The five Amorite kings united all their forces and marched against Gibeon. Thereupon the Gibeonites sent an appeal to Joshua: "Do not abandon your servants; come up here quickly, save us, help us; all the Amorite kings are gathered against us."

So Joshua marched up with all the fighting men and valiant soldiers. Meanwhile, the Lord said to Joshua: "Do not fear them, for I have delivered them into your hands. Not one of them shall hold his own against you." And when Joshua made his surprise attack upon them, the Lord threw them into a panic before the Israelites, who routed them with heavy slaughter. It was on that day, when the Lord handed over the Amorites to the Israelites, that Joshua said: "O sun, stand still at Gibeon; move not, O moon, in the valley of Aijalon." The sun stood still in the middle of the sky, and did not set for about a whole day. Never before or since was there a day like this! The Lord listened to the voice of a man, for the Lord fought for Israel.

When Joshua was old and well advanced in years, the Lord said to him: "You are old, but very much of the land still remains to be conquered. However, allot the land to Israel as I commanded you."

Then the people of Judah came to Joshua, and Caleb said to him: "You know what the Lord said to Moses about you and me. I was forty years old when Moses sent me to spy out the land; I brought back to him a conscientious report. My fellow spies who went up with me discouraged the people, but I was completely loyal to the Lord my God. On that occasion Moses solemnly promised, saying: The land on which your foot has trodden shall be an inheritance for you and your descendants forever.

"And now the Lord has kept me alive for the past forty-five years, ever since the Lord spoke this word to Moses. Here I am today eighty-five years old. I am still as strong today as I was when Moses sent me off; my strength now is as it was then. Give me, then, this hill country of which the Lord spoke on that day."

Joshua blessed Caleb and gave Hebron to him for an inheritance. And the land had rest from war.

A long time afterwards, when the Lord had given rest to the people of Israel from all their enemies round about, and when Joshua was far advanced in years, Joshua summoned all Israel and said to them: "I am about to go the way of all the earth; and you know in your hearts and souls, all of you, that not one thing has failed of all the good things which the Lord promised concerning you. Thus says the Lord God of Israel:

"I took your father Abraham from the other side of the Euphrates River and led him through all the land of Canaan; I gave him Isaac, and to Isaac I gave Jacob and Esau. Jacob and his children went down to Egypt. I sent Moses and Aaron, and I brought your fathers out of Egypt. The Egyptians pursued your fathers as far as the Red Sea, and the Lord engulfed them in it. You lived many days in the wilderness, and I brought you to the eastern side of the Jordan. Then Balak, king of Moab, sent for Balaam to curse you, but he blessed you instead. You crossed the Jordan and came to Jericho, and I put the men of Jericho into your hands; it was not your sword nor bow that defeated them. I have given you a land for which you did not labor, and cities which you did not build, and you eat fruit from vineyards and oliveyards you did not plant. Now therefore revere the Lord and serve him sincerely and faithfully. But if you are unwilling to serve the Lord, then choose today whom you will serve. As for me and my house, we will serve the Lord."

The people answered: "Far be it from us to forsake the Lord and serve other gods!" Then Joshua dismissed the people; every man returned to his own home.

After this, Joshua died at the age of a hundred and ten. He was buried in his own land in the hill country of Ephraim. Israel served the Lord all the days of Joshua and all the days of the elders who outlived Joshua.

Judges

The book of Judges is a story of triumphant faith. It derives its name from the twelve heroic leaders whose deeds and prowess it describes. The Hebrew word for judges (*shoftim*) connotes champions, defenders. The judges, including Eli and Samuel who are described in the book of Samuel, were gifted and courageous persons who strengthened Israel's hold of Canaan against a variety of enemies. These champions of Israel inspired the people to fight against those who threatened their existence. The period of the judges lasted about two hundred and thirty years, during the interval between the death of Joshua and the coronation of Saul.

The book of Judges is replete with character sketches and examples of good traits and bad ones. Deborah, the prophetess who held court and settled disputes among her people, was a dynamic personality in peace and war. The song of Deborah, celebrating the victory over the army of Sisera, is an excellent example of early Hebrew poetry, even though the meaning is not clear in some of its verses. It is the outcome of a powerful imagination and reaches sublime heights of religious emotion.

Gideon was a man of peace, who succeeded in appeasing the fiery Ephraimites by minimizing his own achievements and magnifying their part in the final destruction of the enemy. His daring modesty and good temper make him a glowing personality.

Jephthah was a man of war and, unlike Gideon, fought the Ephraimites back to their Jordan boundary. He seized the fords of the river and set guards to let no Ephraimite pass over. The identity of Ephraimites was easily detected by the way they mispronounced the word "Shibboleth" (stream). They could not pronounce "sh" and said "s" instead.

Samson represents a strange combination of virtue and folly. He is the strong man who is too weak to resist feminine wiles. Delilah has become a symbol of the treacherous woman in whose clutches the strong man is helpless.

After the death of Joshua and all his generation, the people of Israel did evil in the sight of the Lord and served the

Baals. They forsook the God of their fathers, and went after the gods of the various nations around them and worshiped them. So the anger of the Lord flared up against the people of Israel, and he handed them over to their enemies. Then the Lord raised up judges, who saved them from their plunderers. But when a judge died, they would relapse and behave worse than their fathers.

The people of Israel offended the Lord by serving the Baals, so he allowed them to fall into the power of the king of Mesopotamia, whom they served for eight years. But when the people of Israel cried to the Lord, he raised up a champion for them, Othniel, who saved them. The land then was at rest for forty years, until Othniel died.

Again the people of Israel offended the Lord, so he made the king of Moab gain power over them. For eighteen years they were subject to Eglon, king of Moab. Then Israel cried to the Lord, and he raised up a champion for them, Ehud, who was left-handed. He made himself a two-edged dagger, and wore it under his clothes over his right hip.

Ehud once presented the tribute of Israel to Eglon, who was a very fat man. After the presentation, he dismissed the carriers, went back and said: "I have a private message for you, O king." "Silence!" said the king to all his attendants, and they left him. Then Ehud went in to see him, as he sat alone in his cool roof chamber. "I have a message from God for you," Ehud said, and Eglon rose from his seat.

Ehud reached with his left hand, took the dagger from his right hip, plunged it into Eglon's belly, and left it there. He then went out into the vestibule, closed the doors of the room and locked them. After he had gone, the king's servants came—and there lay their lord dead on the floor.

In the meantime, Ehud escaped and sounded the trumpet through the highlands of Ephraim. "Follow me," he said to the people of Israel, "for the Lord has delivered your enemies, the Moabites, into your hands!" So they marched after Ehud and seized the fords of the Jordan leading to Moab, permitting no one to cross. They killed about ten thousand Moabites that day. Moab was brought under the power of Israel, and the land had rest for eighty years.

After Ehud came Shamgar, who killed six hundred Philistines with an oxgoad; he too saved Israel.

After Ehud's death, the people of Israel again did evil in the sight of the Lord, so he delivered them into the power of the Canaanite king, Jabin, whose army commander was Sisera. Jabin had nine hundred iron chariots, and for twenty years he oppressed Israel severely.

At that time Israel was governed by Deborah, a prophetess, who used to sit under a palm tree, where the people came to her for judgment. She summoned Barak from Naphtali and said to him: "The Lord God of Israel commands you to gather ten thousand men. He will deliver Sisera and his chariots and his troops into your power."

Barak said to Deborah: "If you will come with me, I will go; but if you will not come with me, I will not go." She replied: "I will certainly go with you; however, the glory of the course you are undertaking will not be yours, for the Lord will give Sisera over into the hand of a woman."

Then Deborah went with Barak to Kedesh and ten thousand men marched with them.

When Sisera was told that Barak had gone up to Mount Tabor, he summoned his nine hundred chariots and all his forces.

Deborah said to Barak: "Up! This is the day when the Lord has given Sisera into your hand!" So Barak, with his men, charged down from Mount Tabor, and the Lord routed Sisera and all his chariots and all his army. Sisera alighted from his chariot and fled on foot to the tent of Jael, who went out to meet him, saying: "Come in, my lord, come in; do not be afraid." So he went into her tent, and she covered him up with a rug.

He said to her: "Pray give me a little water to drink, for I am thirsty." She opened a bottle of milk, gave him a drink and covered him up again.

He said to her: "Stand at the door of the tent; if anyone comes and asks you if there is a man here, say no." But Jael took a tent peg and a hammer in her hand and, coming quietly up to him, she drove the peg through his temple into the ground while he was sound asleep and exhausted, and he died.

Just then Barak arrived in pursuit of Sisera, and Jael went out to meet him, saying: "Come, and I will show you the man for whom you are looking!" So Barak went inside her tent, and there lay Sisera dead, with the tent peg in his temple.

On that day Deborah and Barak sang:

"Hear, O kings; give ear, O princes! I will sing to the Lord God of Israel. In the days of Jael, caravans ceased and travelers kept to the byways, Israel's hamlets were deserted until I, Deborah, arose, arose as a mother in Israel. My heart goes out to the commanders of Israel, who volunteered among the people! Bless the Lord!

"Awake, awake, Deborah! Awake, awake, utter a song! To your feet, O Barak, and lead away your captives!

"The very stars in heaven were fighting, from their spheres they fought against Sisera. The river Kishon swept them away; then the hoofs of the mighty horses struck, rushing and dashing away.

"Most blessed above women shall Jael be! He asked for water and she gave him milk; she crushed his head and pierced his temple; he sank, he fell, he lay still at her feet.

"Thus may all thy enemies perish, O Lord; may those who love thee be as the rising sun!"

The land was at rest for forty years. But the people of Israel did evil in the sight of the Lord, so the Lord handed them over to Midian for seven years.

Midian gained the upper hand over Israel. Whenever the Israelites had completed their sowing, the Midianites would come and destroy the produce of the country as far south as Gaza. They left Israel nothing to live on. They would come with their cattle and their tents, swarming like locusts; and so the people of Israel cried for help to the Lord.

Gideon, the son of Joash, was beating out some wheat in the winepress, to hide it from the Midianites. And the angel of the Lord appeared to him, saying: "The Lord is with you, mighty man of valor!" But Gideon replied: "Sir, if the Lord is with us, why then has all this befallen us?

Where are all his wondrous deeds of which our fathers told us? The Lord has abandoned us and has delivered us into the power of Midian."

The Lord turned to him and said: "Go, with the strength you have, and save Israel from Midian. It is I who send you."

Then Gideon said to God: "I am putting a fleece of wool on the threshing floor. If dew falls only on the fleece, while all the ground is dry, I shall know that thou wilt save Israel through me, as thou hast promised." This did happen. When he rose early next morning and squeezed the fleece, he wrung enough dew from it to fill a bowl. Gideon then said to God: "Let me make just one more test with the fleece: pray let the fleece alone be dry, and let there be dew on all the ground." That night God did so; the fleece alone was dry, and there was dew on all the ground.

So Gideon and all his men rose early and encamped beside the spring of Harod, south of the Midianite camp. But the Lord said to Gideon: "There are too many men with you. Proclaim now to the people that anyone who is fearful and trembling must return home." And so twenty-two thousand left, and ten thousand remained.

"There are still too many," the Lord said to Gideon; "take them down to the water, and I will sift them there."

When Gideon took them down to the water, the Lord said to him: "Place on one side everyone who laps up the water with his tongue like a dog, and place on the other side everyone who kneels down to drink."

The men who lapped numbered three hundred; all the rest knelt down to drink the water.

Then the Lord said to Gideon: "With the three hundred men who lapped I will save you and put Midian into your hands; let all the rest go home." So he sent all the Israelites home, and retained only the three hundred.

That same night Gideon went down with his servant to the outposts of the Midianites. They lay along the valley in swarms, like locusts. And behold, a man was telling a dream to his comrade. "I had a dream," he said, "that a cake of barley bread tumbled into the camp of Midian. It came to our tent and struck it so that it fell; it turned the tent upside down."

"This can only be the sword of the Israelite Gideon," the other replied. "God has delivered Midian into his power."

When Gideon heard the description of the dream and its interpretation, he returned to the camp of Israel and said: "Arise, for the Lord has delivered the camp of Midian into our hands."

Gideon divided the three hundred men into three companies and provided them all with trumpets, empty pitchers and torches inside the pitchers. "Watch me and do as I do," he told them; "when I and all my men blow our trumpets, you too must blow yours all around the Midianite camp and shout: For the Lord and for Gideon!"

So Gideon, and the hundred men who were with him, came to the outskirts of the camp at the beginning of the middle watch, just when the guard had been posted. They blew the trumpets and smashed the pitchers in their hands. All the three companies blew their trumpets and broke their pitchers. They held the torches in their left hands and the trumpets in their right hands, shouting: "A sword for the Lord and Gideon!"

They all remained standing in place around the camp, while the whole camp fell to running and shouting and fleeing. But the three hundred men kept blowing the horns, and throughout the camp the Lord set the sword of one against another.

The men of Israel were called to pursue Midian. Gideon sent messengers throughout the highlands of Ephraim, saying: "Come down to confront Midian and seize the water courses against them, as well as the Jordan." So all the men of Ephraim were called to arms; they seized the water courses and the Jordan, captured the two chiefs of Midian, and killed them.

The men of Ephraim then asked Gideon: "Why have you treated us like this? Why did you not call us when you started the attack on Midian?" And they quarrelled bitterly with him. But he replied: "What have I accomplished, compared to what you have? God has put the chiefs of Midian into your hands. What have I been able to do in comparison with you?" When he said this, their anger against him subsided.

Then the people of Israel said to Gideon: "Rule over us, for you have saved us from Midian." But Gideon said to them: "I will not rule over you, nor shall my son; the Lord shall rule over you."

So the Midianites were subdued by Israel and they raised their heads no more. The land had rest for forty years in the days of Gideon.

Now the Ammonites gathered for war and encamped in Gilead, while the Israelites assembled and encamped in Mizpah.

There was a chieftain, Jephthah the Gileadite, who was the son of a harlot, and Gilead was his father. The sons of Gilead's wife had driven Jephthah away, saying to him: "You shall inherit nothing in our family, for you are the son of another woman." So Jephthah fled from his brothers and stayed in the land of Tob, where worthless fellows collected round him, and went on raids with him.

When the Ammonites went to war with Israel, the elders of Gilead went to bring Jephthah. "Come, be our commander," they said to Jephthah, "that we may fight the Ammonites." But Jephthah replied: "Did you not hate me and drive me out of my father's house? Why have you come to me now when you are in trouble?"

"We have come back to you," the elders said; "if you go with us to fight the Ammonites, you shall be the leader of all of us who live in Gilead." Jephthah answered: "If you take me back to fight the Ammonites, and if the Lord delivers them into my hands, I will be your leader."

The elders of Gilead said to Jephthah: "The Lord is witness between us that we will do as you say." So Jephthah went with the elders of Gilead, and the people made him their leader and commander.

Then Jephthah sent messengers to the king of the Ammonites, saying: "What have you against me that you come to attack my country?" The king of the Ammonites answered the messengers of Jephthah: "Israel took away my land when they came up from Egypt. Now, then, restore it peaceably."

Again Jephthah sent messengers, saying: "Israel did not take the land of Moab or the land of the Ammonites. Three hundred years have passed; why have you never recaptured them during all that time? No, I have done no wrong to you; it is you who are doing me wrong by making war on me. Let the Lord decide this day between the Israelites and the Ammonites!"

Then Jephthah went to fight against the Ammonites, and the Lord delivered them into his power. Jephthah inflicted a severe defeat on them, and they were subdued by the people of Israel.

The men of Ephraim assembled to ask Jephthah: "Why did you go to fight the Ammonites without calling on us to go with you? We will burn down your house over your head." But Jephthah said to them: "My men and I were engaged in a sharp struggle, the Ammonites were pressing us hard. We summoned you, but you did not rescue us from their power. When I saw that you would not help us, I took my life in my own hand and went to the Ammonites, and the Lord gave them over to me. Why, then, have you come up this day to fight against me?"

Then Jephthah gathered all the men of Gilead and fought with the men of Ephraim, whom they defeated. The Gileadites seized the fords of the Jordan toward Ephraim. When any of the fleeing Ephraimites said, "Let me cross," the men of Gilead would ask him whether he was of the tribe of Ephraim. If he said "No," they asked him to say "Shibboleth." If he said "Sibboleth," not being able to pronounce the word correctly, they knew that he belonged to Ephraim and killed him at the fords of the Jordan.

Jephthah governed Israel for six years. Then Jephthah died and was buried in his town in Gilead.

Again the people of Israel did what was evil in the sight of the Lord, so the Lord handed them over to the Philistines for forty years.

There was a certain man named Manoah whose wife had borne no children. An angel of the Lord appeared to the woman and said to her: "Be careful to drink no wine or strong drink and to eat no unclean food, for you shall bear a son. No razor shall touch his head, for this boy shall be a

Nazirite, consecrated to God from birth; he shall begin the deliverance of Israel from the Philistines." The woman did bear a son, and she called him Samson. The boy grew up, and the Lord blessed him.

Once Samson told his father and mother: "I saw a Philistine woman at Timnah; get her to be my wife." So they said to him: "Can you find no wife among all our people that you must go and take a wife from the Philistines?" But Samson insisted: "Get her for me; I like her!"

Samson went down to Timnah, and a young lion came roaring toward him. He tore the lion in two, although he had no weapon in his hand. After a while he stepped aside to look at the remains of the lion, and there was a swarm of bees and honey in the body of the lion. He scraped the honey into his hands and ate as he went along. He gave some of it to his father and mother, but he did not tell them that he had taken it from the lion's body.

When Samson married the woman in Timnah, he held a feast. He said to the thirty companions who had been sent from Timnah to be with him: "Let me ask you a riddle. If you can solve it within the seven days of the feast, I will give you thirty suits of clothes; but if you cannot guess it, you shall give me thirty suits of clothes." They said to him: "Tell your riddle. Let us hear it." So he said to them: "Out of the eater came something to eat. Out of the strong came something sweet."

For three days they could not guess the riddle. On the fourth day they said to Samson's wife: "Entice your husband to tell us what the riddle means, or we will burn you and your family. Have you invited us here to make us poor?"

She wept and said to Samson: "You hate me. You do not love me. You have proposed a riddle to my countrymen, and you have never told me the answer." She pressed him so hard that, at last, on the seventh day of their feast, he told her. Then she explained the riddle to her countrymen.

That day, before sunset, the men of the town said to Samson: "What is sweeter than honey? What is stronger than a lion?" And he said to them: "If you had not plowed with my heifer, you would not have solved my riddle."

Samson went down to Ashkelon and killed thirty men of the town; he gave their clothes to those who had answered the riddle. Then he went off to his own family in anger. And Samson's wife was given to one of his companions, he who had been his best man.

After some time, Samson went to visit his wife with a present. But her father would not let him enter the house, saying: "I thought that you hated her, so I gave her to your companion. Her younger sister is more beautiful; take her instead."

Samson went and caught three hundred foxes. Turning them tail to tail, he tied between each pair of tails one of the torches he had at hand. He then set fire to the torches, and let the foxes loose in the standing grain of the Philistines. The shocks, the standing grain and the olive orchards were burned to ashes.

When the Philistines were told that Samson, the son-in-law of the Timnite, had done this because his wife had been taken away from him and given to another man, they came up and destroyed her and her family by fire.

"If this is what you do," Samson said to the Philistines, "I will have my revenge on you before I am done." He inflicted a heavy slaughter on them; then he went down and stayed in a cavern.

The Philistines came up and camped in Judah. "Why have you come up against us?" the men of Judah asked. "To seize Samson," the Philistines replied; "to do to him what he has done to us."

So three thousand men of Judah went to the cliff and said to Samson: "Do you not know that the Philistines are our overlords? Why have you done this to us?" He answered: "As they have done to me, so have I done to them."

But the men of Judah declared: "We have come to take you prisoner and hand you over to the Philistines." Samson said to them: "Swear to me that you will not kill me yourselves." They replied: "No, we will not kill you; we will only bind you and hand you over to them." So they bound him with two new ropes and brought him up from the cliff.

When the Philistines came to meet him shouting, the ropes around his arms became like flax that has caught fire, and his bonds melted from his hands. He seized a fresh jawbone of a mule, and with it he slew a thousand men.

After that he fell in love with a woman whose name was Delilah. The Philistine tyrants came to her and said: "Find out the secret of his great strength, and how we may over-power him. If you do this, we will each give you eleven hundred pieces of silver." So Delilah said to Samson: "Tell me the secret of your great strength and how you may be tied up and made helpless." Samson replied: "If I am tied with seven fresh bowstrings that have not been dried, my strength will fail, and I shall be like any other man."

The Philistine tyrants brought her seven fresh bow-strings which had not been dried, and with these she tied up Samson. Then she shouted: "The Philistines are upon you, Samson!" He snapped the bowstrings like a piece of yarn at the touch of fire, and the secret of his strength still remained unknown.

Delilah said to Samson: "You have deceived me! You have told me a lie! Now, do tell me how you may be bound." He said to her: "If they bind me tight with new ropes that have not been used, my strength will fail, and I shall be like any other man." So Delilah took new ropes and bound him. She shouted: "The Philistines are upon you, Samson!" He broke the ropes from his arms like thread.

Delilah said to Samson: "You have been deceiving me all the time; you have told me lies. Tell me why you are so strong." He said to her: "If you weave my seven locks of hair into a web, I shall be as weak as any other man." So while he was asleep, Delilah wove his seven locks of hair into the web, and shouted: "The Philistines are upon you, Samson!" He woke up and pulled out both loom and web.

Then she said to him: "How can you say that you love me when you do not confide in me. Three times you have trifled with me, and you have not told me wherein your great strength lies." At last, when she had pressed and urged him day after day, he became tired to death of it and told her the truth: "A razor has never been used on my head, for I have been a Nazirite to God from birth. If I were to be shaved, my strength would leave me and I should become like any other man."

She made Samson sleep on her lap, and called for a man who shaved off the seven locks of his head. His strength left him, and she shouted: "The Philistines are upon you, Samson!" He woke up and thought he might again shake himself free, not realizing that the Lord had left him. The Philistines seized him and gouged out his eyes; they brought him down to Gaza and bound him with bronze chains. He spent his time in prison grinding at the mill.

Now the Philistine tyrants had gathered for a great sacrifice to their god Dagon, and for merrymaking. "Our god," they said, "has put Samson, our enemy, into our hands." They were in high spirits, and shouted: "Call for Samson that he may amuse us!"

So Samson was called from prison. He was made to stand between the pillars, and he said to the attendant who held him by the hand: "Let me feel the pillars on which the house rests, that I may lean against them." Now the house was full of men and women; all the Philistine lords were there, and on the roof there were about three thousand men and women, looking down in amusement at Samson.

Samson called to the Lord and said: "Lord God, remember me; give me strength, I pray thee, only this once, O God, to wreak vengeance upon the Philistines for one of my two eyes."

Samson grasped the two middle pillars on which the house rested, one with his right hand and the other with his left, and leaned his weight upon them.

"Let me die with the Philistines!" Samson cried. He pulled with all his might, and the temple fell on the tyrants and on all the people that were inside. So those he killed in death were more than he had killed in life.

His kinsmen and all his family came and took him away to be buried in the tomb of his father Manoah. He had championed Israel for twenty years.

Samuel

The two books of Samuel are considered as one book in the Hebrew Bible, and continue the history of Israel from the tribal stage to the development of a united nation. They cover a period of about one hundred years (1070–970). It was one of the most important centuries in the life of Israel. In the long struggle against its surrounding enemies, Israel learned its own strength and prepared to play its part in the history of mankind. Events during this period are centered about three great personalities: Samuel, Saul and David.

The books of Samuel, containing the first records of prophecy, are among the most important sources for the history of religion. The first book records the life of Samuel and the events that occurred during his administration and that of King Saul. It also describes David's good character and his triumphs, spiritual and temporal.

The second book describes the career of David and the expansion of his kingdom. It contains a vivid portrayal of the demoralization in David's family, traceable to David's own moral collapse. The story of Absalom's rebellion against David, and of David's mourning over the death of Absalom is considered to be one of the greatest narratives that has come down to us from ancient times.

There was a man by the name of Elkanah who had two wives, one named Hannah and the other Peninnah. Peninnah had children, but Hannah had none. Year after year this man would go from his town to worship and sacrifice to the Lord at Shiloh.

Upon a certain day, when Elkanah offered a sacrifice, he gave portions to his wife Peninnah and all her sons and daughters; but to Hannah he gave a double portion because he loved her, though the Lord had made her childless. This was done year after year—whenever they went up to the house of the Lord, and Peninnah provoked Hannah, who wept and could not eat. Elkanah said to her:

87

"Hannah why are you weeping? Why are you not eating? Why is your heart sad? Am I not more to you than ten sons?"

After the eating and drinking at Shiloh, Hannah rose to pray, while Eli, the priest, was sitting near the doorpost of the temple of the Lord. With a sad heart she prayed to the Lord and wept bitterly. She vowed, saying: "Lord of hosts, if thou wilt remember me and grant me a son, I will give him to thee for all his life."

As she prayed, Eli watched her. Now Hannah was speaking inwardly; only her lips moved, her voice could not be heard; Eli thought she was drunk. So Eli said to her: "How long will you be drunk? Remove yourself from wine and sober up!"

Hannah replied: "I am a distressed woman; I have drunk neither wine nor any other intoxicating drink. Do not take your servant for a worthless woman; it is because of my great distress that I have spoken so far."

Then Eli answered: "Go in peace; may the God of Israel grant you what you have asked of him." And she said: "May your servant find favor in your eyes." Then the woman went away; she ate, and was sad no more.

Early in the morning they arose, worshiped before the Lord, and returned home. The Lord remembered Hannah, and at the turn of the year she bore a son, whom she named Samuel, meaning: *I asked the Lord for him.*

Elkanah and all his household went up to offer the Lord the annual sacrifice; but Hannah did not go up, for she told her husband: "When the child is weaned I will take him to stay there forever." Elkanah said to her: "Do what seems best to you; and may the Lord carry out his purpose."

So the woman remained, and nursed her son until she weaned him. Then she brought the boy to the house of the Lord at Shiloh and to Eli. She said to him: "As sure as you live, I am the woman who stood beside you praying for this boy, and the Lord has granted my petition. I lend him to the Lord for as long as he shall live." Then Hannah sang this prayer:

"My heart exults in the Lord, my glory is raised by the Lord. There is none holy like the Lord!

"Do not speak boastfully, let no arrogance come from your mouth. The Lord is a God of knowledge, and by him actions are weighed.

"The strong men's bows are broken, while the feeble are girded with strength. Those who had plenty have hired themselves out for bread, while those who were hungry toil no more. The barren woman has seven children, while the mother of many is bereaved.

"The Lord causes death and bestows life; he lowers to the grave and brings up. The Lord makes poor and makes rich. He brings low, he also raises up. He lifts the poor out of the dust, and he raises the needy from the rubbish. He guards the steps of godly men, but the wicked perish in darkness; not by might shall man prevail.

"The foes of the Lord shall be crushed. He will thunder in heaven against them. The Lord will judge all parts of the world!"

The child Samuel ministered in the temple under Eli. And once, when Samuel lay down to sleep beside the ark, the Lord called him. He ran to Eli, saying: "Here I am." But Eli said: "I did not call you; go back and lie down." Again the Lord called him. Samuel got up and went to Eli. "Here I am," he said. But Eli answered: "I did not call you, my son; go back and lie down."

When the Lord called Samuel a third time, Eli understood that the Lord was calling. So he said to Samuel: "Go lie down. If you are called again, say: Speak, O Lord, thy servant is listening."

Then Samuel went and lay down, and when the Lord called, he answered: "Speak, thy servant is listening." And the Lord said to Samuel: "Behold, I am about to do a thing in Israel that will make the ears of everyone who hears it tingle. Eli has known for some time that his sons blasphemed God and he did not stop them, therefore the iniquity of his house shall never be expiated by sacrifice or offering."

Samuel was afraid to reveal the vision to Eli; but Eli

asked: "Samuel, my son, what was it that the Lord said to you? Do not hide it from me." So Samuel told him everything, and Eli said: "He is the Lord; let him do what seems good to him."

Samuel grew up, and the Lord was with him. All Israel from Dan to Beersheba knew that Samuel was a prophet of the Lord.

When Samuel grew old, he made his sons judges over Israel. But his sons did not follow in his footsteps. They took bribes and perverted justice. So the elders of Israel came to Samuel at Ramah and said to him: "You are old, and your sons are not following in your footsteps. Now appoint a king to govern us that we may be like all other nations."

It displeased Samuel to hear them asking for a king, but the Lord said to him: "Listen to the voice of the people; but give them warning and explain to them the ways of the king who shall reign over them."

Samuel then said to the people: "Here are the ways of the king who shall reign over you. He will take your sons and make them his horsemen; some will plow his ground and reap his harvest; some will make his arms and his chariots. He will take your daughters to be cooks and bakers; he will take the best of your fields and vineyards and present them to his officers. He will take a tenth of your grain and give it to his servants; he will use your servants and your cattle for his own work. And you yourselves shall be slaves to him." However, the people refused to listen to the voice of Samuel, and said: "No, we must have a king over us!"

Now, there was a man by the name of Kish, who had a son, Saul, a handsome young man. There was not a man among the people of Israel more handsome than he. Saul was a head taller than any of the people.

When Samuel saw Saul, the Lord said to him: "Here is the man of whom I told you; this man shall rule over my people." So Samuel said to Saul: "Tell your servant to go on ahead; but stop here yourself, that I may reveal to you God's message." Then Samuel poured oil on Saul's head and kissed him, saying: "The Lord has anointed you to be prince over his people Israel. You shall reign over them and save them from the power of their enemies."

God gave Saul another heart, and he prophesied along with the young prophets. On seeing him prophesy, the people who knew him said to one another: "What has happened to the son of Kish? Is Saul also among the prophets?"

When he returned home, his uncle asked him and his servant: "Where have you been?" "In search of the lost donkeys," Saul replied. "When we saw that they were not to be found, we went to Samuel the seer."

Saul's uncle asked: "Pray tell me what Samuel said to you." And Saul replied: "He told us that the donkeys had been found." But concerning the kingdom Saul said nothing.

Samuel called the people together to the Lord at Mizpah, and he said to them: "Do you see whom the Lord has chosen? There is not a man like him among all the people!" And all the people shouted: "Long live the king!"

Then Samuel said to all Israel: "I have listened to your plea and have appointed a king over you. As for me, I have led you from my youth until this day. Here I am! Testify against me in the presence of the Lord and his anointed king. Whose ox have I seized? Whose donkey have I taken? Whom have I defrauded? Whom have I oppressed? From whom have I taken a bribe? Testify against me, and I will restore it to you."

They replied: "You have not defrauded us, nor oppressed us, nor taken anything from anybody."

Then Samuel said to the people: "Stand here, that I may recount all the saving deeds performed by the Lord for you and for your fathers.

"When the Egyptians oppressed your fathers, they cried to the Lord. He sent Moses and Aaron to bring your fathers out of Egypt, and he settled them in this place. But they forgot the Lord their God, so he delivered them into the hands of Sisera and the Philistines and the king of Moab. They cried to the Lord, saying: 'We have sinned, we have worshiped the Baals; but deliver us from our enemies, and we will serve thee.' So the Lord sent Gideon and Barak and Jephthah and Samuel, and rescued you from your enemies.

Yet, when you saw the king of Ammon coming to attack you, you demanded a king, whereas the Lord your God is your King. And now, here is the king you have chosen! If you will revere the Lord and listen to his voice, well and good. But if you persist in doing wrong, both you and your king will be swept away." Then Samuel dismissed all the people, and each one returned home.

Saul had chosen three thousand men for active service. Two thousand were with him, and a thousand were with Jonathan, his son. The rest of the people he had sent home. When all Israel heard that Saul had defeated the garrison of the Philistines, the people were summoned to join Saul at Gilgal.

The Philistines gathered to fight against Israel with troops as numerous as the sands of the seashore, and the people hid in caves and holes and rocks and tombs and pits. Saul waited seven days, the time fixed by Samuel; but Samuel did not come to Gilgal, and the people were trembling and deserting. Saul then offered a burnt-offering himself, without waiting for Samuel. No sooner had he finished offering the burnt-offering than Samuel arrived.

Saul went out to greet him, but Samuel asked: "What have you done?" Saul answered: "I saw that the people were scattering, and you did not come within the appointed time. While the Philistines were massing for an attack, I forced myself to offer the burnt-offering and entreat the favor of the Lord before they pounced on us."

Samuel said to Saul: "You have done foolishly. If you had obeyed the command of the Lord your God, he would have established your kingdom over Israel forever. But now your kingdom shall not continue. The Lord has sought out a man after his own liking, and he has appointed him to be prince over his people."

The Lord said to Samuel: "I have rejected Saul from reigning over Israel; I will send you to Jesse of Bethlehem, for I have chosen me a king among his sons; you shall anoint the man whom I point out to you."

Samuel went to Bethlehem and invited Jesse and his sons to the banquet. When they came, the Lord said to Samuel: "Do not look at his appearance nor at his stature, for the Lord does not see as man sees. Man looks at the outward appearance, but the Lord looks at the heart."

Jesse made seven of his sons pass before Samuel, but Samuel said to Jesse: "The Lord has not chosen these. Are all your sons here?" Jesse answered: "There is still the youngest, and just now he is tending the flock."

"Send and fetch him," Samuel ordered; "we will not sit down to the banquet till he comes." Jesse sent for his youngest son. He was a youth with beautiful eyes and of a handsome appearance.

And the Lord said: "Arise, anoint him. This is the man!" Samuel took the horn of oil and anointed David in the midst of his brothers. From that day onward David was divinely inspired.

Now the spirit of the Lord departed from Saul, and an evil spirit troubled him. Saul's servants said to him: "An evil spirit is tormenting you. Let your servants find a skillful harpist, who will play music whenever the gloomy spirit overpowers you, and you will get well." Saul replied: "Find me a man who plays well, and bring him to me." One of them said: "I have noticed a son of Jesse, who is a skillful player and a brave man, intelligent and with a good presence."

Saul sent messengers to Jesse, requesting: "Send me your son David, who is with the sheep." When David came to Saul and presented himself, Saul loved him greatly and made him his armor-bearer. Whenever the evil spirit overpowered Saul, David took the harp and played until Saul was refreshed and his depression left him.

The Philistines again gathered their armed forces for war, so Saul and the men of Israel drew up in line of battle against them. The Philistines stood on a mountain on one side, and the Israelites stood on a mountain on the other side, with the valley between them. A champion by the name of Goliath came forward from the ranks of the Philistines. He was about ten feet tall. He wore a bronze helmet, and was armed with a coat of mail. The shaft of his spear was like a weaver's beam.

Goliath shouted to the ranks of Israel: "Choose a man from among you, and let him come down to me; if he can

kill me, we will be your servants; but if I kill him, you shall
be our servants. I defy the forces of Israel this day! Give
me a man, and let us have a fight!" When Saul and all
Israel heard the words of the Philistine, they were exceedingly dismayed and very much afraid. For forty days the
Philistine came forward and took his stand, morning and
evening.

David said to Saul: "I will go and fight the Philistine."
Saul replied: "You are not able to fight this Philistine; you
are only a youth, and he has been a warrior from his boy-
hood!" But David said: "I used to keep sheep for my
father, and when a lion came, or a bear, and seized a lamb
from the flock, I went after him and struck him down and
rescued the lamb. If the lion or bear turned against me, I
caught it by the chin and killed it with a blow. I have
killed both lions and bears. This Philistine shall fare like
them! The Lord who rescued me from the paw of the lion
and the paw of the bear, will rescue me from the hand of
this Philistine." "Go," Saul said to David, "and may the
Lord be with you!"

Then Saul clothed David with his armor. He put a helmet of bronze on his head and clad him in a coat of mail.
David girded on his sword over his armor, and he tried to
walk but he could not, for he was not used to wearing
armor. "I cannot move with these," he said, "I am not used
to them." So he removed them, took his staff, picked five
smooth stones from the brook and put them in his shepherd's bag. He then took his sling and went to meet the
Philistine.

When the Philistine saw David, he said disdainfully:
"Am I a dog that you come to me with sticks? Come to me,
and I will give your flesh to the birds of the air and the
beasts of the field."

David said to the Philistine: "You come to me with a
sword and a spear and javelin, but I come to you in the
name of the God of Israel whom you have defied. This day
the Lord will deliver you into my hands, that all may learn
that the Lord does not save by sword and spear."

When the Philistine drew near to attack David, David
hurried forward to meet him. Putting his hand into his

bag, David took out a stone and slung it, striking the Philistine on the forehead. The stone sank into his forehead, and he dropped on his face to the ground. David ran over to the Philistine, drew his sword from its sheath and killed him. When the Philistines saw that their champion was dead, they fled. Then the armies of Saul raised their battle-cry and pursued the Philistines as far as Gath and Ekron.

David returned from killing Goliath the Philistine, and the women came out dancing and singing: "Saul has slain his thousands, David his tens of thousands!" And Saul was very angry. "They give David tens of thousands," he said, "and I get only thousands! What more can he have but the kingdom itself?" From that day on Saul kept his eye on David.

Samuel died, and all Israel mourned for him. Shortly afterwards, the Philistines gathered their forces for war, and Saul gathered together all Israel, and they camped at Gilboa. When Saul saw the Philistine army, his heart trembled greatly. He disguised himself and went to the witch of Endor by night and said to her: "Bring me up the ghost of someone whom I shall name to you."

The woman said to him: "You know what Saul has done, how he has cast the mediums and the wizards from the land. Why, then, are you laying a trap for me? To have me put to death?" But Saul swore to her by the Lord, saying: "As the Lord lives, no punishment shall come upon you for this guilt." So the woman asked: "Whom shall I bring up for you?" And he said: "Bring me up Samuel."

When the woman saw Samuel, she gave a great shriek and said to Saul: "Why have you deceived me? You are Saul!" The king said to her: "Have no fear; what do you see?" The woman replied: "I see a divine being rising out of the earth." And he said to her: "What is he like?"

She said: "It is an old man coming up; he is wrapped in a cloak." Saul realized it was Samuel. He bowed with his face to the ground and prostrated himself.

Then Samuel said to Saul: "Why have you disturbed me by bringing me up?" Saul answered: "I am in great distress, for the Philistines are waging war against me. I have called you to ask what I should do, for the Lord has departed from me and answers me no more." And Samuel said: "Tomorrow you and your sons shall be with me; the Lord will give the army of Israel into the hand of the Philistines."

Saul fell full length upon the ground. He was exceedingly alarmed by what Samuel said. There was no strength in him, for he had eaten nothing all day and all night. When the woman went up to Saul and saw that he was panic-stricken, she said to him: "I have taken my life in my hands by doing what you ordered me to do; now let me put a bite of food before you; eat that you may have strength for your journey." But he refused, saying: "I will not eat." His attendants as well as the woman urged him, and he listened to them. He got up from the ground and sat on the couch. The woman put food before Saul and his attendants, and they ate. Then they went away that very night.

When the Philistines made their attack on Israel, they slew Jonathan and two of his brothers. The men of Israel fled before the Philistines; and Saul, hard pressed in the battle and badly wounded by the archers, said to his armor-bearer: "Draw your sword and run me through with it. I will not be taken prisoner." But his armor-bearer refused. He was terrified! Therefore, Saul took his own sword and fell on it. When his armor-bearer saw that Saul was dead, he also fell on his sword and died with him. Thus Saul and his three sons and his armor-bearer and all his men died together on the same day.

David meanwhile had fought and defeated the Amalekites. Three days after this victory, a man with torn clothes came and threw himself on the ground before David, saying: "I have escaped from the camp of Israel. The people have fled from the field of battle, and Saul and Jonathan are dead!"

Then David tore his garments, as did all the men with him. They lamented and wept and fasted till evening for Saul, his son Jonathan and for the house of Israel, because they had fallen by the sword. Then David uttered this lamentation over Saul and his son Jonathan:

"Your glory, O Israel, is slain! How are the mighty

fallen! Tell it not in Gath, announce it not in the streets of Ashkelon, lest the daughters of the Philistines rejoice.

"Mountains of Gilboa, let there be no dew, no rain upon you! For there the shield of the mighty was defiled, the shield of Saul. Saul and Jonathan, beloved and lovely, never parted in life or in death. They were swifter than eagles, stronger than lions.

"Daughters of Israel, weep over Saul who clothed you in scarlet and jewels. How are the mighty fallen in the midst of battle!

"Jonathan lies slain upon your hills, O Israel! I am distressed for you, my brother Jonathan. You were very dear to me; your love to me was wonderful, far beyond the love of women. How are the mighty fallen!"

After this, David defeated and subdued the Philistines as well as Edom, Moab, Ammon and Amalek. He won a name for himself, reigning over all Israel and administering justice and equity to all his people. Joab was in command of his army. Now Joab and his troops ravaged the Ammonites and besieged Rabbah. David, however, remained at Jerusalem.

One afternoon David walked on the roof of the royal palace and saw a beautiful woman bathing. He sent to make inquiries about her, and someone told him that she was Bathsheba, the wife of Uriah the Hittite. He sent for her, and she came to him. Then she returned to her house.

David sent word to Joab: "Put Uriah in the front line to be struck down and killed." When Uriah's wife heard that her husband was dead, she mourned for him. When the mourning was over, David brought her to his house. She became his wife and bore him a son.

Now what David had done displeased the Lord, and the Lord sent Nathan the prophet to David. Nathan went to him and said: "There were two men in one town, a rich man and a poor man. The rich man had many sheep and cattle; the poor man had nothing but a single lamb. He fed her, and she grew up with him and his children. She ate his bread, drank from his cup, and lay on his bosom; she was like a daughter to him. Now a traveler came to visit the rich man. The rich man refused to take from his own flock or his own herd to prepare for the guest. He took the poor man's lamb and prepared it for the visitor." David's anger blazed against the man, and he said to Nathan: "As the Lord lives, the man who has done this deserves to die!"

Nathan said to David: "You are the man! Thus says the Lord God of Israel: Why have you done what is evil in my sight? You have taken Uriah's wife to be your wife, having slain him by the sword of the Ammonites. Therefore, the sword shall never depart from your house. I will stir up evil against you in your own household. You have acted in secret, but I will act before all Israel, and in the sight of the sun." Then David said to Nathan: "I have sinned against the Lord." And Nathan replied: "The Lord has taken away your sin; you shall not die; but because you have utterly spurned the Lord, the child that is born to you shall surely die."

Then Nathan went home. The Lord struck the child that Uriah's wife bore to David, and it became sick. David prayed to God for the child, fasting and lying on the ground all night. On the seventh day, the child died.

David's servants were afraid to tell him that the child was dead, for fear that he would do something desperate to himself. But when David saw that his servants were whispering to one another, he understood that the child was dead. "Is the child dead?" he asked them; and they answered: "He is dead."

Then David got up from the ground; he washed himself and changed his clothes; he went to the house of the Lord and worshiped; after that he went home, asked for food and ate. "What is the meaning of this?" his servants asked him; "you fasted and wept for the child when it was still alive, but when the child died you got up and ate!" He replied: "When the child was still alive I fasted and wept because I thought that—who knows?—the Lord might have been gracious to me and allowed the child to live. But now he is dead; why should I fast? Can I bring him back again? I am going to him, but he will never come back to me."

Then David consoled his wife Bathsheba, and she later bore him a son whom he named Solomon.

Absalom, one of David's sons, used to rise early and

stand at the entrance of the city, and whenever any man came with a case for the king to judge, Absalom would call to him and say: "From what town are you? Your claims are good and right, but no one has been deputed by the king to hear you. O that I were appointed judge in the land, so that any one with a case or plea might come to me! I would give him justice!" Whenever a man approached to bow to him, he would put out his hand and take hold of him and kiss him. In this way Absalom stole the hearts of the men of Israel.

Absalom sent secret messengers throughout all the tribes of Israel, saying: "As soon as you hear the sound of the trumpet, shout: 'Absalom is king at Hebron!'" The conspiracy was strong; the number of people who joined Absalom increased.

A messenger came to David, saying: "The hearts of the men of Israel are with Absalom." David said to all his officers in Jerusalem: "Let us flee, or else we shall never escape from Absalom!" So the king went forth, and all his household after him. David went up the ascent of the Mount of Olives, weeping as he went, barefoot, with his head covered; and all the people who were with him wept as they went.

David mustered the men who were with him, and set over them commanders of thousands and commanders of hundreds. He divided the troops into three columns, one commanded by Joab, one by Joab's brother, and one, by Ittai the Gittite. The king said to the men: "I will go with you myself." But the men replied: "You shall not. If we run away, or if half of us die, it will not matter to anyone; but you, you are equal to ten thousand of us!" So the king said to them: "I will do whatever you think best." He ordered all his commanders, saying: "Deal gently, for my sake, with young Absalom."

The troops went out into the field against Israel, and the battle was fought in the forest of Ephraim. The men of Israel were defeated there by the soldiers of David. The slaughter that day was heavy—twenty thousand fell. Absalom rode his mule and, as the mule passed below the thick branches of a great oak, his head caught fast in the oak and he was left hanging in the air, while the mule went on without its rider. A certain man saw this and told Joab, who took three spears and thrust them into the heart of Absalom while he was still alive. Then Joab blew the trumpet, and the troops withdrew from pursuing after Israel. Now, Absalom in his lifetime had set up for himself a pillar known as Absalom's Monument, because he had no son to honor the memory of his name.

David was sitting between the gates and, behold, the Cushite came and said: "Good tidings for my lord the king! The Lord has delivered you this day from all who rose against you." The king said to the Cushite: "Is it well with the young man, Absalom?" And the Cushite answered: "May the enemies of my lord the king fare like that young man." The king was deeply moved; he went up to the chamber over the gate and wept. He cried: "O my son Absalom! My son, my son Absalom! O that I had died instead of you, Absalom, my son, my son!"

Joab was told that the king wept and mourned for Absalom. The victory that day turned into mourning for all the people who heard of the king's grief for his son. They stole into the city like people ashamed of having run away in a battle, while the king kept his face covered and cried aloud: "O my son Absalom, O Absalom, my son, my son!"

Then Joab came into the house of the king and said: "Today you have disgraced all your servants who have saved your life and the lives of your sons and daughters, because you love those who hate you, and hate those who love you. You have made it clear today that commanders and troops are nothing to you. If Absalom were alive, and all of us were dead today, you would be pleased. Go out and speak to your servants. If you do not, you will not have a man left on your side tonight; and that will be worse for you than all the evil that has befallen you from your youth until now." So the king got up and sat in the gateway, and all the people came before him.

David sang this song when the Lord had saved him from all his enemies:

"The Lord is my rock, my fortress, my deliverer, in

whom I seek refuge. I call to him, and I am rescued from my foes.

"Waves of death encompassed me, floods of ruin terrified me, deadly nets entangled me. I called the Lord in my plight, and my cry came to his ears.

"He reached from on high, he took me, he drew me out of many waters. He delivered me from my enemies, who were too mighty for me. The Lord rewarded me according to my uprightness, he requited me according to the cleanness of my hands. I was blameless in his sight, and I kept clear of guilt.

"To the kind thou art kind, and true to the true. Thou dost help the humble, and bringest down the haughty. Thou art my lamp, O Lord, lightening my darkness. By thy help I can crush a troop, by God's help I can leap a wall. For this I will extol thee, O Lord, among the nations, and sing praises to thy name."

These are the last words of David, the sweet psalmist of Israel.

"By me the spirit of the Lord speaks; his word is upon my tongue. When a man rules men justly, he dawns on them like the morning light, like the sun shining forth upon a cloudless morning; he is like rain upon the tender grass. But godless men are like thorns that are thrown away; they are utterly consumed with fire."

Once, when David was in the cave of Adullam while the garrison of the Philistines was in Bethlehem, David said longingly: "O that someone would give me a drink of water from the well of Bethlehem." Then three courageous men broke through the camp of the Philistines and drew water out of the well of Bethlehem. But David refused to drink it, saying: "Far be it from me, O Lord, that I should do this. Shall I drink the blood of the men who went at the risk of their lives?"

Kings

The two books of Kings, which tell the history of the kingdoms of Judah and Israel, are treated as one book in the Hebrew Bible. They cover a period of about four hundred years, extending from the last days of David to the destruction of the first Temple. It is the period of Israel's glory, division, decline, disintegration, and fall. The prophets who appeared in the course of history contained in the books of Kings were statesmen as well as ethical teachers.

According to a statement in the Talmud, the books of Kings were written by the prophet Jeremiah, author of the books of Jeremiah and Lamentations. Aiming to set forth the lessons which the history of his people affords, the writer of Kings traces the dire results of disobedience, and the happy consequences of loyalty to the precepts of the Torah. He characterizes the kings of Judah and Israel according to their faithfulness or faithlessness to the divine teachings.

Judah survived by nearly one hundred and fifty years the rival kingdom of Israel, which was the larger and more powerful of the two. The accumulation of large estates in the hands of a few holders, oppression of the poor, perversion of justice, luxury and over-indulgence undermined the kingdom of Israel and hastened its end. In the story of Naboth's vineyard we have the beginnings of the transition from small peasant ownership to that of large estates in the kingdom of Israel, from the privileges of freemen to the ills of a serfdom under large landowners.

When King David was well advanced in years, and his time to die drew near, he charged Solomon his son, saying: "I am about to go the way of all the earth. Be strong and be a man. Keep the commandments of the Lord, so that you may succeed in whatever you do." David reigned over Israel for forty years. When he died, he was buried in the city of David. Solomon sat upon the throne of his father, and his kingdom was firmly established.

One night, the Lord appeared to Solomon in a dream,

and said: "Ask, what shall I give you?" Solomon answered: "Lord my God, I am a mere child; I do not know how to manage. O grant me an understanding heart to govern thy people, that I may discern between good and evil."

God said to him: "Because you have asked neither long life, nor wealth nor the death of your enemies, I shall give you a wise and understanding heart, so that none shall ever be like you. I am giving you, moreover, what you have not asked—both wealth and honor—so that no king shall ever be your equal. Walk in my ways and keep my commandments and I will also give you a long life."

Shortly afterwards, two women came to the king and argued before him. One woman said: "My lord, this woman and I live in the same house. I gave birth to a child, and three days later she bore one; we were together and there was no one else in the house. During the night her child died, so she got up and took mine while I was asleep and put her dead child beside me. When I rose in the morning to nurse my child, behold it was dead; but as I looked at it closely I saw that it was not mine." But the other woman retorted: "No, the living child is mine, the dead one is yours!"

Then the king said: "Fetch me a sword." And the king ordered: "Divide the living child in two and give half to the one and half to the other." At this, the mother of the living child cried out: "My lord, give her the child, do not kill it!" "No!" exclaimed the second woman; "it shall be neither mine nor yours! Divide it!" "Give the child to the first woman; *she* is its mother," the king commanded.

All Israel heard of this decision, and stood in awe of the king, for they saw that the wisdom of God was in him.

Solomon's wisdom surpassed the wisdom of all the people of the east. His fame reached all the nations round about. He composed three thousand proverbs, and his songs numbered one thousand and five. He could talk about all kinds of plants, animals, birds, reptiles and fish. Men came from every nation to hear his wisdom.

Solomon sent word to Hiram, king of Tyre, saying: "You know that my father David could not build a temple for the Lord because of the hostile forces that surrounded him.

But now the Lord has given me peace, and I propose to build a temple. Now order, I pray you, that cedars of Lebanon be felled for me. My servants will join your servants, and I will pay any wage you fix for your servants. There is no one among us who knows how to cut timber like the Sidonians."

Hiram supplied Solomon with all the timber that he needed, while Solomon sent him wheat and oil. Solomon raised a labor force from all Israel, a contingent of thirty thousand men, which he sent to Lebanon in relays of ten thousand a month; one month they were at Lebanon and two months they stayed at home. Solomon also employed seventy thousand carriers, eighty thousand stonemasons and three thousand three hundred foremen who supervised the work. They quarried huge blocks of stone for the foundation of the temple.

In the four hundred and eightieth year after the people of Israel had gone out of Egypt, in the fourth year of Solomon's reign, he began to build the temple of the Lord, and in the eleventh year of his reign it was completed. Solomon also built a palace for himself. It took thirteen years to build it.

When the temple was completed, all the men of Israel gathered before Solomon. The priests brought the ark of the Lord and all the holy vessels. They placed the ark inside the inner sanctuary, the most holy place, underneath the wings of the cherubim. There was nothing in the ark except the two stone tablets which Moses had put there.

Then the king spread forth his hands toward heaven and said: "Lord God of Israel, all the heavens cannot contain thee, how much less this house which I have built! May thy eyes ever be opened toward this house; hearken to the supplication of thy people when they turn in prayer to this place. As for the stranger who does not belong to Israel, when he prays in this house, accept thou his prayer, so that all the nations of the world may know thy name and revere thee."

So Solomon and all Israel held the feast for seven days. On the eighth day he sent the people away; they went home rejoicing, glad with the goodness that the Lord had shown to David, his servant, and to Israel his people.

When the queen of Sheba heard about the fame of Solomon, she came to test him with puzzling questions. She arrived in Jerusalem with a great retinue and with camels bearing spices and gold and precious stones. Solomon answered all her questions. She said to him: "Your wisdom and wealth surpass all that I had heard in my own land. Happy are they who continually stand before you and hear your wisdom!" She gave him a hundred and twenty talents of gold and a huge quantity of spices and precious stones. King Solomon, too, gave the queen of Sheba whatever she desired. Then she went back to her own land.

King Solomon excelled all kings on earth in wealth and wisdom. Men from all parts of the world came to hear his wisdom; everyone brought presents of silver and gold, garments, spices, horses and mules.

King Solomon had seven hundred wives and three hundred concubines. They came from nations against whom the Lord had warned the people of Israel: "You shall not enter into marriage with them, for they will turn your heart after their gods." His wives seduced him to follow their foreign gods. He put up shrines for the idols of the Phoenicians, the Ammonites and the Moabites. He did the same for all his foreign wives, burning incense and offering sacrifice to their gods.

The Lord was angry with Solomon for allowing himself to be seduced, so he said to him: "I will tear the kingdom from you and give it to your servant. Yet for the sake of David your father I will not do it in your days. I will tear it out of the hands of your son. Still, I will not tear away all the kingdom. I will let your son have one tribe, for the sake of David, my servant, and for the sake of Jerusalem which I have chosen."

The Lord raised up an adversary against Solomon, and Jeroboam turned traitor against the king. Jeroboam was a capable man, and Solomon had put him in charge of the entire labor force of the house of Joseph. One day as Jeroboam was leaving Jerusalem, the prophet Ahijah met

105

him and took him aside. The two of them were alone in the open country. Ahijah took the new garment which he was wearing and tore it into twelve pieces, saying to Jeroboam: "Take ten for yourself, for the Lord is about to tear the kingdom of Solomon apart and give you ten tribes." Solomon, therefore, sought to kill Jeroboam, so he fled to Egypt, and remained there till the death of Solomon.

Solomon reigned in Jerusalem over all Israel for forty years. He slept with his fathers and was buried in the city of David. Rehoboam, who succeeded him, went to Shechem where he was to be made king by all Israel. The people said to Rehoboam: "Your father made our yoke heavy; lighten the heavy yoke he imposed upon us and we will serve you." "Go now and come back in three days," he replied.

When the people went away, King Rehoboam consulted the old councillors who had served his father Solomon. And they said to him: "If you will speak kindly to them, they will be your servants forever." But he rejected their advice and took the counsel of the young men, who said: "Tell them: My little finger is thicker than my father's loins. My father lashed you with whips, but I will lash you with scorpions."

On the third day, when Jeroboam and all the people came to Rehoboam, he answered them harshly, speaking to them according to the counsel of the young men. When the people of Israel saw that the king refused to heed them, they exclaimed: "We have no part in David, no share in the son of Jesse. To your tents, O Israel! Look after your own house, David!"

On reaching Jerusalem, Rehoboam assembled all the men of Judah and Benjamin, a hundred and eighty thousand picked troops, to fight against Israel and recover the kingdom. But the word of God came to Shemaiah, the prophet: "Say to Rehoboam: 'You shall not fight against your kinsmen. Return home, every man of you! This thing has come about directly from me.'" So they returned home, as the Lord had told them.

Then Jeroboam thought to himself: "If these people go up to offer sacrifices at the temple in Jerusalem, their heart will again turn toward Rehoboam." So he made two golden calves and said to the people: "You need no longer go up to Jerusalem; here are your gods, O Israel, the gods that brought you out of the land of Egypt!" He placed one of them at Bethel, and the other at Dan. He chose the priests for the shrines from among all the people.

Jeroboam reigned for twenty-two years, and was succeeded by Nadab his son. There was constant war between Rehoboam and Jeroboam. Rehoboam was succeeded by his son Abijam, who reigned for three years in Jerusalem. When Abijam died, Asa his son succeeded him as king.

Asa reigned forty-two years in Jerusalem, and did what was right in the eyes of the Lord. He expelled the sodomites from the land and removed all the idols that his fathers had made. He deposed his mother, Maakah, from the position of queen-mother, because she had made an obscene image of Asherah; he demolished this image and burned it in the Kidron valley. War raged between Asa and Baasha, king of Israel, all their days.

Nadab the son of Jeroboam began his two-year reign over Israel in the second year of Asa king of Judah. Baasha conspired against him, killed him, and reigned in his stead. No sooner did he ascend the throne than he killed all the household of Jeroboam. Baasha reigned twenty-four years, and was succeeded by his son Elah who reigned two years. Zimri, one of his officers, conspired against Elah and struck him down. It was in the twenty-seventh year of Asa king of Judah that Zimri reigned seven days in Tirzah. When it became known that Zimri had conspired and killed the king, the entire Israelite camp at once elected Omri, the commander of the army, to be king. Omri marched with all Israel and besieged Tirzah. When Zimri saw that the town was captured, he set the palace on fire and perished in its flames.

Omri began to reign over Israel in the thirty-first year of Asa king of Judah. Omri died and was buried in Samaria. He was succeeded by his son Ahab. It was in the thirty-eighth year of Asa, king of Judah, that Ahab, the son of Omri, began his twenty-two-year reign over Israel. Ahab did evil in the sight of the Lord, more so than all the kings of Israel before him.

Elijah, the Tishbite, said to Ahab: "As the Lord God of Israel lives, there shall be neither dew nor rain these years except by my word." Now the famine was severe in Samaria, and Ahab summoned Obadiah the overseer of the palace. Ahab said to Obadiah: "Go through the land in search of springs and brooks; perhaps we may find grass and save the lives of the horses and mules." So they divided the country between them; Ahab went in one direction and Obadiah went in another.

As Obadiah went his way, he was met by Elijah who said to him: "Go! Tell your master that Elijah is here." So Obadiah went to Ahab with the news, and Ahab went to meet Elijah. When Ahab saw Elijah, he exclaimed: "Is that you, troubler of Israel?" Elijah answered: "I have not troubled Israel, but you and your family, by forsaking the commands of the Lord and following the Baals. Send now and gather all Israel at Mount Carmel, together with the four hundred and fifty prophets of Baal, who are maintained by Jezebel."

So Ahab sent to all Israel and gathered the prophets at Mount Carmel. Elijah drew near to all the people and said: "How long will you jump from one belief to another? If the Lord is God, follow him; if Baal, then follow him." The people gave no answer. Then Elijah said to them: "I alone am left as a prophet of the Lord, while Baal has four hundred and fifty prophets. Let us have two bullocks. They can choose one bullock for themselves and chop it up, laying the pieces on the wood but putting no fire underneath it. I will prepare the other bullock and lay it on the wood, putting no fire under it. You call to your god, and I will call to the Lord; and the God who answers by fire—he is the real God."

"Well spoken," said the people. So the prophets of Baal took their bullock, prepared it, and called to Baal from morning until noon, crying: "O Baal, answer us!" But not a sound came, there was no answer as they danced about the altar they had made. When it came to midday, Elijah mocked them, saying: "Cry aloud, for he is a god! Perhaps he is asleep and must be wakened!" So they shouted, cutting themselves with knives and lances, as was their custom, until the blood gushed from their bodies. And as midday passed, they raved on until evening; but there was no sound; no one answered, no one heeded.

Then Elijah said to the people: "Come close to me." All the people came close to him, and he repaired the altar of the Lord which had been broken down. He then arranged the wood and laid the pieces of his bullock on the wood. Elijah the prophet came forward and said: "O Lord, God of Abraham and Isaac and Israel, answer me, answer me, that this people may know that thou art God, and that thou hast made their hearts turn to thee again." Then the fire of the Lord fell and consumed the offering, the wood, the stones, and the dust, and licked up the water that was in the trench. On seeing this, all the people fell on their faces, crying: "The Lord is God, the Lord is God!" They seized the prophets and killed them. In a very short time the sky grew black with clouds and wind, and there was a heavy rain.

When Ahab told Jezebel all that Elijah had done, she sent this message to Elijah: "May the gods punish me again and again, if by this time tomorrow I do not make your life as the life of any one of the slain prophets."

Elijah was afraid and ran for his life. When he reached Beersheba, he left his servant there and went into the desert, where he sat down under a broom bush, praying for death. "I have had enough of it," he cried; "O Lord, take away my life now." Then he lay down under the bush and fell asleep; and behold, an angel touched him, saying: "Arise and eat." He opened his eyes, and there was a cake baked on hot stones and a jar of water. He ate and drank, and lay down again. The angel of the Lord came a second time and touched him, saying: "Arise and eat, else the journey will be too much for you." So he rose, ate and drank, and strengthened by the food he went for forty days and forty nights to Horeb, the mountain of God, where he took shelter in a cave. And behold, the Lord passed by. A strong, fierce wind tore the mountain, crashing the rocks, but the Lord was not in the wind. After the wind came an earthquake, but the Lord was not in the earthquake; after the earthquake a fire, but the Lord was not in the fire; after the fire a still small voice. As soon as Elijah heard that, he wrapped his face in his mantle and went out and stood at the entrance of the cave. Then a voice came to him, saying: "What are you doing here, Elijah?" He replied: "I have been very zealous for the Lord. The people of Israel have forsaken thy covenant, thrown down thy altars, and killed thy prophets; I am the only one left, and they are after me, to take my life."

"Go back," the Lord said, "take the desert road of Damascus; when you arrive, you shall anoint Hazael to be king over Syria; you shall anoint Jehu to be king over Israel; and you shall anoint Elisha to succeed you as prophet. Jehu shall slay him who escapes the sword of Hazael, and Elisha shall slay him who escapes the sword of Jehu. But I will spare seven thousand men in Israel—all who have not knelt to Baal or kissed him."

When Elijah had departed from there, he came upon Elisha who was plowing behind twelve yoke of oxen. Elijah passed by and cast his mantle upon Elisha, who left the oxen and ran after Elijah and said: "Let me kiss my father and my mother, and then I will follow you." Elijah replied: "Go back; what have I done to you?" He went back, slaughtered a pair of oxen, used their harness to boil the meat, and gave to the people to eat. Then he started to follow Elijah, acting as his attendant.

Now Naboth of Jezreel had a vineyard close to the palace of Ahab, king of Samaria. Ahab said to Naboth: "Give me your vineyard that I may have it for a vegetable garden, since it is near my house. I will give you a better vineyard for it or I will give you its value in money."

But Naboth said to Ahab: "The Lord forbid that I should part with the inheritance of my fathers." Ahab went home angry and sullen. He lay down on his bed, turned his face to the wall and refused to eat.

His wife, Jezebel, came and asked him: "Why are you so depressed that you cannot eat?" He said to her: "I asked Naboth of Jezreel to sell me his vineyard, or let me give him another vineyard for it, and he refused." Then Jezebel said to him: "Are you not in command of Israel's kingdom? Get up, take some food and cheer up. I will get you the vineyard of Naboth the Jezreelite."

So she wrote letters in Ahab's name and sealed them with his seal. She sent the letters to the elders and the nobles who lived with Naboth in his city. She had written in the letters: "Proclaim a fast, choose two men to bring charges against Naboth, saying that he has cursed God and the king. Then take him out, and stone him to death."

The fellow citizens of Naboth, the elders and nobles who dwelt in his city did as Jezebel had requested. They proclaimed a fast, and two evil men came and brought charges against Naboth in the presence of the people, saying: "Naboth cursed God and the king." So they took him outside the city, and stoned him to death. They sent word to Jezebel: "Naboth has been stoned and is dead."

As soon as Jezebel heard that Naboth had been stoned to death, she said to Ahab: "Arise, take possession of Naboth's vineyard for he is no longer alive." Ahab then went to take possession of Naboth's vineyard.

But the word of the Lord came to Elijah, saying: "Arise, go down to meet Ahab, king of Israel, who is in the vineyard of Naboth. Say to him: You have murdered and now you inherit? Thus says the Lord: Where dogs licked up the blood of Naboth, there shall dogs lick up your blood also."

Ahab said to Elijah: "Have you found me, O enemy of mine?" Elijah answered: "I have found you because you have given yourself over to what is evil in the sight of the Lord.

"Behold, I will bring evil upon you; I will utterly sweep you away and I will make your house like the house of Jeroboam, because you have made Israel to sin." And of Jezebel the Lord said: "The dogs shall eat Jezebel within the bounds of Jezreel."

When Ahab heard these words, he tore his garments and put on sackcloth. He fasted and went about quietly. Then the word of the Lord came to Elijah, saying: "Have you seen how Ahab has humbled himself before me? Because he has humbled himself before me, I will not bring the evil in his day. I will bring evil on his house during the reign of his son."

Now for three years there had been no war between Syria and Israel. But in the third year, Jehoshaphat the king of Judah agreed to join the king of Israel in attacking Ramoth-gilead. The king of Israel disguised himself before he entered the battle. The king of Syria had ordered his thirty-two chariot captains to fight with no one except the king of Israel. When the captains of the chariots saw Jehoshaphat in royal robes, they thought this must be the king of Israel and they surrounded him. Finding that he was not the king of Israel, they turned back from pursuing him. Then a certain man drew his bow and struck Ahab, the king of Israel, between the joints of his armor.

"Turn around," cried the king to the driver of his chariot, "get me out of the battle, for I am wounded." However, the king remained propped up in his chariot facing the Syrians until evening and the blood from his wound flowed into the bottom of the chariot. At about sunset a cry passed through the army: "Back to your towns, back to your country, every man of you, for the king is dead!"

They buried Ahab in Samaria. They washed the chariot at the pool and dogs licked up his blood. His son Ahaziah succeeded him.

In the fourth year of Ahab king of Israel, Jehoshaphat the son of Asa had begun to reign over Judah. He was then thirty-five years of age. He reigned in Jerusalem for twenty-five years, following the ways of his father, Asa, and doing what was right in the eyes of the Lord. He also made peace with the king of Israel. When he died, he was buried with his fathers in the city of David. Jehoram his son succeeded him.

Ahaziah fell through the lattice of his upper chamber in Samaria and lay ill, so he sent messengers to ask the god of Ekron whether he would recover from his illness. The messengers soon returned, and Ahaziah asked why they had come back. They told him that a man had come to meet them and said: "Go back to the king who sent you and tell him this from the Lord: Is it because there is no

God in Israel that you send to consult the god of Ekron? For this you shall never leave your bed; you shall surely die." The king asked: "What kind of a man was he who told you this?" They answered: "He wore a garment of haircloth, with a belt of leather round his waist."

"It is Elijah the Tishbite," the king said, and he sent a captain with fifty men to seize him. Elijah was sitting on the top of a hill, when the captain went up to him and said: "O man of God, the king orders you to come down." Elijah answered: "If I am a man of God, let fire come down from heaven and destroy you and your fifty men." Fire then came down from heaven and destroyed the captain and his fifty men.

Again the king sent another captain with fifty men. He went up to Elijah and said: "O man of God, this is the king's order: Come down at once." But Elijah answered: "If I am a man of God, let fire come down from heaven and consume you and your fifty men." Again the fire of God came down from heaven and consumed him also and his fifty men.

The king sent a third captain with fifty men. The third captain went up and fell on his knees before Elijah, entreating him: "O man of God, pray spare my life and the lives of these fifty men, your servants." Then the angel of the Lord said to Elijah: "Go down with him; do not be afraid of him." He rose and went with him to the king, and said to him: "Thus says the Lord: Because you have sent messengers to consult the god of Ekron, you shall never leave your bed, but you shall surely die." So Ahaziah died and, since he had no son, Jehoram his brother succeeded him.

Now when the Lord was about to take Elijah up to heaven by a whirlwind, Elijah and Elisha went to Bethel and then to Jericho. When they had crossed the Jordan, Elijah said to Elisha: "Before I am taken from you, ask what I shall do for you." Elisha answered: "Let me have a double share of your spirit." Elijah answered: "You have asked a hard thing; if you see me when I am being taken from you, it shall be yours, but not if you fail to see me." Suddenly, as they walked and talked, a fiery chariot with fiery horses drove between them, and Elijah went up by a whirlwind into heaven.

When Elisha saw this, he cried: "My father, my father, the chariot and horsemen of Israel!" And he saw him no more. Then he took up the mantle of Elijah that had fallen from him and went back and stood on the bank of the Jordan. He struck the water, crying: "Where is the Lord God of Elijah?" The water parted right and left, and Elisha crossed over.

When the disciples of the prophets in Jericho saw him at a distance, they said: "The spirit of Elijah rests on Elisha." They came forward and bowed to the ground, saying: "We have fifty strong men; pray let them go in search of your master; perhaps he is upon some mountain or in some valley." Elisha refused their request at first, but when they persisted, he yielded. So fifty men searched for three days but failed to find Elijah. When they returned, Elisha said: "Did I not tell you not to go?"

The wife of one of the disciples of the prophets appealed to Elisha, saying: "My husband is dead, and now a creditor has come to seize my two sons as his slaves." "What shall I do for you?" said Elisha. "Tell me what you have in your house." She replied: "I have nothing in the house except a jar of oil." Then he said: "Go borrow vessels from all your neighbors; shut yourself in the house, you and your sons; pour the oil into all the vessels; and whenever one is full set it aside."

The woman shut herself and her sons in the house. They brought the vessels while she poured the oil. When the vessels were full, she said to her son: "Bring me another vessel," and he said: "There is not another vessel." Then the oil stopped flowing. She told it to the man of God, who said: "Go sell the oil and pay your debts. You and your sons can live on what is left."

One day Elisha went to Shunem. A rich woman, who lived there, persuaded him to partake of her food. After this, he had a meal at her house whenever he went to Shunem. The woman said to her husband: "This is a holy man of God, who continually passes our way. Let us build a small roof-chamber for him, with a bed and a table, a seat and a lamp, so that whenever he comes to us he can go in there."

One day when he came and stayed in the chamber, he said to his servant Gehazi: "Tell the Shunammite: You have taken all this trouble for us; what can we do for you? Would you have a word spoken in your behalf to the king or to the commander of the army?" She answered: "I live safely among my own people." So he asked Gehazi what should be done for her, and Gehazi replied: "She has no son, and her husband is old." Elisha said: "Call her." And as she stood in the doorway, he said: "At this time next year you will be embracing a son." The following year she bore a son, as Elisha had told her.

When the boy grew up, he went out one day to his father among the reapers. He called to his father: "My head, my head!" The father told a servant to carry the boy to his mother. He was taken to his mother, and died sitting on her lap. She carried the boy to the bed of the man of God, laid him on it and closed the door.

She went to Elisha at Mount Carmel. When the man of God saw her coming, he said to Gehazi: "Look, there is the Shunammite; run at once to ask her if she is well and if the child is well." When she came to the man of God, she grasped his feet. Gehazi would have pushed her away, but the man of God said: "Let her alone; she is in bitter distress." Then she said: "Did I ask my lord for a son? As the Lord lives, I will not leave you." So he rose and went with her.

Gehazi went ahead and laid Elisha's staff upon the face of the child, but there was no sound or sign of life. When Elisha went into the house, he saw the child lying dead on his bed. He shut the door and prayed to the Lord. Then he lay down upon the child, put his mouth to the child's mouth, his eyes upon the child's eyes, and his hands upon the child's hands, until the flesh of the child became warm. Then he got up, walked to and fro, and went again and stretched himself over the child. The child sneezed seven times and opened his eyes. Elisha told Gehazi to call the Shunammite, and he said to her: "Take up your son." She fell at his feet; then she took up her son and went out.

Once Elisha went to Gilgal when there was a famine in the land. As the disciples of the prophets were sitting before him, he told his servant to put a large pot on the fire and boil some pottage for the disciples. One of them went out into the field to gather herbs; he cut them up and put them in the pot of pottage, not knowing what they were. The pottage was then poured out for the men to eat. But as they were eating they cried out: "Man of God, there is death in the pot!" They could not eat the pottage. He said: "Bring some flour." He threw it into the pot and said: "Pour out for the men that they may eat." And now there was nothing wrong with the pottage.

Now Naaman, commander of the Syrian army, was highly regarded by the king; he was a valiant man, but he was afflicted with leprosy. The Syrians had carried off from the land of Israel a little girl who waited on Naaman's wife. She said to her mistress: "The prophet who lives at Samaria would cure my lord of his leprosy." Whereupon the king of Syria sent a letter to the king of Israel, which read: "I am sending you my servant Naaman, that you may cure him of his leprosy." When the king of Israel read the letter, he rent his garments and cried out: "Am I God to bring about life and death, that he wants me to cure a man of his leprosy? He is seeking a pretext to start a quarrel with me."

When Elisha heard of the king's despair, he sent word to him: "Let the man come to me, and he shall find there is a prophet in Israel." So Naaman drove his chariot and horses to Elisha's house. Elisha sent out word to him: "Go wash seven times in the Jordan; and your body shall become clean again."

Naaman was enraged and said: "Surely, the rivers of Damascus are better than all the waters in Israel! Could I not wash in them and be clean?" So he drove away in anger. But his servants went up to him and said: "If the prophet had commanded you to do something difficult, would you not have done it? How much rather, then, when he tells you only to wash and be clean?" So Naaman went down and dipped seven times in the Jordan; and his body became clean once more, like the body of a child.

Then he returned to the man of God and said: "Now I know there is no God in all the earth except in Israel! Pray accept a present from your humble servant." But Elisha said: "As the Lord lives, I will not take a single thing." When Naaman had gone a short distance, Gehazi followed him and said: "My master has sent me to say that two young disciples of the prophets have just come to him from the hill country of Ephraim. Give them a talent of silver and two festal garments." "Accept two talents," Naaman said. He tied up the silver and the two festal garments and handed them to Gehazi's two servants.

"Where have you been, Gehazi?" Elisha asked. "Your servant has not been anywhere," he answered. But Elisha said to him: "Was it a time to accept money and garments? Therefore the leprosy of Naaman shall cleave to you forever." He left Elisha's presence stricken with leprosy, white as snow.

Now the disciples of the prophets said to Elisha: "This dwelling of ours is too small for us. Let us go to the Jordan and get each of us a log to build a dwelling-place for ourselves there." Elisha told them to go, and agreed to go along. On reaching the Jordan, they cut down trees. But as one was felling a tree, the head of the axe fell into the water. "Alas, my master," cried the man, "it was borrowed." Then the man of God said: "Where did it fall?" He showed him the place, whereupon Elisha cut off a stick, threw it there, and made the iron float. "Take it," he said. The man put out his hand and took it.

Now Elisha said to the woman whose son he had restored to life: "Move away with your household and stay wherever you can, for the Lord is bringing on the land a famine that will last seven years." So she left and stayed in the land of the Philistines for seven years. When she returned, she appealed to the king for her house and land. Gehazi said to the king: "My lord, here is the woman whose son Elisha restored to life!" The king appointed an official to see that she got back all her property.

Elisha sent a young disciple of the prophets to anoint Jehu king over Israel. The young man poured oil on Jehu's head, saying: "Thus says the Lord God of Israel: I anoint

you king over the people of Israel. You shall strike down
the house of your master Ahab, that I may avenge the
blood of my prophets and my servants. The whole house of
Ahab shall perish, like the house of Jeroboam and the
house of Baasha. Dogs shall eat Jezebel in Jezreel, and
none shall bury her."

Jehu conspired against Jehoram, who had come to
Jezreel to be cured of the wounds he had received in fighting against the king of Syria. He drove off in a chariot to
Jezreel where Jehoram was lying. In the meantime, Ahaziah
king of Judah had come down to visit the ailing king. A
sentinel posted on the tower caught sight of the company
of Jehu. A man on horseback was sent to ask: "Is all well?"
And Jehu said: "Fall in behind me!" The sentinel reported: "The man is not coming back, and the driving is
like the driving of Jehu; he drives like a madman."

Then Jehoram and Ahaziah set out, each in his chariot,
and went to meet Jehu in the field of Naboth the
Jezreelite.

Jehoram asked: "Is it peace, Jehu?" He answered: "What
peace can there be so long as your mother Jezebel goes on
with all her seductions and sorceries?" Jehoram turned
around and fled, calling to Ahaziah: "Treachery, Ahaziah!"
Jehu drew his bow and struck Jehoram. The arrow pierced
his heart, and he sank in his chariot. "Fling him out on the
field of Naboth the Jezreelite!" Jehu commanded.

When Ahaziah king of Judah saw this, he fled. He was
pursued by Jehu, who shouted: "Kill him too! Kill him in
the chariot!" They struck him, but he got away to Megiddo,
where he died. His servants carried him in a chariot to
Jerusalem, and buried him in the city of David.

When Jezebel heard that Jehu had come to Jezreel, she
painted her eyes, adorned her head and looked out of the
window. As Jehu entered the gateway, she cried: "How
are you, murderer of your master?" Jehu looked up to the
window. "Who is on my side?" he inquired. Then he said:
"Throw her down!" They threw Jezebel down and
trampled on her.

When Athaliah saw that her son, Ahaziah, was dead, she
destroyed the entire royal family except Joash, the son of

Ahaziah, who was hidden for six years in the house of the Lord while Athaliah reigned over the land. But in the seventh year, Jehoiada, the priest, armed the guards with the spears and shields belonging to King David, which had been kept in the temple. He brought out Joash the king's son, put the crown upon his head, proclaimed him king and anointed him, while they were clapping their hands and shouting: "Long live the king!"

When Athaliah heard the noise of the guard, she went into the house of the Lord and saw the king standing on the platform with the captains and trumpeters beside him, while all the people were rejoicing and blowing trumpets. She rent her garments and cried: "Treason! Treason!" But Jehoiada, the priest, ordered the captains: "Bring her out, and slay anyone who follows her. Let her not be slain in the house of the Lord." So they seized her, and she was put to death.

Joash was seven years old when he began to reign; he reigned forty years in Jerusalem. When his servants made a conspiracy and slew him, Amaziah his son reigned in his stead.

Jehoahaz the son of Jehu reigned over Israel in Samaria for seventeen years. He had an army of no more than fifty horsemen, ten chariots and ten thousand footmen, for the king of Syria had destroyed the rest. When he died, Joash his son reigned in his stead.

Joash reigned over Israel in Samaria for sixteen years. He recovered from the king of Syria the towns which had been captured from his father Jehoahaz. When Amaziah king of Judah challenged him to an encounter, Joash sent this answer to the king of Judah: "You are proud of having defeated Edom. Stay at home with your pride. Why should you provoke trouble and bring ruin to yourself and to Judah?" But Amaziah would not listen to him, so they had an encounter and Judah was overthrown by Israel. Joash captured Amaziah and took him to Jerusalem, where he seized the gold and silver and all the vessels that were found in the temple, as well as the treasures of the royal palace. When Joash died, Jeroboam his son succeeded him.

Amaziah king of Judah lived fifteen years after the death

119

of Joash king of Israel. A conspiracy was formed against him in Jerusalem, so he fled to Lachish; but men were sent after him, and they killed him. Then the people of Judah took his sixteen-year-old son, Azariah, and made him king. Azariah rebuilt Elath and restored it to Judah. He reigned forty-two years, but he became a leper. His son Jotham managed the royal household and ruled the nation. When Azariah died, Jotham succeeded him.

Zechariah the son of Jeroboam reigned over Israel in Samaria for six months. Shallum conspired against him, killed him, and reigned in his stead for one month. He in turn was struck down by Menahem, who reigned in his stead for ten years. During Menahem's reign, the Assyrian king, Pul, invaded the country. They had to give him a thousand talents of silver before he turned back and left the country. Pekah conspired against Menahem, killed him, and succeeded him as king.

Pekah reigned over Israel for twenty years. In his days, Tiglath-pileser king of Assyria captured Gilead and Galilee, all the land of Naphtali, and carried off the people into exile. Then Hoshea made a conspiracy against Pekah, killed him, and reigned in his stead.

Jotham was twenty-five years old when he began to reign over Judah. When he died, his son Ahaz reigned sixteen years in Jerusalem. He sent messengers to Tiglath-pileser king of Assyria, saying: "I am your servant and your son; come and rescue me from the king of Syria and from the king of Israel, who are attacking me." He sent all the silver and gold, that was in the house of the Lord and in the treasures of the royal palace, as tribute to the king of Assyria. The king of Assyria then marched against Damascus, captured it, and carried off its inhabitants as prisoners.

Hoshea reigned over Israel in Samaria for nine years. He submitted to Shalmaneser king of Assyria who marched against him, and offered tribute. But when the king of Assyria discovered that Hoshea was conspiring against him, he besieged Samaria for three years, and carried Israel off to Assyria; and people from Babylon were placed in the cities of Samaria.

Hezekiah the son of Ahaz reigned twenty-nine years in Jerusalem. He did what was right in the eyes of the Lord. There was none like him among the kings of Judah after him, nor among those who were before him. The Lord was with him; he succeeded wherever he went. He defeated the Philistines as far as Gaza and its surrounding territory.

Sennacherib, king of Assyria, marched against all the fortified towns of Judah and captured them. Then Isaiah sent Hezekiah this message from the Lord God of Israel: "The king of Assyria shall not come to the city of Jerusalem or shoot an arrow there." That night the angel of the Lord slew a hundred and eighty-five thousand in the camp of the Assyrians. Sennacherib departed and went home to Nineveh. When Hezekiah died, Manasseh his son reigned in his stead.

Manasseh was twelve years old when he began to reign, and he reigned fifty-five years in Jerusalem. He did evil in the sight of the Lord, for he rebuilt the shrines which his father Hezekiah had destroyed, and erected altars for Baal. He burned his son as an offering, and practised augury and sorcery. He filled Jerusalem with murders from end to end. When he died, his son Amon reigned two years in Jerusalem. Amon was killed in his house by his servants, who conspired against him. The people then made his son Josiah their king.

Josiah, who was eight years old when he became king, reigned thirty-one years in Jerusalem. In the eighteenth year of King Josiah, Hilkiah the high priest found the book of the Torah in the house of the Lord and handed it to Shaphan, who read it to the king. When the king heard the words of the book of the Torah, he rent his garments and commanded that inquiry be made of the Lord concerning the words of this book.

So Hilkiah and Shaphan went to Huldah the prophetess and talked with her. She said: "Thus says the Lord God of Israel: I will bring evil upon this place and upon its inhabitants, all the words of the book which the king of Judah has read, because they have forsaken me." Then the king went to the temple of the Lord, accompanied by all the men of Judah and all the inhabitants of Jerusalem, young and old. He read aloud to them all the words of the book of the covenant which had been found in the house of the Lord.

The king ordered Hilkiah, the high priest, and the wardens to bring out of the temple all the vessels made for Baal and for star-worship; these he burned outside Jerusalem at the brook Kidron. He commanded all the people: "Keep the Passover in honor of the Lord your God, as it is written in the book of the covenant." Passover had not been kept since the days when the judges had ruled over Israel. Josiah put away the mediums and the wizards, the household idols and all the abominations that were seen in the land of Judah and in Jerusalem.

There had never been a king like him who turned to the Lord with all his heart and with all his soul and with all his might; nor was there a king like him afterwards.

When Pharaoh-nechoh, king of Egypt, marched to fight the king of Assyria, Josiah marched against him and was slain at Megiddo. His servants carried their dead king in a chariot to Jerusalem, where he was buried in his own tomb. Then the people of the land anointed Jehoahaz the son of Josiah and made him king.

Jehoahaz, who was twenty-three years old when he became king, had reigned only three months in Jerusalem when Pharaoh-nechoh imprisoned him and made his brother, Jehoiakim, king. Jehoiakim was twenty-five years old when he became king, and he reigned eleven years in Jerusalem. Nebuchadnezzar, king of Babylon, made Jehoiakim his vassal for three years. The king of Egypt no longer stirred from his country, for the king of Babylon had conquered all that belonged to Egypt.

When Jehoiakim died, his son Jehoiachin became king at the age of eighteen, and reigned three months in Jerusalem. Nebuchadnezzar attacked Jerusalem at that time, and besieged the city. Jehoiachin surrendered to the king of Babylon, who took him prisoner and carried off all the treasures of the temple and the royal palace, cutting to pieces all the golden vessels made by Solomon for the house of the Lord. Nebuchadnezzar exiled all the nobles, all the brave soldiers, ten thousand of them, with all the craftsmen and locksmiths. None remained, except the poorest people of the land.

The king of Babylon made Jehoiachin's uncle, Zedekiah, king over Jerusalem. He reigned eleven years. In the ninth year of his reign, Zedekiah rebelled against the king of Babylon, so Nebuchadnezzar came with all his army against Jerusalem and laid siege to it till the eleventh year of king Zedekiah. By the ninth day of the fourth month, Tammuz, a breach was made in the walls of the city. The king and all the soldiers fled from the city by night, though the Chaldeans surrounded it. They pursued the king and overtook him in the plains of Jericho. He was captured and carried off to the king of Babylon, who passed sentence upon him. The sons of Zedekiah were killed before his eyes. Then they put out Zedekiah's eyes and carried him in chains to Babylon.

On the seventh day of the fifth month (Av), Nebuzaradan, who was chief in command of Nebuchadnezzar's troops, burned the house of the Lord, the royal palace and all the houses of Jerusalem. The Chaldean army demolished the walls around the city, and Nebuzaradan carried off into exile most of the people left in the city as well as those who had already surrendered to the king of Babylon. He left a small number of the poorest people to be vintners and plowmen.

Gedaliah, who was appointed governor over them, said to them: "Do not be afraid; live in the land, serve the king of Babylon, and it shall be well with you." But in the seventh month (Tishri), one of the royal family, Ishmael, came with ten men and killed Gedaliah and those who were with him at Mizpah. Then all the people, young and old, went to Egypt, for they were afraid of the Chaldeans.

In the thirty-seventh year of the exile of Jehoiachin king of Judah, Evil-Merodach king of Babylon freed him from prison. He spoke kindly to him and gave him a seat among the kings who were in Babylon. Jehoiachin changed his prison-dress, and dined with the king every day. A daily allowance was made for him, to maintain him as long as he lived.

Isaiah

Isaiah is considered the greatest of the prophets because of the
grandeur of his style and the great power of his personality.
Isaiah began his prophetic career toward the end of the eighth
century before the common era, at a time when there was
abundant prosperity in Judea, vast stores of silver and gold,
and a tremendous variety of treasure. He witnessed the growth
of large estates, the oppression of the poor, the pursuit of wan-
ton pleasure and the spread of idolatrous practices. Isaiah was
convinced that all this could not continue with impunity. If it
persists, he warned, God will destroy both the kingdom of
Israel and the kingdom of Judah.

According to tradition, Isaiah was of royal blood. He suffered martyrdom by being torn asunder when King Manasseh
persecuted the loyal worshipers of the God of their forefathers.

The book of Isaiah contains sixty-six chapters and is the first
of the three Major Prophets, the other two being the books of
Jeremiah and Ezekiel. The term Major refers to the fact that
these prophetic books are longer than the other prophetic
books in the Bible.

The fortieth chapter of Isaiah introduces the great theme of
deliverance and restoration and has been credited by scholars
to another or second Isaiah. This second Isaiah is referred to
as the great unknown prophet of the exile, because chapters
forty through sixty-six are addressed to the Jews in the Babylonian exile, which occurred more than a century after the
first Isaiah.

The eloquence of the entire book of Isaiah is without parallel
in the literature of the ancient world. In the vision of Isaiah,
the black night of exile is at its end; the period of Zion's
affliction is over; the morning of deliverance dawns before his
eyes.

The vision of Isaiah concerning Judah and Jerusalem.

Wash yourselves; make yourselves clean; remove your
evil doings from my sight; cease to do wrong, learn to do

right; seek justice, restrain oppression; defend the fatherless, plead for the widow.

Let me sing for my Friend a song concerning his vineyard. My Friend had a vineyard on a fertile hill. He trenched it, cleared it of stones, and planted it with choice vines. He built a watchtower in the midst of it, and had a winepress hewn in it; then he looked for good grapes, but it yielded wild grapes.

Now, O citizens of Jerusalem and men of Judah, pray judge between me and my vineyard. What more could have been done for my vineyard? What have I left undone? When I looked for good grapes, why did it yield wild grapes?

Let me tell you now what I will do to my vineyard. I will break down its fence, and it shall be trampled. I will make it a waste; it shall be unpruned, unweeded; it shall be overgrown with thorns and thistles. I will also command the clouds that they drop no rain on it.

The Lord's vineyard is the house of Israel, the men of Judah are his plant of delight; he looked for justice, and behold, violence; for uprightness, and behold, a cry from the oppressed!

In the year that King Uzziah died, I saw the Lord sitting on a high and lofty throne; seraphim hovered round him, each with six wings. They kept calling one to another: "Holy, holy, holy is the Lord of hosts; the whole earth is full of his glory." Then I heard the voice of the Lord saying: "Whom shall I send? Who will go for us?" And I said: "Here I am! Send me."

Woe to those who call evil good and good evil, who regard darkness as light, and light as darkness; who regard bitter as sweet, and sweet as bitter!

Woe to those who are wise in their own eyes, and shrewd in their own sight. Woe to those who are heroes at drinking wine, brave men in mixing strong drink; who clear the guilty for a bribe, and deprive the innocent man of his right!

Thus says the Lord God, the Holy One of Israel: By sitting still and resting shall you be saved; in quietness and confidence your strength shall be.

Woe to those who go down to Egypt for help and rely on horses, who trust in her many chariots and very strong horsemen, but do not heed the Holy One of Israel, and do not seek the Lord. The Egyptians are only men, their horses are flesh; when the Lord strikes, both the helper and the one who is helped shall stumble and collapse.

Strengthen the feeble-handed, make firm the weak-kneed; say to those with fluttering hearts: "Have courage, fear not! Behold, your God comes to save you!"

Then the blind shall see, and the deaf shall hear. Waters shall break forth in the wilderness, and streams in the desert; the burning sand shall become a pool, and the thirsty ground—springs of water. A highway shall be there, and it shall be called the Holy way. No unclean one shall pass over it; no lions shall be there, no wild beasts shall haunt it. On it the redeemed shall walk; those whom the Lord has set free shall return to Zion singing. They shall be crowned with unending joy; sorrow and sighing shall flee away.

Sennacherib, king of Assyria, marched against all the fortified cities of Judah and captured them. He sent his commander with a large army against King Hezekiah at Jerusalem. And the commander shouted in Hebrew: "Hear the words of the great king of Assyria! He warns you not to let Hezekiah deceive you. Do not listen to Hezekiah! Make your peace with me, surrender to me! Then every one of you will eat the fruit of his own vine and his own fig tree, every one of you will drink from his own water supply, until I come and take you away to a land like your own land, a land of grain and wine, a land of bread and vineyards. Beware of letting Hezekiah mislead you by saying that the Lord will save you. Has any god of any nation saved his land from the hands of the king of Assyria, that the Lord should now save Jerusalem from me?"

Upon hearing this, King Hezekiah tore his clothes, put on sackcloth, and went into the house of the Lord. He sent this message to Isaiah: "This is a day of distress and of disgrace. Pray for this remnant of the people." Isaiah replied: "Thus says the Lord: Do not be afraid of the

126

Assyrian king. Behold, he shall hear a rumor; he shall go back to his own land and fall by the sword of his own country. He shall never come into this city, nor shoot an arrow here; by the way he came shall he return, for I will defend this city for my own sake and for the sake of my servant David."

The angel of the Lord went forth and slew one hundred and eighty-five thousand in the camp of the Assyrians. Then Sennacherib, king of Assyria, returned home to Nineveh. And one day, as he was worshiping in the temple of his god, two of his sons struck him down with the sword and escaped.

At that time, the king of Babylon sent envoys with a present to Hezekiah, for he heard that Hezekiah had just recovered from an illness. Hezekiah welcomed them and showed them his treasures, the silver, the gold, the spices, the precious oil, and his whole armory. There was nothing in his palace or in all his realm that he did not show them. Then Isaiah came and asked Hezekiah: "What did these men say? Whence have they come to you?" Hezekiah replied: "They have come to me from a far country, from Babylon."

"And what have they seen in your palace?" Isaiah asked. "They have seen everything in my palace," Hezekiah answered; "there is nothing in my storehouses that I did not show them."

Then Isaiah said to Hezekiah: "Behold, the days are coming, when all that is in your house, with all that your fathers have stored up, shall be carried to Babylon; nothing shall be left, says the Lord. Some of your sons shall be taken away to serve in the palace of the king of Babylon." And Hezekiah said to Isaiah: "The word of the Lord which you have spoken is good," thinking to himself: "At least there will be peace and security in my time."

"Comfort, O comfort my people," says your God; "speak tenderly to Jerusalem, proclaim to her that her guilt is pardoned, that she has received from the Lord's hand double for all her sins . . ."

Get up on a high mountain, O herald of good news to

Zion! Raise your voice strongly, fear not, and tell the towns of Judah: Here is your God! Like a shepherd he tends his flock, gathering the lambs in his arm and carrying them in his bosom.

Do you not know? Do you not hear? Has this not been told you from the first? It is he who sits above the globe of the earth; its inhabitants look like grasshoppers. He brings nobles to nothing, and makes the rulers of the world a thing of nought. Look up and see! Who created these stars? He brings out their host in order, calling them all by name, not one fails to appear.

Why should you say, O Jacob, "My way is hidden from the Lord"? Do you not know? Have you not heard? The Lord is the everlasting God, the Creator of the world from end to end. Young men may faint and grow weary, strong youths may fall exhausted, but those who hope in the Lord shall renew their strength, they shall put forth wings like eagles, they shall run and never weary, they shall walk and never faint.

Israel my servant, you whom I fetched from the ends of the earth, fear not, for I am with you; be not dismayed, for I am your God. I will strengthen you, I will help you, I will uphold you with my victorious right hand.

All who are angry with you shall be put to shame, those who quarrel with you shall perish and vanish. You will not find them when you look for them. I, the Lord your God, will say to you: "Fear not, I will help you."

Fear not, Jacob my servant. For I will pour water on the thirsty land, and streams on the dry ground, I will pour my spirit upon your children, my blessing upon your offspring. They shall grow up like grass amid waters, like willows by flowing streams.

Look around you, look! They all gather together, they come to you, your sons from far away, your little daughters carried in arms! See and be radiant, let your heart thrill and rejoice; for the abundance of the sea shall be turned to you, the wealth of nations shall come to you.

Whoever is thirsty, come to the waters! Whoever has no money, come for food and eat! Why spend your money on what is not food, your earnings on what does not satisfy?

If you but listen to me, you shall eat what is good and be delighted with rich nourishment.

Incline your ear, come to me; listen and you shall live. Seek the Lord while he may be found, call to him while he is near. Let the wicked man give up his way, and the evil man his designs; let him turn back to the Lord who will have mercy on him, to our God who forgives abundantly.

My thoughts are not like your thoughts, nor are your ways like my ways, says the Lord. As the heavens are higher than the earth, so are my ways higher than your ways and my thoughts than your thoughts. As the rain and the snow come down from heaven and return not thither, but water the earth and make it yield seed for the sower and bread for the eater, so is the word that comes forth from my mouth: it does not return to me fruitless, but carries out the plan for which I sent it.

You shall depart with joy, and be led forth in peace; the mountains and the hills shall burst into song before you, and all the trees of the field shall applaud. Instead of the thorn shall come up the cypress; instead of the brier shall come up the myrtle; this shall be a memorial to the Lord, an everlasting monument.

Cry out, spare not, raise your voice like a trumpet; tell my people their guilt, tell Jacob's house their sins. Daily, indeed, they seek me, desiring to know my ways; they keep asking me about righteous ordinances; they seemingly delight to draw near to God. "Why seest thou not when we fast?" they ask. "Why heedest thou not when we afflict ourselves?"

Is that what you call fasting, a day acceptable to the Lord? Behold, this is what I consider precious: Loosen the chains of wickedness, undo the bonds of oppression, let the crushed go free, break all yokes of tyranny! Share your food with the hungry, take the poor to your home, clothe the naked when you see them, and never turn from your fellow.

The Lord will answer you when you call, if you remove from your midst oppression, scorn and malice. If you share your food with the hungry, and clothe the naked, then shall your light rise in darkness and be bright as noon; the Lord will always guide you and nourish you; you shall be like a watered garden, a never-failing spring.

Arise, shine, your light has come! The Lord's splendor has risen upon you. Though darkness covers all the earth, and a black cloud shrouds the nations, yet the Lord shines out upon you. Nations shall walk by your light, and kings by your rising brightness.

For Zion's sake I will not keep silent, for Jerusalem's sake I will not rest until her triumph comes forth clear as light and her deliverance like a blazing torch. The nations shall see your triumph, all the kings shall behold your glory; you shall be called by a new name, a name given by the Lord. You shall be a crown of beauty in the hand of the Lord. No more shall you be named "Forsaken," your land shall no longer be called "Desolate"; you shall be called "My Delight."

I will exult over Jerusalem, and rejoice in my people; no more shall be heard in it the sound of weeping and the cry of distress. No more shall there be in it an infant that lives but a few days, or an old man who has not completed the span of his life.

They shall build houses and inhabit them; they shall plant vineyards and eat their fruit. They shall not labor in vain, nor bring forth children for disaster. Before they call, I shall answer. The wolf and the lamb shall feed together, and the lion shall eat straw like the ox; dust shall be the serpent's food. None shall injure, none shall kill, says the Lord.

Jeremiah

Jeremiah began to prophesy in Jerusalem about seventy years after the death of Isaiah. More is known about his life and teachings than about any other prophet, since the book of Jeremiah contains a mass of historical and biographical material. He was gentle and sensitive. He yearned for the comforts of a normal life; yet he felt impelled to speak the truth and be "a man of strife and contention," delivering messages of doom and foretelling the fall of Jerusalem. He was often imprisoned and in danger of his life, yet he did not flinch. He was cruelly insulted and accused of treason by the people he loved tenderly—those whom he sought to save. After the fall of Jerusalem in 586 before the common era, he was forcibly taken into Egypt by those who fled the wrath of the Babylonian conqueror.

Tradition has it that Nebuchadnezzar, king of Babylon, had instructed his general to treat Jeremiah with consideration and kindness. But the prophet insisted on sharing the hardships and tortures that were inflicted on his people. Afterwards Jeremiah was killed in Egypt, where he had continued his fiery speeches for some time.

Jeremiah also foretold the restoration of Israel, and those who survived the agonies of captivity were promised a safe journey home to Judea. He looked forward to a reunion of deported Israel with the people of Judah, to an ingathering of all the exiles.

The book of Jeremiah is the longest of the prophetic books, even though it has fourteen chapters less than Isaiah. Jeremiah's dictations to his faithful secretary Baruch were written down upon a scroll of leather which the king of Judah slashed with a knife and burned. But the prophet was not easily discouraged. He ordered his scribe to take another scroll and write therein all the words of the book which the king had burned.

The Greek version of the Bible, which was prepared by a group of scholars in the third century before the common era, contains about two thousand and seven hundred words (or about one-eighth of Jeremiah) less than the Hebrew text. This has led to the conjecture that either the translators abbreviated at certain points, or that they had another text from which they made their translation.

The word of the Lord came to me, saying: "Before you were born I set you apart for my service; I appointed you a prophet to the nations." So I said: "Lord God, I cannot speak, I am too young!" But the Lord said to me: "Do not say that you are too young; you shall go to whomever I send you, and you shall speak whatever I command you. Be not afraid of them, for I am with you to help you."

Then the Lord stretched forth his hand and touched my mouth, saying: "Behold, I have put my words in your mouth. See, I have set you this day over nations and over kingdoms to tear up and to break down, to destroy and to overthrow, to build and to plant."

The word of the Lord came to me, saying: "Go and proclaim in the hearing of Jerusalem: I remember the devotion of your youth, the love of your early days, how you followed me in the wilderness. Israel is holy to the Lord, the first-fruits of his harvest; all who ravage him shall be punished, evil shall come upon them.

"Is Israel a slave? Why then has he become a prey? The lions have roared at him, growling loudly. They have made his land a waste; his cities are in ruins, empty of inhabitants.

"You have brought this upon yourself by forsaking the Lord your God! Why do you go to Egypt to drink from the Nile? Why do you go to Assyria to drink from the Euphrates? You shall be put to shame by Egypt as you were put to shame by Assyria, for the Lord has rejected those in whom you trust, and you will gain nothing from them.

"Return, O Israel, for I am merciful; I will not be angry forever. Only acknowledge your guilt in not hearkening to my voice. I will take you, one from a city and two from a family, and I will bring you to Zion. I will give you shepherds after my own heart, who shall feed you with knowledge and understanding. At that time Jerusalem shall be called the throne of the Lord, and all nations shall gather to it, walking no longer in the stubbornness of their evil hearts. In those days the house of Judah shall join the house of Israel and together they shall come from the land of the north to the land that I gave your fathers for a heritage."

Behold, a people is coming out of the north-land, a great nation is stirring from the far ends of the earth! They are cruel and have no mercy; the sound of them is like the roaring sea; they ride upon horses to attack you, O Zion! We have heard the news, and our hands fall helpless; panic has taken hold of us, and pain, as of a woman in travail. Venture not into the field, walk not on the road; for the enemy has a sword, terror is on every side.

Thus says the Lord God of Israel: "Mend your ways and your doings, and I will let you dwell in this place. If you truly mend your ways and your doings, if you really practise justice between man and man, if you do not oppress strangers, orphans or widows, I will allow you to remain in this place, in the land that I gave to your fathers forever."

I went down to the potter's house; there he was at work with his wheel. Whenever the vessel he was making out of clay became spoiled, he remolded it into another vessel. Then the word of the Lord came to me:

"O house of Israel, can I not do with you as this potter has done? Behold, like the clay in the potter's hand, you are in my hand. At one time I may speak of tearing up a nation; but if that nation turns from its evil, I will repent of the evil which I planned to inflict upon it. Again, I may speak of building up a nation; but if that nation does evil in my sight, I will repent of the good which I intended to do for it. Turn, therefore, every one from his evil paths; mend your ways and your doings."

Hear the word of the Lord, O kings of Judah and inhabitants of Jerusalem: "Behold, I am bringing a disaster upon this place, because the people have forsaken me and have filled this place with innocent blood. I will make them fall by the sword before their enemies; I will make this city a desolation; I will break this people and this city just as one breaks a potter's vessel so that it cannot be repaired."

Now when Pashhur, the priest, heard Jeremiah prophesying these things, he beat the prophet and put him in the stocks. The next morning, when Pashhur released Jeremiah from the stocks, Jeremiah said to him: "Thus says the Lord: I will hand over all Judah to the king of Babylon; I will hand over all the wealth of this city and all the treasures of the kings of Judah to their enemies, who shall carry them to Babylon. And you, Pashhur, and all your household, shall go into exile; you shall go to Babylon and die there and be buried there, you and all your friends to whom you have prophesied falsely."

These are the words of the letter which Jeremiah the prophet sent to the people whom Nebuchadnezzar had exiled to Babylon.

"Build houses and live in them; plant gardens and eat their fruit; take wives and beget sons and daughters; get wives for your sons and husbands for your daughters, and multiply where you are. Seek the welfare of the country where you have been exiled; pray to the Lord for it, since your welfare rests on its welfare."

"Days are coming," says the Lord, "when I will restore the fortunes of my people, and I will bring them back to the land which I gave to their fathers, and they shall possess it.

"Sing merrily for Jacob, shout on the hilltops of the nations, ring out your praises and say: Save thy people, O Lord, the remnant of Israel. I am bringing them from the north-land, and will gather them from the uttermost parts of the world; the blind and the lame, women with child and women in travail, a great company shall come back here. They shall come weeping, and I will lead them with grace; I will guide them to streams of water, by a smooth road where they shall not stumble; for I am a father to Israel; Ephraim is my firstborn."

Hear the word of the Lord, you nations, and announce it in far-off islands, saying: "He who has scattered Israel gathers them, and tends them as a shepherd tends his flock." They shall come singing on the heights of Zion, and shall stream to the goodness of the Lord—to the corn, the wine, the oil, the sheep and cattle; they shall be like a watered garden, and they shall languish no more. Then shall maidens delight in dancing, young men and old shall rejoice alike.

134

A voice is heard in Ramah—lamentation and bitter weeping; it is Rachel crying for her children. She refuses to be comforted, for they are gone. Thus says the Lord: "Restrain your voice from weeping, your eyes from tears; your work shall have its reward; they shall return from the land of the enemy. There is hope for your future: your children shall return to their own land.

"I will gather them from all the countries where I drove them; I will bring them back to this place, where I will make them dwell in safety; they shall be my people, and I will be their God. I will rejoice over them and plant them in this land securely. In this land that you call desolate, fields shall again be bought. Men shall buy fields for money in the places round about Jerusalem and in the Negev, for I will restore their fortunes," says the Lord.

The word came from the Lord to Jeremiah, when Nebuchadnezzar and all his army were attacking Jerusalem. "Go to Zedekiah, king of Judah, and say to him that I am giving this city over to the king of Babylon, who shall burn it with fire. You cannot escape from him; you shall be captured and delivered into his hand; you shall face the king of Babylon and speak to him in person, and to Babylon you must go. You shall not die by the sword; you shall die in peace." So Jeremiah spoke these words to Zedekiah when the army of the king of Babylon was fighting against Jerusalem, Lachish and Azekah, the only fortified cities of Judah that remained.

King Zedekiah had made a covenant with all the people in Jerusalem that every one should set free his Hebrew slaves, male or female, so that no one should hold his fellow-Jew in slavery. But afterwards the people turned around and forced back into slavery those they had liberated. Then the word of the Lord came to Jeremiah that he should say to the people: "Since you have not obeyed me by proclaiming freedom, each to his brother and neighbor, I now proclaim you free to fall under the sword, the pestilence, and the famine!"

Pharaoh's army had set out from Egypt, and news of this led the Chaldeans to abandon their siege of Jerusalem. Then the word of the Lord came to Jeremiah: "Thus shall you say to the king of Judah: Behold, Pharaoh's army which came to help you is about to retreat to Egypt, and the Chaldeans shall come back and fight against this city; they shall capture it and burn it in flames. Do not deceive yourselves with the notion that the Chaldeans will leave you alone; they will not stay away."

When the Chaldean forces had abandoned the siege of Jerusalem, in fear of Pharaoh's army, Jeremiah set out from Jerusalem to go to the land of Benjamin. But a sentry, who was posted at the Benjamin Gate, arrested him, saying: "You are deserting to the Chaldeans." Jeremiah replied: "That is not true; I am not deserting to the Chaldeans." However, the sentry would not listen to him. He arrested Jeremiah and brought him to the princes, who in anger had Jeremiah flogged and confined in prison, where he remained for a number of days.

Then King Zedekiah sent for him privately and asked him: "Is there any word from the Lord?" Jeremiah answered: "There is. You shall be handed over to the king of Babylon. What wrong have I done to you or your servants or this nation, that you have put me in prison? I pray you, my lord king, be gracious to my plea; do not send me back to prison, or I shall die there." So King Zedekiah gave orders for Jeremiah to be placed in the guardhouse, where he was given a loaf of bread daily, until all the bread of the city was gone.

Now the princes had heard Jeremiah declaring in public: "Anyone who remains in the city shall die by the sword or by famine or by plague, but anyone who surrenders to the Chaldeans shall live." So they said to the king: "Let this man be put to death, for he is discouraging the people and the soldiers within the city by talking like this! This man is not seeking the welfare of the people, but their harm!" King Zedekiah said: "Behold, he is in your hands," for the king was powerless against them. So they took Jeremiah and cast him into an underground cistern, below the guardhouse, lowering him down with ropes. There was no water in the cistern, only mud, and Jeremiah sank in the mud.

However, an Ethiopian servant, belonging to the royal

house, left the palace to find the king. "Your majesty," he said, "these men have done evil to the prophet by casting him into the cistern; he will die there of hunger, for there is no bread left in the city."

Then the king commanded the Ethiopian to take three men and pull Jeremiah out of the cistern. So he took the men with him and went to the palace, where he got some old rags and worn-out clothes; these he lowered by ropes to Jeremiah in the cistern, saying: "Put the rags and clothes between your armpits and the ropes." Jeremiah did so. And they pulled him up by the ropes out of the cistern.

King Zedekiah sent for Jeremiah and said to him: "I am going to ask you a question; do not hide anything from me." Jeremiah replied: "But if I tell you the truth, you certainly will put me to death. Besides, you will not listen to any advice from me." So King Zedekiah took an oath in secret, saying: "As the Lord lives, I will neither put you to death, nor hand you over to those men who seek your life."

Then Jeremiah said to Zedekiah: "If you surrender to the officers of the king of Babylon, your life shall be spared, and this city shall not be burned in flames; you and your household shall live. But if you do not surrender, this city shall be given over to the Chaldeans to be burned, and you shall not escape from their hands."

King Zedekiah said to Jeremiah: "But I am afraid of the Jews who have deserted to the Chaldeans; they may subject me to indignity and abuse." "You shall not be handed over to the Jews," Jeremiah said; "just listen to what I say, and all will go well with you; you shall live."

Then Zedekiah said to Jeremiah: "Let no one know of this conversation, and your life is safe. If the princes hear that I have been talking with you, and if they come and ask you to tell them what you said to the king and what the king said to you, you shall say to them that you presented a humble plea to the king not to be sent back to die in prison."

All the princes did come to question Jeremiah, and he answered them just as the king had told him; so they said no more. Jeremiah then remained in the guardhouse until the day that Jerusalem was taken.

Nebuchadnezzar with all his army attacked Jerusalem and besieged it. When Zedekiah and the garrison saw that a breach had been made in the walls of the city, they took to flight and left the city during the night. But the Chaldean army pursued them. Zedekiah was caught and brought to Nebuchadnezzar, who slew his sons before his very eyes. The king of Babylon also slew all the nobles of Judea. He then put out the eyes of Zedekiah and bound him with chains to carry him to Babylon.

The Chaldeans burned down the royal palace and the houses of the common people, and demolished the walls of Jerusalem. Then Nebuzaradan, the commander, carried captive to Babylon the rest of the people that were left in the city and the deserters who had surrendered to him. However, he did leave in the land of Judah some poor people who had nothing; he allotted them vineyards and fields.

Nebuchadnezzar had ordered Nebuzaradan to take good care of Jeremiah, so the commander-in-chief took Jeremiah and said to him: "The Lord your God pronounced evil against this place, and has done as he decreed. Well now, I release you today from the chains on your hands. If you like to come with me to Babylon, come, and I will take good care of you. If not, think no more of it; the whole land is before you, go wherever you please. Go back, if you wish, to Gedaliah, whom the king of Babylon has appointed governor over the cities of Judah; stay with him, or go wherever else you choose." Then the commander sent him off with some food and a present. Jeremiah went to Gedaliah and stayed with him among the people who were left in the land.

But Ishmael, the son of Nethaniah, a member of the royal family, came with ten men to Gedaliah at Mizpah. They drew their swords and murdered Gedaliah and all the Jews who were with him at Mizpah, as well as the Chaldean soldiers who happened to be there.

Jeremiah summoned all the people and said to them: "Thus says the Lord God of Israel: If you will remain in this land, I will build you up and not pull you down. Do not fear the king of Babylon, for I am with you. But if

138

you say: 'We will not remain in this country; no, we will go to Egypt where we shall not see war nor hear the sound of the trumpet nor be hungry for bread.' If you really are bent on going to Egypt to live, the sword you dread shall overtake you, the famine you fear shall follow you, and you shall die there. All who are bent on settling in Egypt shall die by the sword, by famine, or by plague. O remnant of Judah, do not go to Egypt!"

When Jeremiah had finished speaking, a group of insolent men said to him: "You are telling a lie; the Lord our God did not send you to forbid us to settle in Egypt—it is Baruch the son of Neriah who has set you against us to deliver us into the hand of the Chaldeans that they may put us to death, or carry us captive to Babylon." So they did not listen to the voice of the Lord, telling them to stay in the land of Judah; but they took the remnant of Judah, the men, women and children, including Jeremiah and Baruch, and went to the land of Egypt.

Then the word of the Lord came to Jeremiah: "Take some large stones in your hands; let some of the men of Judah see you hiding them in the pavement which is at the entrance to Pharaoh's palace, and say to them: Thus says the Lord God of Israel: I am sending for my servant Nebuchadnezzar, king of Babylon, who will set his throne above these stones that you have buried. He shall come to ravage the land of Egypt, inflicting death upon those who are doomed to die, capturing those who are doomed to captivity, and putting to the sword those who are doomed to the sword. He shall set fire to the temples of the gods in Egypt, burning them and carrying off the idols. He shall clean the land of Egypt, and then leave unmolested."

Ezekiel

Ezekiel lived during the last days of Jerusalem and received inspiration from the utterances of Jeremiah, his elder contemporary. Ezekiel prophesied in Babylon for a period of twenty-two years, having been taken into captivity eleven years before the fall of Jerusalem.

Prior to the destruction of the Temple by Nebuchadnezzar in 586, Ezekiel's prophecies were messages of doom; after it, they were messages of hope and assurances of restoration. Ezekiel dwells on a prophet's responsibility for the fate of his people. He maintains that a prophet is a watchman, responsible for warning his people of the consequences of misdoings. He tells us that each man possesses the power to be good or evil regardless of heredity and predisposition, and that the individual is master of his own destiny and responsible for his own deeds. Ezekiel stresses the idea that everybody can turn over a new leaf and look hopefully toward the future. His vision of the dry bones vividly illustrates the hope of restoration and revival of a nation that was given up as dead.

The book of Ezekiel is the third in the division of the Bible known as Latter Prophets, the first two books being those of Isaiah and Jeremiah. Its forty-eight chapters are divided into two equal parts. The first twenty-four chapters contain speeches uttered by Ezekiel prior to the national disaster of 586. The last twenty-four chapters consist of visions that occurred after the destruction of Jerusalem. The final chapters of Ezekiel concerning the glorious future of Israel have provided the Jewish people with a beacon of light through the lonely years of exile.

The word of the Lord came to me, saying: "Son of man, I set you up as a watchman for the people of Israel. If you say nothing to warn the wicked man from his evil course, that his life may be saved, the wicked man shall die for his iniquity, but I will hold you responsible for his death. If, however, you warn him and he does not turn from his

140

evil course, he shall die for his iniquity, but you have saved yourself.

"Son of man, speak to your people and say to them: If I bring down the sword upon a land, and if the watchman blows the trumpet to warn the people, then whoever does not heed the warning, and is swept off by the sword, is to blame for his own death. But if the watchman does not blow the trumpet when he sees the sword coming, and the sword comes and strikes down any one of the people, I will hold the watchman responsible.

"Tell the people of Israel: As I live, says the Lord God, I have no pleasure in the death of the wicked; let the wicked man turn from his way and live. Turn back, turn back from your evil ways! Why should you die, O Israel?"

The word of the Lord came to me, saying: "What do you mean by quoting this proverb in the land of Israel: 'The fathers eat sour grapes, and the children's teeth are set on edge'? By my life, you shall no more use this proverb in Israel. All souls are mine, the soul of the father as well as the soul of the son; he who sins shall die. If a man oppresses no one and robs no one, if he feeds the hungry and clothes the naked, if he abstains from crime and observes strict justice between man and man—he is upright and shall surely live. If he has a son who is a violent man, given to bloodshed, who oppresses the poor and commits robbery, that son shall not live. He has done abominable things, he shall surely die; he is responsible for his own death.

"But if this son, in turn, has a son who, seeing all the sins committed by his father, does not act likewise but lives by my laws, he shall not die for the iniquity of his father, he shall live. His father died for his own iniquity because he practised oppression and outrage and wrongdoing among his fellow men.

"You ask: 'Why should not the son suffer for the iniquity of his father?' If the son does what is right and honest, if he observes and obeys all my laws, he shall live. The person who sins shall die. A son shall not suffer for the iniquity of his father, nor a father for the iniquity of his son.

"But if a wicked man turns away from all the sins which he has committed and keeps all my laws, he shall surely live; he shall not die. None of the transgressions which he has committed shall be remembered against him.

"Again, when a good man turns away from his uprightness and practises iniquity, none of his good deeds shall be remembered; for the sin he has committed he shall die.

"O Israel, repent and turn from all your transgressions, or iniquity will be your ruin; get yourselves a new heart and a new spirit! I have no pleasure in the death of anyone. So repent and live."

"Son of man, prophesy to the mountains of Israel and say: Mountains of Israel, hear the word of the Lord! Because you have been left desolate and crushed on every side, and because you have become the possession of the rest of the nations and the subject of popular evil gossip, I speak in fiery indignation against the surrounding nations who siezed my land for themselves.

"Prophesy concerning the land of Israel, and say to the mountains and hills, watercourses and valleys: Thus says the Lord God: Behold, I speak in my indignation and fury, because you have suffered the reproach of the nations. I swear that the nations that are round about you shall themselves suffer reproach.

"But you, mountains of Israel, shall bear fruit for Israel my people; for they will soon return. I am for you, I will care for you, and you shall be tilled and sown; I will put many people on you—the whole house of Israel; the cities shall be inhabited and the waste places rebuilt. I will multiply both man and beast; they shall increase and be fruitful; I will do more good to you than ever before. Then you will know that I am the Lord. I will let men walk upon you again, the men of my people Israel; they shall possess you, and you shall be their heritage.

"Say to the house of Israel: Thus says the Lord your God: I will take you from the nations and gather you from all countries and bring you back to your own land. A new heart I will give you and a new spirit I will put within you. I will make you live by my laws, and you shall obey and observe my ordinances. You shall dwell in the land which I gave to your fathers; you shall be my people, and I will be your God; I will keep you clear of all your impurities. I will summon the grain and make it abundant, that you may never again suffer the disgrace of famine among the nations. And it will be said that this land which was desolate has become like the garden of Eden. The surrounding nations shall know that I the Lord have rebuilt the ruined places and replanted the desolate land. I the Lord have spoken, and I will do it."

The word of the Lord came to me: "Son of man, set your face toward Gog in the land of Magog; prophesy against him and say: Thus says the Lord God: Behold, I am against you, O Gog! Be ready, you and all the hosts that are assembled about you; hold yourself in reserve for me. In the latter days you will go against the land that has been restored, the land where people have been gathered from many nations. You will advance, coming on like a storm, you will be like a cloud covering the land, you and all your hordes. On that day you will devise an evil plan to invade this land of villages, to attack the quiet people who live in security. You will come from the far north, you and many a nation with you—a huge army, sweeping up against my people Israel like a storm cloud covering the country.

"On that day, when Gog invades the land of Israel, my wrath will be roused. There shall be a mighty earthquake in the land of Israel; mountains shall be torn apart, and cliffs shall topple over, and every wall shall tumble to the ground. I will overwhelm him with utter panic, I will punish him with pestilence and bloodshed.

"Son of man, prophesy against Gog and say: Thus says the Lord God: Behold, I am against you, O Gog! I will strike your bow from your left hand and will make your arrows drop out of your right hand. You shall fall upon the mountains of Israel, you and all your hordes.

"I will restore the fortunes of Jacob and have mercy on the whole house of Israel. They shall forget their shame and all their faithlessness toward me, when they live undisturbed in their own land with none to make them afraid. Then they shall know that I am the Lord their God. I sent them into exile among the nations but now I have gathered them back into their own land."

The hand of the Lord was upon me and carried me off in the spirit, and set me down in the midst of a valley which was full of bones. He made me go all round them, and I saw that they were very many and very dry.

He said to me: "Son of man, can these bones live?" and I answered: "Lord God, thou knowest." Again he said to me: "Prophesy over these bones, say to them: O dry bones, listen to the word of the Lord. Thus says the Lord God: Behold, I will cause breath to enter into you, and you shall live. I will put sinews upon you and cover you with flesh; I will spread skin over you, then I will put breath into you, and you shall live; and you shall know that I am the Lord."

So I prophesied as I was commanded. While I was prophesying, there was a rattling sound—the bones came together, bone to bone. And as I looked, there were sinews upon them! Flesh and skin spread over them, but there was no breath in them. Then he said to me: "Prophesy to the breath, son of man, and say to the breath: Thus says the Lord God: Come from the four ends of the earth, O breath, and breathe into these lifeless bodies that they may live." So I prophesied as he commanded me, and the breath came into them and they lived and stood upon their feet, an exceedingly great host.

Then he said to me: "Son of man, these bones are the people of Israel. Behold, they keep saying: Our bones are dry, our hope is lost, we are undone! Prophesy therefore to them and tell them: Thus says the Lord God: O my people, I will open your graves and bring you back to the land of Israel. You shall know that I am the Lord when I have raised you from your graves, O my people. I will put my spirit into you, and you shall live. I will place you in your own land; then you shall know that I, the Lord, have spoken and performed it."

Hosea

Hosea lived after Amos during the eighth century before the common era, and prophesied in the kingdom of Israel before Isaiah did in the kingdom of Judah. His prophetic work began before the death of Jeroboam II, and he was still living when the kingdom of Israel was destroyed by the Assyrians in 721 before the common era.

The book of Hosea appears as the first among the twelve Minor Prophets, commonly known as "The Twelve." The name Minor Prophets, as compared with Major Prophets, does not refer to value but to volume, that is, the length of the individual books. Since these twelve books were so short, they were gathered into a single collection to safeguard their preservation; hence they count as one book in the Hebrew Bible.

Chronologically, the book of Hosea should come after the book of Amos, but it is placed first because of its length. The length of the Major Prophets likewise determined that they should be placed before the Minor Prophets.

The style of Hosea is highly poetic and difficult to follow. Many passages in Hosea are not clearly understood particularly because we are no longer fully acquainted with certain events to which they allude.

The word of the Lord that came to Hosea during the reign of Jeroboam the son of Joash, king of Israel:

The number of the people of Israel shall be like the sand of the sea that cannot be measured or counted. The people of Judah and the people of Israel shall be gathered together; they shall appoint one leader for themselves, and spread out beyond their land.

"On that day," says the Lord, "I will abolish bow, sword and war from the land, and I will let them lie down in safety. On that day I will answer the heavens, and they shall answer the earth; the earth shall answer the grain, the wine and the oil, and they shall answer Jezreel."

Hear the word of the Lord, O people of Israel, for the Lord has a quarrel with the inhabitants of the land. There is no faithfulness, no kindness, no knowledge of God in the land; there is swearing, lying, killing, stealing, and adultery; one crime follows hard upon another. Hence the land mourns, and its inhabitants languish; even the beasts and birds and the very fish within the sea are perishing. My people are destroyed for lack of knowledge.

I will go back to my place, until they realize their guilt and seek my face, searching me out in their distress and crying: "Come, let us return to the Lord; he has torn, and he will heal us; he has wounded, and he will bind us up; in a day or two he will revive us, to live under his care. Let us know the Lord; he will come to us like spring rain that waters the land."

Ephraim is like a dove, silly and without sense, calling to Egypt, going to Assyria. Woe to them, for they have strayed from me! Ruin to them, for they have rebelled against me! Woe to them when I depart from them!

Like grapes in the wilderness I found Israel. Like the first ripe fig on the fig tree I welcomed your fathers. But when they devoted themselves to Baal, they became as detestable as the thing they loved. Sow justice for yourselves, and reap a harvest of love!

How can I give you up, O Ephraim! How can I hand you over, O Israel! I will not carry out my fierce anger, for I am God and not man; I will not destroy. Come back to the Lord your God, O Israel, for you have stumbled because of your iniquity.

I will heal their faithlessness; I will love them truly, for my anger has turned from them. I will be like the dew to Israel; he shall blossom like a lily, and strike roots like a poplar. Once again they shall dwell beneath my shadow; they shall blossom like a vine.

Whoever is wise, let him understand this: The ways of the Lord are right; good men walk in them, while sinners stumble in them.

Joel

Nothing is known about the personality of the prophet Joel, the author of the second book of the Minor Prophets. Even the date of his book is subject to speculation and is greatly disputed among Bible scholars. Authorities place Joel either in a very early period or in post-exilic times.

The book of Joel consists of three chapters; its style is fluent, clear and of a high order. The general subject of Joel is divine judgment. A plague of locusts, accompanied by a drought of unusual severity, sweeps in successive swarms over Judea and destroys the produce of the fields and vineyards. Remarkably vivid is the description of the locust swarms filling the entire air; their destructiveness is compared with that of a mighty army. Joel summons the people to a penitential fast, and promises that God will bring back prosperity and abundance. The third and last chapter of Joel describes the future glory of Judea.

The word of the Lord that came to Joel:

Hear this, you who are old; listen, all inhabitants of the land! Has such a thing ever happened in your days, or in the days of your fathers? Tell it to your children, and let your children tell their children, and their children to the coming generation.

What the cutting locust left, the swarming locust ate; what the swarming locust left, the hopping locust ate; and what the hopping locust left, the devouring locust ate.

Wake up, you drunkards, and weep for the wine that is snatched from your mouth! An army has invaded our land, powerful and numberless; their teeth are the teeth of a lion, with fangs of a lioness. They have ruined our vines, and splintered our fig trees; they have stripped them clean, till their branches are made white.

Blow the trumpet in Zion; sound the alarm in my holy mountain! Let all the inhabitants of the land tremble, for the day of the Lord is coming, it is near, a day of darkness

147

and gloom. Like blackness spread over the mountains is the huge and powerful army, the like of which has never been before. Before them the land is a paradise, behind them it is a desolate wilderness. Nothing escapes them. They rush on the city, run over the walls, climb into the houses, and enter through the windows like thieves.

"Yet even now," says the Lord, "return to me with all your heart, fasting, weeping, mourning; rend your hearts and not your garments." Turn to the Lord your God, for he is gracious and merciful, slow to anger, rich in kindness, and ready to relent. Blow the trumpet in Zion; gather the people; assemble the old men; collect the children; let the priests, the ministers of the Lord, weep and say: "Spare thy people, O Lord; why should they say among the nations: Where is their God?"

Then the Lord had pity on his people and said to them: "I will now send you grain and wine and oil; I will drive out the northern foe into a parched and desolate land. Fear not, O land, rejoice and be glad. I will make it up to you for the years that the swarming locusts have eaten, that huge army which I sent among you. So you shall eat and eat and be satisfied. My people shall never again be put to shame.

"And it shall come to pass afterward, that I will pour out my spirit on all flesh; your sons and your daughters shall prophesy; your old men shall dream dreams, your young men shall see visions; even upon your servants, both men and women, I will pour out my spirit in those days.

"For in those days and at that time, when I restore the fortunes of Judah and Jerusalem, I will gather all the nations and bring them down into the Judgment Valley, where I shall enter into judgment with them, because they scattered my people Israel among pagans and divided up my land. Then the mountains shall drip wine, the hills shall flow with milk, and all the stream beds of Judah shall flow with water. Judah shall be inhabited forever, and Jerusalem to all generations."

Amos

Amos, the earliest known literary prophet, lived in the village of Tekoa, about twelve miles south of Jerusalem, during the middle of the eighth century before the common era. He left the kingdom of Judah and proceeded to make known the divine warnings in the kingdom of Israel, which had then reached the zenith of its power and prosperity. Though a native of Judah, he addresses himself primarily to the citizens of Israel.

Amos denounces the brutalities and cruel wrongs perpetrated by various nations. He strongly insists upon social justice, respect for the lowly, and the defense of the weak against the powerful. He condemns self-indulgence which breeds cruelty, and compares the pampered women of Samaria to cows grown fat through feeding in the rich pastures of Bashan, east of the Jordan. Their chief delight being luxurious living, they keep saying to their husbands: "Bring, and let us drink!" When the priest of Bethel tells Amos to go back home and prophesy there, he replies that he is not a professional prophet who tries to please people, but simply a shepherd who has been charged to prophesy to the people of Israel.

Though classed as the third of the Minor Prophets, the book of Amos should come first from a chronological point of view. The word "minor" refers to the small size of each of the twelve books of the Minor Prophets in comparison with the so-called Major Prophets, Isaiah, Jeremiah, and Ezekiel.

The words of Amos, a shepherd of Tekoa, who prophesied concerning Israel during the reign of Jeroboam son of Joash, King of Israel, two years before the earthquake:

Do two men walk together, unless they have made an appointment? Does a lion roar in the jungle, unless he has some prey? Does a young lion growl in his lair, unless he has made a capture? Does a bird fall into a snare, unless a trap is set for it? Does the trap spring up, unless there is something to catch? Do not the people tremble when a trumpet is sounded? If there is a disaster in a city, has not the Lord caused it? When the lion roars, who does not shudder? When the Lord God speaks, who can but prophesy?

Hear this, you cows of Bashan, you women in Samaria, who cheat the poor and crush the needy, who tell your husbands: Bring, and let us drink! The time is coming, when you will be dragged out of the city with hooks; out you shall go headlong through breaches in the walls.

Seek good and not evil, that you may live. Hate evil and love good, and establish justice in the gate. Let justice roll down like waters, and righteousness like an ever-flowing stream.

Woe to those who are at ease in Zion, and to those who feel secure in Samaria; woe to those who lie upon beds of ivory and sprawl upon their couches, eating fresh lamb and fatted veal, crooning to the music of the lute, composing songs like David himself, lapping up wine by the bowlful and anointing themselves with the best of oil, but never grieving over the ruin of the nation. So now they shall be the first to be exiled; the dissolute revellers shall disappear.

Amaziah, the priest at Bethel, sent word to Jeroboam, king of Israel: "Amos is conspiring against you in the very midst of Israel, saying that Jeroboam shall die by the sword, and Israel shall go into exile." Amaziah also said to Amos: "You seer, be off to Judah and prophesy there, but never again at Bethel, for it is the royal sanctuary, the national temple."

Then Amos answered Amaziah: "I am no prophet, nor the son of a prophet; I am only a shepherd and a dresser of sycamore trees. But the Lord took me from the flock and said to me: 'Go, prophesy to my people Israel.' Now then, hear the word of the Lord. You say that I am not to prophesy against Israel. The Lord says: Your wife shall be a harlot in the city, your sons and daughters shall fall by the sword, your land shall be divided up, you yourself shall die in a foreign land, and Israel shall go into exile, far from its own country."

Hear this, you who would destroy the poor of the land, saying: "When will the new-moon festival be over, that we may sell our grain? When will the sabbath be done, that we may offer wheat for sale?" You deal deceitfully with false balances; you sell the very refuse of your grain.

"On that day," says the Lord, "I will make the sun go down at noon, and darken the earth in broad daylight. I will turn your feasts into mourning, and all your songs into lamentation."

"The days are coming," says the Lord, "when I will send a famine on the land; not a famine of bread, not a thirst for water, but of hearing the word of the Lord. Men shall wander from sea to sea, and run from north to east; they shall run to and fro, in quest of the Lord's word, but they shall not find it.

"On that day I will raise again the fallen booth of David, repair its breaches and rebuild it as in the days of old.

"Behold, the days are coming, when the plowman shall overtake the reaper, when he who treads the grapes shall overtake the sower; the mountains shall drip sweet wine, and all the hills shall be aflow with milk. I will restore the fortunes of my people Israel, and they shall rebuild the ruined cities and inhabit them; they shall plant vineyards and drink their wine, and they shall make gardens and eat their fruit. I will plant them upon their land, and they shall never again be uprooted from the land which I have given them," says the Lord.

Obadiah

The shortest of all prophetical books, Obadiah contains only one chapter of twenty-one verses. The unknown author predicts the destruction of Edomites, who will be treated measure for measure as they treated Israel when they helped the Babylonians to bring about the downfall of Jerusalem. From their mountainous strongholds, south of the Dead Sea, the warlike and cruel Edomites, the archenemies of Israel, looked down upon their neighbors. Obadiah's prophecy brings to mind Psalm 137, where we read: "Remember, O Lord, Jerusalem's fall against the Edomites, who said: Raze it, raze it, to its very foundation!"

Thus says the Lord God concerning Edom: "I will make you least among the nations, you shall be utterly despised. Your pride of heart has deceived you, thinking none could pull you down. Though you soar aloft like an eagle, though you set your nest among the stars, I will pull you down.

"All your allies shall betray you; your trusted friends shall set a trap under you. On that day I will destroy the wise men from Edom; your heroes shall be dismayed. For the outrage to your brother Jacob, shame shall cover you, and you shall be cut off forever. On that day you stood aloof, when strangers carried off his wealth and cast lots for Jerusalem; you were like one of them.

"You should not have gloated over your brother's fate on the day of his misfortune; you should not have rejoiced over the people of Judah on the day of their disaster; you should not have laughed aloud on the day of distress; you should not have entered the gates of my people on the day of their calamity; you should not have looted their goods on the day of their calamity; you should not have stood at the passes to cut off their fugitives; you should not have delivered up their survivors on the day of distress. As you have done, it shall be done to you; your deeds shall return upon your own head."

152

Jonah

The book of Jonah contains the noblest expression of the universality of religion. It is designed to show that kindness of heart and readiness to repent may be found everywhere amongst men.

The episode of the great fish swallowing Jonah has been interpreted figuratively as the captivity which swallowed up Israel. The deliverance from exile has been likened to being disgorged alive from the mouth of the devouring beast. Jonah's reluctance to denounce the heathen city of Nineveh was prompted perhaps by fear of exposing himself to the wrath of the king and the people.

The book of Jonah is recited as the prophetic lesson (Haftarah) in the afternoon service of Yom Kippur to show that the compassion of God extends to all his creatures, even those who are as sinful as the people of Nineveh.

Jonah is included among the Minor Prophets, even though it is not actually a prophecy but a short story about a prophet. Jonah, son of Amittai, is mentioned in II Kings 14:25 as having lived during the reign of Jeroboam II, about the middle of the eighth century before the common era.

The Lord spoke to Jonah, saying: "Arise, go to the great city of Nineveh and proclaim against it; their wickedness has come up before me." But Jonah went down to Jaffa and found a ship bound for Tarshish. He paid his fare and went aboard in an attempt to get away from the presence of the Lord.

The Lord then hurled a furious wind upon the sea; the ship was about to be smashed to pieces. The sailors were frightened, each cried to his own god, and they threw overboard the cargo that was in the ship in order to lighten it. But Jonah was fast asleep on the lower deck. The captain came and said to him: "Why are you sleeping? Get up and call upon your God! Perhaps God will think of us and we shall not perish."

153

They said to one another: "Come, let us cast lots to find out on whose account this evil has come upon us." They cast lots, and the lot fell on Jonah. Then they said to him: "Tell us now, you who are the cause of our present distress, what is your occupation? Where do you come from? What is your country? To what people do you belong?" He told them: "I am a Hebrew; I revere the Lord God in heaven who made the sea and the dry land." The men were terrified, and said to him: "What have you done?"; for they knew that he was running away from the Lord's presence. Jonah had told them that. They asked him: "What shall we do with you, so that the sea may again be calm for us? It is growing more and more stormy." He told them :"Take me and throw me overboard so that the sea may calm down for you, for I know that on my account this great tempest is upon you." Nevertheless, the men rowed hard to get back to land; they could not, however, for the seas ran higher and higher against them.

They cried to the Lord: "O Lord, let us not perish for this man's life, let us not be guilty of shedding innocent blood; for thou, O Lord, hast done as it pleased thee." Then they lifted Jonah and threw him overboard, and the sea ceased from its raging. The men feared the Lord exceedingly. They offered a sacrifice to the Lord and made vows.

Now the Lord ordered a great fish to swallow Jonah, and for three days and three nights Jonah lay inside the fish. He prayed to the Lord his God. Then the Lord spoke to the fish, and it threw Jonah out upon the dry land.

The Lord spoke to Jonah for the second time, saying: "Arise, go to the great city of Nineveh and proclaim what I tell you." Jonah started for Nineveh, as the Lord had commanded. He entered the city proclaiming: "Forty days more and Nineveh shall be overthrown!"

The people of Nineveh, great and small alike, believed God, so they proclaimed a fast and put on sackcloth. When the news reached the king of Nineveh, he rose from his throne, threw off his robe, covered himself with sackcloth, and sat in ashes. He published this proclamation: "By order of the king and his nobles! Let neither man nor beast, neither cattle nor sheep, taste any food or drink water: they shall put on sackcloth and cry earnestly to God. All must turn from their evil ways and from their acts of violence. Who knows but that God may relent and turn from his fierce anger and we shall not perish?"

When God saw what they were doing and how they turned from their evil ways, he relented and did not inflict upon them the evil he had threatened.

Jonah was painfully distressed and prayed to the Lord: "O Lord, this is what I foresaw when I was still in my own land; I therefore hastened to run away to Tarshish, for I knew that thou art a gracious and merciful God, patient and abundant in kindness. Now, O Lord, take my life away! It is better for me to die than to live."

Jonah made a tent for himself and sat in its shade, waiting to see what would happen to the city. The Lord God made a gourd grow up over Jonah to shade his head and alleviate his discomfort, and Jonah was exceedingly pleased with it. But next morning, at dawn, God caused a worm to attack the gourd and it withered. At sunrise, God sent a hot east wind and the sun beat on Jonah's head until he fainted. He longed for death, saying: "It is better for me to die than to live." Thereupon God said to Jonah: "Are you sorely grieved about the gourd?" He replied: "I am grieved enough to die."

Then the Lord said: "You would spare the gourd though you spent no work upon it. You did not make it grow—it sprang up in a night and perished in a night. Should I not then spare the great city of Nineveh with more than a hundred and twenty thousand human beings, who do not know their right hand from their left?"

Micah

Micah was a younger contemporary of Isaiah. Both envisioned the messianic future when war among nations would be no more. The fact that the prophecy concerning universal peace is phrased alike in both Isaiah and Micah has raised the question whether Micah quotes from Isaiah, or Isaiah from Micah, or both quote the same prophecy from an earlier unknown prophet. It was Micah who set forth the perfect ideal of religion when he said: "The Lord requires of you only to do justice, to love mercy and to walk humbly with your God."

Woe to those who devise iniquity and work evil. They covet fields and seize them; they covet houses and snatch them.

"I will surely assemble all of you, O Jacob, I will gather the remnant of Israel, all together like sheep in a fold, a noisy multitude of men, led by their King, by the Lord at their head."

It shall come to pass in the latter days that the mountain of the Lord's house shall be established as the highest mountain, towering over every hill, and peoples shall stream to it.

Many nations shall say: "Come, let us go up to the mountain of the Lord, to the house of the God of Jacob; he will teach us his ways, and we will walk in his paths."

Out of Zion shall go forth Torah, and the word of the Lord from Jerusalem.

They shall beat their swords into plowshares, and their spears into pruning hooks; nation shall not lift up sword against nation, neither shall they learn war any more.

They shall sit each under his vine and under his fig tree, and none shall make them afraid.

"On that day," says the Lord, "I will assemble the lame; I will gather those who have been cast off and those whom I have afflicted. I will make the lame and the sick into a mighty nation."

Now what does the Lord ask of you? Only to do justice, to love mercy, and to walk humbly with your God.

Nahum

The prophet Nahum, whose name signifies consolation, limits himself to the graphic description of the downfall of the Assyrian empire. His book, containing only three chapters, is one of the best productions of biblical literature in terms of style and sublimity of thought. Nahum's message is a permanent expression of the cry for justice. He speaks in the name of outraged humanity, trampled by the ruthless armies of tyrannical Assyria. Nahum's breathless account of the destruction of Nineveh, the Assyrian capital, in the year 612, must have been written during or immediately after this historic event. Unlike other prophets, Nahum does not allude to the sins of his own people.

An oracle concerning Nineveh; the vision of Nahum.

The Lord is an avenging God, he takes vengeance upon his enemies. The Lord is slow to anger and of great might; he will by no means clear the guilty. The Lord is good to those who wait for him, a stronghold in the day of trouble; he cares for those who trust in him.

Behold, upon the hills, the feet of the messenger who brings good news, who proclaims peace! Keep your feasts, O Judah, for never again shall the villain invade you; he is utterly destroyed.

The shatterer has come up against you! The shields of his mighty men are crimson, his soldiers are clad in scarlet, his armored chariots gleam like fire. The chariots rage in the streets, flashing like torches, darting like lightning.

The palace is in panic, the queen is stripped and carried off, her ladies lamenting, moaning like doves, beating their breasts. And Nineveh is like a pool of water, desolate, dreary, drained; hearts are fainting, knees are shaking, all faces grow pale.

What has become of the lion's den, the lion who tore enough for his whelps and strangled prey for his lionesses? He filled his caves with prey, his dens with torn flesh.

157

"Behold, I am against you, Nineveh," says the Lord of hosts. "I will burn your chariots, and the sword shall devour your young lions; I will wipe your prey from the earth, and the voice of your envoys shall be heard no more."

O city, bloody throughout, full of lies and plunder! "Behold, I am against you," says the Lord of hosts. "I will expose you to nations; I will show kingdoms your shame. I will throw filth at you and treat you with contempt. Everyone who sees you will flee from you and say: Nineveh is ruined; there is none to lament her; where can I find comforters for her?"

Will you fare better than Thebes that sat by the Nile, with water around her? Yet she was exiled, she went away captive, at every street corner her infants were dashed to the ground; all her great men were bound in chains. You too shall reel and swoon, you too shall seek refuge from the foe; all your fortresses are like fig trees with ripe figs —if they are shaken they drop into the hungry mouth. The people inside you are but women! The gates of your land are wide open to your foes; your bars are burned by fire.

Draw water for the siege, strengthen your forts, plunge into the mud, trample the clay, take hold of the brick mold! But there fire shall devour you, the sword shall cut you down. Multiply yourselves like locusts, multiply like grasshoppers! Locusts spread their wings and fly away. Your officers are like grasshoppers, settling on the fences in a cold day—when the sun rises they fly away; no one knows where they are.

King of Assyria, your shepherds are asleep, your heroes slumber! Your people are scattered all over the hills, with none to rally them. There is no healing for your disaster, fatal is your wound. All who hear the news about you shall clap their hands over you; for upon whom has not your malice passed unceasingly?

Habakkuk

Nothing is known of the personal life of Habakkuk, the great prophet who, like Job, asked searching questions and received answers from God. Some scholars maintain that Habakkuk was a younger contemporary of Isaiah; others place him later, as a younger contemporary of Jeremiah. The three chapters of Habakkuk are well worth repeated readings, for they contain some of the noblest utterances in the history of religious experience. The book is full of force, thought, and poetic expression.

Habakkuk complains against the cruelties and inhumanities of the oppressors. Their continued victories and successes seem to him inconsistent with divine justice. He stations himself on a watchtower and looks hopefully for a divine answer. The tower is not a literal tower, but the inner light of revelation whereby he ponders the problem. The answer is that evil shall ultimately perish from the earth, and the upright shall live by their faithfulness.

How long, O Lord, shall I cry for help and thou wilt not hear? I complain to thee of wrongs, and thou dost not help. Why dost thou show me evil and make me look upon misery? Oppression and outrage confront me; strife and contention arise. The law is slack, and justice never appears; the wicked beset the righteous, so justice goes forth twisted.

Thou art eternal, Lord my God, my Holy One; we shall not die. Thy eyes are too pure to behold evil; thou canst not gaze upon wrongdoing. Why then dost thou look on faithless men and keep silent when the wicked swallow up the innocent? Thou hast made men like the fish in the sea, like crawling things without a ruler. The foe hooks all of them, drags them out with his net, and joyfully gathers them up. Through them he lives in luxury, and his food is plentiful. Shall he keep on emptying his net, murdering people without pity? I will station myself on the tower, and look forth to see what God will say to me!

The Lord answered me and said: Write down this vision on your tablets plainly, that one may read it swiftly: If it seems slow, wait for it; it will surely come without delay. The good man lives by reason of his faithfulness; the arrogant man shall not abide. His greed is as wide as the netherworld; like death he never has enough. Woe to him who heaps up what is not his own—for how long? Woe to him who acquires unjust gain, seeking to set his nest on high, safe from the reach of calamity. You have brought disgrace upon your house, you have forfeited your life. The stone shall cry from the wall, and the beam in the woodwork shall echo the call.

Woe to him who builds a city by bloodshed and founds a town on crime! The toil of nations ends in smoke, and peoples wear themselves out for naught. The knowledge of the Lord's glory shall fill the earth, as waters cover the sea.

O Lord, I have heard of thee; thy work, O Lord, I fear. In wrath, remember to be merciful. I have heard, and my body trembles; my lips quiver at the sound. Decay enters my bones; my steps totter beneath me. I will calmly await the day of trouble that comes upon people who assail us.

Though the fig tree may not blossom, and no fruit is on the vines; though the olive crop has failed, and the fields yield no food; though the flock is cut off from the fold, and there are no cattle in the stalls—yet I will exult in the Lord, I will rejoice in the God who saves me. The Lord God is my strength.

Zephaniah

Zephaniah, an older contemporary of Jeremiah, was of royal blood, and lived in Jerusalem during the reign of Josiah. He aimed to arouse the moral sense of his people, who had adopted the religion and customs of their Assyrian conquerors. Zephaniah was one of the first to break the long silence of more than fifty years which followed the death of the great prophet Isaiah.

The brief book of Zephaniah, consisting only of three chapters, stresses the demand for purity of heart and conduct. It contains also the idea that suffering has a disciplinary value. Zephaniah's prophecy was occasioned by the Scythian invasion of western Asia, which marked the beginning of the end to the Assyrian empire. Zephaniah pictures the approaching calamity and predicts the future glory of Jerusalem.

The word of the Lord which came to Zephaniah during the reign of Joshiah, king of Judah:

"I will utterly sweep away everything from the face of the earth. I will sweep away man and beast, birds of the air and fish of the sea. I will strike at Judah and all the inhabitants of Jerusalem. I will punish those who enrich the palace by violence and fraud. I will punish those who are at ease, who say to themselves that the Lord will do neither good nor ill. Their goods shall be plundered, and their houses laid waste. They shall not live in the houses they build, nor drink wine from the vineyards they plant."

The great day of the Lord is near, a day of distress and anguish, a day of ruin and devastation, a day of trumpet blast and battle cry against the fortified cities. No silver and no gold shall avail to protect them on the day of the Lord's wrath.

Seek the Lord, seek righteousness, seek humility; perhaps you may be hidden on the day of the Lord's wrath.

Gaza shall be deserted, and Ashkelon shall become a

161

desolation; Ashdod shall be exiled, and Ekron shall be up-rooted. The seacoast shall belong to those left of the house of Judah; in the houses of Ashkelon they shall lie down at evening. For the Lord their God will remember them and restore their fortunes.

Moab shall become like Sodom, and Ammon like Go-morrah, lands overrun by weeds and salt pits, desolate for-ever. Those left of my people shall possess them. They shall be paid back for their pride, for taunting the people of the Lord.

And this was the exultant city that sat so secure, that thought herself supreme, saying: "I am and there is none else." What a desolation she has become! All who pass by her hiss and shake their fist. Woe to her, the defiled and oppressing city! Her officials are roaring lions; her prophets are faithless men; her priests do violence to the law. The unjust are shameless.

Sing, O Zion! Shout, O Israel! Rejoice with all your heart, O Jerusalem! The Lord is in your midst; you shall fear evil no more. "I will deal with all your oppressors. I will save the lame, and gather the outcast; I will lift them out of their shame to world-wide praise and fame. At that time I will bring you home; I will grant you praise and renown among all the peoples of the earth," says the Lord.

Haggai

Haggai, one of the last three literary prophets, was a contemporary of Zechariah and Malachi. His prophetic activity centered around four months of the year 520, eighteen years after Cyrus had permitted the exiles to return to Judea. The work of rebuilding the Temple had been at a standstill for seventeen years, because of the hostile Samaritans who interfered with the work of restoration. Haggai sent four messages urging the returning exiles to rebuild the Temple in Jerusalem. They had lost courage, and needed renewed enthusiasm and hopefulness. Haggai roused the energies and aspirations of the people who started a new life in Judea.

In the second year of King Darius, the word of the Lord came to Haggai the prophet.

The people say that the time has not yet come to rebuild the house of the Lord. Is it a time for you to live in panelled houses of your own, while this house lies in ruins? Consider how you have fared. You have sown much and harvested little; you eat and yet you never have enough; you drink, but you never have your fill; you clothe yourselves but cannot keep warm; and he who earns wages puts them into a bag with holes.

"Now then, go up to the hills and bring wood to build the house. You expected a rich harvest, and it came to little; and when you brought it home, I blew it away. Why? Because of my house that lies in ruins, while each of you runs to his own house. Therefore the sky withholds its dew and the earth withholds its produce."

The people obeyed and went to work on the temple. And the Lord told Haggai the prophet to say to Zerubbabel, governor of Judah, and to the high priest Joshua, and to the rest of the people: "You who saw the temple in its former splendor, what do you think of it now? You think nothing of it? Yet, take courage, all you people of the land; work, for I am with you. Once again the treasures of all nations shall come in, and I will fill this house with splendor. The silver is mine, the gold is mine; the future splendor of this house shall be greater than the former; and upon this place I will bestow prosperity."

The word of the Lord came again to Haggai: "Speak to Zerubbabel, governor of Judah, tell him that I am about to shake the heavens and the earth; I will overthrow royal thrones, and shatter the power of empires; I will overthrow chariots and their riders; horses and their riders shall be struck down, each falling by the sword of his fellow. But on that day I will take you, O Zerubbabel my servant, and make you like a signet ring that is highly cherished, for I have chosen you as mine, says the Lord of hosts."

Zechariah

The book of Zechariah consists of fourteen chapters. The first eight chapters, generally referred to as part one, contain a series of eight visions, by means of which the prophet expresses his assurance that the Lord will restore Israel's former glory. The last six chapters, generally referred to as part two, include prophecies concerning the advent of Messiah, deliverance, final victory, and God's reign of peace.

Some scholars are of the opinion that the last six chapters belong to a much earlier anonymous author, a "Second Zechariah"; others, however, maintain that the so-called Second Zechariah lived at a much later period than the original Zechariah who, like his older contemporary Haggai, urged the immediate rebuilding of the Temple in Jerusalem during the years 520–518.

In the second year of King Darius, the word of the Lord came to Zechariah the prophet, bidding him tell the people: "Turn to me, and I will turn to you; be not like your fathers, who did not listen to me."

I raised my eyes and looked. There was a man with a measuring line in his hand! "Where are you going?" I asked him. He replied: "To measure Jerusalem, to see how broad and how long it should be." Another angel came forward and said: "Jerusalem shall be unwalled, like an open village, because of the multitude of men and cattle in it. For I, says the Lord, I will be a wall of fire around her, and I will be the glory within her. Sing and rejoice, O Zion, for I am coming, I will dwell in the midst of you, says the Lord."

Once more the angel came and waked me like a man roused from sleep, and he asked me: "What do you see?" I answered: "I see a lampstand, all of gold, with seven lights on it; there are two olive trees beside it, one to the right and the other to the left." Then I asked: "What are these, sir?" The angel replied: "These seven are the eyes of the

Lord; they range over the whole earth." I asked him:
"What are these two olive trees?" He replied: "These are
the two anointed who stand before the Lord of all the
earth."

The word of the Lord came to Zechariah, saying: "Ad-
minister true justice; practise kindness and compassion
toward each other; oppress not the widow, the orphan, the
stranger or the poor; do not plot evil in your hearts against
each other.

"Old men and old women shall again sit in the streets
of Jerusalem. The streets of the city shall be full of boys
and girls playing there. I will save my people from the
land of the east and from the land of the west, and I will
bring them home to dwell within Jerusalem; they shall
be my people and I will be their God. I will sow peace and
prosperity; the vine shall yield its fruit, the ground shall
give its produce, and the skies shall drop their dew. I will
save you, O house of Israel, and you shall be a blessing.
Fear not, but let your hands be strong."

Thus says the Lord of hosts: "These are the things you
must do: Speak the truth to one another; render judgments
that are true and for the common good; do not plot evil in
your hearts against one another, and never give yourselves
to any perjury."

Thus says the Lord of hosts: "The fast of the fourth
month, and the fast of the fifth, and the fast of the seventh,
and the fast of the tenth shall become seasons of joy and
gladness to the house of Judah, cheerful feasts. Only love
truth and peace."

Malachi

Malachi, signifying "my messenger," is not a personal name but a pseudonym alluding to the promise: "Behold, I will send my messenger" (Malachi 3:1). The Socratic method of developing an idea through question and answer is a prominent feature of the style of Malachi, who often makes a statement and asks a question. This unidentified prophet, who was active about the middle of the fifth century before the common era, stresses personal religion, emphasizes mercy and faith. He deals with questions which have to be faced repeatedly, and analyzes the proper way of life. The book of Malachi, regarded as the finale of the Bible from a chronological viewpoint, contains the firm belief that ultimately all wrongs will be righted.

The word of the Lord to Israel through Malachi:

"I have loved you," says the Lord. But you ask: "How hast thou loved us?" "Is not Esau Jacob's brother?" says the Lord; "yet I loved Jacob and hated Esau. I laid waste his hill country and left his heritage to jackals of the desert.

"A son should honor his father, and a servant should honor his master. Now, if I am a Father, where is my honor? If I am a Master, where is my reverence?" says the Lord of hosts to you, O priests, who despise his name. The lips of a priest should treasure wisdom, and men should seek direction from his words. But you have turned aside from the way, you have caused many to stumble by your instruction; "you have violated the covenant of Levi," says the Lord of hosts; "so I too will make all the people despise and degrade you."

Have we not all one Father? Has not one God created us? Why then are we faithless to one another? "Take heed to yourselves, and let none be unfaithful to the wife of his youth; for I detest divorce and cruelty," says the Lord God of Israel.

"Behold, I send my messenger to clear the way for me; the Lord whom you seek will suddenly come to his temple; the messenger of the covenant, in whom you delight, is coming. But who can endure the day of his arrival, who can stand when he appears? He will sit as a refiner and purifier of silver, and he will cleanse the sons of Levi; he will refine them like gold and silver. Then the offering of Judah and Jerusalem will be pleasing to the Lord, as in the days of old. Return to me, that I may return to you," says the Lord of hosts.

"Behold, the day is coming, burning like an oven; all the arrogant and all evildoers shall be stubble; the day to come shall burn them up, leaving them neither root nor branch. But for you who revere my name, the saving sun shall rise with healing in its wings.

"Remember the Torah of my servant Moses, the rules and regulations that I gave him at Horeb for all Israel. Behold, I will send you Elijah the prophet, and he will turn the hearts of fathers to their children and the hearts of children to their fathers."

Psalms

The book of Psalms, consisting of 150 stirring hymns, is the first book in the third division of the Bible known as Hagiographa (Sacred Writings). The word *Psalms* is derived from the Greek version of the Bible, the Septuagint, where it is used in the sense of songs accompanied by the playing of musical instruments. The keynote of the psalms is simplicity of heart, faith in God and good conduct. In them we find the human heart in all its moods and emotions—in penitence, in danger, in desolation, and in triumph. The psalms are as varied as human life; they are enlightened in their ethics as they are lofty in their religious spirit.

Psalm 15 has the most perfect description of a good man. According to the Talmud, the six hundred and thirteen precepts of the Torah are summed up in this psalm, that is to say, the moral purpose of the Torah is clearly defined here.

Psalm 19 has been epitomized in the saying: "The starry sky above me and the moral law within me are two things which fill the soul with ever new and increasing admiration and reverence." According to Maimonides, this psalm contains a description of what the celestial spheres actually do; the heavens themselves are declaring God's wonders without words.

Psalm 23, portraying God's tender care and abundant love, has been the world's favorite psalm for many centuries. With quiet beauty and simple, unquestioning and unclouded confidence, the Psalm describes how all man's needs are met on his journey through life in a vast and dangerous world. God is presented first as a shepherd and next as a host, ever affording guidance and protection.

Psalm 27 consists of two parts. The first part expresses fearless confidence in the face of hostile armies, while the second part is the prayer of one in deep distress, beset by malicious accusers.

Psalm 34 is arranged alphabetically in the Hebrew text, each line begins with a letter of the alphabet in consecutive order. The essential message of the psalm is confidence and trust in God.

Psalm 39, of great pathos and beauty, has been said to be

"the finest of all the elegies in the Psalter." This short hymn reveals a variety of moods: faith, rebellion, despair, penitence, resignation and trust.

Psalm 90, contrasting the eternity of God with the brevity of human life, is ascribed to Moses and bears a resemblance to the book of Deuteronomy.

Psalm 104 is closely similar to the story of creation in Genesis. The psalmist celebrates God's glory as seen in the forces of nature. It has been declared that it is worthwhile studying the Hebrew language for ten years in order to read Psalm 104 in the original.

Psalm 107 has a universal appeal. It begins by calling upon the exiles, brought back to their homes, to give thanks. Then it describes God's goodness in taking care of lost travellers, prisoners, the sick, and sea-voyagers. At the end of each of the four stanzas, Psalm 107 uses the double refrain: "They cried out to the Lord in their trouble, and he delivered them from their distress. Let them thank the Lord for his kindness and his wonders toward men." Hence the talmudic statement that all who escape serious danger arising from illness, imprisonment or a perilous voyage, must offer public thanks.

The description of a storm at sea is the part of the psalm often recited by seafaring men. The storm is of exceptional violence, and the sailors realize in terror that they are in real danger. Their technical skill has become useless; they are at the mercy of the sea until the roar of the storm dies away, and nothing but a gentle, whispering wind remains.

Psalm One

Happy is the man who walks not in the counsel of the wicked, nor stands in the road of sinners, nor sits in the company of scoffers; but his delight is in the law of the Lord, and he meditates on it day and night.

He is like a tree planted by streams of water, that bears fruit in due season, with leaves that do not fade; whatever he does shall succeed.

Not so the wicked! They are like the chaff which the wind sweeps away. Hence, the wicked shall not stand when judgment comes, nor shall the sinful be among the upright.

Truly, the Lord favors the way of the just, but the way of the wicked shall perish.

Psalm Six

O Lord, punish me not in thy anger; chastise me not in thy wrath. Have pity on me, O Lord, for I languish away; heal me, O Lord, for my health is shaken. My soul is severely troubled; and thou, O Lord—how long?

O Lord, save my life once again; save me for the sake of thy grace. For in death there is no thought of thee; in the grave who can give thanks to thee?

I am worn out with my groaning; every night I drench my bed with tears. My eye is dimmed from grief; it grows old and weak because of all my foes.

Depart from me, all you evildoers! For the Lord has heard my weeping; the Lord accepts my prayer. All my foes shall turn back; they shall suddenly be put to shame.

Psalm Fifteen

O Lord, who may dwell in thy temple, who may reside in thy sanctuary? The blameless man who acts uprightly, and speaks truth in his heart. He neither slanders nor hurts nor insults his neighbor. He has contempt for a rogue, and honors those who revere the Lord. He keeps his word at his own risk, and does not retract. He lends money without interest, and does not accept a bribe against the innocent. He who does these things shall never be shaken.

Psalm Nineteen

The heavens proclaim the glory of God; the sky declares his handiwork. Day unto day pours forth speech, and night unto night reveals knowledge. There is no speech, there are no words; their voice is unheard. Yet their message extends through all the earth, and their words reach the end of the world.

The law of the Lord is perfect, refreshing the soul; the testimony of the Lord is trustworthy, making wise the simple. The precepts of the Lord are right, gladdening the heart; the commandment of the Lord is clear, enlightening the eyes. The Lord's faith is pure, enduring forever; the Lord's judgments are all true, all just. They are more desirable than gold; sweeter are they than honey from the honeycomb.

Thy servant is careful of them; in keeping them there is great reward. But who can discern his own errors? Hold thou me guiltless of unconscious faults. Restrain thy servant also from wilful sins; let them not have dominion over me. Then I shall be blameless, I shall be clear of grave transgressions.

May the words of my mouth and the meditation of my heart be pleasing to thee, O Lord, my stronghold and my redeemer.

Psalm Twenty-three

The Lord is my shepherd; I am not in want. He makes me lie down in green pastures; he leads me beside refreshing streams. He restores my life; he guides me by righteous paths for his own sake. Even though I walk through the darkest valley, I fear no harm; for thou art with me. Thy rod and thy staff—they comfort me. Thou spreadest a feast for me in the presence of my enemies. Thou hast perfumed my head with oil; my cup overflows. Only goodness and kindness shall follow me all the days of my life; and I shall dwell in the house of the Lord forever.

Psalm Twenty-four

The earth and all it contains belong to the Lord! He has founded it upon the seas, and established it on the floods.

Who may ascend the mountain of the Lord? Who may stand within his holy place? He who has clean hands and a pure heart; he who strives not after vanity and swears not deceitfully.

Who is the King of glory? The Lord of hosts. He is the King of glory.

Psalm Twenty-seven

The Lord is my light and my aid; whom shall I fear? The Lord is the strength of my life; of whom shall I be afraid? Though war should rise against me, still will I be confident.

One thing I ask of the Lord, one thing I desire: that I may dwell in the house of the Lord all the days of my life, to behold the goodness of the Lord and to meditate in his temple.

O Lord, hear my voice when I call; be gracious to me and answer me. Teach me thy way, O Lord, and lead me in a straight path, in spite of my enemies. Deliver me not to the will of my adversaries.

Truly I trust to see the goodness of the Lord in the world of the living. Hope in the Lord! Be strong! Let your heart be brave! Hope in the Lord!

Psalm Thirty-three

Rejoice in the Lord, you righteous; it is fitting for the upright to give praise. The word of the Lord is right; all his work is done with faithfulness. He loves righteousness and justice; the earth is full of the Lord's kindness. By the word of the Lord the heavens were made, and all their host by the breath of his mouth.

Let all the earth revere the Lord; let all the inhabitants of the world stand in awe of him. For he spoke, and the world came into being; he commanded, and it stood firm.

From heaven the Lord looks down, and sees all of mankind. He fashions the hearts of all, he notes all their deeds. A king is not saved by the size of an army; a warrior is not rescued by sheer strength. Our soul waits for the Lord; he is our help and our shield. In him our heart rejoices; in his holy name we trust.

May thy kindness, O Lord, rest on us, even as our hope rests in thee.

Psalm Thirty-four

I bless the Lord at all times; his praise is ever in my mouth. Exalt the Lord with me, and let us extol his name together! I sought the Lord and he answered me; he delivered me from all my fears.

O consider and see that the Lord is good; happy is the man who takes refuge in him. Young lions may suffer want and hunger, but those who seek the Lord shall lack nothing.

Come, children, listen to me; I will teach you how to

revere the Lord. Who is the man that desires life, and loves a long life of happiness?

Keep your tongue from evil, and your lips from speaking falsehood. Shun evil and do good; seek peace and pursue it. The Lord is near to the broken-hearted, and saves those who are crushed in spirit.

A good man may have many afflictions, but the Lord delivers him from them all. The Lord saves the life of his servants; none of those who trust in him are ever desolate.

Psalm Thirty-nine

O Lord, let me know my end, the number of days that I have left; let me know how short-lived I am. Thou hast made my days no longer than a span; my lifetime is as nothing in thy sight. Every man, at his best, is an empty breath. Man walks about as a mere shadow, making much ado about vanity; he heaps up riches and knows not who will possess them.

What then can I expect, O Lord? My hope is in thee! Save me from all my sins; let me not become an object of reproach. Hear my prayer, O Lord, listen to my cry, answer thou my tears; for I am but a guest of thine, a sojourner, like all my forefathers. Have mercy upon me that I may recover my strength before I depart to be no more.

Psalm Forty-nine

Hear this, all you peoples; listen, all you inhabitants of the world, both low and high, rich and poor alike. My mouth speaks wisdom, and my heart's meditation is deep insight.

Why should I be afraid in days of evil, when the iniquity of my foes surrounds me, men who trust in their wealth, and boast of their great riches?

Even wise men die, the stupid and senseless perish alike, and leave their wealth to others. Man abides not in his splendor; he is like the beasts that perish.

Such is the fate of those who trust in themselves, the end of those who are pleased with their own mouthings. Like sheep they are destined to die. Death shall be their shepherd.

So fear not when a man grows rich, when the splendor of his house increases; for he will take nothing with him when he dies; his wealth will not follow him down to the grave. The man who lives in splendor but lacks understanding is like the beasts that perish.

Psalm Ninety

O Lord, thou hast been our shelter in every generation. Before the mountains were brought forth, before earth and world were formed,—from eternity to eternity thou art God.

Thou turnest man back to dust, and sayest: "Return, you children of man." A thousand years in thy sight are like a day that passes. Thou sweepest men away and they sleep. They are like grass that grows in the morning; in the evening it fades and withers.

All our days pass away in thy displeasure; we spend our years like a fleeting sound. The length of our days is seventy years, or, if we are strong, eighty years. It is speedily gone, and we fly away.

O teach us how to number our days, that we may get us a heart of wisdom. Have pity on thy servants. Gladden us in proportion to the days wherein thou hast afflicted us, the years wherein we have seen evil. May thy favor, Lord our God, rest on us; and establish thou the work of our hands.

Psalm Ninety-two

It is good to give thanks to the Lord, and to sing praises to thy name, O Most High; to proclaim thy goodness in the morning, and thy faithfulness at night.

Thou, O Lord, hast made me glad through thy work; I sing for joy at all that thou hast done. How great are thy works, O Lord! How very deep are thy designs! A stupid man cannot know, a fool cannot understand this. When the wicked thrive like grass, and all evildoers flourish, it is that they may be destroyed forever.

But thou, O Lord, art supreme for evermore. For lo, thy enemies, O Lord, shall perish; all evildoers shall be dispersed. The righteous will flourish like the palm tree;

175

they will grow like a cedar in Lebanon. Vigorous and fresh they shall be, to proclaim that the Lord is just! He is my Stronghold, and there is no wrong in him.

Psalm Ninety-four

Lord God of retribution, appear! Arise, thou Judge of the earth, render to the arrogant what they deserve. How long shall the wicked, O Lord, how long shall the wicked exult?

They speak arrogantly; all the evildoers act boastfully. They crush thy people, O Lord, and afflict thy heritage. The widow and the stranger they slay, and the fatherless they murder. They think the Lord does not see, the God of Jacob does not observe.

You fools, when will you understand? He who sets the ear, does he not hear? He who forms the eye, does he not see? He who punishes nations, shall he not punish you?

The Lord will not abandon his people, nor forsake his heritage. Judgment shall again conform with justice, and all the upright in heart will follow it.

They band themselves against the life of the righteous, and condemn innocent blood. But the Lord is my stronghold; my God is the rock of my safety. He will requite them for their crime, and destroy them for their wickedness.

Psalm One Hundred Four

Lord my God, thou art very great; thou art robed in glory and majesty. Thou wrappest thyself in light as in a garment; thou spreadest the heavens like a curtain. Thou makest winds thy messengers, the flaming fire thy servant.

Thou sendest forth streams into the valleys; they run between the mountains. They furnish drink for all the beasts of the field. Beside them the birds of the sky dwell; from among the branches they sing. Thou waterest the mountains from thy upper chambers; the earth is full of the fruit of thy works.

Thou makest grass grow for the cattle, and fodder for the working animals of man, to bring forth bread from the earth, and wine that cheers man's heart.

How manifold are thy works, O Lord! In wisdom hast thou made them all; the earth is full of thy creations. There is the sea, vast and broad, wherein are creeping things innumerable, creatures small and great. When thou takest away their breath, they die and turn again to dust. When thou sendest forth thy spirit they are created, and thou renewest the face of the earth.

Psalm One Hundred Seven

Give thanks to the Lord, for he is good; his mercy endures forever. Let the redeemed of the Lord say praise, for he has delivered them from the hand of the oppressor. He has gathered them from far lands, from east and west, from north and south. They wandered in the wilderness, on a desert road, without finding an inhabited town. They were hungry and thirsty, and were fainting away. Then they cried out to the Lord in their trouble, and he delivered them from their distress. He guided them in the right way, that they might reach an inhabited city. Let them thank the Lord for his kindness and his wonders toward men. He satisfies the longing soul, and gratifies the hungry heart.

Some sat in darkness and in gloom, bound in misery and iron, because they had rebelled against the words of God and scorned the counsel of the Most High. He humbled their heart by toil; they stumbled, with none to help. Then they cried out to the Lord in their trouble, and he delivered them from their distress. He delivered them from darkness and gloom, and broke their chains. Let them thank the Lord for his kindness and his wonders toward men. He breaks gates of bronze, and shatters iron bars.

Some, fools in their sinful ways, were sick and suffering because of their iniquities. They loathed all food, and reached the gates of death. Then they cried out to the Lord in their trouble, and he delivered them from their distress. He sent his word and healed them; he saved them from their graves. Let them thank the Lord for his kindness and his wonders toward men. Let them bring offerings of thanksgiving, recounting joyfully what he has done.

Those who crossed the sea in ships, trading in great waters, saw the works of the Lord and his marvels in the deep. He commanded and raised the stormy wind, which lifted the waves on high, soaring to the sky, sinking to the depths. Their soul melted away in distress. They reeled and staggered like drunken men, and were at their wit's end. Then they cried out to the Lord in their trouble, and he delivered them from their distress. He stilled the storm, and the waves were hushed. They rejoiced because the waves were calmed; he brought them to their desired haven. Let them thank the Lord for his kindness and his wonders toward men. Let them extol him in crowds of people; let them praise him in the council of the elders.

He turns rivers into a desert, fountains into parched land, and a fruitful country into a salt waste, because of the wickedness of its inhabitants. He turns a desert into pools of water, and dry land into fountains; there he settles the hungry, who establish a town for habitation. They sow fields and plant vineyards, which yield fruits for harvest. He blesses them and they multiply greatly; he does not diminish their herds. And when they are decreased and brought low through oppression, evil and distress, he pours contempt on lords and sets them in a pathless waste astray. But he lifts the needy from their affliction, and makes their families [as numerous] as a flock. Let the upright see this and rejoice, and all wickedness shut its mouth. Whoso is wise, let him observe these things and consider the gracious acts of the Lord.

Psalm One Hundred Fourteen

When Israel went out of Egypt, Judah became God's sanctuary and Israel his dominion. The sea beheld and fled; the Jordan turned backward; the mountains skipped like rams, and the hills like lambs.

What ails you, O sea, that you flee? Why, O Jordan, do you turn backward? You mountains, why do you skip like rams? You hills, why do you leap like lambs?

Tremble, O earth, at the Lord's presence, at the presence of the God of Jacob, who turns the rock into a pool of water, the flint into a flowing fountain.

178

Psalm One Hundred Eighteen

Out of distress I called upon the Lord; he answered me by setting me free. The Lord is with me; I have no fear. What can man do to me? The Lord is my helper; I shall see the defeat of my foes.

It is better to seek refuge in the Lord than to trust in man. It is better to seek refuge in the Lord than to trust in princes.

They swarmed like bees about me, but they were extinguished like a fire of thorns; relying on the Lord, I routed them. The Lord is my strength and my song; he has delivered me indeed. The right hand of the Lord does valiantly; the Lord's right hand triumphs. I shall not die, but live to recount the deeds of the Lord. The Lord has indeed punished me, but he has not left me to die. Open for me the gates of righteousness, that I may enter and praise the Lord. This is the gateway of the Lord; the righteous alone may enter.

Psalm One Hundred Twenty-one

I lift my eyes to the hills; oh, whence will my help come? My help comes from the Lord who made heaven and earth.

He will not let your foot slip; he who guards you does not sleep. Behold, he who keeps Israel neither slumbers nor sleeps.

The Lord is your keeper; the Lord is your shelter upon your right hand. The sun shall not harm you in the day, nor the moon by night.

The Lord will keep you from all evil; he will preserve your life. The Lord will protect you as you come and go, henceforth and forever.

Psalm One Hundred Twenty-five

Those who trust in the Lord are like Mount Zion which cannot be shaken, but abides forever. The mountains are round about Jerusalem, and the Lord is round about his people, henceforth and forever. Do good, O Lord, to those who are good, to those who are upright in heart. Peace be in Israel!

179

Psalm One Hundred Twenty-six

When the Lord brought the exiles back to Zion, we were like those who dream. Our mouth was filled with laughter, and our tongue with ringing song; then it was said among the nations: "The Lord has done great things for them." The Lord had done great things for us, and we rejoiced. Restore our fortunes, O Lord, like streams in the Negev. Those who sow in tears shall reap in joy.

Psalm One Hundred Twenty-eight

Happy is everyone who reveres the Lord, who walks in his ways. When you eat the toil of your hands, you shall be happy and at ease. Your wife shall be like a fruitful vine in your house; your children like olive plants, around your table. The Lord bless you from Zion; may you see the welfare of Jerusalem all the days of your life; may you live to see your children's children. Peace be upon Israel!

Psalm One Hundred Thirty

Out of the depths I call to thee. O Lord, hear my voice; let thy ears be attentive to my supplications. If thou, O Lord, shouldst keep strict account of iniquities, who could live on? But there is forgiveness with thee, that thou mayest be revered.

I hope in the Lord, my whole being hopes; I wait for his word. My soul waits for the Lord more eagerly than watchmen for the dawn. O Israel, put your hope in the Lord, for with the Lord there is kindness; with him there is great saving power. He will redeem Israel from all its iniquities.

Psalm One Hundred Thirty-seven

By the rivers of Babylon we sat down and wept when we remembered Zion. There upon the willows we hung our harps. Our captors demanded of us songs, saying: "Sing us some of the songs of Zion!"

How shall we sing the Lord's song in a foreign land? If ever I forget you, O Jerusalem, may my right hand wither! May my tongue cleave to my palate, if I ever stop thinking of you, if ever I do not set Jerusalem above my greatest joy!

Psalm One Hundred Thirty-nine

O Lord, thou hast searched me and dost know me. Thou knowest me sitting or rising; thou dost discern my very thoughts from afar. Even before a word is on my tongue, O Lord, thou knowest it all. Thou art on every side, behind me and before, laying thy hand on me.

Where could I go from thy spirit? Where could I flee from thy presence? If I ascend to heaven, thou art there! If I make my bed in the netherworld, thou art there! If I dwell in the uttermost parts of the sea, even there thy hand shall lead me, thy right hand shall hold me.

Thou didst form my being, didst weave me inside my mother. I praise thee for the awe-inspiring wonder of my birth; thy work is wonderful! Search me, O God, and know my heart; try me and test my thoughts; do thou lead me in the way everlasting!

Psalm One Hundred Forty-four

Blessed be the Lord, my stronghold, who trains my hands for war, my fingers for battle. He is my refuge and my deliverer.

O Lord, what is man that thou shouldst regard him? What is mortal man that thou shouldst consider him? Man is like a breath; his days are like a passing shadow.

O Lord, flash lightning and scatter my foes; send forth thy arrows and destroy them. Send down thy help from on high; rescue me from the great floods, from the hands of barbarians.

May our sons be like full grown plants, our daughters like sculptured pillars in a palace. May our barns be filled with all kinds of produce; may our sheep increase by tens of thousands. May there be no riot, no cry of distress in our streets. Happy are the people whose God is the Lord!

Psalm One Hundred Forty-five

I extol thee, my God, O King, and bless thy name forever and ever. One generation praises thy works to another, and recounts thy mighty acts. They spread the fame of thy great goodness, and sing of thy righteousness.

Gracious and merciful is the Lord, slow to anger and of great kindness. The Lord is good to all, and his mercy is over all his works.

Thy kingdom is a kingdom of all ages, thy dominion is for all generations.

The Lord upholds all who fall, and raises all who are bowed down.

The eyes of all look hopefully to thee, and thou givest them their food in due season. Thou openest thy hand, and satisfiest every living thing with favor.

The Lord is righteous in all his ways, and gracious in all his deeds. The Lord is near to all who call upon him sincerely. The Lord preserves all who love him, but all the wicked he destroys.

Let all creatures bless his holy name forever and ever.

Psalm One Hundred Forty-six

Praise the Lord! Praise the Lord, O my soul! I will praise the Lord as long as I live; I will sing to my God as long as I exist.

Put no trust in princes, in mortal man who can give no help. When his breath goes, he returns to the dust, and on that very day his designs perish.

Happy is he who has the God of Jacob as his help, whose hope rests upon the Lord his God, Maker of heaven and earth and sea and all that is therein. The Lord sets the captives free.

The Lord opens the eyes of the blind, raises those who are bowed down, and loves the righteous. The Lord protects the strangers, and upholds the fatherless and the widow; but the way of the wicked he thwarts.

The Lord shall reign forever; your God, O Zion, for all generations. Praise the Lord!

Psalm One Hundred Forty-seven

Praise the Lord! It is good to sing to our God, it is pleasant; praise is comely. The Lord rebuilds Jerusalem;

he gathers together the dispersed people of Israel. He heals the broken-hearted, and binds up their wounds.

Great is our Lord and abundant in power; his wisdom is infinite. The Lord raises the humble, casts the wicked down to the ground, provides rain for the earth, and causes grass to grow upon the hills. He gives food to the cattle, and to the crying young ravens.

Praise the Lord, O Jerusalem! Praise your God, O Zion! He has fortified your gates; he has blessed your children. He sends forth his command to the world; his word runs very swiftly. He declares his word to Jacob, his statutes and ordinances to Israel. He has not dealt so with any of the heathen nations; his ordinances they do not know. Praise the Lord!

Psalm One Hundred Forty-nine

Praise the Lord! Sing a new song to the Lord; praise him in the assembly of the faithful. Let Israel rejoice in his Maker; let the children of Zion exult in their King. Let them praise his name with dancing; let them make music to him with drum and harp. For the Lord is pleased with his people; he adorns the meek with triumph. Let the faithful exult in glory; let them sing upon their beds. Let the praises of God be in their mouth, and a double-edged sword in their hand, to execute vengeance upon the heathen, punishment upon the peoples; to bind their kings with chains, and their nobles with fetters of iron; to execute upon them the written judgment. He is the glory of all his faithful. Praise the Lord!

Psalm One Hundred Fifty

Praise the Lord! Praise God in his sanctuary; praise him in his glorious heaven. Praise him for his mighty deeds; praise him for his abundant greatness. Praise him with the blast of the horn; praise him with the harp and the lyre. Praise him with the drum and dance; praise him with strings and flute. Praise him with resounding cymbals; praise him with clanging cymbals. Let everything that has breath praise the Lord. Praise the Lord!

Proverbs

The book of Proverbs, together with the books of Job and
Ecclesiastes, belongs to the Wisdom Literature of the Bible.
It contains maxims and aphorisms for the better conduct of
everyday life. In Proverbs, the ideal of life is a composite of
honesty, diligence, helpfulness toward the distressed and consideration for one's fellow man. At the end of the book there
is the poem which describes the perfect wife, trusted by her
husband, obeyed by her servants, and admired by everyone.
She is kind to the poor and gentle to all. She is self-respecting
and dignified. Husband and children prize her as the source
of their happiness.

Hear, my son, your father's instruction, and reject not
your mother's teaching.

Happy is the man who gathers wisdom; no treasure can
compare with it.

Go to the ant, you sluggard; look at her ways and learn
wisdom. Though she has no leader, no ruler nor chief,
she prepares her food in the summer, and gathers sustenance during the harvest season.

How long will you sleep, you sluggard? When will you
rise from your slumber?

A little sleep, a little slumber, a little folding of the
hands to rest, and poverty will pounce on you, want will
overpower you.

Six things the Lord hates; seven he loathes: haughty
eyes, a lying tongue, hands that shed innocent blood, a
mind that plots wicked plans, feet that are quick to run
after evil, a false witness who tells lies, and one who sows
discord among brothers.

Can a man carry fire in his bosom without burning his
clothes? Can one walk upon hot coals without scorching

his feet? So is he who touches a neighbor's wife; he shall not go unpunished.

Do not reprove a scoffer, for he will hate you; reprove a man of sense, and he will love you.

Reverence for the Lord is the first thing in wisdom.

A sensible son is a joy to his father; a senseless son is a grief to his mother.

Where words abound, sin is not lacking; he who controls his tongue is a wise man.

The good man is delivered from trouble; the bad man takes his place.

A good man cares for the life of his beast; the bad man has a cruel heart.

The way of a fool is right in his own eyes, but a wise man listens to advice.

There are those whose reckless words wound like a sword, but the tongue of the wise brings healing.

A cautious man conceals his knowledge, but a fool comes out with his folly.

Worry weighs a man down; a kind word cheers him up.

He who guards his lips guards his life; he who talks freely comes to ruin.

One man pretends to be rich, though he has nothing; another pretends to be poor, though he has great wealth.

Wealth won in haste will dwindle, but he who gathers little by little will increase it.

Associate with wise men and you will be wise; a companion of fools will suffer harm.

He who spares the rod hates his son; the man who loves his son disciplines him.

The simpleton believes every thing; the prudent man watches where he goes.

In a multitude of people there is glory for a king; in a scarcity of people there is ruin for a prince.

He who oppresses a poor man insults his Maker; he who is kind to the poor honors his Maker.

Righteousness exalts a nation; evil brings a people low.

A soft answer turns wrath away, but a harsh word stirs up anger.

For the depressed every day is hard, but the cheerful heart enjoys a continual feast.

Better a little with reverence for the Lord than a great treasure with worry.

Better a dish of vegetables with love than the best beef served with hatred.

Pride ends in disaster, haughtiness means a downfall.

Better be modest among the poor than divide plunder with the proud.

He who is slow to anger is better than the mighty; he who controls himself is better than a conqueror.

Better a morsel of dry bread and peace than a house full of feasting and quarrels.

A rebuke goes deeper into a man of sense than a hundred lashes into a fool.

Even a fool may pass for wise if he says nothing; with closed lips he may be counted intelligent.

To answer a question before hearing it is foolish and shameful.

Many seek the favor of a generous man; all are friends of a man who gives presents.

Even a child makes himself known by his acts.

Better live in a lonely desert than beside a nagging, fretful woman.

Reputation is better than riches; esteem means more than silver and gold.

Train a child in the way he should go, and he will not leave it even when he grows old.

You see a man skillful in his work? He will stand before kings.

Do not eat the bread of a niggardly man; "eat and drink" he says to you, but his heart is not with you.

Never talk to a fool, for he will despise your words of wisdom.

Do not rejoice when your enemy falls, do not exult when he is overthrown.

Like clouds and wind without rain is a man who does not give what he promises.

Go seldom to your neighbor's house; he may grow tired of you and hate you.

186

If your enemy is hungry give him food; if he is thirsty give him water.

Like snow in summer and rain in harvest, so honor is unbecoming to a fool.

You see a man who is wise in his own eyes? There is more hope for a fool than for him.

The sluggard says: "There is a lion in the street."

As the door turns on its hinges, the lazy man turns upon his back.

Never boast about tomorrow; you never know what the day may bring.

The wicked flee when no one pursues, but the righteous are bold as lions.

He who hates unjust gain will prolong his life.

He who gives to the poor will not come to want.

The man who flatters his neighbor spreads a net for his feet.

A fool gives full vent to his temper, but a wise man restrains it.

Open your mouth, defend the rights of the poor and the needy.

The Ideal Wife

Who can find a good wife?
She is worth far more than rubies.
Her husband trusts in her,
And he never lacks gain.
She brings him good, and not harm,
All the days of her life.
She seeks out wool and flax,
And works willingly with her hands.
She is like the merchant ships—
She brings her food from afar.
She rises while it is yet night,
And gives food to her household,
And rations to her maids.
She considers a field and buys it;
With her earnings she plants a vineyard.
She girds herself with strength,
And braces her arms for work.

187

She finds that her trade is profitable;
Her lamp goes not out at night.
She sets her hands to the distaff;
Her fingers hold the spindle.
She stretches out her hand to the poor;
She reaches out her arms to the needy.
She is not afraid of the snow for her
    household,
For all her household is clad in scarlet
    wool.
She makes her own tapestries;
Her clothing is fine linen and purple.
Her husband is known at the gates,
As he sits among the elders of the land.
She makes linen cloth and sells it;
She supplies the merchants with belts.
Dignity and honor are her garb;
She smiles, looking at the future.
She opens her mouth with wisdom,
And kindly counsel is on her tongue.
She looks after her household;
She eats not the bread of idleness.
Her children rise and bless her,
And her husband praises her, saying:
"Many women do worthily,
But you excel them all."
Charm is deceptive, and beauty is vain;
Only a God-fearing woman shall be
    praised.
Give her due credit for her
    achievement;
Let her own works praise her at the gates.

Job

The book of Job deals with the problems of human suffering and contains some of the deepest thoughts that have come down from antiquity. Written in poetry, which is always more difficult than prose, the book of Job is not known and read as it deserves to be.

The forty-two chapters consist of three parts: a prologue, a poem, and an epilogue. The poem contains the debates between Job and his three friends; a speech by a bystander named Elihu; an address by God and a penitent confession by Job. In true humility, Job acknowledges the divine supremacy and learns the value of perfect trust and patience. God vindicates him and does not forsake him.

In chapter thirty-one, the virtues enumerated by Job are: a blameless family life, consideration for the poor and weak, charity, modesty, generosity, hospitality to strangers, honesty and just dealings.

The function of Satan, the Adversary, is described in the prologue as that of testing the sincerity of man's character. In talmudic literature, Satan was transformed into the *yetser ha-ra,* the evil impulse, whose function it is to strengthen man's moral sense by leading him into temptation. Man's heart is pictured as an arena where the good and evil wrestle in perpetual conflict.

In midrashic literature, Job is represented as a most generous man. He built an inn at the crossroads with four doors opening in four directions, so that transients might have no trouble in finding an entrance. He took the greatest care to keep himself aloof from every unseemly deed. However, Rabbi Yohanan ben Zakkai used to say that Job's piety was only the result of his fear of punishment (Sotah 27a). Job's chief complaint was, according to a talmudic opinion, that although man is driven to sin by the *yetser ha-ra* or evil impulse, yet he is punished. But Eliphaz answered him that if God created the *yetser ha-ra,* he also created the Torah by which a man can subdue the evil impulse (Baba Bathra 16a). The Rabbis ascribed the book of Job to Moses.

Once there was a man in the land of Uz, whose name was Job, a blameless and upright man who revered God and shunned evil. He had seven sons and three daughters, and possessed seven thousand sheep, three thousand camels, five hundred pair of oxen, five hundred donkeys, and a large number of servants. He was the greatest man in all the East.

One day the heavenly beings presented themselves before the Lord, and among them was Satan. "Whence do you come?" said the Lord to Satan. Satan answered: "From roaming and roving about the earth." And the Lord said to Satan: "Have you noticed my servant Job, a perfect and upright man who reveres God and shuns evil?" Satan replied: "But is it for nothing that Job reveres God? Hast thou not hedged him safely round about, his house and all that belongs to him? Thou hast blessed the labor of his hands, and his wealth is spread abroad in the land. Only put out thy hand and touch whatever he has; surely he will blaspheme thee to thy face!" Then said the Lord to Satan: "Well, all that he has is in your power; but lay no hand upon the man himself." Then Satan went away from the presence of the Lord.

One day, when Job's sons and daughters were eating and drinking in the house of their eldest brother, a messenger came to Job and said: "The oxen were plowing, the donkeys were grazing close by, when the Sabeans made a raid and carried them off; they killed the servants and I alone have escaped to tell you." He was still speaking when another came and said: "Lightning fell from the sky and consumed the flocks and the servants; I alone have escaped to tell you." He was still speaking when another came and said: "The Chaldeans formed three divisions and made a raid upon the camels. They carried them off and killed the servants; I alone have escaped to tell you." He was still speaking when another came and said: "Your sons and daughters were eating and drinking in the house of their eldest brother, when a mighty wind came from the wilderness and struck the four corners of the house. It fell upon the young people, and they were killed; I alone have escaped to tell you."

Then Job arose, tore his mantle, shaved his head and fell to the ground crying: "Naked I came from my mother's womb, and naked I shall return; the Lord gave and the Lord has taken away; blessed be the name of the Lord." In all this, Job did not sin nor did he give offense to God.

Again on another day the heavenly beings presented themselves before the Lord, and among them was Satan. "Whence do you come?" said the Lord to Satan, and Satan answered: "From roaming and roving about the earth." And the Lord said to Satan: "Have you noticed my servant Job, a perfect and upright man, who reveres God and shuns evil? He still holds to his integrity, though you have led me to ruin him without cause." But Satan answered: "His own skin has been saved! A man will give all that he has to preserve his life. Only put out thy hand and touch his flesh and bones; surely he will blaspheme thee to thy face." And the Lord said to Satan: "Behold, he is in your hands; only spare his life."

Satan went away from the presence of the Lord, and he smote Job with leprosy from the soles of his feet to the crown of his head. Job took a potsherd with which to scrape himself as he sat among the ashes. His wife said to him: "Do you still hold fast to your integrity? Blaspheme God, and die." But he said to her: "You speak like a worthless woman. Shall we receive good at the hand of God, but not receive evil?" In all this, Job did not sin with his lips.

When Eliphaz, Bildad and Zophar, the three friends of Job, heard of all the trouble that had befallen him, they came to comfort him. When they saw him from a distance and could not recognize him, they wept aloud. For seven days and seven nights they sat beside him on the ground, and no one spoke a word to him, for they saw that his suffering was very great.

After this Job opened his mouth and cursed the day of his birth: "Perish the day I was born! Why did I not die at birth? I would have been lying still, I would have slept in peace, with the kings and counselors of the world. High and low are there alike, and the slave is free from his master. Why is light given to him who is in misery, and life to men in bitter despair, who long for death, but it comes not?"

Then Eliphaz replied: "If one ventures a word with you, will you be offended? Yet who can keep from speaking? Think now, what guiltless man has ever perished? When have the just ever been swept away? As I see it, men reap the evil that they plow, the trouble that they sow. Can mortal man be just before God? Can man be pure before his Maker? Were I in your place, I would turn to God who does great things beyond our understanding. He gives rain upon the earth and sends waters upon the fields; he sets on high those who are lowly, and those who mourn are exalted to victory. In famine he will rescue you from death, and in war from the power of the sword. You shall come to the grave in ripe old age, as a shock of grain comes to the threshing floor in the harvest season."

Job answered: "Would that God were pleased to crush me! What strength have I to hold out? Is my strength the strength of stones? Is my flesh made of bronze? Teach me, I will be silent; make me understand where I have gone wrong.

"I am forced to live through empty months, and nights of misery are allotted to me. I lie down thinking, 'When shall I arise?' The night is long, and till the day dawns I keep tossing to and fro. I will not restrain my mouth; I will speak in the anguish of my spirit; I will complain in the bitterness of my soul. When I think, 'My bed will comfort me, my couch will ease my complaint,' then thou scarest me with dreams, terrifying me with nightmares, till I would fain be strangled, I would prefer death to my being. Let me alone, for my days are but a breath. What is man, that thou dost make so much of him, punishing him every morning, testing him moment by moment? If I sin, what harm is that to thee? Why dost thou not pardon my transgression, why not let my sin pass?"

Then Bildad replied: "How long will you talk like that? Does God pervert justice? If you are pure and upright, he will reward you and prosper your righteous house. And though your beginning was small, he will amply enrich

192

you in the end. God will not reject a blameless man; he will yet fill your mouth with laughter and shouts of joy."

Then Job answered: "Yes, it is true; I know it; but how can a man be just before God? Though I am innocent, I cannot answer him; I must appeal for mercy to my accuser. Though I am blameless, he would prove me wrong. He destroys the blameless and the bad alike. The world is handed over to the wicked; he makes the rulers of men blind to justice! I am bound to be held guilty; why, then, should I struggle in vain? I am sick of life; I will give free utterance to my complaint; I will speak in the bitterness of my soul. I will say to God: 'Do not condemn me; let me know why thou dost quarrel with me. Does it seem good to thee to oppress and to despise the work of thy hands? Thy hands fashioned and made me; and wilt thou try to destroy me? Remember that thou madest me like clay; and wilt thou grind me into dust again?' "

Then Zophar replied: "Should a multitude of words go unanswered? Are men to be silenced by your babbling? When you mock, shall no one rebuke you? If God would only speak, and open his lips against you, you would know that God exacts of you less than your guilt deserves. If you will turn your mind to God, banishing sin from your life and evil from your house, you will be calm and fearless. You will forget your misery, remembering it no more than waters that have flowed away. Your life will be brighter than the noonday, your darkness will be like the dawn. You will lie down, and none will disturb you; and many will entreat your favor."

Then Job spoke: "No doubt you are the wise men, and wisdom will die with you. But I have understanding as well as you. Men at ease sneer at the unfortunate; when men stumble, there is contempt for them. The homes of robbers are at peace; those who provoke God are secure. I have seen all this; my ear has heard and understood it. What you know, I know too. But I would appeal to the Almighty; I desire to argue my case with God. You white-wash everything with lies. If only you would keep silent, you might pass for wise men. Will you speak falsely for

God? Will you show partiality toward him? Can you deceive him as one deceives a man?

"Let me have silence and I will speak, and let come on me what may. What are my iniquities? Let me know my offense and my sin. Why dost thou hide thy face and count me as thy enemy? Wilt thou frighten a driven leaf? Wilt thou pursue a withered straw? Man wastes away like a rotten thing, like a garment that is moth-eaten. Man born of woman lives but a few days and is full of trouble. He comes forth like a flower and withers; he is a fleeting shadow. There is hope for a tree that is felled; it may flourish yet again. Though its root decays in the soil, though its stump is dead in the ground, it may bud at the scent of water and put forth branches like a young plant. But man dies, and his strength is gone; man breathes his last, and where is he? Man lies down and rises not again; till the skies are no more he will not awake, he will not stir from his slumber. If only man might die and live again.

"But the mountain falls and crumbles away, the rock is removed from its place; stones are worn out by waters, torrents wash the soil away; even so thou destroyest the hope of man. Thou dost overpower him, and he has to go. His sons come to honor, but he does not know it; they are brought low, but he does not perceive it.

"Terrors are let loose on me; like a cloud my welfare has disappeared. My soul within me melts with sorrow; days of affliction lay hold of me. The night racks my bones; the pain that gnaws me never slumbers. God has plunged me into the mire, I am reduced to dust and ashes. I cry to thee and thou dost not answer me. Thou hast turned cruel to me; thou tossest me before the wind. I hoped for good, and evil came; I waited for the light, and darkness fell.

"If ever my step turned from the right way, if ever my heart went after my eyes, if ever I took to fraud, may others eat up what I sow, may my crops be uprooted.

"I never ignored the rightful claim of my servants when they complained against me—did not my Maker make my servant too, forming us both alike? I never begrudged a poor man anything, or caused a widow to pine in want or ate my food alone without sharing it with the fatherless.

194

For, like a father, God has brought me up, caring for me since ever I was born.

"If ever I saw anyone perish for lack of clothing without giving him fleece from my sheep; if ever I lifted up my hand against the fatherless; then let my shoulder drop from its socket, my arm snap from the collar-bone!

"If ever I relied on gold, or rejoiced because my wealth was great; if ever I exulted over my foe's ruin when evil overtook him, or practised the sin of cursing him and praying for his death; if ever I concealed my sins from men, covering up my guilt; if ever I was afraid of the great multitude and kept quiet within doors—well, here I enter my own plea of innocence.

"If ever my land accused me, if the furrows complained with tears that I ate the products without paying, and snuffed out the life of those who owned the land, may thorns grow up instead of wheat, and weeds instead of barley."

The three men ceased speaking to Job, because he considered himself in the right. Elihu became angry with Job. His anger was kindled also against Job's three friends, because they had found no answer to Job's railing against God. Elihu had waited to speak to Job because the men were older than he, but now he spoke:

"I am young and you are old, so I was timid and afraid to tell you my opinion. However, it is the spirit in men, the breath of the Almighty, that makes them understand. The old are not always wise, nor do the aged always understand what is right. Therefore I say: Listen to me; let me also express my opinion. I waited while you spoke, I listened to your arguments; I paid attention carefully to you, but none of you confuted Job. I must speak, that I may find relief; I must open my lips and answer. I will show partiality to no man. I will not flatter anyone. I do not know how to flatter.

"Give heed, O Job, listen to me; be silent, and I will speak. If you have anything to say, answer me; speak, for I desire to justify you. If not, be silent, and I will teach you wisdom. Far be it from God to do evil, far be it from the Almighty to do wrong. He makes man answer for his deeds, and fare exactly as he may deserve. Were he to withdraw his spirit, were he to gather in his breath, all flesh would perish at once, and man would return to dust. Could one who is opposed to justice govern? Would you denounce him who is righteous and mighty, who never favors princes, and who never prefers the rich to the poor? All men are the work of his hands. In a moment they are dead; in the middle of the night people are shaken and pass away; the mighty are taken away by an unseen hand.

"God's eyes are upon the ways of man, he watches every step that a man takes. There is no darkness, there are no black shadows, where evil-doers can hide themselves. He shatters the mighty and sets others up in their place. He strikes them down for their wickedness in the sight of men, because they turned aside from following him and heeded none of his ways. They caused the poor to cry to him, and he heard the groaning of the oppressed.

"Look at the heavens and see, behold the skies above. If you have sinned, how does it affect him? What are your many misdeeds to him? If you are upright, what do you give to him? What does he receive from your hand? Behold, God is exalted in his power; who is a teacher like him? Who can prescribe for him his way? Who can say: 'Thou hast done wrong?'

"Behold, God is great, and we know him not. He draws up water from the sea, and pours the rain down from the clouds, and provides food in abundance. Can any one understand the spreading of the clouds, the thunderings of his pavilion? He hurls the lightning from an unseen hand, and commands it to strike the mark. The thunder tells of him whose anger blazes against iniquity. To the snow he says: 'Fall on the earth,' and to the downpour and the rain: 'Be strong.' Then the beasts go into their lairs, and remain in their dens. Storms blow out of the south, and cold comes from the north. By the breath of God ice is formed, and the broad waters are frozen fast. He loads the thick cloud with moisture, and from the clouds his lightning scatters, turning as he directs it, doing whatsoever he commands it over all the world.

"Listen to this, O Job; stop and consider the wonders of God. Do you know how God makes the lightning of his cloud to flash? Do you know how the clouds are poised? Tell us what we shall say to him; we cannot argue with our darkened minds. The Almighty is beyond our reach; he is great in power and justice; he violates no right. He has no regard for those who are wise in their own conceit."

Then the Lord answered Job out of the whirlwind, saying: "Who is this that darkens my design by thoughtless words? Gird up your loins like a man, answer me the questions I will ask you. When I founded the earth, where were you then? Tell me, if you have understanding. Who fixed its measurements—do you know that? Have you discovered the fountains of the sea? Have you set foot upon the depths of ocean? Have you ever entered the storehouses of the snow? Have you ever seen the arsenals of hail? Do you know the laws of the heavens? Can you describe their sway over the earth? Can you lift up your voice to the clouds, that a flood of waters may cover you? Can you send out lightnings on a mission? Do they say humbly to you: 'Here we are'? Who provides for the raven its prey, when its young ones cry to God for lack of food?

"Do you know how wild goats breed upon the hills? Do you know the time when they bring forth? They bend down as they bring forth their young—robust offspring, thriving in the open; they run off and return not to the herd. Can you give strength to the horse? Do you make him leap like the locust, with majesty and terrible snorting? He mocks at fear and is not frightened, but on he charges in wild rage, he cannot stand still at the sound of the trumpet. Is it by your wisdom that the hawk soars and spreads its wings for the south? Does your word make the eagle fly high to nest aloft among the hills? Will the faultfinder still argue with the Almighty? He who argues with God, let him answer it."

Then Job replied to the Lord: "I am of small account; how shall I answer thee? I put my hand over my mouth. I will not answer. I know that thou canst do all things, and that nothing is too difficult for thee. I have said what I did not understand, things too wonderful for me, things

197

which I did not know. I despise myself, in dust and ashes I repent."

Then the Lord said to Eliphaz: "My anger is hot against you and your two friends, because you have not spoken sincerely of me, as my servant Job has."

The Lord restored the fortunes of Job when he had prayed for his friends, and the Lord doubled all that Job had possessed before. His brothers and sisters and all who had known him before came and ate bread with him in his house; they comforted him for all the evil that the Lord had brought upon him.

In the end, the Lord made Job more prosperous than he had been before. He had fourteen thousand sheep, six thousand camels, a thousand pair of oxen, and a thousand donkeys. He had also seven sons and three daughters. In all the land there were no women as beautiful as Job's daughters. Job lived to see his grandsons and great-grandsons—four generations. Then Job died, old, after a full life.

Song of Songs

The Song of Songs has been accepted throughout the ages as an allegory of the relations between God and Israel. Some nineteen centuries ago, Rabbi Akiba declared that the Song of Songs is the holiest of all the sacred writings. According to the Targum, the Song of Songs portrays the history of Israel. It has been regarded also as a representation of the affection of Israel for the Sabbath.

O kiss me with your lips, for your caresses are better than wine. Sweet is the fragrance of your perfumes; your very self is a precious perfume; therefore do maidens love you.

I am dark but lovely, maidens of Jerusalem. Do not stare at me because I am dark, for the sun has tanned me. My brothers were angry with me, so they made me keeper of the vineyards, and I did not look after my own vineyard.

Tell me, you whom my soul loves, where you feed your flocks, where you bring them to rest at noon. Why should I have to wander among your companions' flocks?

You are beautiful, my love, you are beautiful; your eyes are like doves. Like a lily among thorns, so is my loved one among maidens.

Like an apple tree among trees of the forest, so is my beloved among youths. In his shadow I long to sit; his fruit is sweet to my taste.

I hear the voice of my beloved! Here he comes, leaping across the mountains, bounding over the hills! My beloved is like a gazelle, like a young deer. There he stands, behind our wall, gazing through the windows, peering through the lattice.

My beloved called and said to me: Rise, my love, my beauty, come away. For, lo, the winter is over, the rain is

199

past and gone; the flowers appear on the earth, the time of song has come! The call of the turtle-dove is heard in our land; the fig tree is ripening its early figs, and the vines in blossom give forth their fragrance. Rise, my love, my beauty, come away. O my dove, in the clefts of the rock, in the cover of the cliff, let me see your form, let me hear your voice; for sweet is your voice, and your form is lovely.

On my bed at night I looked for him whom my soul loves; I searched for him, but I did not find him. I will rise, I said, and go through the city—I will seek him whom my soul loves.

I looked for him, but I did not find him. I asked the watchmen: "Have you seen him whom my soul loves?" Scarcely had I left them than I found him. I held him and would not let go of him until I had brought him into my mother's house.

You are beautiful, my love, you are beautiful! Your eyes are dove-like behind your veil; your hair is like a flock coming down from Mount Gilead. Your teeth are like a flock of sheep all shaped alike, which have come up from being washed; they are evenly matched, and not one is missing. Your lips are like a thread of scarlet, and your mouth is lovely.

I was asleep, but my heart was awake. Hark! My beloved is knocking. "Open to me, my sister, my love, my dove, my innocent one; for my hair is drenched with dew, my locks with the drops of night."

I opened to my beloved, but he had turned away and was gone. I searched for him, but could not find him; I called him, but he did not answer. The watchmen struck me and wounded me, the guardians of the walls stripped me of my mantle.

Where has your beloved gone, O fairest of women? Where has he turned, that we may seek him with you?

My beloved has gone down to his garden, to the flower-beds of balsam, to gather lilies. I am my beloved's, and he is mine.

Come, let us go into the fields, let us stay in the villages. Let us go early to the vineyards, to see whether the grapevine has budded, whether the vine blossoms have opened, whether the pomegranates are in flower. There I will give my love to you.

O that you were my brother! I would meet you in the street and kiss you, and none would despise me. I would bring you into my mother's house; I would give you some wine to drink, some of my pomegranate juice.

Love is strong as death itself; its flashes are flashes of fire, a flame of the Lord. Floods cannot quench love, rivers cannot drown it. If a man offered all his wealth for love, he would be utterly scorned.

Make haste, my beloved! Be like a gazelle, or like a young deer, on the mountains of spices.

Ruth

The book of Ruth takes its name from Ruth who clung to her mother-in-law Naomi with all the unselfishness of true-hearted affection. The narrative is one of idyllic beauty. It is the most charming short story in the Bible, and presents a pleasing picture of life in Israel during the period of the judges.

Naomi is an example of faithfulness and loyalty, self-sacrifice and moral integrity. Widowed and bereft of her two sons, Naomi returned to Bethlehem from Moab, where they had lived during a famine in Judea. Anxious to provide for Ruth and to see her married, she successfully arranged the marriage of Ruth to Boaz.

About two-thirds of the narrative is in dialogue. In the Hebrew Bible, the book of Ruth is placed among the five *Megilloth* or Scrolls (Song of Songs, Ruth, Lamentations, Ecclesiastes, Esther), which are recited in the synagogue on special occasions.

The book of Ruth is recited annually on Shavuoth (Pentecost), the harvest festival commemorating the giving of the Torah, because the scene of its story is the harvest field and its leading character embraces Judaism.

In the time when the judges ruled, there was a famine in the land of Judah; so a man named Elimelech from Bethlehem went to live in Moab, he and his wife Naomi and their two sons. Elimelech died, and Naomi was left with her two sons, Mahalon and Kilion, who married Moabite women, one named Orpah, and the other—Ruth. After about ten years, both Mahalon and Kilion died, so that the woman was bereft of her two children as well as her husband.

When she heard that the Lord had remembered his people in Judah and given them food, she left Moab together with her daughters-in-law to return to her own

202

country. But, as they were setting out, Naomi said to her two daughters-in-law: "You go back, each of you to her mother's house. May the Lord treat you as kindly as you have treated the dead and me. May the Lord help each of you find a home in the house of her husband." Then she kissed them. "No," they replied, "we will go back with you to your people."

"Turn back, my daughters," Naomi said, "why should you go with me? Have I any more sons to be husbands to you? No, my daughters, my plight is worse than yours; the hand of the Lord has gone forth against me." Again they wept; Orpah kissed her mother-in-law goodby, but Ruth clung to her.

Naomi said: "Look, your sister-in-law has turned back to her people and to her gods; turn back after her." But Ruth said: "Entreat me not to leave you and to turn back from following you; wherever you go, I will go; wherever you stay, I will stay; your people shall be my people, and your God shall be my God; wherever you die, I will die, and there will I be buried. May the Lord punish me time and again if anything but death parts me from you!" When Naomi saw that she was determined to go with her, she said no more.

The two went on until they came to Bethlehem. Upon their arrival in Bethlehem the whole town was stirred, and the women said: "Is this Naomi?" But she said to them: "Do not call me Naomi; call me Mara, for the Almighty has dealt very bitterly with me. I left here when I was rich, and the Lord has brought me back empty-handed."

The barley harvest was just beginning when Naomi and Ruth reached Bethlehem. So Ruth said to Naomi: "Let me go to the fields and glean ears of corn after one who will be kind to me." "Go, my daughter," Naomi answered. So Ruth went and gleaned in the fields after the harvesters, and she happened to come to the field belonging to Boaz, a kinsman of Naomi's husband. Just then Boaz came out from Bethlehem and said to the harvesters: "May the Lord be with you!" They replied: "May the Lord bless you!"

"Whose girl is this?" Boaz asked the foreman of the

harvesters. The foreman replied: "It is the Moabite girl who came back with Naomi. She asked to be allowed to glean among the sheaves after the harvesters, and she has been working ever since morning, without resting even for a moment."

Then Boaz said to Ruth: "Now listen, my daughter. Do not go to glean in another field; do not leave this one, but stay close to my maidservants. Keep your eyes on the field they are reaping and follow them. Whenever you are thirsty, go to the water jars and drink. I have been well informed of all that you have done for your mother-in-law since the death of your husband, of how you left your father and mother and the land of your birth and came to a people who were strange to you. May the Lord reward you for what you have done; may you receive full recompense from the Lord God of Israel, under whose wings you have taken refuge."

She answered: "Thank you, my lord, for speaking kindly to me, even though I am not one of your own servants."

At mealtime Boaz said to her: "Come here and eat some of our bread; dip your slice in the vinegar." So she sat beside the harvesters, and he handed her roasted grains. She ate till she was satisfied, and had some left over. When she got up to glean, Boaz gave orders to his servants: "Let her glean even among the sheaves, and do not be rude to her."

So she gleaned in the field till evening. Then she beat out what she had gleaned and took it away with her to the town. Her mother-in-law asked her: "Where did you glean today? Where did you work? A blessing on the man who was friendly to you!" So she told her mother-in-law that the man's name was Boaz. Then Naomi said: "May he be blessed by the Lord, who has not ceased to be kind to the living and to the dead! The man is a relative of ours; he is one of our near kinsmen."

"Furthermore," said Ruth, "he told me to keep close to his servants till they have finished all his harvesting." But Naomi said: "It is well, my daughter, that you go out with his girls, so as not to be molested in another field." So she kept close to the girls of Boaz as she gleaned until the end of the barley and wheat harvests.

Then Naomi said to her: "Boaz is winnowing barley tonight at the threshing floor. Wash yourself, put on your best clothes, and go down to the threshing floor, but do not reveal your presence to the man until he has finished eating and drinking. Note the place where he lies down; then uncover his feet and lie down there; and he will tell you what to do."

She went down to the threshing floor and did just as her mother-in-law had told her. At midnight the man was startled; he discovered a woman lying at his feet. "Who are you?" he asked. She replied: "I am Ruth; take me in marriage, for you are a close relative." And he said: "May the Lord bless you, my daughter. Have no fear, my daughter, I will do for you all that you ask. It is true that I am a kinsman, but there is a nearer kinsman than myself. If he will do his duty, good and well; if not, I will."

So she lay at his feet until morning, then she went back to the city. "How did you fare, my daughter?" her mother-in-law asked. And she told her all that Boaz had done for her, saying: "He gave me these six measures of barley, for he said that I must not go back empty-handed."

Boaz found the kinsman and asked him if he would buy the parcel of land which belonged to Elimelech. "I will," the man replied. Then Boaz said: "When you buy the field from Naomi, you are also buying Ruth, the widow, so as to carry on the name of her dead husband along with his inheritance." But the kinsman answered: "I cannot, for fear of injuring my own inheritance. Take over my right of redemption yourself, for I cannot redeem the property."

Boaz married Ruth, and she bore a son. Then the women said to Naomi: "Blessed be the Lord who has not left you this day without a kinsman! May the boy's name be renowned in Israel! He will renew your life and nourish your old age, for he is the child of your daughter-in-law, who loves you and is better than seven sons to you." They named the baby Obed. He was the father of Jesse, who in turn was the father of David.

Lamentations

The book of Lamentations consists of five lyric poems describing the fall of Jerusalem in 586 before the common era. In the Hebrew Bible, four of these dirges are alphabetical acrostics. The fifth poem, even though it is not an alphabetical acrostic, has twenty-two verses, corresponding to the number of letters in the Hebrew alphabet.

These poems are among the finest examples of biblical Hebrew. They are attributed to Jeremiah who was an eyewitness to the agony of Jerusalem and the despair of its inhabitants during the invasion of Nebuchadnezzar, when Solomon's Temple was destroyed after it had been in existence for four hundred and ten years.

The Greek version of the Bible, known as the Septuagint, begins the book of Lamentations with these words: "After Israel was carried into captivity, and Jerusalem was laid waste, Jeremiah sat down and wept, and sang this song of woe over Jerusalem." The book is recited in the synagogues on the ninth day of Av, the day on which the Temple was destroyed.

How lonely is the city, once so full of people! She has become like a widow, once so great among the nations! She weeps bitterly in the night. Of all her friends there is none to comfort her. They have all betrayed her. They have become her enemies.

Judah has gone into exile; she finds no rest; her pursuers have all overtaken her in the midst of her distress. Jerusalem recalls all the precious things that were hers; the enemy has laid his hands on all her treasures; she has seen pagans invade her sanctuary. All her people are moaning in their search for bread; they trade their treasures for food to keep themselves alive.

You who pass by, look all of you and see if there is any

sorrow like my sorrow which was brought upon me by the Lord on the day of his wrath. For all this I weep, tears stream from my eyes; my children are desolate, for the enemy has prevailed. Zion stretches out her hands, but there is none to comfort her.

Cry aloud to the Lord, O Zion! Pour out your heart like water before the Lord! Look, O Lord, and see! All over the streets they lie, both young and old. My maidens and my young men have fallen by the sword; not one escaped or survived on the day of thy anger.

The kindnesses of the Lord never cease, his mercies never fail; they are new every morning; great is thy faithfulness! The Lord is good to those who look hopefully to him, to a soul that seeks him. It is good to wait in silence for the salvation of the Lord.

Why should a man complain when he is punished for his sins? Let us scan and test our ways, let us return to the Lord! Let us lift up our hearts and hands to God in heaven. Without cause, my enemies have hunted me like a bird.

Happier were the victims of the sword than the victims of hunger. Compassionate women have cooked their children with their own hands; they became their food at the downfall of my people. The Lord lit a fire in Zion which consumed its foundations. Our eyes failed as we looked vainly for help.

Our pursuers were swifter than the vultures of the air; they hunted us on the hills, they lay in wait for us in the wilderness. Remember, O Lord, what has befallen us; look and see our disgrace! Our heritage has been turned over to strangers; we have become orphans and are fatherless.

Our fathers sinned and are no more; and we must bear their guilt. Slaves rule over us; there is none to free us from their power. But thou, O Lord, dost reign forever; thy throne endures through all generations. Restore us, O Lord, and let us return to thee. Renew our days as of old.

Ecclesiastes

The book of Ecclesiastes was composed by Koheleth, who is traditionally identified with King Solomon. It contains twelve chapters of maxims and wise observations on the purpose of life.

Koheleth counsels patience, endurance and discretion. He examines the value of wisdom, wealth, and pleasure, and finds life unsatisfying. He declares that wealth does not yield happiness. It is often lost even before it is enjoyed. At death, it is left to people who have not toiled to acquire it; hence, all is a vain pursuit.

How are we to gain happiness? Shall we follow wisdom or unrestrained pleasure? Human existence is monotonous: there is nothing new in the entire world. We should therefore alternate wholesome work with reasonable pleasures of life while we can, since there is no telling when the end comes.

This book concludes with this counsel: "Revere God and keep his commandments, for this is the whole duty of man." Koheleth is recited in the synagogues on the eighth day of the Sukkoth festival.

Vanity of vanities, says Koheleth, all is vain. What does a man gain from all his toil under the sun? One generation goes and another comes, but the earth remains forever. The sun rises and the sun sets, only to rise again. All the rivers flow into the sea, but the sea is never full. There is nothing new under the sun. Men may say of something: "See, this is new!"—but it existed long ago before our time.

I was king of Israel in Jerusalem. I set my mind to search and survey all that is done under the sun. It is a sorry task given to the sons of men by God! I have seen all the things done under the sun—they are vain and futile. The more you know, the more you suffer; an increase of knowledge is an increase of sorrow.

I built mansions, planted vineyards, and laid out gardens and parks. I made pools to water the trees in my

plantations; I acquired servants; I amassed silver and gold.
Richer and richer I grew, more than any before me in
Jerusalem. My wisdom also remained with me. I denied
myself nothing that I desired. I withheld no pleasure from
my heart. But when I turned to look at all I had achieved,
at my toil and trouble—it appeared all vain and unreal.
There was nothing to be gained under the sun. Then I saw
that wisdom excels folly as light excels darkness.

There is a time for everything: a time to be born and a
time to die; a time to plant and a time to uproot; a time
to kill and a time to heal; a time to break down and a time
to build up; a time to weep and a time to laugh; a time to
mourn and a time to dance; a time to cast away stones and
a time to gather stones; a time to embrace and a time to
repel; a time to seek and a time to discard; a time to keep
and a time to throw away; a time to rend and a time to
mend; a time to keep silent and a time to speak; a time to
love and a time to hate; a time for war and a time for peace.

I know that there is nothing better for men than to be
happy and enjoy themselves as long as they are alive. It is
indeed God's very gift to man that he should eat and drink
and be happy as he toils.

There is one fate for man and beast; as the one dies so
the other dies; the same breath is in all of them. All go to
one place; all are from the dust, and all return to the dust.
Who knows whether the spirit of man goes upward and the
spirit of the beast goes down to the earth? So I saw that it is
best for man to enjoy his work and be happy.

I looked again and saw all the oppression that prevails
under the sun. So I thought that the dead are more
fortunate than those who are still alive. I saw another futile
thing under the sun—a person who has no one, either son
or brother, yet there is no end to all his toil. He cannot
satisfy himself with what he gains, and he never asks himself: "For whom am I toiling and depriving myself of
pleasure?" Two are better than one—if either of them
should fall the other will raise him up; but woe to him
who is alone.

Never be rash with your mouth. Better not vow at all
than vow and fail to pay.

A lover of money will never be satisfied with his money.

Sweet is the sleep of the worker, whether he eats much or little; but the surfeit of the rich man does not let him sleep.

Naked he came from his mother's womb, and naked he must return; for all his toil he has nothing to take with him. What does he gain by all his toil for the wind, spending all his days in darkness and grief, in much anger and sickness and distress?

There is an evil that lies heavy upon mortals: a man to whom God gives riches, wealth and honor, and he lacks nothing of all that he desires, yet God does not permit him to enjoy it, but a stranger enjoys it.

A good name is better than precious oil.

It is better to hear the rebuke of the wise than the praise of fools.

Let your garments be always spotless.

Cast your bread upon the waters; after many days you shall find it.

As you do not know how the wind blows, nor how a child within the womb grows, so you do not know how God works, God who makes everything.

Sweet is the light of life; it is pleasant for the eyes to see the sun.

If a man lives many years, let him have joy throughout all of them; let him remember that the days of darkness will be many.

Rejoice in your youth, young man; follow your heart's desire and the sight of your eyes, but know that for all this God will bring you to account.

Remove all worries from your mind, and keep your body free from pain.

Remember your Creator in the days of your youth, before the evil days come and the years approach of which you will say: "I have no joy in them." Revere God and keep his commandments, for this is the whole duty of man.

Esther

The book of Esther, one of the most cherished works in Jewish literature, is the last of the five sacred scrolls that are part of the third division of the Bible known as Hagiographa (Holy Writings). The scroll of Esther tells the story of a Jewish girl who used her influence as queen of Persia to save her people from a general massacre which Haman had plotted against them on purely racial grounds. It is a tale of plot and counter-plot, showing the downfall of the arrogant and the vindication of the innocent.

Queen Esther is depicted as dutiful toward Mordecai, her guardian, and faithful to her people. Haman, with his vanity, malice and cruelty, is a masterpiece of portraiture. His fate reminds us that pride goes before a fall. Ahasuerus, who agrees to Haman's plot without thought, is painted as a pompous and feeble-minded monarch. Some scholars identify him with Xerxes, who reigned from 486 to 465. Others believe him to be Artaxerxes II, who reigned from 404 to 361, and who is mentioned in Ezra 4:6.

Explaining the origin of the social and convivial festival of Purim, the scroll of Esther is recited aloud in the synagogues at the eve of Purim and again the next morning. The feast of Purim, universally observed by the Jewish people even to this day, has been considered strong evidence that the book of Esther is an historical document. Though the name of God is not mentioned in the book, the author clearly implies that God used Mordecai and Esther as instruments for the deliverance of a persecuted people.

King Ahasuerus, who reigned over a hundred and twenty-seven provinces from India to Ethiopia, gave a banquet to the nobles and officers of the army and displayed his royal treasures. The banquet lasted one hundred and eighty days, and was followed by a seven-day banquet for all the people in Shushan, the capital. Queen Vashti also gave a banquet for the women. On the seventh day, when the king's heart was merry with wine, he commanded Queen Vashti to appear in order to show off her beauty, but Queen Vashti refused to go before the court. Enraged, the king asked his wise men what should be done with her. "Let the king assign her royal position to a better woman," Memucan advised, and the king acted accordingly. He also sent letters to every province directing that every man should be lord in his own house.

There was a Jew in Shushan by the name of Mordecai. He had adopted his orphaned cousin Esther and brought her up as his own daughter. Beautiful and lovely, she was taken into the royal house where she became a favorite. She said nothing about her people or her descent, for Mordecai had told her not to reveal it. The king loved Esther more than all his wives and he made her queen instead of Vashti.

After these events, King Ahasuerus promoted Haman and advanced him above all his officers. All bowed low before Haman, but Mordecai would not bow to him. This infuriated Haman so much that he decided to destroy all the Jews throughout the empire of Ahasuerus. He said to the king: "There is a certain people dispersed in every province of your kingdom whose laws are different from those of other people and they do not obey the king's laws. The king should not tolerate them in the land. If it please the king, let it be decreed that they be destroyed, and I will pay ten thousand talents of silver into the royal treasury."

"Keep your money," the king said to Haman, "and do what you like with the people." Then instructions were sent to all the king's provinces to massacre and destroy all the Jews, young and old, women and children in one day, the thirteenth day of the month of Adar. The king and Haman sat down to drink, but the city of Shushan was perplexed.

When Mordecai learned all that had been done, he rent his garments, put on sackcloth and went about the city, crying bitterly. There was great mourning among the Jews in every province, wherever the king's command was heard. Esther ordered Hathach to go and find out from Mordecai what was the meaning of it all. Mordecai told him all that had happened and gave him a copy of the decree, which he was to show to Esther, charging her to intercede with the king on behalf of her people.

When Hathach told Esther what Mordecai had said, she gave him this message for Mordecai: "Everybody knows that there is one penalty for any person who goes to the king without being summoned; it is death. I have not been summoned for thirty days." Whereupon Mordecai replied: "Do not imagine you will escape inside the royal palace any more than the rest of the Jews on the outside. If you keep silent at a time like this, relief and deliverance will arise from another quarter; but you will perish, you and your father's house. Who knows whether it was not for a time like this that you have been raised to royalty."

Then Esther sent this reply to Mordecai: "Go gather all the Jews of Shushan and fast on my behalf; eat and drink nothing for three days and three nights; I and my maids will fast likewise. Then I will go to the king, though it is against the law; and if I perish, I perish." Mordecai did as Esther ordered him.

On the third day Esther stood in the inner court of the royal palace. When the king saw Esther standing in the court, he held out the golden scepter to her; Esther approached and touched it. "What is your wish, Queen Esther," the king asked, "what is your request? It shall be given you were it even half of my kingdom." Esther said: "If it please the king, let the king and Haman come today to a banquet which I have prepared for the king."

"Bring Haman at once," the king ordered, "that we may do as Esther desires." So the king and Haman came to the banquet that Esther had prepared. As they were drinking wine, the king said to Esther: "What is your petition? It shall be granted; were it even half of my kingdom, it shall be fulfilled." But Esther replied: "My petition and my request—well, if it please the king, let the king and Haman come tomorrow to the banquet which I will prepare for them; tomorrow I will do as the king has said."

That day Haman was joyful and glad of heart. He told his friends and his wife Zeresh: "Queen Esther invited no

213

one except myself along with the king to the banquet she had prepared, and she has invited me again tomorrow together with the king. But all this does me no good as long as I see Mordecai the Jew sitting at the king's gate." Then his wife and all his friends said to him: "Let a gallows be made, and in the morning tell the king to have Mordecai hanged upon it; then go merrily with the king to the banquet." This pleased Haman, and he had the gallows made.

On that night the king could not sleep, so he had the book of records brought and read in his presence. It was found that Mordecai had saved the king's life. The king asked: "What honor, what dignity has been bestowed on Mordecai for this?" "Nothing has been done for him," the king's attendants replied. Then the king asked: "Who is in the court?" Haman had just entered the outer court to speak to the king about hanging Mordecai. So the king's attendants said: "Haman is standing in the court." And the king said: "Let him come in."

Haman came in, and the king asked him: "What should be done to the man whom the king delights to honor?" Haman said to himself: "Whom would the king delight to honor more than me?" So he said to the king: "For the man whom the king delights to honor, let a royal robe be brought which the king has worn, and a horse on which the king has ridden, with a royal crown upon its head; let the robe and the horse be entrusted to one of the king's noblest officials. He shall see that the man whom the king delights to honor is arrayed and led on horseback through the streets of the city, proclaiming: 'This is done for the man whom the king delights to honor.'"

The king said to Haman: "Make haste, take the robe and the horse, as you have said, and do all this to Mordecai the Jew; leave out nothing of what you have spoken." So Haman took the robe and the horse and arrayed Mordecai and led him on horseback through the streets of the city, proclaiming: "This is done for the man whom the king delights to honor."

Then Haman hurried home lamenting, and told his wife Zeresh and all his friends everything that had befallen him.

214

They said to him: "If Mordecai, before whom you have begun to fall, is of the Jewish people, you will never defeat him, but you will keep falling before him." Just as they were talking, the king's attendants arrived and hurried Haman to the banquet that Esther had prepared.

So the king and Haman came to feast with Queen Esther. On the second day of the banquet, the king again asked Esther: "What is your petition, Queen Esther? It shall be granted you. What is your request? Were it half my kingdom, it shall be fulfilled." Queen Esther replied: "If I have found favor in your sight, O king, and if it pleases the king, let my life be given me—that is my petition! Grant me my people—that is my request! I and my people are to be destroyed, to be slain, to be annihilated." King Ahasuerus asked Esther: "Who is it? Where is the man who has dared to do this?" Esther replied: "A foe, an enemy, this wicked Haman!"

Haman trembled before the king and the queen. The king rose in fury from the feast and went into the palace garden. Haman came forward to beg Queen Esther for his life, for he saw that the king had determined evil against him. When the king came back from the palace garden, Haman had fallen on the couch where Esther sat! "Will he even violate the queen in my presence, in my own house?" said the king. One of the royal attendants, Harbonah, said: "At Haman's house a gallows is standing, which he prepared for Mordecai who saved the king's life." "Hang him on that!" the king ordered. So they hanged Haman on the gallows which he had prepared for Mordecai.

Then Esther spoke again to the king; she fell at his feet and begged him with tears to avert the evil design of Haman against the Jews. She said: "If it please the king, let an order be written to revoke the letters sent out by Haman, in which he commanded the destruction of the Jews throughout the king's empire. How can I bear to witness the calamity that befalls my people? How can I endure the destruction of my kindred?" Thereupon King Ahasuerus said to Esther and Mordecai: "Write as you please about the Jews, write it in the name of the king and seal it with the signet of the king."

The king's secretaries were summoned, and an edict was written to the governors and officials of the provinces, from India to Ethiopia, to every province in its own script and to every people in its own language, and also to the Jews in their script and their language. The writing was in the name of King Ahasuerus and sealed with the king's signet ring. Letters were sent by mounted couriers riding on swift horses. By these the king gave the Jews permission to gather and defend their lives on the thirteenth day of the twelfth month, which is the month of Adar.

The couriers rode out in haste, and the decree was issued in Shushan. The Jews had light and joy and gladness and honor. In every province and in every city, wherever the king's edict arrived, there was gladness and joy among the Jews. Indeed, many pagans became Jews.

Mordecai sent despatches, giving to the Jews in every city the king's permission to defend their lives and destroy any armed forces that might attack them. On the thirteenth day of Adar, the Jews triumphed over their adversaries. In Shushan they fought for their lives on the thirteenth and the fourteenth, resting on the fifteenth and making that a day of feasting and rejoicing and sending gifts to one another.

Mordecai charged all the Jews to keep both the fourteenth and the fifteenth of the month of Adar, every year, as days of feasting and rejoicing. These days are called *Purim* after *pur,* lot, for Haman had cast the lot to destroy and annihilate the Jews, but his wicked plot recoiled upon his own head. Mordecai was great and popular among the Jews, for he sought their welfare and peace.

Daniel

The book of Daniel is made up of two parts. The first six chapters, written chiefly in Aramaic, tell of the miraculous deliverance of Daniel and his three friends who were exiled to Babylon by Nebuchadnezzar before the fall of Judea; they also include Daniel's interpretations of Nebuchadnezzar's dreams.

Daniel lived at the royal court and survived till the days of Cyrus, the Persian conqueror of Babylon, who authorized the return of the Jewish exiles and permitted them to rebuild the Temple at Jerusalem in 538.

The story of Daniel's three friends who were cast into the burning furnace is similar to the incident of Abraham and Nimrod. The last six chapters, written chiefly in Hebrew, consist of visions concerning four great empires, probably Babylon, Persia, Greece, and Syria.

Belshazzar is referred to as the son of Nebuchadnezzar, even though cuneiform inscriptions make it clear that he was the eldest son of and co-regent with Nabonidus, the last king of the Babylonian empire (556–539). Belshazzar was probably a descendant of Nebuchadnezzar, and in the Bible the word for "son" sometimes denotes "descendant."

The four Aramaic words, which were written by a mysterious hand on the wall at Belshazzar's feast, may have appeared in the form of anagrams. According to the Talmud, the inscription *mene mene tekel upharsin,* which could not be read by anyone except Daniel, appeared like this:

M M T L R
E E E U S
N N K P I
E E E A N

The initial "u" of the word *upharsin* is a conjunction, meaning *and.* After such a conjunction, the letter "p" changes to "ph," in keeping with rules of Hebrew grammar. The word *parsin* is the plural of *peres,* which denotes division and is spelled exactly like the Hebrew word for Persia. Hence, instead of *upharsin* the word should be transliterated *uparsin.*

King Nebuchadnezzar commanded his chief officer to bring to him some youths of Jewish nobility. They were to be handsome and intelligent, scholarly and competent, and able to serve in the royal palace. They were to be trained for three years before entering the king's service. Among these young men were Daniel, Hananiah, Mishael, and Azariah, who were renamed Belteshazzar, Shadrach, Meshach, and Abednego.

Daniel, who refused to defile himself by eating the king's food, said to the steward: "Let us have vegetables to eat and water to drink for ten days, and you will then compare our appearance with that of the youths who eat the king's fare." The steward agreed and did as they asked. At the end of ten days, they looked better and healthier than the youths who ate the king's fare. So he withheld meat and wine and served them vegetables. At the end of their training the four young men became the personal attendants of Nebuchadnezzar, who found them ten times better than all the magicians in his realm.

Nebuchadnezzar often had strange dreams. His spirit was troubled and he could not sleep. The king asked Daniel: "Can you explain the dream I have had and what it means?" Daniel answered: "There is a God in heaven who reveals mysteries, and he has disclosed to King Nebuchadnezzar what is to happen in days to come. You saw, O king, a mighty statue of exceeding brightness standing before you, terrible to behold. The head of this statue was made of fine gold, its breast and arms of silver, its belly and thighs of bronze, its legs of iron, and its feet were part iron and part clay. As you looked, a stone struck the feet of the image and shattered them to pieces; then the iron, the clay, the bronze, the silver, and the gold were shattered, and the wind swept them away so that not a trace of them remained. But the stone that struck the image became a great mountain and filled the whole earth.

"This was the dream; now we will tell the king what it means. You, O king, are the golden head. After you shall arise another kingdom, less powerful; then a third kingdom of bronze, which shall rule over all the earth. The fourth kingdom shall be strong as iron; it shall be a divided

kingdom, for you saw iron mixed with the clay. The
vided kingdom will not hold together, just as iron does
mix with clay. In the days of these kings, God will set up a
kingdom which shall never be destroyed. It will smash all
the kingdoms and bring them to an end. For you saw a
stone cut out of the mountain by no human hand and it
broke to pieces the iron, the bronze, the clay, the silver,
and the gold. Great God has revealed to the king what
shall happen in the future."

Then King Nebuchadnezzar gave Daniel high honors
and many great gifts. He made him ruler over the entire
province of Babylon and prefect over all the wise men of
Babylon.

King Nebuchadnezzar once made a golden image, ninety
feet high and nine feet broad. He summoned the officials
of the provinces to appear at its dedication. When they arrived and stood before the image, the herald proclaimed
aloud: "When you hear the sound of the horn and other
kinds of music, you are commanded to fall down and worship the golden image that King Nebuchadnezzar has set
up. Whoever does not bow down and worship shall instantly be cast into a fiery furnace." So, whenever the people heard the sound of the horn and the rest of the music,
they knelt down and worshiped the golden image.

Some Chaldeans maliciously accused Shadrach, Meshach
and Abednego of defying the king's orders. They said to
King Nebuchadnezzar: "These men have paid no heed to
you, O king; they do not serve your gods, and they do not
worship the golden image which you have set up." At this,
Nebuchadnezzar was filled with fury, and his face became
distorted with rage. He ordered the soldiers to bind Shadrach, Meshach and Abednego and cast them into the burning furnace. So hot was the furnace the flames killed the
men who lifted Shadrach, Meshach and Abednego; but
these three fell bound into the flames of the furnace.

Then King Nebuchadnezzar became alarmed, and said:
"I see four men walking in the midst of the flames, and
they are not hurt. The appearance of the fourth is like that
of an angel." Nebuchadnezzar went towards the door of
the fiery furnace, calling: "Shadrach, Meshach and

219

Abednego, servants of the Most High God, come forth and come to me!" The three came out of the fire, and when the governors and the king's ministers gathered round, they saw that the fire had had no effect upon their bodies; their hair had not been singed, and there was no smell of burning about them.

Nebuchadnezzar said: "Blessed be the God of Shadrach, Meshach and Abednego! He has sent his angel to save his servants who trusted in him and surrendered their bodies to the fire rather than serve any god other than their own God." Then the king promoted them in the province of Babylon.

King Nebuchadnezzar to all the nations of the world: "I was at ease in my house, when I saw a dream which alarmed me. I told it to Daniel, saying:

"I saw a tree in the midst of the earth, and its height was great. The tree grew and became strong, till its top reached to heaven and was visible to the very end of the earth. Its leaves were lovely and its fruit was abundant; the beasts of the field took shelter in its shadow, and the birds of the air dwelt in its branches; it provided food for all. And an angel came down from heaven and called aloud: 'Hew down the tree and cut off its branches; shake off its leaves and scatter its fruit. Let the beasts flee from under it and the birds from its branches. Yet leave the stump of its roots in the earth, with a band of iron and bronze round it, amid the tender grass of the field. Let him be drenched with the dew of heaven. Let him share the grass of the earth with the beasts. Let his mind be changed from man's, and let a beast's mind be given to him.'

"I, King Nebuchadnezzar, had this dream. Now, Belteshazzar, tell me what it means. All the wise men of my kingdom are unable to tell me its meaning, but you are able, for the divine spirit is in you."

Then Daniel, whose name was Belteshazzar, replied: "My lord, may the dream be for those who hate you, and its interpretation for your enemies! The tree you saw, which grew and became strong till it was high as heaven and visible to all the word, the tree whose leaves were lovely and whose fruit was rich, providing food for all, the tree under

220

which the beasts of the field sheltered and in whose branches the birds of the air dwelt—it was you, O king! You have grown and become strong. Your power and your dominion stretch to the world's end. O king, it is a decree of the Most High, that you shall be driven from among men, and your dwelling shall be with the beasts of the field. You shall be made to eat grass like an ox, and you shall be drenched with the dew of heaven, and seven years shall pass over you, till you learn that the Most High rules the kingdom of men, and that he gives power to anyone he chooses. Therefore make an end of your sins by practising justice and showing mercy to the oppressed."

Now all this came upon King Nebuchadnezzar. Twelve months later he was walking on the roof of the royal palace in Babylon, saying to himself: "This great Babylon I have built by my vast power and for my glorious majesty." The words had not left his lips when a voice fell from heaven: "O King Nebuchadnezzar, here is your sentence: your kingdom is taken from you! You shall be driven from among men and shall dwell with the beasts of the field; you shall be forced to eat grass like an ox, and seven years shall pass over you until you have learned that the Most High reigns over the realm of men, and gives it to anyone he chooses."

The sentence was carried out instantly upon Nebuchadnezzar. He was driven away from among men. He ate grass like an ox, and his body was drenched with the dew of heaven until his hair resembled the feathers of an eagle, and his nails looked like the claws of a bird.

"When the time had passed, I, Nebuchadnezzar lifted my eyes to heaven, and my reason returned to me. I regained my majesty and splendor and was firmly seated on my throne. Now I praise and honor the King of heaven, for all his deeds are right and his ways are just, and those who walk in pride he is able to humble."

King Belshazzar made a great banquet for a thousand of his lords. Carried away by the wine he drank, Belshazzar commanded that the gold and silver vessels which his father Nebuchadnezzar had taken from the temple in Jerusalem be brought before him. The sacred vessels were brought, and the king, his lords, wives and concubines, drank from them.

That very hour, the fingers of a man's hand appeared and wrote upon the wall of the royal palace, and the king saw the hand as it wrote. The king's color changed, his thoughts alarmed him. His knees knocked against each other. Not one of all the king's wise men could read the writing or explain the meaning of it to him.

Daniel was then brought into the king's presence. He said: "O king, God gave Nebuchadnezzar, your father, greatness and glory and majesty; all nations trembled before him. But when he became arrogant, when his spirit became defiant, he was deposed from his royal throne and deprived of his glory; he was driven away from among men, and his mind was made like that of a beast. He ate grass like an ox, until he learned that the Most High God rules the kingdom of men and that he sets over it whom he chooses. Yet you, his son, O Belshazzar, have not humbled your heart. Though you knew all this, you lifted yourself up against the Lord of heaven. The vessels of his house were brought before you, and you and your lords, your wives and your concubines have drunk wine from them! You have praised the gods of silver and gold which do not see or hear or know; but the God in whose hand is your breath of life and all your destiny you have not honored.

"This is the writing that was inscribed upon the wall: *Mene, Mene, Tekel, Uparsin*. The meaning of it is: *Mene* (numbered), God has numbered the days of your kingdom and brought it to an end; *Tekel* (weighed), you have been weighed in the scales and found wanting; *Peres* (divided), your kingdom is divided and given to the Medes and Persians."

That very night Belshazzar, the Chaldean king was slain, and Darius the Mede captured the kingdom.

The windows in Daniel's room were opened toward Jerusalem, and three times a day he got down upon his knees and prayed to God. Daniel's foes surged in and found him offering prayers and supplications to his God. They went before King Darius and asked: "Did you not sign an edict that any man who makes petition to any god or man within thirty days, except to you, O king, shall be cast into the den of lions?"

"It is true," the king replied. Then they said to the king: "Daniel pays no heed to you, O king; he recites his prayers three times a day to his own god."

When the king heard these words, he was greatly distressed. He worked hard until sundown trying to save Daniel's life, but the men reminded the king that, according to the statutes of the Medes and the Persians, no law laid down by the king could be changed. So Daniel was cast into the den of lions. A stone was brought and laid upon the opening of the den, and the king sealed it with his own signet and with the signet of his lords. Then the king went to his palace, and spent the night fasting.

At daybreak, the king went in haste to the den of lions. When he came near the den, he cried in a tone of anguish: "O Daniel, has your God been able to deliver you from the lions?" Daniel replied: "O king, live forever! My God has sent his angel and shut the mouths of the lions; they have not hurt me. He has found me innocent; nor have I done you any wrong, O king." The king was exceedingly glad, and commanded that Daniel be lifted out of the den. The men who had accused Daniel were then brought and cast into the den of lions; and before they reached the bottom of the pit, the lions crushed their bones to pieces.

Ezra

The books of Ezra and Nehemiah are counted as a single book because they owe their existence to a single compiler. This combined work is called *Ezra* in the Talmud. It is the main authority for that period of Jewish history with which it deals. A considerable part of Ezra-Nehemiah contains the memoirs left by the two leaders who organized Jewish life in Judea.

The book of Ezra describes the activities of a new figure in Judaism—the scribe, who took the place of the prophet after the return of the Jews from the Babylonian captivity. The scribes made available copies of the Scriptures, and carefully interpreted and taught them to the people.

Accompanied by fifteen hundred exiles, Ezra, the scribe, arrived in Jerusalem in 450. According to talmudic tradition, Ezra was the founder of the Great Assembly, a body of spiritual leaders, described as the successors to the prophets in keeping alive the knowledge of the Torah.

The book of Nehemiah, however, is written mostly in the first person singular. It tells of the experiences of Nehemiah, a cupbearer of the Persian king, Artaxerxes, who was twice governor of Jerusalem in 445 and 433. The noble character of Nehemiah, his strong self-reliance combined with a serene trust in God, are vividly portrayed in the story of his zealous endeavors to restore the ruined city of Jerusalem and rebuild its walls.

The Lord inspired Cyrus king of Persia to issue a proclamation permitting the Jews of his realm to return to Jerusalem and rebuild the temple.

The tribes of Judah and Benjamin, the priests and the Levites, prepared to go. Their neighbors helped them with silver and gold, goods and beasts of burden and costly things—all freely offered. The entire company numbered forty-two thousand three hundred and sixty, besides seven thousand three hundred and thirty-seven servants and two hundred singers. They had seven hundred and thirty-six horses, two hundred and forty-five mules, four hundred and thirty-five camels, and six thousand seven hundred and twenty donkeys.

They hired masons and carpenters to rebuild the temple. They traded food, drink, and oil with the Sidonians and Tyrians for cedars brought down from Lebanon to the sea-coast at Jaffa. Zerubbabel appointed Levites to superintend the work on the house of the Lord. When the builders laid the foundation of the temple, the priests and the Levites came forward with trumpets and cymbals to praise the Lord with the refrain: "He is good, his kindness endures forever." All the people raised a mighty shout as they praised the Lord. But many of the priests and Levites, old men who had seen the first temple, wept aloud at the sight of this house.

When the enemies of Judah and Benjamin heard that the returned exiles were building a temple, they came and said to Zerubbabel and the heads of the tribes: "Let us build with you, for we worship your God as you do; we have been sacrificing to him ever since the king of Assyria brought us here." But Zerubbabel and the other leaders told them: "You can have nothing to do with building a house to our God; we will build it ourselves, as King Cyrus has commanded us."

The people of the land harassed the men of Judah and terrorized them. In a letter to Artaxerxes king of Persia, they wrote: "Be it known to the king that the Jews have come to Jerusalem. They are rebuilding that rebellious and wicked city. Be it known to the king that if this city is rebuilt, they will not pay tribute, tax, or toll, and the royal revenue will suffer; you will also lose all your territory west of the Euphrates." This put an end to the work on the temple. The rebuilding of the temple did not begin again until the second year of the reign of Darius, king of Persia.

Zerubbabel and Jeshua, aided by the prophets Haggai and Zechariah, started once more to rebuild the temple of God at Jerusalem. Then came the governor of the province, and his associates and asked: "Who gave you permission to build this temple? What are the names of the men who are building here?" However, they did not stop the construction but reported the matter to Darius, who replied with these instructions:

"Let the governor and the elders of the Jews rebuild the house of God on its site. The cost is to be covered from the royal treasury without delay. Day by day without fail, let them have whatever they require, that they may offer sacrifices and pray for the life of the king and his children." The governor and his associates acted promptly on the king's instructions and the elders of the Jews built and prospered. The temple was finished in the sixth year of the reign of King Darius.

The people of Israel, the priests and the Levites and the rest of the returned exiles, celebrated the dedication of this house of God with joy. On the fourteenth day of the first month the returned exiles observed the Passover. For seven days the festival of unleavened bread was celebrated with joy, for the Lord had made them joyful by turning the heart of the king of Assyria towards them, to encourage them in their work on the temple of the God of Israel.

It was after this that Ezra, who was a scribe skilled in the Torah of Moses, came from Babylon to Jerusalem accompanied by Israelites, priests, Levites, singers, wardens and temple attendants. He had set his heart upon studying the Torah, upon obeying it and upon teaching it in Israel.

Then the leaders approached Ezra and said: "The people of Israel and the priests and the Levites have not separated themselves from the abominable practices of the Canaanites, the Ammonites, and the Egyptians; they have married their daughters and married their sons to their daughters." When Ezra heard this, he rent his garments, tore his hair, and sat down aghast. At the evening offering he rose from his fasting, and spread out his hands to the Lord God, saying:

"O my God, I am ashamed, I blush to lift my face to thee; our guilt has mounted up to the skies. O our God, what shall we say? We have forsaken the commandments which thou didst send through thy servants the prophets, saying: 'The land which you are entering to possess is polluted with the abominations of the peoples, who have filled it with their uncleanness from end to end. Therefore give not your daughters to their sons, neither take their daughters for your sons, that you may be strong and eat the good of the land.' O Lord God of Israel, here we stand guilty before thee; none of us can stand before thee because of this."

As Ezra prayed and made confession, weeping and prostrating himself before the house of God, he was joined by a very large gathering of men, women and children, who wept bitterly. Shecaniah said to Ezra: "We have broken faith with our God and have married foreign wives from among the natives. Still, there is some hope for Israel in spite of all this. Let us put away our wives and their children. Let us act according to the Torah. We are with you; be strong and take action."

Then Ezra withdrew from the house of God into a room of Johanan, where he neither ate bread nor drank water, for he was mourning over the faithlessness of the returned exiles. A proclamation was then issued throughout Judah that all should assemble at Jerusalem and, if anyone failed to appear within three days, all his property should be confiscated and he himself excommunicated.

Within three days all the men of Judah and Benjamin assembled at Jerusalem. They sat in the open square before the house of God, shivering from fear as well as from the chill of the heavy rain. Ezra, the priest, rose and said to them: "You have broken faith and married foreign wives. Now make confession to the Lord God of your fathers and do his will; separate yourselves from the natives and from your foreign wives." The assembly answered with a loud voice: "Truly, we shall do as you have said. But the people are many, and it is the rainy season; we cannot stand in the open; and this is not work for a day or two, for we have greatly transgressed in this matter. Let all in our towns who have married foreign wives come at appointed times before the judges and elders." Then the returned exiles took action and by the first day of the first month all had divorced their foreign wives.

Nehemiah

These are the words of Nehemiah:

It happened in the month of Kislev, when I was in Shushan the capital, that one of my kinsmen came from Judah with a few men. I asked them about the Jews and about Jerusalem. They told me that the returned exiles were suffering great misery and shame; that the wall of Jerusalem was broken down and that the gates were destroyed by fire. When I heard this, I sat down and wept.

I was cupbearer to the king. He said to me: "Why is your face sad? You are not ill. This must be sadness of heart." I replied: "May the king live forever! Why should not my face be sad, when the city of Jerusalem lies waste and its gates have been destroyed by fire?" Then the king said: "What request have you to make?" I answered: "If it please the king, pray let me go to the city where my fathers are buried, that I may rebuild it." The king asked: "How long will you be gone?" I proposed a certain time to him, and it pleased him to allow me to go.

I also requested that letters be given me to the governors west of the Euphrates, permitting me to proceed to Judah and, also, a letter to Asaph, the keeper of the king's forest, to give me timber for the gates of the fortress of the temple, for the wall of the city and for the house in which I would live.

The king granted my request, for the good hand of my God was upon me. The king also sent with me some army officers and horsemen. When Sanballat the Samaritan and the Ammonite slave, Tobiah, heard of this, they were greatly incensed that a man had come to promote the welfare of the people of Israel.

After spending three days in Jerusalem, I got up during the night and inspected the broken walls and the gates. I came back and said to the people: "You see how Jerusalem lies in ruins. Come, let us rebuild the wall." "Let us start to build," they replied, and they set about their task with vigor. But when Sanballat heard that we were rebuilding the wall, he was furious. He said to his fellow Samaritans: "What are these feeble Jews doing? Will they restore things? Will they revive the stones out of the heaps of rubbish?" Tobiah, the Ammonite, added: "Let them build! If a fox stepped on that stone wall of theirs, he would knock it down!"

So we rebuilt the wall to half its height all round, for the heart of the people was in their work. But when Sanballat and Tobiah and the Ammonites and the Ashdodites heard that the walls of Jerusalem were being repaired, they were extremely angry. They then conspired to fight against Jerusalem. But we offered prayers to our God and posted guards to watch both day and night. I stationed men armed with sword and spear and bow and said to them: "Do not be afraid of them! Remember the Lord and fight for your sons, your daughters, your wives and your homes."

Half of my retinue worked on construction, and half held the spears, shields, bows, and coats of mail, protecting all those who were building the wall. The laborers were armed. Each of them worked with one hand, and held a weapon in the other. Each mason was girded with a sword. The bugler stood beside me. I said to the people: "The work is widely spread and we are far apart from each other on the wall; so, whenever you hear the bugle sound, rally to us there. Our God will fight for us." As for myself and my associates, none of us took off our clothes, and each of us kept his weapon in his hand at all times.

Then a loud outcry arose among the people. Some demanded: "Let us have food to keep us alive!" Others complained: "We are mortgaging our fields, our vineyards, and our houses to get food in the famine." Others cried: "We had to borrow money to pay the king's tax. We forced our sons and daughters to be slaves and we have no money to buy them back, for our fields and vineyards are in the hands of others."

When I heard their complaints, I was deeply moved. I brought charges against the nobles and officials, and said to them: "You are taking interest from your own people. We have done all we could to buy back our fellow Jews who have been sold to the heathens, and you would sell them back to us!"

They were silent, and could not find a word to say. So I went on: "The thing you are doing is not good. Come, let us stop taking interest from the people. Restore to them, this very day, their vineyards, their olive yards and their houses with the interest on the money and the food that you have been taking from them."

They replied: "We will do as you say." I summoned the priests, and took an oath of the money-lenders to do as they had promised.

From the time that I was appointed to be the governor in the land of Judah, for twelve years neither I nor my associates ate the food allowance of the governor. The governors who were before me had laid heavy burdens upon the people, and taken food and wine from them. Even the servants lorded it over the people. But I did not; I revered the Lord. I entertained at my table a hundred and fifty Jews who had come to us from the surrounding lands. My daily provision was one ox and six choice sheep. My God, remember all that I have done for this people.

Once the wall was built, I put Jerusalem in charge of Hanani and Hananiah. I said to them: "The gates of Jerusalem are not to be opened until the sun is high. Arrange guards from among the inhabitants of Jerusalem, each to be posted opposite his own house." The city was wide and large, but there were few people and houses had not been built.

On the first day of the seventh month, Ezra the scribe brought the Torah before the community, both men and women and all who could listen intelligently; he read from it, in the open space in front of the water gate, from early morning until noon, and all the people listened closely. Ezra stood on a wooden platform; and when he opened the book, all the people rose. Then Ezra blessed the Lord, and all the people answered "Amen, Amen," raising their hands; they bowed their heads and worshiped the Lord with their faces to the ground.

Chronicles

The first and second books of Chronicles count as one book. They contain a historical record dating from the creation of the world to the end of the Babylonian captivity. Unlike the book of Kings, which covers the history of the kingdoms of Israel and Judah, Chronicles is confined to the story of the kingdom of Judah only, and completely ignores the northern kingdom of Israel. The religious view presented by Chronicles is the conviction that history is not made by chance. Only those events are treated which illustrate a divine purpose and providence.

David defeated the Philistines and subdued them; he defeated Moab, and the Moabites became his subjects. He defeated the king of Zobah, and captured a thousand chariots. When the Syrians came to aid the king of Zobah, David slew twenty-two thousand of them, and then posted a garrison in Syria. This made the Syrians subject to David, and they brought him tribute. He posted garrisons throughout Edom, and all the Edomites became his subjects. Indeed, wherever David went, the Lord gave him victory.

Now David sent messengers to condole with Hanun, the Ammonite king, whose father had died. But the Ammonite princes said to Hanun: "Do you think that David is honoring your father by sending you comforters? His officers have come to explore and overthrow the country." So Hanun seized David's officers, shaved them, cut off their robes as far as their waists, and sent them away. When David was told what had happened to the men, he sent messengers to meet them, for they were greatly ashamed. "Stay at Jericho," he counseled, "until your beards are grown, and then return." In the spring, Joab besieged Rabbah, the capital city of Ammon; he stormed and overthrew it. Then the royal crown of the Ammonites was placed on David's head.

David told Joab to go and number Israel from Beer-sheba to Dan. So Joab went throughout all Israel and came back to Jerusalem. He reported to David that in all Israel there were one million one hundred thousand men-at-arms, while the tribe of Judah numbered four hundred and seventy thousand men-at-arms. Joab did not include the tribes of Levi and Benjamin in the numbering, for the king's order was detestable to him.

God was displeased with this action, so the seer, Gad, told David: "Thus says the Lord: Three things I offer you; choose one of them: three years of famine, three months of sweeping defeat by your foes, or three days of the Lord's sword and pestilence in the land." Then David said to Gad: "Let me fall into the hand of the Lord, for his mercy is very great; but let me not fall into the hand of man."

So the Lord sent a pestilence, and there fell seventy thousand men of Israel. Then the Lord said to the destroying angel: "It is enough; now stay your hand." When David raised his eyes, he saw the angel of the Lord standing between earth and heaven, holding a drawn sword over Jerusalem, so he said to God: "It was I who gave command to number the people. It is I who have sinned and acted wickedly. But these sheep, what have they done? Let thy hand, Lord my God, be against me and against my father's house, not against my people." Then the Lord commanded the angel, and the angel put the sword back into its sheath. And David said: "Here shall be the house of the Lord God."

David charged Solomon his son to build a house for the Lord God of Israel, saying: "My son, I myself intended to build a temple for the Lord my God. But the word of the Lord came to me: 'You have shed much blood, you have waged great wars; you shall not build a house to my name, because you have shed so much blood on earth. Behold, a son shall be born to you who shall be a man of peace. I will grant him peace from all his enemies round about, for his name shall be *Sh'lomoh*, Solomon, and I will give peace and quiet to Israel in his days. He shall build a house for my name. He shall be my son, and I will be a father to him; I will establish his royal throne over Israel.' Now, my son, may the Lord be with you, that you may succeed in building the temple of the Lord your God, as he has directed you. Be strong and of good courage. Fear not, be not dismayed. You have plenty of workmen, masons, carpenters, and all kinds of craftsmen. There is no end of gold, silver, bronze, and iron. Set to work, and may the Lord be with you!"

David blessed the Lord before all the assembly and said: "Blessed art thou, O Lord, God of Israel our Father, forever and ever. Thine, O Lord, is the greatness and the power, the glory and the victory and the majesty, for all that is in heaven and on earth is thine; thine, O Lord, is the kingdom, and thou art supreme over all. Riches and honor come from thee; thou rulest over all; in thy hand are power and might, and it is in thy power to make all great and strong. Hence, our God, we ever thank thee and praise thy glorious name."

Then Solomon began to build the house of the Lord in Jerusalem on Mount Moriah. When the temple was finished, Solomon brought in the things which David his father had dedicated, the silver and the gold, and all the other articles, and placed them in the treasuries of the temple of God. Then all the men of Israel assembled before the king at the festival in the seventh month. The Levites brought up the ark, the tent of meeting, and all the holy vessels that were in the tent. The priests brought the ark of the covenant of the Lord to its place, in the inner sanctuary of the house, in the most holy place, underneath the wings of the cherubim.

At the end of twenty years, in the course of which Solomon had built the house of the Lord and his own palace, he rebuilt the towns which Huram had given to him, and settled Israelites in them. He built Tadmor in the wilderness and all the store-towns, the towns for his chariots, the towns for his cavalry, and whatever he was pleased to build in Jerusalem, in Lebanon, and anywhere throughout his dominion. Then Solomon went to Ezion-geber and Eloth on the seacoast, in the land of Edom. Huram sent him ships and expert seamen, who accompanied Solomon's men to Ophir and brought back to King Solomon over nineteen tons of gold. The amount of gold that came to Solomon in one year was nearly twenty-nine tons, in addition to what was derived in taxes from traders and merchants. Arabian kings and princes, too, brought gold and silver to Solomon. In wealth and in wisdom King Solomon excelled all kings on earth.

After a period of nearly four hundred years, King Zedekiah did what was evil in the sight of the Lord his God. He would not humble himself before the prophet Jeremiah, and he rebelled against King Nebuchadnezzar; he hardened his heart and obstinately refused to turn to the Lord God of Israel. The leading priests and the people were likewise exceedingly unfaithful, copying the abominable practices of the pagans and defiling the temple which the Lord had hallowed in Jerusalem. They mocked God's messengers, despised his words, and scoffed at his prophets, until the wrath of the Lord burst upon the people, till there was no remedy. He brought down on them the king of the Chaldeans, who killed their young and old and had no compassion. All the treasures of the temple of the Lord, and the treasures belonging to the king and to his nobles, the Chaldean king took away to Babylon. The house of God and all the buildings of Jerusalem were burned; all the costly vessels were destroyed. The Chaldean king carried the survivors off to Babylon, where they became servants to him and to his sons until the establishment of the Persian empire. All this, in fulfillment of what the Lord had foretold through Jeremiah, that the land was to lie desolate for seventy years.

Then the Lord stirred up the spirit of Cyrus, king of Persia to issue a proclamation throughout all his kingdom, permitting reconstruction of the House of God at Jerusalem.

Apocrypha

The books of the Apocrypha represent a substantial and remarkable religious-ethical literature compiled and written during the period of the Second Temple. They reflect the developments of social and religious life among the Jewish people and the foreign influences to which they were subjected during the second commonwealth.

These books are referred to as *Apocrypha* (hidden away) because they were produced after the time of Ezra, the scribe, and were not included in the Hebrew Bible, since direct revelation had ceased with the passing of the prophets.

The Talmud refers to the apocryphal books as *sefarim hitzonim,* "outside books." Though these books were originally produced by Jews, some in Hebrew and some in Aramaic, they have come down to us in the ancient Greek version of the Bible known as the Septuagint.

The book of Tobit is the earliest of all the apocryphal books. It introduces the reader to the kind of home in which the Jew lived more than two thousand years ago. In this book are enshrined the high ideals of the Jewish people, such as the purity of family life and the duty of kindness to the poor. It has in its plot the framework of a complete novel.

The book of Ben Sira, known as Ecclesiasticus, was translated from Hebrew into Greek by the author's grandson in the year 132. Some sixty years ago, about two-thirds of the Hebrew text was recovered in manuscripts found in the famous Genizah or hiding place of Cairo, Egypt, where it had been customary for many centuries to deposit old Hebrew books.

Much of Ben Sira's counsel, from which many of us can profit, concerns practical affairs, physical health and good manners. The proverbs in this book are an admirable collection covering a wide range of subjects and should be read slowly, a little at a time, for a true appreciation of their full meaning.

Containing fifty-one chapters, and written by a man who had the gift for clear and forceful expression, the book of Ben Sira reminds one of the biblical books of Proverbs, Ecclesiastes and Job.

Tobit

I, Tobit, did many acts of charity for my people who were exiled to Nineveh with me. One of the Ninevites informed King Sennacherib that I was burying many Judeans whom he had killed, so he tried to put me to death; but I escaped. After two months Sennacherib was killed, and I returned home. I said to my son: "Go and bring any poor man of our brothers, and I will wait for you." He came back and said: "Father, one of our people has been strangled and thrown out in the marketplace." I rushed out and brought him into a room; when the sun was set, I dug a grave and buried him. That same night I became blind. I called my son Tobias and said:

My son, do not neglect your mother; provide for her as long as you live; try to please her—do not be a cause of grief to her. Remember that she faced many dangers for your sake.

Act uprightly all your life and do not follow the ways of wrongdoers. You will succeed in life if you are truthful.

Do not give to charity grudgingly. God will not ignore you if you do not ignore the poor.

Give to charity according to your means; if you have little, do not hesitate to give little. Charity saves a person from death.

Do not marry a stranger who does not belong to your father's people, for we are descendants of the prophets. Remember that our forefathers long ago married wives from among their own kindred.

You must not keep overnight the wages of any man who works for you; you must pay him immediately.

Do not do to anyone else that which is hateful to you.

Ben Sira

A man who keeps silent is considered wise.
A man who talks excessively is detested.
Healthy sleep results from moderation in eating.
A thief is better than a habitual liar.
A fool raises his voice when he laughs.
Happy is the man who has a good wife.
A quiet, silent wife is a gift from the Lord.
The man who sets a trap for others will be caught in it himself.
Sorrow has destroyed many; there is no profit in it.
Envy and anger shorten a man's life.
Worry makes a man old before his time.
When you are at the table, do not be the first to help yourself.
Speak concisely; say much in a few words.
Do not sell yourself to anybody as long as you have breath.
It is better that your children should ask for things from you than that you should ask from them.
The man who fears the Lord will fear no man.
Be on your guard against advisers.
Conceal your plans from those who envy you.
Do not be known as a talebearer or as one who sets an ambush with his tongue.
Do not follow your impulses, but curb your longing.
Do not indulge in too much luxury, or be tied down by its expenses.
Flee from sin as you would from a serpent, for like a serpent it will bite you if you go near it.
Forgive your fellow man for his wrongdoings, then your own sins will be forgiven.

The Twelve Testaments

The Testaments of the Twelve Patriarchs belong to the Apocalyptic Literature which had a marked influence on the development of Jewish life and thought. The word *apocalypse* signifies revelation, vision. The apocalyptic books are based on a moral and religious interpretation of the history of the world. Originally written in Hebrew or Aramaic, the Testaments of the Twelve Patriarchs are represented as a record of the dying declarations and instructions of the twelve sons of Jacob. Each in turn recounts the story of his life and asks his descendants to emulate his virtues and shun his vices.

My children, pay no heed to the beauty of lewd women; do not let your mind dwell on them, but rather set yourself to the performance of good works.

Beware of deceit and envy. Envy controls the whole mind of a man and does not let him do anything good. It goads him into frenzy, causes tumult in his soul and trembling in his body.

Work diligently to acquire wisdom. Cities and lands may be destroyed; gold, silver and possessions may perish; but no one can take away a person's wisdom. Whoever teaches noble things and performs them shall rise high.

Both the works of truth and the works of deceit are written in the hearts of men, and the Lord knows each and everyone of them. The sinner is consumed by his own conscience and cannot raise his head before the judge.

Lead a life of sincerity. A single-minded man does not covet money or cheat his neighbor. He is not ruled by the spirit of deceit. There is no envy in his thoughts nor is he overcome by insatiable desires. Love the Lord and your neighbor. Have pity on the poor and the weak.

Be compassionate toward all persons and animals. Do not hesitate to show kindness and mercy to all creatures. When waters flow together, they sweep along stones, trees and earth; but if they are divided into many streams, the earth swallows them up and they become of no account. So shall you be if you are divided.

Anger is blind and does not permit one to see the face of anyone as it really is. An angry person behaves even toward his own father and mother as if they were enemies; he has no regard either for a good man or a personal friend. Do not become angry when someone speaks against you; do not become vain when you are praised. Do not be distressed if you suffer a loss. Shun anger; hate lying; speak the truth to your neighbor, and love each other with a true heart.

Sun, moon and stars do not change their course; nor shall you change the law of God by disorderly behavior. You shall recognize in the sky, in the earth, in the sea and in all created things, the Lord who made all things.

Hatred is evil; it goes hand in hand with lying; it makes small things appear great; it leads to slander and stirs up war; it fills the heart with evil and poison. Thrust hatred from your heart; love one another from the heart. If someone commits a sin against you, speak peaceably to him; if he repents and confesses, forgive him. If a man is more successful than you, do not become vexed over it. Put envy out of your souls, and love one another with singleness of heart.

There are two sides to every matter; the one is hidden by the other. Greed is hidden in wealth; drunkenness in conviviality; grief in laughter; lechery in wedlock. Death succeeds life; dishonor succeeds glory; night follows day; and darkness follows light.

Be patient with one another's faults and overlook them. If someone tries to wrong you, treat him well and pray for him; the Lord will keep you from all harm.

A good man shows mercy to everyone, even to sinners. He is neither envious nor jealous of others, but rejoices always in their good fortune. He does not have two tongues —one for blessing and another for cursing; one for hypocrisy and another for truth. In everything he does or says, he remembers that the Lord looks into his soul.

239

Second Maccabees

The first book of Maccabees describes the rise of the Maccabean revolt and covers the period between 175 and 135 before the common era.

The second book of the Maccabees is a summary of a larger work composed by one Jason of Cyrene about whom nothing is known. The author of this book writes in chapter two:

"All that has been related by Jason of Cyrene in five books we will try to condense into one volume . . . We have aimed at attracting those who like to read . . . For us, who have taken upon ourselves the painful task of abridgment, the thing is not easy . . . just as it is no easy matter for a man to prepare a banquet and strive to benefit others."

The second book of the Maccabees describes the events of the Maccabean uprising, a period of fifteen years, from 175 to 160. Filled with stories of defiant martyrdom, this book leads us through the heroic struggle of the Jews against pagan forces, a struggle which proved decisive in forming the character of the Jewish people and has enabled many to face persecution with triumphant courage.

The third book of Maccabees has nothing to do with the Maccabees or their time. It received its name probably from the fact that its narrative concerns the persecution of the Jews by a foreign king. According to this narrative, Ptolemy assembled the Jews of Alexandria, Egypt, in the hippodrome to be massacred. They escaped death because the necessity of writing down their names exhausted the supply of paper. After another attempt to destroy the Jews, the king underwent a change of heart and bestowed great favor on them.

The fourth book of Maccabees is a philosophic discourse on the supremacy of piety and reason. The only connection this book has with the Maccabees is in the fact that the author's illustrations are drawn from the second book of the Maccabees.

King Antiochus sent one of his henchmen to compel the Jews to forsake the laws of their forefathers. They were no

240

longer allowed to keep the Sabbath or celebrate their festivals, or even bear Jewish names. A decree was issued that anyone who refused to adopt the heathen customs of the Greeks was to be put to death. Two women were publicly murdered for having circumcised their children. Jews, who gathered in a cave to keep the Sabbath in secret, were burned alive.

Elazar, a leading scholar of advanced age and noble appearance, chose to die a martyr rather than eat forbidden food. He was privately urged to pretend that he was eating, and thus escape the death penalty; but he refused, declaring that he would not lead his people to suppose that he, at the age of ninety, had embraced paganism. "By manfully giving up my life now," he said, "I will prove myself worthy of my great age and leave to the young people a noble example of how to die willingly and nobly for the sake of the holy way of life."

With these words he went straight to the torture wheel. And so he died, leaving, in his death, a memorial of virtue to his entire nation.

Seven brothers and their mother were arrested and urged by the king to taste the forbidden food. "We are ready to die," one of them cried out, "rather than transgress the laws of our forefathers." Infuriated, the king commanded that his tongue be cut out in the presence of his brothers and his mother. However, his family encouraged him to die nobly.

"Will you eat, or have your body torn limb from limb?" the tormentors asked the second brother. When he answered no, he was made to undergo the same torture that his brother had suffered. And so they tormented each one in turn while the mother stood by surpassingly courageous. Filled with a noble spirit, she encouraged each one of them. When Antiochus appealed to the youngest brother, promising him a rich reward if he would give up the ways of his forefathers, he too refused. Mocking the cruel tyrant, his mother whispered to him: "I beseech you, my child, do not be afraid of this butcher; show yourself worthy of your brothers and accept death."

Before she could finish speaking, the young boy shouted:

"What are you waiting for? I will not obey the command of the king! I will obey the command of the Torah! You will not escape the hands of God for having designed every kind of evil against the Jewish people." In a rage, the king tortured him more than the others, whereupon the mother went up to a nearby roof top and threw herself to the ground.

Judah Maccabee secretly enlisted six thousand loyal Jews, and told them not to fear the vast heathen multitude but to fight nobly. "They trust in arms," he said, "but we trust in the Almighty God." He put each of his four brothers in command of a division consisting of fifteen hundred men. Then he joined battle with Nicanor, who was in command of some twenty thousand heathen of various nationalities striving to annihilate the Jewish people.

But the Almighty was the ally of the Jews, who disabled most of Nicanor's army and forced them all to flee. They captured the money of a thousand slave-dealers whom Nicanor had brought along to buy Jewish captives. They gave some of the spoils to the wounded and to the widows and orphans. Nicanor fled to the city of Antioch, where he made it known that the Jews were invulnerable because of their religion and way of life.

Now Judah Maccabee and his followers regained the Temple and the city, and tore down the altars that had been built up by the pagans. Having purified the sanctuary, they offered sacrifices after an interval of two years. The dedication of the sanctuary took place on the twenty-fifth day of Kislev. They celebrated it for eight days, and recalled how a little while before, during the Sukkoth festival, they had been wandering about in the mountains and caverns like wild animals. They passed a decree that all the people of Israel should observe these eight days every year.

Scroll of the Hasmoneans

The Scroll of the Hasmoneans, known also as the Scroll of Antiochus, has come down to us in both Aramaic and Hebrew. The Hebrew version is a literal translation from the Aramaic original which was composed probably in the seventh century. Rav Saadyah Gaon of the tenth century attributed its authorship to the five sons of Mattathias. It still forms part of the liturgy of the Yemenite Jews.

Concerning the Scroll of the Hasmoneans, otherwise known as *Megillath Antiochus,* Dr. Julius H. Greenstone writes in his Jewish *Fasts and Feasts:* "Among the Jews of the Middle Ages, another source for the story of the Maccabees was known under the name of Scroll of Antiochus, often found included in the more complete editions of the Prayer Book. The first reference to this scroll is found in the works of Saadyah (tenth century). Names and events are here confused and legends are given as historic occurrences. The author apparently drew largely upon the midrashic interpretations of the Hanukkah story, although the first book of the Maccabees was not unknown to him. It is strange that this was the chief source for a knowledge of the Maccabean struggle, known to the Jews of the entire period of the Middle Ages up to modern days. It is quite likely that its legendary nature and the many stories which it graphically depicts contributed to making it popular and acceptable to medieval Jewry."

During the Middle Ages this *Megillah* or scroll was read in the Italian synagogues on Hanukkah, the festival of lights celebrated for eight days in memory of the Maccabean victory, as the book of Esther is read on Purim.

King Antiochus was a powerful ruler who subdued many and mighty sovereigns. He destroyed their castles, burned their palaces and imprisoned their men. Since the reign of Alexander there had not been a king like him beyond the Euphrates.

In the twenty-third year of his reign, Antiochus determined to march on Jerusalem. He said to his officers: "You are aware that the Jews neither offer sacrifices to our gods nor observe our laws. They hope moreover for the day when kings and tyrants shall be crushed. It is a disgrace for the royal government to let them remain on the face of the earth. Come now, let us attack them and abolish the covenant made with them: their sabbath, their festivals and circumcision."

Immediately King Antiochus dispatched his general with a large body of troops, who came to Jerusalem and massacred many people and set up a heathen altar in the Temple. When Mattathias heard of this deed, he was filled with rage. He set out and fought the enemy, inflicting heavy slaughter on them. Upon returning, he erected a column with the inscription: "Maccabee, Destroyer of Tyrants."

When Antiochus heard that his general had been slain, he was bitterly distressed. He sent for general Bagris and ordered him to attack the Israelites. Thereupon wicked Bagris and his hosts invaded Jerusalem, murdered the population and proclaimed an absolute decree against the sabbath, the festivals and circumcision. So drastic was the king's edict that when a man was discovered to have circumcised his son, he and his wife were hanged along with the child.

A woman gave birth to a son after her husband's death and had him circumcised when he was eight days old. With the child in her arms, she went up on top of the wall of Jerusalem and cried out: "We say to you, wicked Bagris: This covenant of our fathers which you intend to destroy shall never cease for us nor for our children's children." She cast her son to the ground and flung herself after him so that they died together. Many Israelites of that period did the same, refusing to renounce the covenant of their fathers.

Some of the Jews said to one another: "Come, let us keep the Sabbath in a cave lest we violate it." When they were betrayed to Bagris, he dispatched armed men who sat at the entrance of the cave and said: "You Jews, surrender to us! Eat of our bread, drink of our wine, and do what we do!" But the Jews said to one another: "It is better for us to die than to desecrate the Sabbath." When they failed to come out, wood was brought and a fire set at the entrance of the cave. About a thousand men and women died there. Later the five sons of Mattathias, Yoḥanan and his four brothers, set out and routed the hostile forces, whom they drove to the coast.

Wicked Bagris invaded Jerusalem for the second time. He broke through the wall, shattered the gateway, made thirteen breaches in the Temple, and ground the stones to dust. He thought to himself: "This time they shall not defeat me; my army is numerous, my hand is mighty." However, God did not think so.

The names of the five sons of Mattathias were: Judah, the firstborn; Simeon, the second; Yoḥanan, the third; Jonathan, the fourth; Elazar, the fifth. Their father blessed them, saying: "Judah my son, I compare you to Judah the son of Jacob who was likened to a lion. Simeon my son, I compare you to Simeon the son of Jacob who slew the men of Shechem. Yoḥanan my son, I compare you to Abner the son of Ner, general of Israel's army. Jonathan my son, I compare you to Jonathan the son of Saul who defeated the Philistines. Elazar, my son, I compare you to Phinehas the son of Elazar, who was zealous for his God and rescued the Israelites."

Soon afterward the five sons of Mattathias attacked the pagan forces, inflicting severe losses upon them. One of the brothers, Judah, was killed. When the sons of Mattathias discovered that Judah had been slain, they returned to their father, who asked: "Why did you come back?" They replied: "Our brother Judah, who alone equalled all of us, has been killed." "I will join you in the battle against the heathen," Mattathias said, "lest they destroy the house of Israel; why be so dismayed over your brother?" He joined his sons that same day and waged war against the enemy. God delivered into their hands swordsmen and archers, officers and high officials. Many others were compelled to seek refuge in the coastal cities. When King Antiochus heard that Bagris and the army officers had been killed, he boarded a ship and fled. Wherever he went the people rebelled and called him "The Fugitive," so he drowned himself in the sea.

The Hasmoneans entered the sanctuary, rebuilt the gates, closed the breaches and cleansed the Temple court from the slain and the impurities. They looked for pure olive oil to light the Menorah, and found only one bottle with the seal of the high priest so that they were sure of its purity. Though its quantity seemed sufficient only for one day's lighting, it lasted for eight days owing to God's blessing. Hence, the Hasmoneans and all the Jews alike instituted these eight days as a time of feasting and re-joicing, like any festival prescribed in the Torah, and of kindling lights to commemorate the victories God had given them.

From that time on the Greek government was stripped of its renown. The Hasmoneans and their descendants ruled for two hundred and six years, until the destruc-tion of the Temple.

Thus, the Jews everywhere observe this festival for eight days, beginning on the twenty-fifth of Kislev. These days, instituted by priests, Levites and sages of Temple times, shall be celebrated by their descendants forever.

Josephus

Josephus Flavius (37–105) was born in Jerusalem and died in Rome. He was one of the military leaders of the Jews in their struggle for independence against Rome, and later he became their historian.

According to his own account, Josephus spent three years in the desert as an ascetic, denying himself the pleasures of life. He probably lived among the Essenes, who despised trade and wealth and considered it their duty to help the poor, the weak and the aged. This Jewish sect disappeared with the destruction of the Second Temple.

Josephus wrote his autobiography, which makes us more familiar with him than with any other Jewish author of antiquity. After the outbreak of the Jewish revolt against Rome, Josephus was made a general in Galilee, but he proved a complete failure. He surrendered to the Romans, and later acted as an adviser to Titus during the siege of Jerusalem. After the fall of Jerusalem he accompanied the victors to Rome, where he devoted himself to the writing of two works: a history of the war with Rome, and a history of the Jewish people from the time of creation until the outbreak of the revolt against Rome. His account of Jewish history is tinged with admiration for the Romans, whom he excuses for burning the Temple in the year 70. Josephus did not have a very good reputation among his own people, and was completely ignored by the authors of the Talmud.

Philo of Alexandria, the famous philosopher of Hellenistic Judaism, visited Jerusalem in his youth, about the beginning of the first century, and he may have come in personal contact with the Essenes, described by Josephus in the following selection.

According to a description by Philo, the Essenes were a sect of Jews, numbering more than four thousand, who lived in villages and avoided cities, in order to escape the contagion of evil. No maker of war weapons was to be found among them. They felt that the law of nature made all men free and that slavery was a violation of this law. They were chiefly pre occupied with ethics, and taught piety, holiness, justice, love of God and man. Their love of virtue revealed itself in their indifference to money, worldly position and pleasure. No one lived in a private house, but shared his dwelling with all the rest. They threw open their doors to any of their sect who happened to stop by. The aged among them were treated with reverence and honor.

In the war against the Romans, many of the Essenes died under torture rather than blaspheme Moses the lawgiver or eat unclean food. Some scholars have recently identified the Essenes with the Qumran sectarians, whose colonies were near the place where the Dead Sea Scrolls were discovered in the spring of 1947.

The Sect of the Essenes

The Essenes shun pleasure as a vice. They adopt other men's children and train them according to their own principles. They despise riches, and there is no one among them who owns more than another. They have a rule that new members must surrender their property to the brotherhood. You will never see them either in dire poverty or excessive wealth. Like brothers, they share equally in whatever the community possesses. The interests of the community are taken care of by selected officers.

There are many Essenes in every town. Members of the sect who arrive from other places have at their disposal all the resources of the community. They enter the homes of people they have never seen before, as though they were intimate friends. For this reason, they carry nothing with them on a journey except weapons to protect them against robbers.

In every city there is a special official whose duty it is to welcome strangers and provide them with everything they need. They do not throw away their clothes or shoes until they are worn to shreds. There is no buying or selling among them; each gives what he has to those in need and receives in exchange what he himself can use. They can also take from their members without making a return.

The Essenes do not speak about worldly things before sunrise, but recite prayers that have been handed down to them from their forefathers. Immediately afterward, they set out to do the various tasks assigned to them. They work strenuously for four hours. Then they gather in one place, bathe in cold water and go to a special building which the uninitiated may not enter. Here they meet in the dining room as solemnly as though it were a sacred shrine.

After they have taken their seats in silence, the baker hands out loaves of bread to them, and the cook serves each person a single course. Before and after the meal the priest offers a prayer. Thus, at the beginning and at the end of each meal they do homage to God as the bountiful giver of life. Removing their garments, they again apply themselves to their work until evening. On their return they dine in the same manner, and any guest who may have arrived during the day joins them at the table. No noise ever desecrates the house; each speaks in his turn. The silence that prevails in this house is both mystifying and awe-inspiring.

The Essenes do nothing without orders from their superiors, but members are permitted to help the needy and give food to those in want. They are forbidden, however, to send presents to relatives without the consent of the administrators. The Essenes are masters of their temper, champions of fidelity and true servants of peace. One word of theirs has more force than an oath by others. They display extraordinary interest in the writings of the ancients.

A candidate wishing to join their sect is not immediately accepted. First he must live outside the brotherhood for a year in the same manner as the members of the order. Having given proof of his moderation during this probationary period, the would-be member is brought into closer contact with the community, but he is not admitted to the meetings of the order. His character is tested for two years more, and only then, if he is found worthy, can he be enrolled in the society.

Before he is permitted to share the common meal, he must take a solemn oath that he will worship God, do justice, never inflict harm on his fellow men, and always champion the cause of the just. He will forever love truth and conceal nothing from the members of the sect nor report any of their secrets to others, even though it means martyrdom and death.

Those who are convicted of serious misdemeanors are expelled from the order; and the man who is thus ousted often comes to a most miserable end. For, being bound by the oath he has taken, he is not free to accept food from anyone but Essenes and, consequently, he is forced to live on herbs. This has led the Essenes to take back many of these unfortunates who are almost dead of exhaustion, considering the torments they have endured as sufficient atonement for their misdeeds.

Next to God, they revere Moses. It is a point of honor with them to obey their elders, and to abide by the decisions of the majority. For instance, if ten of them sit together, one will not speak if the other nine prefer silence. They are stricter than all other Jews in abstaining from work on the Sabbath. They are divided into four classes. Senior members are considered so superior to junior members that they must take a bath if they are so much as touched by one.

They enjoy long life, many of them living to be more than a hundred years old, possibly because of the simplicity and regularity of their way of living. They make light of danger; they triumph over pain by their resolute will. They prefer a glorious death to an inglorious life. This attitude of theirs became evident in the war with the Romans. Racked and twisted, burned and broken, made to endure every instrument of tortute, they refused to blaspheme Moses, their lawgiver, or eat forbidden food. Nor did they cringe before their persecutors or shed a tear in their presence. Smiling in their agony, scorning their tormentors, they gave up their souls cheerfully, confident that they would receive them back again.

Ethics of the Fathers

The Mishnah was compiled and edited by Rabbi Judah Hanasi and his colleagues at the beginning of the third century. It consists of sixty-three books called tractates, each of which is divided into chapters and subdivided into paragraphs. The tractate *Avoth* ("Fathers") deals with the ethical principles given by the fathers of Jewish tradition, who flourished over a period of five centuries, from the time of the last prophet to the end of the second century.

The world is based on three principles: Torah, worship and kindliness.

Do not be like servants who serve the master for the sake of receiving a reward; be like servants who serve the master without the expectation of reward.

Let your house be a meeting-place for the wise; sit at their feet; and drink in their words thirstily.

Let your house be wide open; treat the poor as members of your own family; and do not engage in gossip with women.

Provide yourself with a teacher; get yourself a colleague; and judge all men favorably.

Stay away from a bad neighbor; do not associate with an evil man; and do not despair when you meet with disaster.

When the parties in a lawsuit are before you, regard them both as wicked but after they have left, regard them both as innocent.

Love work and hate public office.

Be a disciple of Aaron, loving peace and striving for peace, loving people and attracting them to the Torah.

He who does not increase his knowledge decreases it.

If I do nothing for myself, who will do it for me? But if I care only for myself, what good am I? and if not now, when?

251

Make study a regular habit; say little and do much; and receive all men cheerfully.

Do not be aloof from the community; do not condemn your fellow man until you have been in his same position; do not say *I shall study when I find time,* for you may never find time.

The bashful cannot learn, nor can the quick-tempered teach.

The more flesh (gluttony), the more worms; the more property, the more anxiety; the more schooling, the more wisdom. One who has acquired a good name has done so for his own benefit; one who has acquired Torah has won life in the world to come.

Greed and hatred shorten a man's life.

The day is short, the task is great, and the Master is insistent. You are not called upon to complete the work, yet you are not free to evade it.

One who is liked by men is liked by God; one who is not liked by men is not liked by God.

Everything is given on pledge; the store is open, and the storekeeper [God] allows credit; the ledger is open and the hand writes; whoever wishes to borrow may come and borrow, but the collectors go around regularly and exact payment from man, whether or not he realizes [that he is punished for his sins].

He who learns from every man is wise; he who controls his impulse is strong; the man who is content with his lot is rich; the man who honors his fellow men is honored.

One good deed leads to another; one misdeed leads to another. Do not despise any man.

Be exceedingly humble, for the end of man is the grave.

Let the honor of your pupil be as dear to you as your own; respect your colleague as you respect your teacher; revere your teacher as you revere God.

Be careful in teaching, for an error in teaching amounts to willful sin.

Be first in greeting every man; be the tail of lions rather than the head of foxes.

Do not try to pacify a friend when he is in a rage; avoid seeing him in the hour of his disgrace.

Knowledge gained when one is young is like ink used on clean, fresh paper; knowledge gained in old age is like ink used on crumpled paper.

He who learns from the young is like one who eats unripe grapes; he who learns from the old is like one who eats ripe grapes or drinks old wine.

Envy, lust and vainglory shorten a man's life.

There are seven characteristics of a stupid person and seven of a wise man. The wise man does not speak before one who is greater than he in wisdom; he does not interrupt the speech of his companion; he is not hasty to answer; he asks questions and gives answers to the point; he speaks on the first point first, and on the last point last; regarding that which he has not learned he says: "I have not learned it"; and he acknowledges the truth. The reverse of all this is to be found in a stupid person.

There are four types of men: He who says "what is mine is mine and what is yours is yours" is an average man; he who says "what is mine is yours and what is yours is mine" is a boor; he who says "what is mine is yours and what is yours is yours" is a saintly man; he who says "what is yours is mine and what is mine is mine" is a wicked man.

There are four kinds of dispositions among men: He who is easily angered and easily pacified offsets his loss by his gain; he who is hard to anger but also hard to pacify offsets his gain by his loss; he who is hard to anger and easy to pacify is a saintly man; he who is easy to anger and hard to pacify is a wicked man.

There are four types of pupils: Those who are quick to learn and quick to forget counterbalance their gain by their loss; those who are slow to learn and slow to forget counterbalance their loss by their gain; those who are quick to learn and slow to forget possess a rare gift; those who are slow to learn and quick to forget have a serious shortcoming.

There are four types of donors to charity: He who gives but does not want others to give begrudges others; he who wants others to give but will not give himself begrudges himself; he who gives and wants others to give is a saintly man; he who will not give and does not want others to give is a wicked man.

There are four types of students: The sponge, the funnel, the strainer, and the sieve. The sponge absorbs all; the funnel receives at one end and spills out at the other; the strainer lets the wine drain through it, and retains the dregs; and the sieve which lets out the flour dust and then retains the fine flour.

Be bold as a leopard, light as an eagle, swift as a deer and strong as a lion to do the will of your Father in heaven.

Study the Torah again and again, for it contains everything. Contemplate it, grow old and gray over it, and swerve not from it; for there is nothing that excels it.

According to the effort is the reward.

Anyone who applies himself to the study of the Torah shall be exalted.

None can be considered free except those who devote themselves to the Torah.

He who learns a single expression from his fellow man should treat him with respect.

Do not seek greatness for yourself and do not crave honor; let your good deeds exceed your learning; do not desire the table of kings, for your table is greater than theirs, your crown is more glorious than theirs.

The Holy One, blessed be he, desired to purify the people of Israel, so he gave them a Torah rich in rules of conduct.

Man's Importance

Witnesses who are called on to testify in matters of life and death should be given a solemn charge when they are brought into court. The court should address them as follows:

"Perhaps what you are about to say is mere conjecture or hearsay based on second hand information or on what you heard from a trustworthy person. Perhaps you are not aware that we shall, in the course of the trial, subject you to close examination and searching inquiry.

"You must know that cases of capital punishment are not like trials concerning monetary matters in which one may make restitution and redeem his guilt by money. In cases of capital punishment the witness is accountable for the blood of the person wrongfully condemned and for the blood of his potential posterity until the end of time.

"Adam was created alone to show that should anyone destroy a single life he shall be called to account for it as though he had destroyed the entire world; and if anyone saves a life he is rewarded as though he had saved the whole world.

"Furthermore, all men are fashioned after the pattern of the first man, yet no two faces are exactly alike. Hence, every person may well say: For my sake the world was created."

Self-Respect

It once happened that a man let down a woman's hair in the street, and Rabbi Akiba told him to pay her four hundred silver pieces as compensation for the embarrassment he had caused her. The man said: "Rabbi, give me time," so he gave him time.

The man noticed the woman standing at the entry of her courtyard, and he broke a bottle of perfume in front of her. She let down her hair, and scooping up the perfume in her hand, she applied it to her hair. The man had posted witnesses to testify against her, and he came before Rabbi Akiba, asking: "Rabbi, do I have to give four hundred silver pieces to a woman like this?"

"Yes," Rabbi Akiba answered, "because he who inflicts a wound on himself, even though he does not have the right to do so, is not punishable; but if others have wounded him, they are punishable. So too, if a man cuts down his own plants, even though he does not have the right to do so, he is not punishable; but if others cut them down, they are."

Talmud

The Talmud has been the chief source of education for Jews in many lands since the middle of the sixth century. There are indeed two Talmuds which differ from each other in style and contents, namely: the Babylonian Talmud and the Palestinian Talmud. The Babylonian Talmud contains about two million five hundred thousand words, and is often referred to as "Shas," from the initials of the Hebrew *shishshah sedarim* (six orders). The vastness of the Babylonian Talmud has given rise to the expression *Yam ha-Talmud*, "the ocean of the Talmud."

The Talmud consists of two parts: the Mishnah and the Gemara. Unlike the Mishnah which is written in Hebrew and was completed in Palestine at the beginning of the third century, the Gemara in both Talmuds is written in Aramaic dialects with a considerable admixture of Hebrew. The Gemara of the Babylonian Talmud was completed in the year 500, whereas the Gemara of the Palestinian Talmud was edited in haste and made available one century earlier on account of the persecutions. Less than one-third of the size of the Babylonian Talmud, the Palestinian Talmud lacks the comprehensiveness of the Babylonian Talmud, which is an encyclopedia covering the whole gamut of human life.

The subject matter of the Talmud is classified into *Halakhah* and *Aggadah*, the legal element and the didactic element. About thirty percent of the Babylonian Talmud is taken up with *Aggadah*, which includes everything that is *not* of a legal nature, such as descriptions of historical events and legends, proverbs and aphorisms that illustrate moral duties, and scientific data concerning medicine, mathematics, astronomy and other branches of knowledge.

Compassion

Nahum of Gimzo was blind and crippled. His whole body was covered with sores. Once his students asked him: "Master, if you are righteous, why has all this come upon you?"

"All this," he replied, "I have brought upon myself. Once I was going on a visit to my father-in-law. I had with me a load of provisions carried by three donkeys. A poor man stopped me on the road and said: 'Rabbi, give me something to eat.' I told him to wait until I unloaded the donkeys.

"I had barely managed to unload them when I found that the man was dead. I threw myself upon his body and wept bitterly. 'Let these eyes which had no pity on you be blind,' I said; 'let my hands and feet be crippled because they delayed in giving you aid; and may my whole body be covered with sores.'"

Then the students said to him: "Alas, that we must see you in such a condition."

"It would be even more grievous to me if I were not in this condition," declared Nahum.

Contentment

Every day a heavenly voice proclaims: "The entire world is sustained on account of my son Hanina, while he is content with a small measure of carob fruit from one Sabbath to another."

Every Friday his wife would light the oven to produce smoke. Her neighbors would see the smoke and think that she was preparing a meal. But an evil neighbor said to herself: "I know she has nothing to bake; I will go and see why there is all this smoke." She went in and found the oven full of bread. She cried out: "Hurry, bring a shovel! Your bread is getting burned!"

Once she said to her husband: "How long shall we go on suffering so much poverty?" He asked: "What shall we do?" She replied: "Pray to God that he should give us some of the reward which is reserved for the righteous in the world to come."

He prayed, and suddenly there appeared a leg of a golden table. That night, in a dream, he saw people in paradise eating at tables with three legs, while he ate at one having only two legs. He said to his wife: "Are you satisfied to have others eat at a perfect table while ours has only two legs?" "What shall we do?" she asked; then she added:

257

"Pray that the golden leg should be taken back." He prayed, and it was taken away.

Lessons in Personal Conduct

Once there was a drought and the Rabbis sent two scholars to Abba Hilkiah to ask him to pray for rain. When the scholars came to his house and did not find him at home, they went to look for him in the fields and found him plowing. They greeted him, but he paid no attention to them. Toward evening he gathered some wood. On his way home, he carried the wood and the spade on one shoulder, and his cloak on the other. He walked barefoot all the way, but when he reached a stream he put his shoes on. Whenever he came to thorns and shrubs he lifted up his clothes.

Finally he reached the city, where his wife came to meet him dressed in her best. At the door of his house, he let her enter first, then he went in and after him the two scholars who were with him all this time. He sat down to eat, but did not invite the scholars to join him. He distributed cakes among the children, giving the elder child one and the younger, two. Then he whispered to his wife: "I know that these scholars have come to see me about rain. Come, let us go up on the roof and pray for rain. Perhaps God will answer our prayer. However, we will claim no credit for the rain."

So they went up to the roof, where they prayed, each in a separate corner. As they were praying, a cloud appeared in the sky above the Rabbi's wife, and it began to rain. He went down to the scholars and asked: "Why have you come here?" They replied: "The Rabbis have sent us to ask you to pray for rain." Whereupon he exclaimed: "Blessed be the Lord who has made you no longer dependent on Abba Hilkiah's prayer!"

"We know very well," they said, "that the rain has come because of you, but we would like you to explain to us the meaning of your strange behavior. Why did you not answer when we greeted you? Why did you carry the spade and the wood on one shoulder and your cloak on the other? And why did you go barefoot throughout the journey but put on your shoes when you came to a stream?"

"I hired myself out for the day," the Rabbi explained, "so I reasoned that I had no right to interrupt my work. The cloak I wore was a borrowed garment; it was loaned to me to wear, but not to carry things in. As for putting on my shoes when I came to the stream, I did it because I could not see what I was stepping on in the water; but I could see on the road."

The scholars again asked: "Why did you lift up your clothes when you came to thorns and shrubs? And why did your wife come to meet you so well-dressed? Why did she enter the house first, and then you, and lastly we? And why did you not invite us to join you in the meal?"

Abba Hilkiah explained: "A scratch on the body heals up; a tear in a garment does not. My wife came to meet me well-dressed so I would not pay attention to other women. She entered the house first because I did not know if I could trust you. I did not invite you to eat with us because there was not enough food for all of us. And it is a great sin to be insincere in one's speech, to say one thing and mean another, to receive undeserved thanks for a false invitation."

The two scholars asked again: "Why did you give one cake to your elder child and two to the younger? And why did a cloud appear first at the corner where your wife stood praying and then at yours?"

Abba Hilkiah replied: "My elder child stays at home and can eat whenever he likes, while the younger one goes to school. My wife's merits are superior to mine because she usually stays at home and gives food to the poor, so that the hungry find immediate relief, while I give them money which they cannot immediately enjoy."

Hillel's Gentleness

Once a man made a bet, saying that he could make Hillel angry. He was to receive four hundred silver pieces if he succeeded.

One Friday afternoon, as Hillel was getting ready for the Sabbath, the man went to Hillel's door and shouted: "Are you there, Hillel? Are you there?"

Hearing his name called, Hillel went out to see who it was. "What do you wish, my son?" he asked.

"I want to ask you a question," the man replied. "Ask, my son, ask whatever you like," Hillel said.

"Why are the Babylonians round-headed?" asked the man.

"You have asked a difficult question, my son. They have round heads because they are delivered by unskilled midwives."

The man listened and went away. A little later he came back shouting: "Are you there, Hillel? Are you in?" Hillel came out to him again, saying: "My son, what do you wish?"

"I have a question to ask," the man said. "Ask whatever you like, my son," Hillel prompted.

"Why do the people of Palmyra have dim eyes?" the man asked again.

"You have asked a great question, my son," Hillel replied. "They have dim eyes because they live in sandy places."

The man listened and went away. After a short while he came back again, shouting: "Hillel, are you there? Are you there, Hillel?" Again Hillel came out to him and said: "What do you wish, my son?"

"I want to ask a question," the man said. "Ask, my son," Hillel prompted, "ask whatever you like."

"Why do the Africans have broad feet?"

"My son, you have asked an important question. The Africans have broad feet because they live in watery marshes."

"I have many questions to ask," the man exclaimed, "but I am afraid you will grow angry!" Whereupon Hillel sat down and said kindly: "You may ask me all the questions you like, and I will answer them as best I can."

"Are you the Hillel who is known as the prince of Israel? If you are, may there not be many like you in Israel!"

"Why, my son?" Hillel asked.

"Because I have lost four hundred silver pieces on account of you," the man complained.

"Be careful of your temper," Hillel warned him. "It is far better that you should lose twice the amount of four hundred silver pieces than that Hillel should lose his temper."

Three Proselytes

A heathen once came to Shammai and asked him: "How many Torahs have you?" He replied: "We have two, the Written Torah and the Oral Torah. The written one consists of the five books of Moses; the oral one is composed of the traditional interpretations handed down by word of mouth from generation to generation."

"I believe you with respect to the Written Torah," said the heathen, "but not with respect to the Oral Torah. I wish to become a proselyte, but on condition that you teach me only the Written Torah." Shammai rebuked him sharply and sent him away in anger.

The heathen then appeared before Hillel, and he accepted him as a proselyte. On the first day, Hillel taught him: *Alef, beth, gimmel, daleth,* the first four letters of the Hebrew alphabet. The next day, he reversed the order of these letters.

"But yesterday you did not teach them to me like this," the proselyte protested. "Should you not rely on me?" Hillel said. "A certain reliance on authority is necessary if anything at all is to be learned. Depend on me, then, with respect to the Oral Torah too."

On another occasion, it happened that a heathen appeared before Shammai and said to him: "I wish to become a proselyte but only on condition that you teach me the whole Torah while I stand on one foot." Shammai drove him away. The man then went to Hillel, who received him cordially and said: "It is very simple: Do not to your neighbor that which is hateful to you. That is the whole Torah, while the rest is merely its commentary; go learn it."

On still another occasion a heathen heard of the honor paid to the high priest, and thereupon wished to become a

Jew. Shammai rejected him, saying that it was ridiculous for him to aspire to the office of high priest. But Hillel received him with the understanding that he must first learn all that was required of him. "Should anyone be made king before he knows the art of government?" Hillel asked.

So the heathen studied the Torah and he came to the passage: "Any outsider who approaches the sanctuary shall die." He was told that even David, the king of Israel, had not been allowed to approach the altar of God and serve as priest. Whereupon he gave up his ambition to become a high priest and simply became a Jew.

Some time later the three proselytes met in one place. They remarked: "Shammai's impatience nearly drove us from the future world, but Hillel's patience brought us under the wings of divine faith."

Flexible Like a Reed

Rabbi Elazar ben Rabbi Simeon once returned home from his school. He rode leisurely on a donkey along the lake shore and felt greatly elated because he had acquired much learning. While in this mood, he chanced upon a man who was extremely ugly. He failed to respond to the man's greeting, but exclaimed: "What an ugly man you are! Are all the people of your town as homely as you?" The man replied: "I do not know. Go tell the craftsman who made me: 'What an ugly thing you have made!'"

Rabbi Elazar realized his error at once. He got off his donkey, prostrated himself before the man and said: "I have sinned against you. Forgive me." But the man replied: "No, I will not pardon you until you say to the craftsman who made me: 'What an ugly thing you have made!'" Rabbi Elazar followed him until they reached the man's town. When they arrived there, the inhabitants of the town came out to meet the Rabbi, and greeted him with the words: "Peace be with you, Master!"

The man who preceded the Rabbi asked: "Whom are you addressing as Master?" They replied: "The man who is walking behind you." "If he is a teacher, may there be few like him in Israel!" he said. "Why do you say that?" the people asked. "What has he done to you?"

He told them what had happened. "Nevertheless, forgive him," the people pleaded, "for he is a great scholar." "I will forgive him," the man said, "but on the condition that he shall never act in this manner again."

Rabbi Elazar soon arrived at the school where he lectured as follows: "A man should always be as flexible as a reed, not rigid like a cedar tree."

From Shepherd to Scholar

Rabbi Akiba was once a poor shepherd in the employ of Kalba Savua, one of the richest men in all Jerusalem. While engaged in that lowly occupation, his master's only daughter, Rachel, fell in love with him. Hearing of it, her father threatened to disinherit her and turn her out of the house if she did not break off her engagement. How could she think of marrying an ignorant fellow who could neither read nor write and old enough to be her father?

Rachel determined to be true to Akiba and brave the consequences. She married him, exchanging her father's mansion for her husband's wretched hovel. After a short spell of married life she prevailed upon Akiba to attend certain schools in a distant city, where she felt sure his hidden talents would be fully developed.

After he left home, he began to have misgivings as to the wisdom of the step he was taking, and more than once thought of returning. But pausing one day before a waterfall, he noticed how the water, by its continuous flow, was wearing away the solid rock. At once he applied the lesson to himself. "So may the Torah," he reasoned, "work its way into my hard and stony mind." Encouraged, he went on and pursued his journey.

Under the guidance of Rabbi Eliezer ben Hyrcanus and Rabbi Joshua ben Hananyah, his native ability soon began to appear. He rose step by step until he became the head of the very college which he had entered as a poor student. After some twelve years of hard study, he returned home. On nearing the dwelling of his devoted wife he heard the sound of voices in eager conversation. He paused and listened at the door; he overheard a gossiping neighbor scolding Rachel for having married a man who left her for twelve long years on the pretext of going to college. He listened in breathless curiosity, wondering what Rachel's reply would be. To his surprise, he heard his self-sacrificing wife exclaim: "I wish my husband were here and could listen to me. I would permit, even urge him to stay away another twelve years if it would benefit him."

Strange to say, Akiba took his wife's hint, turned around and left the place without even seeing her. He stayed away for another twelve-year period and then returned, so the story goes, with twice twelve thousand students.

Nearly all the inhabitants of the city turned out to do him honor, every one striving to welcome him. Kalba Savua, who had repented of the hasty resolution which had cost him both his daughter and his own happiness, went to Rabbi Akiba to ask his opinion about annulling his vow to disinherit his daughter. Rabbi Akiba replied by making himself known to Kalba Savua as his rejected son-in-law. The two were at once reconciled, and Kalba Savua looked upon himself as one of the happiest parents in Israel.

Kindness Rewarded

Rabbi Akiba had a daughter of whom the astrologers predicted that on the day of her marriage she would be bitten by a serpent and die. Rabbi Akiba was extremely worried about this prophecy.

On her wedding-day, a poor man came to the door. Everyone was at the banquet tables and nobody paid any attention to him. So the bride took her own portion and gave it to the beggar. Then she happened to remove the ornamental clasp from her hair and stuck it into a crevice of the wall. By chance, it penetrated the eye of a serpent that was concealed there and killed it.

The following morning, when she took out the ornamental clasp, the serpent came trailing after it. She called her father's attention to this, and he asked her what good deed she had performed that day. When she told him that she had given her own portion of her wedding-feast to a poor man, he remarked that her good deed had delivered her from death.

Escaping Injury

Rabban Gamaliel said: I was once at sea and saw a ship wrecked and going to pieces. I was in great distress because of Rabbi Akiba who was on board the ill-fated vessel. When I reached shore safely, Rabbi Akiba appeared before me and began to discuss a legal problem with me.

I asked him: "My son, who has brought you up from the sea?" He replied: "A board of the ship was provided for me, and as I floated on it I bowed my head every time a wave came, and so it passed by and caused me no harm." Hence the saying: "If evildoers would injure a man, let him bow his head to them."

Investment

Rabbi Tarfon was not as liberal as a man of his wealth was expected to be. Once Rabbi Akiba said to him: "Shall I invest some money for you in real estate?" Rabbi Tarfon assented and brought to Rabbi Akiba a considerable sum of money for investment. Rabbi Akiba immediately distributed it among the poor. When Rabbi Tarfon asked to be shown where the real estate was located, Rabbi Akiba showed him a little boy who recited this verse: "He has given to the poor; his uprightness endures forever."

"There," said Rabbi Akiba, "your property has been invested in charity which endures forever." Rabbi Tarfon thanked him heartily for this lesson and gave him additional funds to be distributed among the poor.

All for the Best

A man should develop the habit of saying: "Whatever the Merciful One does is for the best." Once, when Rabbi Akiba was on a journey, he came to a town where he looked for a lodging but was refused. He said: "Whatever the Merciful One does is for the best," and he spent the night in an open field. He had with him a donkey, a rooster and a lamp. The wind came and blew out his lamp, but he said: "Whatever God does is for the best." Then a lion came and devoured the donkey, and a cat killed the rooster, but he constantly repeated: "Whatever the Merciful One does is for the best."

That same night the town was invaded by robbers who carried off the inhabitants into slavery. Rabbi Akiba remarked to his companions: "Whatever the Merciful One does is for the best. The light of the lamp, the braying of the donkey and the crowing of the rooster might have disclosed my whereabouts to the robbers."

Defeated by Three

Rabbi Joshua ben Hananyah said: "I have never been defeated by anyone except by a woman, a little boy and a little girl. I once was staying at an inn where the hostess served beans at the table. The first day I ate all and left nothing. The next day too I left nothing. The third day she overseasoned the beans. When I tasted them, I stopped eating. 'Rabbi,' the hostess said, 'why have you suddenly stopped eating?' 'Because I have already eaten during the day,' I replied. 'You should have eaten less,' she remarked. 'Perhaps you left the dish today because you left nothing the last two days, for the sages have laid down a rule that nothing should be left in the pot, but one should leave some food in the dish for the poor.'

"On another occasion, while I was walking in the middle of a field, a little girl said to me: 'Rabbi, is there not a law that one should not walk across a sown field?' I replied: 'This is a beaten path.' 'Yes,' she remarked, 'robbers like you have made it a trodden path.'

"My experience with a young boy is as follows: Once on a journey, I saw a little boy sitting at a crossroads. I said to him: 'My son, which of the roads leads to the town?' He replied: 'This road is short and yet long, while the other is long and yet short.' I took the road which was short and long. When I reached the outskirts of the town, I found it surrounded by vineyards and gardens so that I had to turn back to where I had started. I said to the boy. 'My son, you told me this road was short.' The boy replied: 'Rabbi, when I told you that it was short and yet long I meant that, though it was closer to the town, one has to make a long

266

detour in order to enter the town because of the vineyard.' I kissed the boy on the forehead and said: 'Happy are you, O Israel, that the highest and the lowest among you are indeed clever.' "

Martyrdom and Eternal Life

The Romans condemned Rabbi Hananya ben Teradyon to be burned alive wrapped in the scroll of the Torah from which he had taught the people despite the decree of the emperor. He was placed on a pyre of green brushwood; his chest was drenched with water in order to prolong his agony by a slow fire. "Father!" cried his daughter who stood nearby, "Woe is me that I should see you in such a condition."

"Daughter," replied the martyr serenely, "I should indeed despair if I were to be burned alone; but since the scroll of the Torah is burning with me, I am sure that God, who will avenge the offense against the Torah, will also avenge my painful death." His disciples, who stood near, noticed a smile upon his face. Heart-broken, they asked: "Master, what do you see?" He answered: "I see the parchment burning while the letters soar upward."

"Open your mouth, that the flames may enter and the sooner put an end to your torments," his students advised. But he said: "No, it is best that God who has given the soul should take it away; none may commit suicide." The executioner at once removed the sponge and fanned the flame, thus hastening the end, and then plunged himself into the fire and died. A heavenly voice was heard saying: "Rabbi Hananya ben Teradyon and his executioner have acquired life in the hereafter."

When Rabbi Yehudah Hanasi heard this he wept and said: "One wins life eternal after a struggle of many years, while another obtains it in one moment."

Faithfulness

Once it happened that a pretty, well-dressed girl lost her way and was unable to reach home. After wandering around in the fields for quite a while she became exhausted. Presently she noticed a well that was equipped with a rope and a bucket. Being thirsty, she slid down the rope to get some water; but she could not pull herself up again. Soon her cries attracted the attention of a young man who was passing by. He offered to help her if she would promise to marry him. This she did, and he pulled her up. Since there were no witnesses to this pact, as was required by Jewish law, the girl suggested that the well and a weasel, that happened to be nearby, should be their witnesses. So, after they exchanged mutual promises, the couple parted.

However, the young man broke his promise and married another girl who bore him a son. At the age of three months the baby was smothered to death by a weasel. Later, a second boy was born to the couple, and he fell into a well and drowned. The mother, alarmed by these accidents, asked her husband the meaning of their misfortune. He told her the story of his breach of promise, whereupon she sought and obtained a divorce.

During all this time, the young man's former fiancee waited for him to return and she discouraged everyone who asked to marry her. When the young man, after a long search, finally returned to her, she refused him, not realizing who he was. But when he reminded her of the weasel and the well, she recognized and accepted him at once. They were married and lived happily ever after.

Torah and Humility

Why is the Torah likened to water? Just as water leaves high places and goes to low ones, so the Torah leaves the arrogant and stays with the humble.

Why is the Torah likened to water, wine and milk? Just as these three liquids are preserved in the cheapest receptacles, so will the Torah be preserved only in the humble.

Rabbi Joshua ben Hananyah was once mocked by a princess who said of him: "What brilliant wisdom in such an ugly container!" Whereupon he retorted: "Your father is a king, and yet he puts wine in vessels of clay!"

"Where then should he put it?" she asked. "You nobles should put it in vessels of gold and silver," he replied. So she went home and told her father, who ordered his wine put into vessels of gold and silver, but the wine became sour.

Thereupon Rabbi Joshua was summoned before the king and asked: "Why did you give the princess such advice?" "As she spoke to me, so I spoke to her," Rabbi Joshua replied.

"But there are also handsome people that are learned!" they said. "If the same people were ugly, they would be still more learned," was Rabbi Joshua's reply.

Education and Learning

Joshua ben Gamala should be gratefully remembered, because had it not been for him the Torah would have been forgotten.

In ancient times each father taught his own child. The child who had no father grew up without an education. Then schools were established in the city of Jerusalem, where a father could bring his child for instruction. The fatherless, however, still remained without schooling. Later, schools were established in each district and boys of sixteen and seventeen were enrolled. But it often happened that a pupil, rebuked by a teacher, rebelled and left school. At last Joshua ben Gamala established elementary schools in each and every town, and all children of six or seven, including orphans, were enrolled.

Teaching Methods

Rav said: Do not accept pupils before the age of six and upward. Take the child from six and upward and cram knowledge into him as if you were fattening an ox. When you must punish a child, do not strike him with anything more than a bootstrap. If the pupil makes progress, good and well; if not, put him next to a studious companion.

Rava said: When there are two teachers in a place, one teaching the children more than the other, the one that teaches less is not to be dismissed, because having no competition to fear, the other is likely to grow negligent. When there are two teachers, one teaching much, but carelessly; and the other teaching little, but carefully, the former is to be preferred. The errors will correct themselves in time.

269

Rav Dimi, however, maintained that when once an error has crept in, it is hard to eradicate.

Kamtza and Bar Kamtza

There was a man who had a friend named Kamtza and an enemy named Bar Kamtza. The man once gave a dinner and sent his servant to invite Kamtza, but the servant brought Bar Kamtza.

Finding Bar Kamtza seated among the invited guests, the host said to him: "You have always been my enemy; what are you doing here? Get up and begone!"

But Bar Kamtza pleaded: "Since I am already here, let me stay, and I will pay for whatever I eat and drink." The host sternly refused. "Then I will give you half the cost of the entire banquet," said Bar Kamtza. "No!" replied the other. "Then let me pay you for the whole banquet." The master still refused and, seizing hold of him, thrust him out of the house.

The humiliated man muttered to himself: "The Rabbis sat there without intervening, it is evident therefore that my host's conduct was agreeable to them. I will go to Rome and inform on them to the imperial government." So he made his way to the emperor and said: "The Jews have rebelled against you!" Upon being asked for proof, he said: "Send a sacrifice to the Temple, and you will see whether it will be accepted."

So the emperor sent a calf with Bar Kamtza, who disqualified it as an offering by inflicting an injury on its upper lip. The Rabbis, in order not to offend the emperor, were inclined to sacrifice the animal in spite of its blemish; but Rabbi Zechariah ben Avkulas said to them: "If we do this people will say that blemished animals may be offered on the altar." It was then proposed Bar Kamtza be killed so that he might not return to Rome and report to the emperor, but Rabbi Zechariah said: "If we do that people might think that a man who mutilates an offering is punished by death."

Bar Kamtza then took the calf and returned it to the emperor as proof that the Jews were in rebellion against him.

Now, the emperor sent Nero against Jerusalem. As Nero approached Palestine he endeavored to guess what luck he would have: He shot an arrow towards the east, and it fell in Jerusalem. He then shot one towards the west, and again it fell in Jerusalem. He shot his arrows toward all four points of the compass, and each time they fell in Jerusalem.

After this, he chanced to meet a Jewish boy and said to him: "Recite for me the biblical verse you have learned today." The boy recited: "I will lay my vengeance upon Edom by the hand of my people Israel." Whereupon Nero fled and became a proselyte to Judaism. The emperor then sent Vespasian, who besieged Jerusalem for three years.

Now, there were three men of great wealth in Jerusalem. The first volunteered to supply the city with wheat and barley; the second undertook to supply it with wine, oil and salt; the third promised to provide it with wood. These provisions would have been enough for twenty-one years, but the zealots burned the stores of grain in order to force the inhabitants to come out and fight. Famine naturally resulted.

Martha was the richest woman in Jerusalem. She sent one of her servants to buy some fine flour; but he returned from the market and reported that all the best flour was sold out, except some white flour which was yet to be had. "Go bring me some," she told him. By the time he got there he found the white flour was also sold out. He returned and told his mistress: "There is only coarse flour left." She sent him to get that; but that too was gone, and only barley flour remained. Again his mistress sent him, and again he returned empty-handed. She decided to go herself, but so delicate was she that, having set her foot on something filthy, she died of shock.

Rabbi Zadok fasted forty years, that Jerusalem might not be destroyed, and so emaciated did he become that when he ate, the movement of the food could be seen as it went down his throat. Every evening he broke his fast by sucking on a fig, which he afterwards threw away. The delicate, but starving Martha is said to have picked up one of these castaway figs and to have died from eating it. Before her death, she gave orders that her immense treasures of gold and silver should be thrown into the streets, saying: "Of what use are all these to me?"

Abba Sikra, the leader of the war party, was the nephew of Rabbi Yohanan ben Zakkai. Rabbi Yohanan sent for him secretly and asked him: "How long are you going to carry on this way, killing the people with starvation?"

He replied: "What can I do? If I should venture to say one word to them, they would kill me!"

Rabbi Yohanan then said: "Devise some plan for me to escape. Perhaps I shall be able to save the situation."

"Pretend to be ill," said the leader of the zealots, "and let your friends circulate a rumor that you are dead. Then let your own disciples carry you out of the city in a coffin so that the device shall not be detected, since it is known that a live person is lighter than a corpse. The guards at the gate will then allow the funeral procession to pass, and in this way you can get out of the city."

Rabbi Eliezer and Rabbi Joshua carried the coffin and, on their arrival at the gate, the guards were about to pierce the body, to see whether it was really a corpse, but Abba Sikra prevented them by saying: "People will say that you have pierced your own Rabbi." Then they wanted to shake the coffin, but this also was prevented by Abba Sikra. The gate was opened and the procession passed through, and thus Rabbi Yohanan ben Zakkai escaped alive.

He then presented himself before the Roman general, and saluted him saying: "Peace be with you, O king!" The general said to him: "You deserve death on two counts: first because you gave me the false title of king, and secondly, if I am king, why did you not come to me before?" The Rabbi replied: "In truth you are born to be a king, otherwise Jerusalem would not be delivered into your power, for it is written: Lebanon shall fall to a majestic one. *Majestic one* means a king, and *Lebanon* means the Temple at Jerusalem." He added: "I would have come to you before, but the zealots prevented me."

At this point a messenger came to the general from Rome, saying: "Arise, for the emperor is dead, and the nobles of Rome have proclaimed you his successor." At the time, the new emperor was putting on his boots. He had already one on but could not get the other one on; nor could he pull the first one off. "What is the meaning of this?" he asked.

Rabbi Yohanan said to him: "Do not worry, O king; the good news you have just received is the cause of this, for it is written: 'Good news makes the bones fat.' Let someone whom you dislike pass before you and your sudden fatness will disappear, for it is written: A downcast spirit dries up the bones!" The general did as Rabbi Yohanan recommended and was able to put on his other boot at once.

As a reward for such wisdom the emperor granted to Rabbi Yohanan the preservation of Yavneh and its sages, the family of Rabbi Gamaliel and a physician to heal Rabbi Zadok from the effects of his forty years' fast. The emperor then left for Rome, and Titus succeeded him.

Titus blasphemed God and entered the Holy of Holies together with a harlot. As he slashed the curtain of the most holy shrine with his sword, blood miraculously spurted from it. He took the curtain, wrapped the vessels of the Temple in it and shipped them to Rome. While at sea, a storm arose and threatened to sink the ship. "It seems," he said, "the God of the Jews has no power anywhere but at sea. He drowned Pharaoh, he drowned Sisera and now he is about to drown me also. If he is really mighty, let him come up on dry land and fight me there."

Then a voice from heaven said: "You wicked man, son of a wicked man and descendant of wicked Esau, go ashore! I have a tiny creature in my world—a gnat. Go make war with it." When he landed, a gnat flew into his nostrils and made its way into his brain, on which it fed for seven years.

Once he happened to pass a workshop and the noise of the hammer caused the gnat to stop boring into his brain. "I see there is a remedy!" he said. So every day he ordered a blacksmith to hammer constantly in his presence, paying him four pieces of silver a day if he was a non-Jew, but paying nothing to a Jewish blacksmith, to whom he would say: "You are well paid by seeing me in such a wretched condition." For thirty days he felt relief but, after that period, the creature got used to the hammering and went on with its work.

Titus willed that his body be cremated after his death, and his ashes scattered over the seven seas, so that the God of the Jews might not find him and bring him to judgment.

Proverbial Sayings

The hope of the world lies in its school children.

A town that has no school children is headed for ruin.

Jerusalem was destroyed because the instruction of its children was neglected.

A single light will do for a hundred men as well as for one.

As iron whets iron, so mind sharpens mind.

I have learned much from my teachers, even more from my colleagues, but I have learned the most from my pupils.

He who studies but does not review his work is like one who sows but does not reap.

He who knows that he knows nothing possesses knowledge indeed.

A teacher should give instruction concisely.

If a man says to you: "I have searched for wisdom but have not found it," do not believe him. If he says: "I have not searched for it but have found it anyhow," do not believe him then either. But if he says: "I have searched for wisdom and have found it," believe him, for he speaks the truth.

He who does not teach his son a trade is as guilty as though he teaches him to steal.

Pay special attention to the children of the poor, for it is from them that knowledge will come.

Descend a step in choosing a wife; ascend a step in choosing your friend.

All the blessings of a home come through its mistress.

Love your wife as much as yourself; honor her more than yourself.

Men should be careful not to give their wives any cause for tears, for God counts their tears.

He who marries for money shall have incorrigible children.

If your wife is short, bend your head and take her advice.

A lovely wife, a splendid home and beautiful furniture cheer a man's heart.

A man should eat and drink beneath his means, clothe himself within his means, and honor his wife above his means.

When a bride has beautiful eyes her figure needs no inspection.

Even if a wife should have a hundred servants she should do some work herself, for idleness leads to mental disturbance.

Life is a passing shadow—the shadow of a bird in flight; when the bird has flown, its shadow is gone too.

The noblest charity of all is that which enables the poor to earn their living.

Support the old without reference to religion; respect the learned regardless of their age.

A house that is not open to the poor will open to the physician.

The world is a dismal place to the man who has to accept charity.

No man dies with even half his desires realized.

Adversity reveals man's inner strength, but prosperity weakens his will.

Do not let care enter your heart, for care has killed many.

No man should be held responsible for words uttered in his grief.

No man sins unless a spirit of foolishness has entered into him.

He who has committed a sin twice no longer considers it a sin.

God turns away from four types of men: the scoffer, the liar, the hypocrite and the slanderer.

No one should taunt a reformed sinner about his past.

A man notices the weaknesses of others but not his own.

Adorn yourself before you adorn others.

Teach your tongue to say: "I do not know."

A liar finds his punishment in being disbelieved even when he tells the truth.

If you tell a secret to three people, ten will know it.

Your friend has a friend, and your friend's friend has a friend, so be careful with what you say.

A little coin in a big jar makes a lot of noise.

A slanderous tongue kills three people: the slanderer, the slandered and the one who listens to the slander.

A man who injures his fellow man commits a worse sin than one who robs a temple.

He who seeks a friend without faults will remain friendless.

There are many brothers and friends at the gate of abundance, but at the gate of misery there are neither brothers nor friends.

Love the one who shows you your faults more than the one who praises you.

Kindliness is the beginning and the end of the Torah.

If two men ask for your help, and one of them is your enemy, help your enemy first.

He who neglects to visit a sick friend is as guilty as if he sheds his blood.

A man should cast himself into a flaming furnace rather than embarrass someone in public.

The man who can feel shame will not easily go wrong.

There is a great difference between the man who can feel ashamed before his own conscience and the one who is only ashamed before his fellows.

When good people die, they are not truly dead, for their example lives.

The best preacher is the heart; the best teacher is time; the best book is the world; the best friend is God.

Rabbi Akiba said: "The greatest commandment in the Bible is: "Love your neighbor as yourself."

God loves three types of men: the one who does not get angry, the one who does not become intoxicated, and the one who is generous.

Do not weep in the presence of those who laugh, and do not laugh in the presence of those who weep; wake not among those who sleep, and sleep not among those who are awake; stand not while others sit, and sit not while others stand.

Midrash

Midrash (investigation) signifies study and interpretation. Hence, *Beth ha-Midrash* (house of learning) denotes a talmudic school. For the most part, the purpose of the Midrash is to explain the biblical text from the ethical or devotional point of view. It is then referred to as *Midrash Haggadah,* in contrast to *Midrash Halakhah* which is mainly concerned with the derivation of laws from the words of the Scriptures.

Haggadah is a form of teaching that seeks to admonish and edify. It penetrates deeply into the spirit of the Bible by means of its broad interpretations of the text. From the wealth of haggadic literature the Jewish people continue to receive comfort and strength as they have for many generations.

For the religious Jew, the Midrash retains today the significance attached to it in the ancient saying: "If you wish to know him at whose command the world came into existence, learn Haggadah, for thereby you shall know the Holy One, blessed be he, and cling to his ways."

The historical themes of the Bible are midrashically interpreted in such a religious and national sense that the entire story of Israel becomes a continuous revelation of God's love and justice. The Midrash has ever proved an unfailing spring with the power to sustain and strengthen the Jewish thirst for the word of the living God. Ever since the third century, the most flourishing period of haggadic activity in Palestine, the Midrash has represented an important medium for the expression of Jewish thought.

The Alphabet and the Creation

When God was about to create the world, each of the twenty-two letters of the Hebrew alphabet pleaded: "Create the world through me!"

The letter Tav said: "O Lord of the universe, may it be thy will to create the world through me; it is through me that thou wilt give the Torah to Israel." God replied: "No, because in days to come I shall place you as a sign of death upon the foreheads of men."

The Shin pleaded: "Lord of the universe, create thy world through me; thy own name *Shaddai* begins with me." Unfortunately, it is also the first letter of *sheker*, falsehood, and that disqualified it.

The Resh had no better luck, because it was the initial letter of *ra*, evil.

The Koof was rejected because *kelalah*, curse, outweighs the advantage of being the first in *Kadosh*, the Holy One.

In vain did the Tsadde draw attention to *Tsaddik*, the Righteous One; there was *tsaroth*, misfortunes, to testify against it.

The Peh had *podeh*, Redeemer, to its credit; but *pesha*, transgression, discredited it.

The Ayin was declared unfit because, though it begins *anavah*, humility, it performs the same service for *erwah*, immorality.

The Samekh said: "O Lord, may it be thy will to begin the creation with me, for thou art called *somekh*, the Upholder of all that fall." But God replied: "You are needed right where you are; you must continue to uphold all that fall."

The Nun introduces *ner*, lamp, the lamp of the Lord, which is the spirit of men, but it also brings to mind the lamp of the wicked which will be put out by God.

The Mem starts *melekh*, king, one of the titles of God. But as it is the first letter of *mehumah*, confusion, it had no chance of achieving its desire.

The Lamed advanced the argument that it was the first letter of *luhoth*, the celestial tablets of the Ten Commandments. It forgot that the tablets were dashed to pieces by Moses.

The Kaf was sure of victory: *kisseh*, the throne of God, *kavod*, his honor, and *kether*, his crown, all begin with it. God had to remind it that he would clap his hands, *kaf*, in despair over the misfortunes of Israel.

The Yod seemed to be the proper letter for the beginning of creation on account of its association with *Yah*,

God; but *yetser ha-ra,* the evil impulse, begins with it too.

The Teth is identified with *tov,* good. However, permanent good is reserved for the world to come.

The Heth is the first letter of *hanun,* the Gracious One; but this advantage is offset by its place in the word for sin, *hattath.*

Zayin was disqualified because it is the word for weapon, the doer of mischief.

Wav and Hey compose the Ineffable Name of God; they are therefore too exalted to be pressed into the service of a mundane world.

Daleth stands for *din,* justice; but justice untempered by mercy would bring the world to ruin.

The Gimmel would not do, because *gemul,* retribution, starts with it.

When the claims of all these letters had been disposed of, the Beth stepped before the Holy One, blessed be he, and pleaded: Lord of the universe, may it be thy will to create thy world through me, since all the inhabitants of the world will give praise daily unto thee through me, for it is written: "Blessed (*barukh*) be the Lord forever." God at once granted the petition of Beth, and created the world through it, and so it is written: "*Bereshith,* in the beginning, God created the heaven and the earth."

The only letter that had refrained from making any claims was the modest Alef, and God rewarded it later for its humility by giving it the first place in the Ten Commandments, which begin with *Anokhi.*

Adam and Eve

The world was made for man, though he was the last to be created. Man's late appearance on earth is a lesson in humility: Be not proud, O man, for the gnat was created before you.

When God was about to create Eve, he said: "If I create her from the head, she will be overbearing; from the ear, she will be an eavesdropper; from the neck, she will be impudent; from the mouth, she will be a gossip; from the heart, she will be envious; from the hand, she will be a

meddler; from the foot, she will be a gadabout." Hence he
created her from the rib, a modest part of the body.

The intelligence of woman matures more quickly than
that of man. A man is easily reconciled, not so a woman.
The man must ask the woman to be his wife, because he
must make good the loss of his rib.

When Adam awoke from his profound sleep and saw
Eve before him in all her beauty and grace, he knew that
she would seek to carry her point with man either by en-
treaties and tears or flattery and caresses.

Abraham

The first test to which Abraham was subjected was his de-
parture from his native land. The hardships were many
and severe and, besides, he was reluctant to leave his home.
God told him: "Do not worry about your kinsmen.
Though they speak words of kindness to you, they are all
determined to ruin you."

When Abraham was first commanded to leave his home,
he was not told to what land he was to journey but placed
his trust in God and said: "I am ready to go wherever thou
sendest me." He rejoiced when he reached Canaan, where
the people devoted themselves to the cultivation of the
land. Each altar that Abraham built became a center for
his activities as a teacher of true religion.

Scarcely had Abraham established himself in Canaan
when a famine devastated the land. He was compelled to
leave Canaan and go to Egypt where he was to learn the
wisdom of the priests. His stay in Egypt was of great service
to the inhabitants of that country because he introduced
the wise men to new views of religion and science, hitherto
unknown in Egypt.

On his return to Canaan, strife developed between his
herdsmen and the herdsmen of Lot. After he and Lot separated, Abraham received assurance from God that Canaan
would belong to his descendants who would multiply as
the sand of the seashore. Just as the sand fills the whole
earth, so would his descendants be scattered over the whole
earth; just as the earth is blessed only when it is moistened

with water, so would his descendants be blessed through the Torah which is likened to water; and just as the earth endures longer than metal, so would his descendants endure forever.

Written and Oral

When God revealed himself at Sinai to give the Torah to Israel, he communicated to Moses the Bible, Mishnah, Talmud, and Haggadah, and told him to teach it all to the people. "Shall I write it down for them?" Moses asked. God replied: "I do not wish to give it to them in writing, because I foresee a time when the heathen will have dominion over them and take it away from them and they will be despised by the idolaters. I will give them in writing only the Bible; but the Mishnah, Talmud and Haggadah, I will give them orally, so that when the idolaters enslave them they will remain distinct from them."

There is a proverb: "If you go into a city, you should adopt its customs." When Moses ascended on high, he followed the heavenly example and did not eat or drink for forty days and forty nights. When the angels descended to earth to visit Abraham, they ate and drank, that is, it seemed as if they ate, since each of the courses disappeared.

Birth and Death

The day on which a great man dies is better than the day on which he was born, because no one knows on the day of the child's birth what deeds he will perform; but at his death, his good deeds are acclaimed by all. This may well be compared to two ocean-going ships—one leaving the harbor and the other entering. Everybody seemed to rejoice over the one setting out on her voyage, while only few greeted with pleasure the one arriving. Upon seeing this, a wise man reflected: People should not rejoice at the ship leaving the harbor, since they do not know what seas she may traverse and what winds she may have to face. On the other hand, everybody should rejoice for the ship that has safely returned to the harbor. When a man is born, every year of his life brings the day of his death nearer, and

281

he is constantly haunted by the certainty of death; but when he dies, he is solaced by the hope of immortality and he looks forward to his revival.

The Revelation

Before God gave the Torah to Israel, he offered it to every tribe and nation. He went to the descendants of Esau and asked: "Will you accept the Torah?"

"What is written in it?" they wanted to know. "You shall not kill," he answered. "We live by our sword; we cannot accept the Torah," they said.

He went to the descendants of Ishmael, asking them: "Will you accept the Torah?"

"What is written in it?" they inquired. "You shall not steal," was the answer. "We live by pillage and plunder; we will not accept thy Torah," declared the children of Ishmael.

When all the other nations had rejected the Torah, he offered it to the people of Israel, who asked: "What is written in it?"

"Six hundred and thirteen precepts," he said. "All that the Lord has spoken we will do, and we will be obedient," they responded.

Then they continued: "Lord of the world, we acted in accordance with thy commandments before they were revealed to us. Jacob fulfilled the first of the Ten Commandments by telling his sons to put away the strange gods that were among them. Isaac observed the commandment to honor his father and his mother when he allowed Abraham to bind him on the altar as a sacrifice. Judah observed the commandment not to kill when he said to his brothers: "What is the good of killing our brother and concealing his blood?" Joseph observed the law which forbids adultery.

The fifth commandment was stressed in these words: "Honor your parents, to whom you owe existence, as you honor me; maintain your parents, for your parents took part in your creation." Man owes his existence to God, to his father and to his mother. God not only commanded that we love and revere our parents as himself, but in some

282

respects he places the honor due to parents even higher than that due him.

Gentle Mercy

Rabbi Yosé of Galilee had a malicious and spiteful wife, who used to insult and disgrace him before his students. So they said to him: "You should divorce this wicked woman; she treats you with such contempt."

"What can I do?" sighed Rabbi Yosé. "If I divorce her, I must pay her a large sum of money, and that I cannot afford."

At one time Rabbi Yosé and Rabbi Elazar ben Azaryah were engaged in a lengthy legal discourse. When they had finished, Rabbi Yosé invited Rabbi Elazar to dine with him. As soon as they had entered the house, the wife glared at them and walked out.

As she was leaving the house, Rabbi Yosé asked her if there was anything to eat. "There is a carrot stew," she said. But when he uncovered the pot he found roast chicken, which he served at the table.

"Master," inquired the guest, "did not your wife say that she had prepared a carrot stew? Where did you get the chicken?" "It was a miracle," explained Rabbi Yosé.

After the meal, Rabbi Elazar said: "You should get rid of this woman; she is so disrepectful to you." "But," replied Rabbi Yosé despairingly, "I am helpless. If I divorce her, I must pay her a large sum of money; and I am not in a position to raise that sum."

'We, your disciples, will raise the necessary amount," volunteered Rabbi Elazar. The required sum was collected by the students, and Rabbi Yosé was able to divorce her. This done, he married a more worthy woman.

The divorcee, too, remarried. Her choice was the town watchman. Shortly after this marriage, he became blind, and his wife had to lead him through the streets begging for alms. Whenever they reached the street where Rabbi Yosé lived, she would turn back. Being familiar with the town, the blind man wanted to know why she shunned that street. "I have heard," he said, "that Rabbi Yosé is a very charitable man. Why don't you take me there?"

283

"I am his divorced wife," she replied, "and I am ashamed to face him."

One day they were begging in Rabbi Yosé's vicinity, and she again carefully avoided the Rabbi's house. The next day she did the same thing, and the blind man began to beat her. It was a tragic and disgraceful scene, one which outraged the whole neighborhood.

Her cries were heard by Rabbi Yosé who recognized her voice and came out to investigate. He was shocked to see his former wife in such a wretched plight. "Why do you beat her?" demanded Rabbi Yosé sternly.

"Because every day I lose money on account of her," declared the sightless man. Thereupon Rabbi Yosé let him live in one of his houses and supported them as long as they lived.

Moral Justice

Rabbi Joshua ben Levi fasted and prayed to God that he might be permitted to gaze on the prophet Elijah who had ascended alive into heaven. God granted his prayer, and Elijah appeared before him.

"Let me journey with you in your travels through the world," the Rabbi entreated Elijah; "let me observe your doings so that I may gain in wisdom and understanding."

"No," answered Elijah; "you would not understand my actions; my doings would trouble you. They are beyond your comprehension."

But still the Rabbi implored: "I will neither trouble nor question you; only let me accompany you on your way."

"Come, then," said Elijah; "but let your tongue be mute. With your first question, your first expression of astonishment, we must part company."

So the two journeyed through the world together. They approached the house of a poor man, whose only treasure and means of support was a cow. As they came near, the man and his wife hastened to meet them, begged them to come into their house, eat and drink of the best they had and to pass the night under their roof. This they did, received every attention from their host and hostess. In the morning Elijah prayed to God that the cow belonging to

284

the poor people should die, and the animal died. Then the travelers continued on their way.

Rabbi Joshua was amazed. "Why did you kill the cow of this good man?" he asked.

"Look, listen, and be silent," Elijah replied; "if I answer your questions we must part."

They continued on their way together. Toward evening they arrived at a large and imposing mansion, the residence of an arrogant and wealthy man. They were coldly received; a piece of bread and a glass of water were placed before them. They remained there during the night. In the morning Elijah saw that a wall of the house had collapsed and he immediately restored it.

Rabbi Joshua again was filled with wonder but said nothing, and they proceeded on their journey.

As the shades of night were falling, they entered a city where there was a large and imposing synagogue. They went in at the time of the evening service and admired the rich adornments, the velvet cushions, and gilded carvings of the interior. After the service, the president arose and called out: "Who is willing to take these two poor men to his house?" None answered, and the travelling strangers had to sleep in the synagogue. In the morning, however, Elijah shook hands with the members of the synagogue and said: "I hope that you may all become presidents."

Next evening the two entered another city. The sexton of the synagogue came to meet them and notified the members of the congregation of the coming of the two strangers. The best hotel of the place was opened to them, and all showed them attention and honor. On parting with them, Elijah said: "May the Lord appoint but one president over you."

Rabbi Joshua could resist his curiosity no longer. "Tell me," he said to Elijah, "tell me the meaning of all these actions which I have witnessed. To those who have treated us coldly you have extended good wishes; to those who have been gracious to us you have made no suitable return. Even at the risk of parting, please explain to me the meaning of your acts."

Elijah explained: "We first entered the house of the

poor man who treated us so kindly. Now it had been decreed that on that very day his wife should die. I prayed the Lord that the cow might die instead. God granted my prayers, and the woman was saved. The rich man, whom we visited next, treated us coldly and I rebuilt his wall. For had he rebuilt it himself he would have discovered a treasure which lies underneath. To the members of the synagogue who were not hospitable I said: 'May you all be presidents,' and where many rule there can be no peace. But to the others I said: 'May you have but one president'; with one leader, no dissension will arise. Now, if you see the wicked prospering, be not envious; if you see the righteous in poverty and trouble, be not doubtful of God's justice."

With these words Elijah disappeared, and Rabbi Joshua ben Levi was left alone.

A Better Sense of Justice

When Alexander the Great reached a distant country beyond the dark mountains of Africa, he was offered by the king of the land golden bread on a golden tray. "Do I need your gold?" Alexander asked. "Have you had nothing to eat in your country that you have come here?" the king retorted. "I came only to see how you dispense justice here," Alexander explained.

While the two were conversing, a man came to them with a complaint against his companion, saying: "This man sold me a piece of land and I found a treasure buried in it. I want to return the treasure to him but he refuses to accept it from me, maintaining that he has sold me the land together with everything it contains. However, I am certain that I have no right to the treasure, because I have purchased from him only the land and nothing else."

"Have you a son?" the king asked the plaintiff. "Yes," he replied. "And have you a daughter?" the king turned to the defendant. "Yes," was the answer. Thereupon the king announced his decision: "Let them get married and share the treasure between them."

When the king became aware of Alexander's amazement at this decision, he asked: "Why, have I given a wrong decision?" "Yes," came the reply. "And how would you have judged in a case like this?" the king asked. "I would have killed the two fools and kept the treasure for myself," Alexander answered.

"Does it rain in your country?" the king asked. "It does," replied Alexander. "Does the sun shine there?" he inquired. "Yes," was the answer. "Have you sheep and goats?" the king continued. "We have," said Alexander. "Then I am certain," concluded the king, "that all the blessings of nature are intended for the cattle rather than for the citizens of your country who must share your sense of justice."

Three Proofs of Wisdom

A man of Jerusalem with a large sum of money in his possession went into a foreign country on business. In a certain small town he put up at an inn where he had been used to staying. While there, he became seriously ill. So he called the host and entrusted to him all that he had, making him promise to hand it over to his son.

"You will know my son," said the dying man, "by his extraordinary wisdom, which will show that he is indeed my son and not a swindler. Test him on three points of wisdom, and if you are satisfied with the results, give my legacy to him."

The man died, and the news of his death and bequest reached Jerusalem. Meanwhile, the trustee exacted from the people of the town the promise not to give his address to any stranger who might ask about him.

After some time, the son of the deceased man arrived at the place where his father had died. He knew the name of the person with whom his father had usually lodged, but he did not know the man's address, and the people of the town refused to give it to him. In this predicament, he met a man selling wood. This he bought, ordering the woodman to carry it for him to the house of the man whose address he did not know. On arriving there, the woodman put down his load.

"What is this?" exclaimed the master of the house; "I have not ordered any wood!"

287

"True," said the woodman, "but the young man behind me has." The stranger at once stepped up and made himself known to the master of the house and told him about the trick he had used in order to find him. Pleased with the young man's cleverness, the host invited him to be his guest, and the young Jerusalemite gladly accepted his offer.

Dinner was just then ready. Those sitting at the table consisted of the host, hostess, his two sons, his two daughters and the visitor from Jerusalem. When they were all seated, a dish containing five squabs was placed on the table, and the host asked his guest to serve the portions.

This he did in the following manner: One of the squabs he divided between the host and the hostess, another between the two sons, and a third between the two daughters; the remaining two squabs he took for himself. This strange conduct came as an utter surprise to all of them, but no one commented on it, hoping that the wisdom of it would soon be understood.

At supper-time a fine chicken was placed before the company, and the host again invited the guest to distribute the portions. This he did as follows: The head of the bird he gave to the host, the stuffing to the hostess, a leg to each son, and a wing to each daughter; the remainder he took for himself.

"Sir," said the host at last, "have you any reason for your method of serving? At dinner I thought your method very strange, but now it seems still more extraordinary."

"Have patience with me," replied the Jerusalemite, "and I will explain it all to you. At dinner there were seven of us and only five squabs; as these could not be divided with mathematical exactness, I thought it best to divide them numerically. You and your wife with one squab made three. Your two sons and one squab made another three, and so did your two daughters with one squab. To make up another three, I was obliged to take the other two squabs for myself.

"At supper I was obliged to act on a different principle, according to the altered circumstances. Since you are the head of the family, I gave you the head of the fowl; the inner part of the fowl I gave to your wife, as a sign of her fruitfulness; the legs, symbolic of pillars, I gave to your two sons as the future supporters of your home; the wings that I gave to your daughters were meant to show that they will soon fly away with their husbands; and the body of the fowl, which resembles a ship, I kept for myself. In doing this I meant to indicate that as soon as you give me my father's property I shall set sail for home."

These three proofs of wisdom convinced the host that his guest was the rightful heir, and he thereupon handed him his father's legacy and sent him away in peace.

Measure for Measure

A Jerusalemite went to see a merchant in Athens. On his arrival, he went to an inn where he found three persons sitting and drinking wine. He ordered a meal, and after he had eaten he asked if he might spend the night there too. Those sitting in the inn said to him: "We have agreed among ourselves not to accept a guest unless he has jumped three times first."

"I do not know how to jump," said the man of Jerusalem; "show me how to do it."

So one of the men jumped and landed in the middle of the inn; a second jumped from the spot where the first had come down, and found himself at the front door; the third one jumped and landed outside. The first two men followed the third to see how far he would get, whereupon the Jerusalemite bolted the door and called out to them: "See! I have done to you what you intended to do to me."

More than Enough

An Athenian went to Jerusalem, where he gave some money to a child, saying to him: "Go bring me something to eat, and get enough so that I can eat my fill and also have some left over to take on my journey." The boy went, but came back only with some salt. The man asked him: "Did I tell you to bring me salt?" The child replied: "Did you not tell me to bring you something of which you could eat your fill and have some left over to take on your journey. That is exactly what I have done."

The Foolish Parent

A man once left a will which read as follows: "My son shall not receive his inheritance until he becomes foolish." The embarrassed judges of the probate court, after long deliberation, came to Rabbi Joshua ben Korha, who lived about the middle of the second century, to get his advice in the difficult case.

As they approached his house, they saw him crawling on all fours with a cord in his mouth, held by his little son, who was playing horse with his father. When the judges finally were ushered into the presence of the Rabbi, they placed before him the difficult question that was the cause of their visit.

Laughingly the Rabbi said: "I have given you a concrete illustration of your case: everyone becomes foolish as soon as he has children." The will was therefore interpreted as meaning that it was the wish of the deceased to have his son married and the father of children before he received his heritage.

Israel's Tragedy and Hope

When God sought to destroy the Temple, he said: "So long as I am in its midst, the nations of the world will not touch it; but I will close my eyes so as not to see it." Then came the enemy and destroyed it. God said: "Woe for my house! My children, where are you? What shall I do with you, seeing that I warned you but you did not repent?" God said to Jeremiah: "I am now like a man who had an only son, for whom he prepared a marriage-canopy, but the son died under it. Go, summon Abraham, Isaac, Jacob and Moses from their graves, for they know how to weep. Go, stand by the bank of the Jordan, raise your voice and call out: Son of Amram, son of Amram, arise and behold your flock which the enemies have devoured."

Then and there Jeremiah went to the cave of Machpelah and said to the patriarchs of the world: "Arise, for the time has come when your presence is required before the Holy One, blessed be he."

"For what purpose?" they inquired. He said that he did

not know, fearing that they might say: Such a thing has happened to our children in your lifetime!

Jeremiah left them and stood by the bank of the Jordan and called out: "Son of Amram, son of Amram, arise; the time has come when your presence is required before the Holy One, blessed be he." When Moses asked why, Jeremiah replied that he did not know. Moses then asked the ministering angels, who replied: "Son of Amram, do you not know that the Temple is destroyed and that Israel has gone into exile?" He cried aloud and wept until he reached the patriarchs.

Abraham spoke before the Holy One, blessed be he: "Sovereign of the universe, why hast thou exiled my children and delivered them over to heathen nations who have put them to death and who destroyed the Temple, the place where I offered my son Isaac before thee?" God replied to Abraham: "Your children have sinned and transgressed against the whole Torah. Let the Torah come and testify against Israel."

When the Torah came to testify, Abraham said: "My daughter, have you come to testify against Israel that they have transgressed your commandments and you are not ashamed? Remember the day when God offered you to every nation on earth but they refused to accept you, whereas my children accepted you cheerfully. And now you come to testify against them in the day of their trouble!" When the Torah heard this, she stepped aside and offered no testimony against them.

Moses said to Jeremiah: "Walk before me, so that I may go and see what has happened to them." Jeremiah replied: "It is impossible for me to walk along the road because of the slain."

"Nevertheless, let us go," said Moses. He went with Jeremiah, the prophet leading the way, until they arrived at the rivers of Babylon. When the exiles beheld Moses, they said one to another: "The son of Amram has come from his grave to redeem us from the hand of our adversaries."

A heavenly voice issued forth and announced: "This is a decree from me." Thereupon Moses said to them: "My

children, it is not possible to take you back now since it is
so decreed, but the Almighty will soon bring you back."

When Moses came to the patriarchs of the world, they
asked him: "What has the enemy done to our children?"
He replied: "Some of them were killed; the hands of
others were tied behind their backs; some were fettered
with iron chains; others were stripped naked; some died
by the way and their corpses became food for birds and
beasts; others were exposed to the sun, hungry and thirsty."
Hearing this, they all began to weep and lament.

Moses lifted up his voice, saying: "A curse on you, O
sun! Why did you not become dark when the enemy entered the Temple? O captors, I charge you, do not completely exterminate my people; do not slay a son in the
presence of his father nor a daughter in the presence of
her mother. A time will come when the Lord of heaven
will demand a reckoning of you."

Rachel burst forth into heart-rending lamentation.
"Sovereign of the universe," she moaned, "thou knowest
that thy servant Jacob loved me exceedingly and toiled for
my sake seven years. When those seven years were completed and the time arrived for my marriage, my father
substituted my sister for me. I suppressed my desire and
had pity upon my sister that she should not be exposed to
shame. In the evening I revealed to my sister all the secret
signs which I had arranged with Jacob, that he might think
he was consorting with me. I did her a kindness; I was not
jealous of her and did not expose her to shame. And if
I, a creature of flesh and blood, formed of dust and ashes,
was not envious of my rival and did not expose her to
shame and contempt, why shouldst thou, eternal and merciful King, be jealous of idols which are absolutely unreal?
Why dost thou exile my children, letting them be slain by
the sword?"

God's mercy was stirred, and he said: "For your sake, O
Rachel, I will restore the people of Israel to their place."
It is written in Jeremiah: "A voice is heard in Ramah,
lamentation and bitter weeping: Rachel is weeping for her
children, because they are not. Thus says the Lord: Keep
your voice from weeping, and your eyes from tears; your

work shall be rewarded, and they shall come back from the land of the enemy. There is hope for your future. Your children shall come back to their own land."

Midrashic Maxims

Man enters the world with closed hands, as if to say: "The world is mine." He departs from it with open hands, as if to say: "I take nothing with me."

At first, sin is like a thin thread; but in the end, it becomes like a thick rope.

Do not despise a man who abandons his wickedness and repents.

God loves the persecuted and hates the persecutors.

It is easy to acquire an enemy, but difficult to win a friend.

He who turns his enemy into a friend is the bravest hero.

He who hates a man is as if he hated God.

He who steals people's confidence is the worst thief.

Man's friends are: children, wealth, and good deeds.

Learn to receive blows, and forgive those who insult you.

There is no absolute good without some evil in it.

The greater the man, the humbler he is.

He who has nothing to do can quickly die.

A person can forget in two years what he has learned in twenty.

Bad neighbors count a man's income but not his expenses.

Slander is as bad as murder.

Gossipers begin with praise and end with abuse.

When trouble comes into the world, Israel feels it first.

One empire comes and another passes away, but Israel continues forever.

In prosperity, people feel brotherly toward one another.

A man's love goes to his parents before he is married; after he is married, his love goes to his wife.

Every man is a king in his home.

When you come into a town, follow its customs.

Zohar

The Zohar, written in Aramaic in the form of a commentary on the five books of Moses, is the fundamental book of the mystic teachings of Judaism. The Zohar first became known in the thirteenth century as the work of Rabbi Simeon ben Yohai who lived in the second century. The Zohar's mystic interpretation of the Torah is based on the principle that the biblical narratives contain deeper and more vital truths than they ostensibly express.

Soon after the first appearance of the Zohar in Spain through the efforts of Rabbi Moses de Leon, its influence spread among the Jewish people with remarkable speed. The enthusiasm felt for the Zohar was shared by many non-Jewish scholars. Its teachings have played a great part in the lives and writings of many saintly rabbis.

Human Relations

To withhold the wage of a poor man is like taking both his life and that of his family. Even if a long life and many blessings have been decreed for the employer who commits that sin, they are all withdrawn for cutting short the life of the poor. The same thing holds true if he violates the rights of a rich man.

If a man curses his neighbor, he is as guilty as if he sheds his blood.

The command "You shall not place an obstacle in front of the blind" is addressed to a man who leads another into sin.

Happy are those who know the ways of the Torah, for they plant trees of life which are superior to any healing medicine.

In the absence of competent teachers, one should study the Torah from those less qualified to teach, so that one may develop an interest in it, and eventually study under better teachers.

294

Allegory

The story of Jonah may be interpreted as an allegory of man's life in this world. As Jonah descends into the ship, so the soul of man descends from heaven into his body. Man, in this world, is like a ship crossing the vast ocean and in danger of being smashed to pieces by strong winds and stormy waters. Man sins thinking the Lord pays no attention to him. But a raging storm of misfortune is unleashed, and his accusers relentlessly seek his punishment.

He is caught in this tempest and tries to hide from it, just as Jonah went down below deck and fell fast asleep. The captain—his better nature—says to him: "Why are you sleeping? Get up and pray to your God! This is no time to sleep; you are about to stand trial for all your deeds in this world. Repent of your sins, and return to your Lord. Do not be arrogant, but consider that you are dust, and that to dust you shall return."

When man is brought before the heavenly tribunal, some of the King's counsellors will plead for him, others will testify against him. Those who plead for him present arguments in his favor and seek to return him to this world, but they fail. The sea grows more and more stormy, the prosecution is roused to fury against him and overwhelms the defense, and man stands convicted of his transgressions.

And just as the sea ceased from its raging when Jonah was thrown overboard, so the doom of judgment ceases to rage only when man is finally lowered into the grave.

God of Truth

Blessed be the name of the Lord of the Universe! Blessed be thy crown and thy dominion. May thy good will ever abide with thy people Israel. Reveal thy saving power to thy people in thy sanctuary; bestow on us the good gift of thy light, and accept our prayer in mercy. May it be thy will to prolong our life in happiness.

Let me also be counted among the righteous, so that thou mayest have compassion on me and shelter me and mine and all that belong to thy people Israel. Thou art

295

he who nourishes and sustains all; thou art he who rules over all; thou art he who rules over kings, for dominion is thine. I am the servant of the Holy One, blessed be he, before whom and before whose glorious Torah I bow at all times. Not in man do I put my trust, nor do I rely on any angel, but only in the God of heaven who is the God of truth, whose Torah is truth and whose Prophets are truth, and who performs many deeds of goodness and truth. In him I put my trust, and to his holy and glorious name I utter praises. May it be thy will to open my heart to thy Torah, to fulfill the wishes of my heart and of the heart of all thy people Israel for happiness, life and peace.

The Nutshell

When King Solomon went down to the nut garden, which is mentioned in the Song of Songs, he drew an analogy from the layers of a nutshell to the spirits which arouse sensual desires in human beings. God created them to insure the continued existence of the world. The whole universe is constructed on this principle: a brain encircled by many membranes, upper and lower. They are all coverings to one another, brain within brain and spirit within spirit, so that one is a shell to another. The innermost light is of a purity passing comprehension.

Sayings

The love of grandchildren is appreciated more than the love of children.

The man who praises himself shows that he knows nothing.

There is no true justice unless mercy is part of it.

He who praises no one is an arrogant man.

When a dog is hit by a stone he bites a fellow dog.

The ideal man has the strength of a male and the compassion of a female.

296

Siddur-Prayerbook

The Siddur is the most popular book in Jewish life. It is a mirror that reflects the development of the Jewish spirit throughout the ages. The Daily Prayerbook went through a long process of evolution until it finally emerged as a rich anthology of the Hebrew classics. The poetic and philosophic compositions of numerous known and unknown authors constitute a considerable part of the Siddur which contains passages from the Bible, the Mishnah, the Talmud and the Zohar.

Here is a brief description of a number of prayers that follow.

Adon Olam (Eternal Lord) treats of God's omnipotence, and has been part of the morning service since the fifteenth century. It is frequently chanted at the conclusion of Sabbath and Festival services. *Adon Olam* has been attributed to various poets, particularly to Rabbi Solomon ibn Gabirol of eleventh century Spain.

Yigdal is a summary of the thirteen principles of faith formulated by Moses Maimonides in his commentary on the Mishnah. This poem was written by Rabbi Daniel ben Judah of Rome (fourteenth century).

The first two meditations are taken from the Talmud. *Alenu* is the proclamation of God as King over a united humanity. An old tradition claims Joshua, the successor of Moses, as its author. It has been used as the closing prayer of the daily services since the thirteenth century.

With a Great Love is regarded as one of the most beautiful prayers in the liturgies of the world. It is a very old prayer, and probably dates back to the early period of the Second Temple. A profound love for God and the Torah is echoed in this prayer, in which the Merciful Father is entreated to open our eyes and our minds that we may understand his teachings.

Nishmath is a composite poem, consisting of three independent parts. The first paragraph was known during the period of the Mishnah, the second was composed in talmudic times, and the concluding part was added during the early period of the Geonim.

Avinu Malkenu (Our Father, Our King) is mentioned in the Talmud as the prayer of Rabbi Akiba, who died a martyr's death in 135. Since this prayer directly refers to a long series of human failings and troubles, it is omitted on Sabbath when one is expected to be cheerful.

Kaddish was composed in Aramaic, the language spoken by the Jews for about a thousand years after the Babylonian Captivity. The Kaddish is used in the liturgy to mark the conclusion of sections of the service. Though the Kaddish contains no reference to the dead, it is recited for eleven months after the passing away of parents and on the anniversary day of their deaths. The underlying thought in the Kaddish is hope for the redemption and ultimate healing of suffering mankind.

Adon Olam

He is the eternal Lord who reigned before any being was created.

At the time when all was made by his will, he was at once acknowledged King.

And at the end, when all shall cease to be, the revered God alone shall still be King.

He was, he is, and he shall be in glorious eternity.

He is One, and there is no other who can compare with him or be equal to him.

He is without beginning, without end; power and dominion belong to him.

He is my God, my living Redeemer, my stronghold in times of distress.

He is my guide and my refuge, my share of bliss the day I call.

To him I entrust my spirit when I sleep and when I wake.

As long as my soul is with my body the Lord is with me, I am not afraid.

Yigdal

Exalted and praised be the living God! He exists; his existence transcends time.

He is One—there is no oneness like his; he is unknowable—his Oneness is endless.

He has no semblance—he is bodiless; beyond comparison is his holiness.

He preceded all that was created; the First he is though he never began.

He is the eternal Lord; every creature must declare his greatness and his kingship.

His abundant prophecy be granted his chosen men in whom he glories.

Never has there arisen in Israel a prophet like Moses who beheld God's image.

The Torah of truth God gave to his people through his prophet, his own faithful servant.

God will never replace nor ever change his eternal Law for any other law.

He looks into and knows all our secret thoughts; he foresees the end of things at their birth.

He rewards the godly man for his deeds; he repays the evil man for his evil.

At time's end he will send our Messiah to save all who wait for his final help.

God, in his great mercy, will revive the dead; blessed be his glorious name forever.

Meditation

My God, the soul which thou hast placed within me is pure. Thou has created it; thou hast formed it; thou hast breathed it into me. Thou preservest it within me; thou wilt take it from me, and restore it to me in the hereafter. So long as the soul is within me, I offer thanks before thee, Lord my God and God of my fathers, Master of all creatures, Lord of all souls.

Lord our God and God of our fathers, make us familiar with thy Torah and cause us to cling to thy precepts. Let us not fall into sin, temptation or disgrace. Let no evil impulse have power over us. Keep us away from bad companions. Make us cling to good deeds, and bend our will that we may submit to thee. Grant us grace, favor and mercy today and every day. Blessed art thou, O Lord, who bestowest lovingkindness on thy people Israel.

Master of all worlds, it is not because of our righteousness that we can approach thee with our supplications, but only because of thy great compassion toward us. What good are we? What do our lives amount to? What our goodness? What our strength? What can we say in thy presence, Lord our God and God of our fathers? Even heroes are as nothing before thee, men of renown are as though they never existed, wise men are as though they were empty of knowledge, for most of their deeds are worthless to thee, and their lives are but a vain show in thy sight. They are hardly superior to beasts. All is vanity.

Great Love

With great love hast thou loved us, Lord our God. Thou hast showered us with thy great and abundant mercy. Our Father, our King, teach us the laws of life, as thou didst teach our fathers who trusted in thee, and be gracious to us for their sakes. Merciful Father, thou who art always compassionate, have pity on us; give us understanding and discernment, so that we may gladly fulfill all the precepts of thy Torah. Enlighten our eyes to appreciate thy Torah, make our hearts cling to thy commandments, and unite us in a love and reverence for thy name. May we never be put to shame. We trust in thy great and revered name. We thrill with joy over thy salvation. O bring us home in peace from the four corners of the earth and lead us upright into our homeland, for thou art the God who performs triumphs. Blessed art thou, O Lord, who hast graciously chosen thy people Israel.

Alenu

Lord our God, we hope to behold soon thy majestic glory, when the earth shall be cleansed of all its abominations, and false gods shall be destroyed forever; when the world shall become perfect under thy reign, Almighty God; when all mankind shall call upon thy name, and all the wicked men shall turn to thee. May all people realize, that every knee must bow and every tongue pledge allegiance to thee. May they prostrate themselves before thee, Lord our God, and give honor to thy glorious name. May they accept the yoke of thy kingdom. Reign thou over them forever and ever, for the kingdom is thine and thou wilt reign through all eternity, for it is written in thy Torah: "The Lord shall be King forever and ever." And it is written: "The Lord shall be King over all the earth; on that day the Lord shall be One, and his name One."

Nishmath

Every living being shall bless thy name, Lord our God; every mortal shall always glorify and extol thy fame, our King. From eternity to eternity thou art God. Besides thee we have no king who redeems, rescues and sustains, showing mercy in all times of trouble and distress. We have no king but thee.

God of the first and the last, thou who guidest thy world with kindness and thy creatures with mercy, be thou endlessly praised. Thou, O Lord, dost never slumber, but rousest those who sleep. Thou enablest the speechless to speak, and settest the captives free. Thou supportest all who fall and raisest up all who are bowed down. To thee alone we give thanks.

Were our mouths filled with song as the sea is with water, and our tongues with ringing praise as are the waves with roaring sound; were our lips full of adoration as boundless as the wide expanse of heaven, and our eyes sparkling with ecstasy like the sun or moon; were our hands spread out in prayer like the wings of the eagles in the air, and our feet as swift as deer—we would still be unable to thank thee enough, Lord our God and God of our fathers, nor could we bless thy name for a thousandth part of the countless favors which thou hast bestowed on our fathers and on us. Thou hast delivered us from Egypt and redeemed us from slavery. Thou hast nourished us in famine and provided us with plenty. Thou hast rescued us from the sword, caused us to escape the plague and kept us free from severe diseases. To this very day, thy mercy has helped us, and thy kindness has not abandoned us. Do not forsake us ever, Lord our God.

301

High Holyday Prayers

Remember us to life, O King who delightest in life; inscribe us in the book of life for thy sake, O living God.

Thou sustainest the living with kindness; thou supportest all who fall, and healest the sick; thou settest the captives free, and keepest faith with those who sleep in the dust. Thou bringest death and restorest life, and causest salvation to flourish.

Who is like thee, merciful Father? In mercy thou rememberest thy creatures to life.

Lord our God, place thy awe upon all whom thou hast made, thy dread upon all whom thou hast created; let thy works revere thee, let all thy creatures worship thee; may they all blend into one brotherhood to do thy will with a perfect heart. Iniquity shall shut its mouth, wickedness shall vanish like smoke, when thou wilt abolish the rule of tyranny on earth.

Our God and God of our fathers, reign over the whole universe in thy glory; be exalted over all the earth in thy grandeur; shine forth in thy splendid majesty over all the inhabitants of thy world. May every existing being know that thou hast made it; may every creature realize that thou hast created it; may every breathing thing proclaim: "The Lord God of Israel is King, and his kingdom rules over all."

Our God and God of our fathers, sanctify us with thy commandments and grant us a share in thy Torah; satisfy us with thy goodness and gladden us with thy deliverance. Purify our heart to serve thee in truth, for thou art the God of truth.

Avinu Malkenu

Our Father our King, we have sinned before thee.

Our Father our King, abolish all evil decrees against us.

Our Father our King, rid us of every oppressor and adversary.

Our Father our King, bring us in perfect repentance to thee.

Our Father our King, send a perfect healing to the sick among thy people.

Our Father our King, inscribe us in the book of a good life.

Our Father our King, remember that we are but dust.

Our Father our King, fill our hands with thy blessings.

Our Father our King, have compassion on us and on our children.

Our Father our King, deal charitably with us and save us.

Un'thanneh Tokef

Let us tell how utterly holy this day is and how awe-inspiring. It is the day when thy dominion shall be exalted, thy throne shall be established on mercy, and thou shalt occupy it in truth. True it is that thou art judge and arbiter, discerner and witness, inscribing and recording all forgotten things. Thou openest the book of records and it reads itself; every man's signature is contained in it.

The great shofar is sounded; a gentle whisper is heard; the angels, quaking with fear, declare: "The day of judgment is here to bring the hosts of heaven to justice!" Indeed, even they are not guiltless in thy sight. All mankind passes before thee like a flock of sheep. As a shepherd seeks out his flock, making his sheep pass under his rod, so dost thou make all the living souls pass before thee; thou dost count and number thy creatures, fixing their lifetime and inscribing their destiny.

On Rosh Hashanah their destiny is inscribed, and on Yom Kippur it is sealed, how many shall pass away and how many shall be brought into existence; who shall live and who shall die; who shall come to a timely end, and who to an untimely end; who shall perish by fire and who by water; who by sword and who by beast; who by hunger and who by thirst; who by earthquake and who by plague; who by strangling and who by stoning; who shall be at ease and who shall wander about; who shall be at peace and who shall be molested; who shall have comfort and who shall be tormented; who shall become poor

303

and who shall become rich; who shall be lowered and who shall be raised.

But repentance, prayer and charity cancel the stern decree.

Confession on Day of Atonement

Thou knowest the mysteries of the universe and the dark secrets of every living soul. Thou dost search all the inmost chambers of man's conscience; nothing escapes thee, nothing is hidden from thy sight.

May it be thy will, Lord our God and God of our fathers, to forgive all our sins, pardon all our iniquities, and grant atonement for all our transgressions.

For the sin we committed in thy sight unintentionally,

And for the sin we committed against thee by idle talk.

For the sin we committed in thy sight by lustful behavior,

And for the sin we committed against thee publicly or privately.

For the sin we committed in thy sight knowingly and deceptively,

And for the sin we committed against thee by offensive speech.

For the sin we committed in thy sight by oppressing a fellow man,

And for the sin we committed against thee by evil thoughts.

For the sin we committed in thy sight by lewd association,

And for the sin we committed against thee by insincere confession.

For the sin we committed by contempt for parents or teachers,

And for the sin we committed against thee willfully or by mistake.

For the sin we committed in thy sight by unclean lips,

And for the sin we committed against thee by foolish talk.

For the sin we committed in thy sight by fraud and falsehood,

And for the sin we committed against thee by bribery.

For the sin we committed in thy sight by scoffing,

And for the sin we committed against thee by slander.

For the sin we committed in thy sight in dealings with men,

And for the sin we committed against thee in eating and drinking.

For the sin we committed in thy sight by casting off responsibility,

And for the sin we committed against thee in passing judgment.

For the sin we committed in thy sight by plotting against men,

And for the sin we committed against thee by sordid selfishness.

For the sin we committed in thy sight by running to do evil,

And for the sin we committed against thee by talebearing.

For the sin we committed in thy sight by swearing falsely,

And for the sin we committed against thee by groundless hatred.

Forgive us all sins, O God of forgiveness, and grant us atonement.

Modim

We ever thank thee, who art the Lord our God and the God of our fathers. Thou art the strength of our life and our saving shield. In every generation we will thank thee and recount thy praise—for our lives which are in thy charge, for our souls which are in thy care, for thy miracles which are daily with us, and for thy continual wonders and favors—evening, morning and noon. Beneficent One, whose mercies never fail, Merciful One, whose kindness never ceases, thou hast always been our hope.

Kaddish

The Kaddish contains no reference to the dead. The earliest allusion to the Kaddish as a mourners' prayer is found in Mahzor Vitry, dated 1208, where it is said plainly:

305

"The lad rises and recites Kaddish." One may safely assume that since the Kaddish has as its underlying thought the hope for the redemption and ultimate healing of suffering mankind, the power of redeeming the dead from the sufferings of *Gehinnom* came to be ascribed in the course of time to the recitation of this sublime doxology. Formerly the Kaddish was recited the whole year of mourning, so as to rescue the soul of one's parents from the torture of *Gehinnom* where the wicked are said to spend no less than twelve months. In order not to count one's own parents among the wicked, the period for reciting the Kaddish was later reduced to eleven months.

The observance of the anniversary of parents' death, the Jahrzeit, originated in Germany, as the term itself well indicates. Rabbi Isaac Luria, the celebrated Kabbalist of the sixteenth century, explains that "while the orphan's Kaddish within the eleven months helps the soul to pass from *Gehinnom* to *Gan-Eden,* the Jahrzeit Kaddish elevates the soul every year to a higher sphere in Paradise." The Kaddish has thus become a great pillar of Judaism. No matter how far a Jew may have drifted away from Jewish life, the Kaddish restores him to his people and to the Jewish way of living.

Glorified and sanctified be God's great name throughout the world which he has created according to his will. May he establish his kingdom in your lifetime and during your days, and within the life of the entire house of Israel, speedily and soon; and say, Amen.

May his great name be blessed forever and to all eternity.

Blessed and praised, glorified and exalted, extolled and honored, adored and lauded be the name of the Holy One, blessed be he, beyond all the blessings and hymns, praises and consolations that are ever spoken in the world; and say, Amen.

May there be abundant peace from heaven, and life, for us and for all Israel; and say, Amen.

He who creates peace in his celestial heights, may he create peace for us and for all Israel; and say, Amen.

Beliefs and Opinions

BY RAV SAADYAH GAON

Rav Saadyah Gaon (882–942) is regarded as the pioneer of Judeo-Arabic culture in the Middle Ages. He was born in Egypt, where he also spent his early youth. His fame as a great scholar and leader in Israel soon spread far and wide. He was the first non-Babylonian to be appointed to the exalted position of Gaon, or head, of the renowned Talmudic Academy of Sura. This took place in 928, when he was barely forty years old.

At twenty, Rav Saadyah had completed a Hebrew dictionary called *Agron,* and some years later produced an Arabic translation of the Bible, accompanied by a lengthy commentary, which exercised a profound influence on countless Arabic speaking Jews.

Rav Saadyah's *Beliefs and Opinions,* translated into Hebrew under the title of *Emunoth we'Deoth,* is one of the standard works of Jewish religious philosophy. This book, completed in 933, deals with the ten cardinal principles of Judaism, namely: Creation, God, Revelation, Divine Justice, Divine Commands, Resurrection, Messiah, Reward and Punishment and Right Living. In all these he presents, besides his own view, a summary of the most important divergent opinions about them which he refutes on the basis of Scripture, tradition, and rational proof.

There are some people who think that a man should lead a life of self-denial, that he should wander off into the mountains and bewail this perishable world where fortune changes so quickly, where joy turns into sorrow and success into failure. Since a man's whole life is spent in the midst of fraud and falsehood, some say, he should reject this world and seek solitude in the mountains until he dies.

But if all men were to follow such a course of action the world would become a wilderness, and human intellect would degenerate into brute instinct. Self-restraint is indeed commendable if it is properly practised, but a too solitary individual is likely to become so shy of other human beings that he suspects them of wanting to kill him. He nourishes a hatred for them and considers them evil.

Then there are those who believe that one should indulge in eating and drinking, since food and drink keep one alive. These contend that if a person fasts for a day, his strength fails, his eyes become dim, and his power of thinking is weakened. Wine is beautiful, fragrant, and pleasant-tasting; it makes the miser generous and the coward brave.

But the people who advance these arguments stress only the advantages of eating and drinking and ignore the ill effects of over-indulgence. They fail to consider the indigestion and mental sluggishness resulting from overeating; they forget that excessive drinking dulls the nerves and eventually causes intense pain. The person who expends all his energy in obtaining food and drink will try to get them under any circumstances, however unlawful.

Some people are of the opinion that a man should devote himself to amassing money, since the necessities of life, as well as all business transactions, are made possible by it alone. And too, those who are financially successful can afford to be generous, charitable and philanthropic.

Now, the acquisition of money would be perfectly all right if it were to come to a person easily. But the quest for wealth entails great mental exertion, and brings with it many hardships. Sleep may become difficult. Quarrels, contentions and animosities spring up, reminding one of fierce lions attacking their prey. The man who is completely devoted to amassing money pays no attention to the cries of the orphan and widow, to the poor and the oppressed. He breaks his promises and takes false oaths because of his greed, with the result that truth becomes alien to him.

Others, again, are of the opinion that men ought to dedicate themselves earnestly to the propagation of children. If there were no children, they say, the world would not perpetuate itself. Children serve as a provision against old age, and parents receive affection and honor from them. Every distinguished prophet implored God for children.

But, on the other hand, what good are children to a person who is unable to provide them with food, clothing and shelter? One must consider, too, the mother's pain and discomfort during pregnancy and childbirth. Hardships must be endured by the father solely for the purpose of providing food for his family. It is a trouble to raise children, and especially to care for them when they get sick. If they are disobedient and become delinquent, the parents' hearts are broken. Love for their children has been implanted in the hearts of men in order that they may not lose patience with them.

There are those people who hold the view that the highest aim of man's endeavor in this world should be to increase his life-span, since in the course of a long life a person may realize all of his wishes in spiritual as well as in material matters. Life, in their opinion, is lengthened by regular eating and drinking, moderate sex habits, cheerfulness, and the avoidance of dangerous activities. However, we find many people with strong constitutions who are short-lived even though they fulfill these conditions, while others who are comparatively weak live to a ripe old age. Aside from this, the longer a person lives, the more numerous are his cares, worries and troubles.

When a man is old, all his desires cease; his youthful sparkle, his fresh color and good looks fade, and he becomes thoroughly useless, like a cloud from which the rain has fallen. A righteous man loves the life of this world because it serves as a stepladder to the next. Love for life has been implanted in man so that he will not commit suicide when severe trouble assails him.

Some people maintain that one should devote oneself wholly to the pursuit of scientific knowledge, and thereby be acquainted with nature and astronomy. Knowledge of this sort gives pleasure to the soul and is an adornment equal to pearls and jewels worn by kings.

All that is said of scientific knowledge is true. But if a

309

person should fail to concern himself with his everyday needs, his knowledge would be of little use to him, since his existence depends on food, clothing and shelter. If he were to impose himself on other people for his necessities, he would be rejected by them, and his advice would be no longer accepted. Besides this, if he were to be preoccupied exclusively with physical science he would neglect that of religious law. Love for physical science was implanted in man to give support to religious science; they form an excellent combination.

Many people say that a servant of God should dedicate himself exclusively to the service of the Lord. That is, he should fast during the day and praise and glorify God at night, forgetting all his worries in the belief that God will provide for his needs. However, if a person did not bother to eat, he would die.

Service for God consists in fulfilling the precepts of the Torah. But which of the laws of measures, weights and balances is the saintly hermit able to fulfill? What chance has he, in his seclusion, to obey rules concerning what is permitted or forbidden in such matters as the eating of meat? And why should he not study so that he may instruct others that they may comply with the law? But in that case, they and not he would be serving God, since the service of God would be performed by them and not him.

True, a person must rely on God in matters of health and food. But it is impossible to vacate the need for earning a livelihood. Work was designed by God to help mankind. Of course, there are occasions when God miraculously provides us with the things we need. However, as a rule, he does not change the laws of nature established by him.

Orhoth Hayyim

Orhoth Hayyim ("Paths of Life") is attributed to Rabbi Eliezer ben Isaac the Great of eleventh century Germany. He was a pupil of Rabbi Gershom Me'or ha-Golah ("Light of the Exile"), founder of talmudic learning in Germany.

Rabbi Gershom came from France and settled in Mayence, where he gathered many students around himself and taught them the Talmud in the form of a running commentary. This commentary was gradually committed to writing by Rabbi Gershom's disciples, who, in turn, became teachers of the Talmud and influenced subsequent commentators like Rashi.

Orhoth Hayyim has also been attributed to Rabbi Eliezer ben Hyrcanus, one of the most prominent scholars of the first and second centuries. He became known as Eliezer the Great. He attended the college of Rabbi Yohanan ben Zakkai until the fall of Jerusalem in the year 70. Then he became a member of the new Sanhedrin and the academy of learning in Yavneh, south of Jaffa. Referring to his retentive mind, Rabbi Yohanan styled him "a cemented cistern that does not lose a drop" and declared him to be unequaled by his colleagues.

My son, render homage to the Lord and give praise to him. He created you and brought you into the world. You have need of him; he has no need of you. Be not too sure of yourself until your dying day. Do not rely on your physical well-being; many have gone to bed and failed to rise again; many have gone to bed sound and happy and awakened in violent pain.

Worship the Lord God of your fathers, and recite the evening and morning prayers. Be ever among the first ten to arrive in the synagogue. Enter the presence of your Creator in deep reverence. When you pray, know before whom you stand. In the house of learning, do not engage in idle talk; incline your ear to the learned discussion of the students. Consider nothing too trivial, and do not look down on anyone.

Visit the sick and lighten their suffering. Pray for them and leave. Do not stay long, for you may inflict upon them additional discomfort. And when you visit a sick person, enter the room cheerfully.

Do not enter your house suddenly, certainly not the house of your neighbor. Do not make yourself an object of terror in your home. Fear is the cause of many evils. Drive anger out of your heart; it is only fools who cherish wrath. Love the wise and follow them. Greet every person cheerfully and speak the truth. Be discreet in all your actions.

Be trustworthy to all, and do not betray another's secret even when you are on bad terms with him. Eat sparingly rather than be dependent on others. Prefer death to making yourself a burden on people.

Keep away from a bad neighbor and a person of unsavory reputation. Be not like a fly that dwells on sore spots. Cover up the failings of your neighbor and never reveal them. Do not stay among those who speak ill of their fellow men.

Rabbi Solomon ibn Gabirol

Rabbi Solomon ibn Gabirol, the famous poet-philosopher who lived in Spain during the eleventh century is believed to be the author of *Mivhar ha-Peninim* (Select Pearls), which has survived in a Hebrew translation made in the twelfth century. This work was originally composed in Arabic.

Rabbi Solomon ibn Gabirol began to write Hebrew poetry at an early age. During his short life, of which little is known, he won for himself a place among the greatest Hebrew poets of all time. Judah Alharizi of the thirteenth century has this to say about Ibn Gabirol: "The poets who succeeded him strove to learn from his poems, but were unable to touch even the dust of his feet . . . If he had lived longer he would surely have accomplished wondrous things in poetry, but he was snatched away when still young . . . and his light was extinguished before he had completed his thirtieth year."

In a Hebrew poem written at the age of sixteen, Ibn Gabirol declares: "From my youth I labored in the cause of wisdom . . . She has been my sister from my childhood, and of all men she chose me as her friend." He may well refer to his *Select Pearls* when he writes: "I gather stray phrases into strings of thought, and from scattered words I collect pearls of wisdom."

Select Pearls

He who humbles himself in quest of wisdom will be honored by those who seek it of him.

A man's worth is in proportion to his knowledge.

A man is wise when he pursues wisdom, but if he is conceited by his attainment of it he becomes a fool.

Do not be ashamed to ask questions. When asked about things you do not know, do not hesitate to say: "I do not know."

Why are the wise more often at the doors of the rich than the rich at the doors of the wise? Because the wise appreciate the advantage of wealth, while the rich do not know the value of wisdom.

Wisdom gained in old age is like a mark made on the sand; wisdom gained in youth is like an engraving on stone.

Accept the truth from whatever source it comes, even from your inferiors.

None is more deserving of sympathy than a wise man subjected to the judgment of a fool.

The mark of an intelligent man is humility; the mark of a fool is impudence; the result of humility is peace.

Silence is the best answer to a fool.

He who craves more than he needs cannot enjoy what he has.

There are three types of friends: one type is like food without which you cannot exist; another is like medicine, which you need only occasionally; a third is like a disease which you can dispense with altogether.

A companion who tells you your faults privately is better than one who flatters you whenever he sees you.

If you wish to know who is your friend and who your enemy, look into your own heart.

If you keep a secret it is your prisoner; but if you disclose it, you become its prisoner.

Before I utter a word, I am its master; but after I utter it, it becomes my master.

If you want people to dislike you, visit them frequently; if you wish them to like you, visit them rarely.

None is so poor as the man who is afraid of becoming poor.

Everyone can enjoy life except the man who envies others; only the misfortune of others pleases him.

Moral Qualities

At the age of twenty-four, Ibn Gabirol composed one of his major works entitled "The Improvement of the Moral Qualities," emphasizing the principles of ethics independently of religious belief and dogma. According to Ibn Gabirol, man's intelligence must control his natural impulses. The very effort that a man puts forth to control his animal impulses affords him happiness.

Many become displeased with the man who is pleased with himself.

314

What is intelligence? Modesty. What is modesty? Intelligence.

The intellect is the dividing line between man and beast; it masters man's natural impulses and subdues his passion.

Lust is preferred by foolish men because of the immediateness of its delight. They do not consider the suffering and the wretchedness that follow in its wake.

He who hates men is hated by them and suffers injury through their hostility.

Plato said: "He who seeks to be avenged upon his enemies should add a degree of excellence to himself."

If it is impossible for a man to have what he desires, he should desire what he has.

He who desires the impossible will have his wish denied, and he whose wish is denied is miserable.

The surest reason for a man's success is the alertness with which he conducts his affairs.

He who is hasty rushes to destruction; the man of haste is never safe from disappointment.

Be more prompt to do what you have not promised than to promise what you will not do.

The wise man should not be niggardly in imparting his knowledge to others, for knowledge is not lessened in the giving.

The very limit of courage is shown in the strength and endurance with which you bear the things you abhor.

The coward says: "I will not travel, for fear of highwaymen and wild beasts. I will not do business, lest I meet with losses. I will not fast, lest I become ill. I will give no alms, lest I become poor."

Where escape is impossible, it is permissible to use caution which might appear to be cowardice. A man refused to go to a dangerous place, saying to the one who would have sent him: "It is better that you revile me when living than praise me when dead."

Duties of the Heart

BY RABBI BAHYA IBN PAKUDA

Rabbi Bahya ibn Pakuda of eleventh century Spain was the most popular Jewish philosopher of the Middle Ages. His famous book, *Hovoth ha-Levavoth* (Duties of the Heart), became one of the most widely read and deeply loved ethical works. The book is written in ten sections, each representing one of the duties of the heart or spirit as opposed to those of the body. Rabbi Bahya makes the Torah part and parcel of the inner life of the Jew. The first systematic presentation of the ethics of Judaism, Rabbi Bahya's *Duties of the Heart* is an attempt to present the Jewish faith as a great spiritual truth founded on reason, revelation and tradition.

Rabbi Bahya was thoroughly familiar with the entire philosophical and scientific literature of his period. He combined depth of emotion, poetic imagination, eloquence and exquisite diction with a keen intellect. The purpose of his work was to appeal to the sentiments and to stir the hearts of the people. He declared that a man may be as holy as an angel, yet he will not equal in merit the one who leads his fellow man to uprightness. Rabbi Judah ibn Tibbon of twelfth century Spain translated the *Duties of the Heart* from Arabic into Hebrew, hence the famous Hebrew title *Hovoth ha-Levavoth*.

Man consists of a body and a soul, both of which reveal the Creator's goodness; one is seen, the other unseen. Hence, the service we owe to the Creator must be visible as well as invisible.

The outward service includes such visible observances as prayer, almsgiving, and learning and teaching the Torah. The inward service consists of acknowledging the Oneness of God in our hearts, believing in him and obeying his laws, revering and loving him, trusting in him and offering our very lives for him. Even the practical outward duties

316

cannot be adequately performed without a sincere and reverent heart.

Tradition alone, without the support of scientific proof, is sufficient for those who are not able to study. However, anyone who is able to investigate the truth of tradition and fails to do so, because of indolence or disrespect for God's precepts, is guilty of neglect and punished. This may well be illustrated by the following story:

A king once commissioned an officer to receive moneys collected by the officials of his kingdom. He gave the officer special instructions to count, weigh and test the coins. The royal servants brought him the money and assured him that it was correct in amount, weight and value as currency. The officer believed them and was too indolent to ascertain for himself the truth of their report, and thus he violated the royal command. The matter came to the king's notice, and he condemned him for relying on the statement of the servants when he could have ascertained the facts himself.

So too, if you are a man of intellect and understanding, able to verify what you have learned from the sages with regard to the basic principles of religion, you are obligated to use your own faculties to gain clear and definite knowledge of the truth so that your faith and conduct may rest on a foundation of tradition, reason and personal understanding. If you ignore this duty, you fail in your obligation to your Creator.

A king, wishing to test the intelligence of his servants, distributed among them quantities of silk. One servant, more diligent and sensible than his fellows, sorted and resorted the portion allotted to him. He divided it according to its quality into three parts: fine, medium, inferior. With each of these he did the best he could, and had the materials made up by skilled workmen into luxurious garments of different styles and colors, suitable to various occasions and places. The fool among the king's servants turned all his silk into that which the wise servant had made out of the worst weaves, sold it for whatever it would fetch, and hastened to squander the proceeds in eating and drinking. The king was pleased with the conduct of the intelligent servant, promoted him to a position near himself and raised him up to the rank of a favorite. But, displeased with the action of the fool, he drove him away and had him transported to a desolate part of his realm to keep company with those who had incurred his wrath.

God, too, has given the Torah of truth in order to test his servants. The wise man will classify its contents under three headings. First he will try to understand the subtle, spiritual themes which underlie the science that pertains to the inner life—the duties of the heart and the discipline of the soul—and will make a continual effort to fulfill these duties. Then he will select the second part, the practical duties, which he will endeavor to perform, each in its due time and place. He will also make use of the third part, the historical portions of the Bible in an effort to know various types of men, their history in chronological order, the events of past generations, and the problems that beset them. He will apply every item in this third part at the right time, and as occasion requires.

There are men who say that the world came into existence by chance, without a Creator who caused and formed it. I wonder how any rational person in a normal state of mind can entertain such a notion. If, in regard to a revolving water-wheel which irrigates a field or garden, a man were to say he thinks it has been set up without intention on the part of a mechanic who labored to put it together and adjust it, the hearer would promptly charge him with lying.

Now, if such a statement is rejected with regard to a small and insignificant wheel which serves to improve a small portion of the earth, how can anyone permit himself to harbor such a thought concerning the whole world with all the creatures in it? How can one say that the universe came into existence without a wise, purposeful and mighty designer? If ink were poured out accidentally on a blank sheet of paper, legible writing could hardly result. If someone were to bring us a fair copy of a script that could only have been written with a pen and were to tell us that ink had been spilled on paper and these carefully written characters had come of themselves, we would charge him to his face with falsehood. How, then, can one assert that something far finer in its art could have come about without the purpose, power and wisdom of a wise and mighty designer?

Human beings are surrounded by a superabundance of divine favors which are essential to life. When men reach maturity, they foolishly ignore the benefits the Creator has bestowed on them. They may be compared to a little boy found in the desert by a kindhearted person who compassionately took him home and brought him up, feeding and clothing him, and providing him generously with everything he needed till he was old enough to understand the many benefits he had received. When this same kindhearted person heard of a man who had fallen into the hands of an enemy and had for a long time been treated with extreme cruelty, he set the prisoner free and showed him kindness, but to a smaller extent than that shown to the foundling. Yet, the man was more grateful for what had been done for him than the child who had been surrounded with benefits from early infancy.

The reason for this is that the prisoner passed from wretchedness and destitution to a state of happiness and tranquillity at a time when his mental faculties were mature. Hence, he fully appreciated the goodness and kindness of his benefactor. The foundling, however, did not realize the value of the benevolence he had experienced, even after his power of perception had become fully developed, because he had been accustomed to favors from earliest childhood. Still, no one with intelligence will doubt that the kindness to the child was greater in scope.

In the beginning of a man's existence, the Creator designated the mother's body as a couch for the infant so that it might abide in a safe place, a strongly guarded fortress, as it were, where no hand can touch it, where it cannot be affected by heat or cold, but is shielded and sheltered. Here it continues to grow and develop, gradually becoming capable of movement, receiving nourishment without any effort or exertion on its part.

When the infant emerges into the world, the Creator provides it with food from its mother's breast. The blood, which was its nourishment before it was born, is now converted into milk in the mother's breast. As the infant's physical faculties grow stronger, it is able to distinguish sight and sound. God inspires the parents with kindness, love and compassion for their offspring, so that rearing it is not a burden to them. They are more sensitive to its needs than to their own requirements.

It is a great blessing that during childhood one cannot distinguish good from evil. For were a child endowed in its early years with a ripe intellect and mature powers of perception, he would die of grief. Remarkable too is the fact that crying, as learned physicians assert, is beneficial to an infant.

Later on he meets with painful experiences and thereby gains knowledge of the world. In this way man is put on guard against a too implicit trust in the world. He learns not to let his lusts have dominion over him, lest he become like the brutes that have neither knowledge nor understanding.

One should reflect upon the uses of the limbs and organs and the various ways in which each functions—the hands are for taking and giving, the feet for walking, the eyes for seeing, the ears for hearing, the nostrils for smelling, the tongue for speaking, the mouth for eating, the teeth for masticating, the stomach for digesting, the liver for purifying the food, the kidneys for removing superfluities. The heart is the reservoir of natural heat and the well-spring of life; the brain is the seat of all spiritual faculties, the center of sensation, and the root from which the nerves branch out. And so it is with the rest of the bodily organs. They all have their specific functions.

The humble man does not think of himself as having any special merit; hence, whatever he receives of the world's goods suffices for his maintenance. This induces tranquillity of spirit and diminishes anxiety. He eats what is offered to him, wears the apparel he finds, sleeps where he can, and is content with only a few of this world's goods. The opposite is the case of the proud and arrogant man. However much he obtains, it is not enough.

The humble man is patient when troubles befall him and when he meets with reverses in his affairs. But the fear of the proud man is great and his patience is small when troubles beset him. The humble man is beloved by his fellow men. It is easy for him to share their views and adopt their usages. It is related of a certain king that he was in the habit of walking fast. When asked the reason, he replied: "I thus keep myself far away from the path of pride and arrive sooner at my destination."

A sage was once asked: "How did you come to be accepted as leader of your contemporaries?" He answered: "I never met anyone in whom I did not see some quality in which he surpassed me. If he was wiser than I, I concluded that because of his superior wisdom he must also be more God-fearing. If he had less wisdom than I, I considered that on the Day of Judgment he will be held the less accountable."

Life and death are brothers that dwell together; they cling to each other and cannot be separated. They are joined by the two extremes of a frail bridge over which all created beings travel. Life is the entrance; death is the exit. Life builds, death demolishes; life sows, death reaps; life plants, and death uproots.

Provide abundantly for yourself while you are yet alive and able. Say not: "I shall make provision tomorrow," for you do not know what the next day may bring forth. Know that yesterday shall never come back and that whatever you have done therein is being weighed, numbered and counted. Nor should you say: "I shall do it tomorrow," for the day of death is hidden from all the living. Hasten to do your task every day, for death may at any time send forth its arrow-like lightning. Delay not to do your daily task, for like a bird that strays from its nest is a man that strays from his home. Seek the Lord your Maker with all your might and strength; seek uprightness, seek meekness.

Kuzari

BY RABBI YEHUDAH HALEVI

The Kuzari, written in the form of a discussion at the court of the king of the Khazars, is the work of the foremost Hebrew poet, Rabbi Yehudah Halevi (1085–1142), who had an excellent practice as a physician in Toledo, Spain.

The story of his life as physician, philosopher and poet has come down to us in small fragments. In her introduction to the *Selected Poems of Yehudah Halevi,* Nina Solomon writes: Yehudah Halevi was "God-intoxicated" or, to use Heine's phrase, "God-kissed." God, not the physician, was to him the Healer; God, not human reason, was the source of truth. The physician was but God's servant. He took the poet's view of Judaism and of the Jews. Israel is to him the heart of mankind, filling the same function in the world at large as does the heart in the body of man. Halevi's songs to Zion are his most beautiful works, displaying the deepest of his emotions. Singing to Zion, he said of himself: "I am a harp for your songs."

The chief purpose of the *Kuzari* is to show that the continuity of Jewish tradition is the best proof of the validity of the Jewish faith. Many of the Khazars, in what is now southeastern Russia, embraced the Jewish religion in the seventh century.

Upon completing his Arabic *Kuzari,* Rabbi Yehudah Halevi made a pilgrimage to Jerusalem where, according to a tradition, he was ridden down and killed by an Arab horseman.

We know from historical records that the king of the Khazars became a convert to Judaism about four hundred years ago. He had repeatedly dreamed of an angel who addressed him in these terms: "Your intentions are pleasing to the Creator, but your actions are not." He devoted himself wholeheartedly to the temple service and the sacrifices, yet the angel came one night and repeated: "Your intentions are pleasing to the Creator, but your actions are not." This led him to give careful examination to the different faiths and religions. Finally he became a convert to Judaism, together with many other Khazars.

Since he was commanded to seek work that might please God, he invited, in turn, a philosopher, a Christian, and a Muslim to his residence, and questioned them concerning their respective beliefs. Then he invited a rabbi and asked him about his religion.

The rabbi declared: I believe in the God of Abraham, Isaac and Jacob, who with signs and wonders, led the people of Israel out of Egypt; who sustained them in the wilderness and gave them the promised land; who brought them across the Red Sea and the Jordan in a miraculous way. He sent Moses with the Torah, and after him thousands of prophets who confirmed its truth.

The people of Israel lived in Egypt as slaves. They looked forward to the promise, given to their ancestors, that the land of Canaan would become their heritage. While they groaned in the depths of Egyptian slavery, the promised land was in the possession of seven mighty and prosperous nations.

Pharaoh could not protect himself against the ten plagues which befell the Egyptians, affecting their streams, land, air, plants, animals, and even their own bodies. The most beloved member of their households, the firstborn son, died instantly at midnight. All these plagues were preceded by warnings, which proves that they were ordained of God, who does what pleases him.

Up to that time the people of Israel had had only a few laws handed down to them from Adam and Noah. Moses did not abolish these laws, but rather added to them. It is a long and well-known story.

When the people of Israel came to the parched wilderness, God sent them daily food, which they ate for forty years. Although the people believed in the message of Moses, they still remained a little doubtful as to whether God really ever spoke to mortals. They suspected that it was merely divine inspiration. They could not associate speech with a divine being, since speech is a corporeal function.

God, however, desiring to remove this doubt, commanded them to ready themselves spiritually as well as physically to hear his words. These were preceded by overwhelming phenomena: lightnings, thunders, earthquake and fire. The fire remained visible to the people for forty days; they also saw Moses enter and emerge from it. They distinctly heard the giving of the Ten Commandments, which are the very essence of the Torah. God engraved them on two tablets of precious stone and handed them to Moses.

I do not say that this is exactly how these things occurred. Maybe they happened in another way which is too deep for me to understand. But the result was that every one who witnessed these phenomena was convinced that the whole revelation was definitely of God.

Israel among the nations is like the heart among the organs of the body. Israel is at one and the same time the weakest and the healthiest of them all. Even as the heart may be affected by the disease of other organs, so Israel is affected by the troubles and wrongs of other nations. The tribulations which we experience are meant to cleanse us and to remove all taint of evil from us.

Rational laws are indispensable in the administration of every human society. Even a gang of robbers must have some code of justice; otherwise mutual fellowship could not exist. The function of divine law will be incomplete unless social and rational laws are perfected. Divine law imposes no asceticism on us; it desires rather that we should grant our every mental and physical faculty its due, without overburdening one at the expense of another. If a person gives in to licentious desires, he blunts the edge of his mental keenness; if he leans toward violence, he injures some other faculty.

Long fasting is not a suitable form of worship. Our Torah as a whole is based on reverence, love and joy. Through any of these you may approach God. Your contrition on a fast day is not more effective in drawing you near to God than is your joy on the Sabbath and on holy days. Observance of the Sabbath is an acknowledgment of God's omnipotence as the Creator and Originator of all things; it brings you closer to God than asceticism and retirement do. The influence of divine power is not seen in choice phrases and raised eyebrows, in weeping and praying and uttering empty words, unsupported by charitable deeds; it is only made manifest by a pure heart and good works which, although difficult, are performed with utmost zeal and love.

The servant of God does not detach himself from secular contacts and does not despise life, which is one of God's bounties to him. On the contrary, he loves the world and desires a long life because they give him opportunities for achieving eternal life. The more good he does, the greater his claim to life in the future world. Philosophers love solitude, for in solitude they can refine their thoughts. Nevertheless, they seek the society of disciples in order to stimulate their research and reasoning. Such was the case of men like Socrates.

But in this day and age, the man who desires ascetic solitude can count only on pain of soul and body. He is sick and miserable, living as a prisoner and hating life purely out of disgust with his solitude and pain, not because he enjoys his seclusion. How could it be otherwise? He has not received prophetic light, nor has he acquired knowledge to stimulate his interest and enjoyment of life as the philosophers did. Suppose he is God-fearing, humbling himself and reciting as many prayers as he can remember, his satisfaction in these things lasts but a few days, only as long as they are new experiences to him. Frequently repeated words lose their effect on the soul and do not make for humility and submission.

Like a prince who is obeyed by his subjects, the godly man is obeyed by his mental and physical faculties over which he has full control. He is fit to rule. If he were the prince of a country he would be as just to his people as he is to his own body and soul. He satisfies his desires moderately, restraining them from excess. He further subdues his urge toward superiority by allowing it only as much freedom as is required for the discussion of scientific or practical views. He always acts and speaks in the realization that he is being observed by God, who rewards and punishes, calling man to account for everything objectionable in word or deed. He is aware that every part of his body was formed with infinite wisdom. He notices how well his limbs obey his will when he wishes to get up or sit down or assume any other posture.

If God's providence and guidance were removed for even one instant, the whole world would perish. Deeply convinced of God's justice, the pious man finds in it protection and help from the world's woe and trouble. He knows that the Creator sustains and guides his creatures with wisdom surpassing our intellect. The perfection of creation reveals the purpose of an all-wise God, who has endowed great and small, with all their essential organs. He gave speed to the timid hare and stag that they might have safety in flight. He gave the ferocious lion power to claw and tear its enemy. Anyone who considers the formation and use of his limbs and their relation to the animal instinct, sees in them so perfect a proportion and so precise an arrangement that no doubt or uncertainty whatever can remain in his mind concerning the justice of the Creator.

Reason refutes those who see injustice in the fact that a hare falls prey to a lion and a fly to a spider. How can I charge the supremely wise Creator with injustice? Divine injustice is out of the question. I see only that this wise and just Master of the world has equipped the lion with ferocity and strength, with teeth and claws; that he has furnished the spider with cunning and designated the fly to be its food, just as some fish are food for others. I cannot but conclude that I am unable to fathom the wisdom and justice of the Almighty. Everyone should therefore follow the example of Nahum of Gimzo who, no matter what happened to him, was in the habit of saying: "This too is for the best." The man who does this will live happily and bear lightly all the tribulations of life.

Ethical Will

BY RABBI JUDAH IBN TIBBON

Rabbi Judah ibn Tibbon of the twelfth century was born in Spain, whence he fled because of religious persecution. He settled in France, where he devoted himself to the translation of philosophic works from Arabic into Hebrew.

He translated a series of epoch-making books, including Rabbi Bahya's *Duties of the Heart,* Rav Saadyah Gaon's *Beliefs and Opinions,* and Rabbi Yehudah Halevi's *Kuzari.*

Ibn Tibbon addressed the following admonition to his son, Samuel ibn Tibbon, who later translated Maimonides' *Guide for the Perplexed,* one of the world's most influential books.

My son, ability is of no avail without inclination. Exert yourself while still young; awake from your sleep. Devote yourself to science and religion; accustom yourself to moral living. There are two sciences: ethics and physics; strive to excel in both.

Let not the prospect of great gain blind you to risk your life; do not be like a bird that sees the grain and not the net. Respect yourself and your family by providing decent clothes according to your means.

My son, show your kindness to all human beings. Tend those who are sick and heal the poor gratuitously. Thus you will win the respect of high and low.

Read through a second time whatever you write; no one can avoid errors. A man's mistakes in writing bring him into disrepute; they are remembered against him all his days.

Take good care of your health; do not be your own destroyer.

Honor your wife to your utmost capacity.

If you give orders, let your words be gentle.

All I ask of you is to attain a higher degree of wisdom; to behave in a friendly spirit toward all; to gain a good name; to deserve praise for your dealings with your fellow men; to revere God and perform his commandments. Thus you will honor me in life and in death.

Devote yourself to your children; be tender to them; be not indifferent to any slight ailment in them or in yourself.

My son, if you hear fools disparaging me, be silent and make no reply. Take no notice of anything that they may say against me. Remember: "The fruit of hearing others in silence is peace of mind, confidence, and joy."

Arrange your library in fair order so as not to weary yourself in your search for the book you need. Never refuse to lend books to anyone who can be trusted to return them. Honor your teachers and attach yourself to your friends. Treat them with respect in all places and under all circumstances.

My son, make your books your companions. Let your shelves be your treasure grounds and gardens. If you are weary, change from garden to garden. Your desire will renew itself, and your soul will be filled with delight.

Moses Maimonides

Rabbi Moses ben Maimun, usually called *Rambam* (from the initials of his name and that of his father), lived scarcely sixty-nine years (1135–1204). His youth was spent in wandering from place to place with his father and his brother David. He experienced religious persecutions in Spain and North Africa from the time he was thirteen years old until he established himself in Cairo, Egypt, as the court physician of the Sultan Saladin.

During the trying periods of wandering, sickness and tragedies in the family, he managed to devote himself to a systematic study of Talmud, logic, mathematics, astronomy, medicine, and the other natural sciences. At the age of sixteen he wrote a book on the terminology of logic, which has been repeatedly translated and interpreted from the original Arabic.

His commentary on the Mishnah, which has served as a guiding light to countless students of the Talmud, was begun when he was twenty-three years old and completed ten years later, at the age of thirty-three. Concerning this work, he writes: "The task I undertook was not easy of fulfillment. I was troubled by the distress of the exile which God had inflicted upon us, so that we were being driven from one corner of the world to the other. I started part of the work on the road; some parts I wrote during the sea voyage. . . ."

In 1172, during a crisis through which the Jews of Yemen in south-western Arabia were passing, Maimonides wrote his *Letter to Yemen* known as *Iggereth Teman,* which has come down to us in three Hebrew translations from the Arabic. A forced conversion to Islam threw the Jews of Yemen into panic, and Maimonides succeeded in supplying guidance and encouragement to the Yemenites. The *Letter to Yemen* was sent to Jacob Alfayyumi with the request that it be circulated widely and read publicly in all the congregations of Yemen. Roused to enthusiasm and gratitude for the spiritual and material help Maimonides extended to them, the Yemenite Jews included a complimentary allusion to Maimonides in the daily Kaddish prayer.

Maimonides spent ten years writing his Jewish code of laws and ethics, the *Mishneh Torah*, which consists of fourteen books in lucid and superb Hebrew. This gigantic work penetrated every Jewish community shortly after its appearance in 1180. All rabbinic writings of the past seven centuries have been greatly affected by it. In the *Mishneh Torah*, which is indeed the full summary of Judaism in all its varied aspects, Maimonides condensed the Jewish lore contained in the Bible, the two Talmuds, the Midrash, and the responsa literature of the Geonim. About four hundred commentaries have been written on the *Mishneh Torah*, which has exercised the greatest influence on Jewish life.

In answer to a letter from one of his correspondents, who had expressed regret that the *Mishneh Torah* was not intelligible to him because it was not written in Arabic, Maimonides wrote that his Hebrew style was so easy that it would take one only a short time to grasp it. He added: "After having become familiar with one of the fourteen books you will easily understand the whole work. By no means would I render it into Arabic, for it would lose its flavor in the translation." The numerous commentaries and super-commentaries are not concerned for the most part with *what* Maimonides says but rather *why* he says it. What he says is clear. The questions and arguments raised by scholars refer to the sources of Maimonides' code.

Mishnah Commentary

Let us suppose that a young boy is brought before a teacher. The purpose of instructing the boy obviously is to enable him to receive knowledge, which is the greatest good! But the boy is too tender in years and too weak in understanding to appreciate the good which is intended for him and the advantages which he will reap from his progress.

Since the teacher is wiser than the boy, he will encourage his pupil to study by offering such things as appear desirable and worthwhile to the child. He will say: "Read, and you shall have nuts and figs and honey." The little one reads with zest, not because he finds pleasure in the book or understands that he will be the better for reading it, but because he wants the sweets which have been promised him, and which mean more to him than all his studies.

When he becomes a little older, those first objects of his desire will appear to him insignificant and contemptible; and if he is to be urged to further effort, he must be offered a greater reward. Then the teacher will say: "Read, and you shall have splendid shoes and magnificent clothes." The prize is tempting and the boy works hard. Later the prize is again changed and he is promised a certain amount of money for every lesson he learns.

At last, when he is grown up, these rewards tempt him no longer and the teacher exhorts him, saying: "Study, and you may become a president or a judge, and people will bow before you." Then the young man studies, keeping in view the honor and glory which men may bestow on him.

All of this is unworthy, but it is necessary, because the human spirit is narrow and, while acquiring wisdom, hopes for other, more material advantages.

In searching for truth, the goal is truth itself. Torah is truth. The aim in knowing the commandments is the practice of them. Hence the saying: "Do not be like servants who serve their master for the sake of receiving a reward, but rather be like those who serve their master without expecting a reward." This is called serving in the spirit of love.

Our sages say with the Psalmist: "Blessed is the man who glorifies God and takes pleasure in his commandments and not in the reward which he might expect." This thought is expressed even more clearly in an early Midrash: "Lest you say: I will learn the Torah so that I may become rich, that I may become a rabbi, that I may be rewarded in the world to come, it is written: *Love the Lord your God.* That is, all that you do should be done only out of your love for God."

However, since man is accustomed to act or not to act according to the good or the harm which may result, he loses nothing by shaping his conduct with a view to reward and punishment until, by habit and zeal, he arrives at an understanding of the truth and serves purely out of love. Our sages of old said: "A man should by all means learn Torah and do good deeds, even if it is only to gain a reward or avoid punishment, for eventually he will arrive at a stage of doing good for its own sake."

Eight Chapters

Just as a physician must have perfect knowledge of the human body and be acquainted with the means by which a patient may be cured, so a person who tries to cure the soul must have a thorough knowledge of it in order to improve its moral qualities. He should know how to prevent disease and how to maintain health.

The sensations of one species are not, of course, like those of another, for each species has its own characteristic soul distinct from every other. Let us imagine that three dark places are lit up: one by the sun, the second by the moon, and the third by a flame. In each of these places there is light; but the cause in the one place is the sun, in the other the moon and in the third the fire. So it is with sensation and its causes. In man it is the human soul, and in the eagle it is the soul of an eagle.

Sensation in man comes from the five well-known senses —sight, sound, taste, smell, and touch. The mind retains impressions of things after they have ceased to affect the senses, and the imagination then constructs new ideas of which the mind has never received any impression. For instance, one may imagine a man whose head reaches the sky while his feet are on the ground, or an animal with a thousand eyes or any other impossibility.

A man's likes or dislikes give rise to the following activities: the pursuit of an object or flight from it, inclination and avoidance, anger and affection, fear and courage, cruelty and compassion, love and hate.

Reason, the faculty peculiar to man, enables him to understand and reflect, to acquire knowledge of the sciences and to distinguish between right and wrong.

The soul, like the body, is subject to health and illness. It is healthy when it constantly strives to do what is good; it is ill when it craves to do wrong. Now, just as those who

332

are physically ill imagine that the sweet is bitter and the bitter sweet, so those who are ill in spirit imagine that evil is good and the good, evil.

When people realize they are sick, they consult a physician who tells them what they must do, and prescribes medicines which are often unpleasant and bitter. So too, those who have become spiritually ill should consult the sages—ethical physicians—who will advise them not to indulge in evils which seem good only to those who are corrupt. Eventually they will be healed, and their moral qualities will be restored to normal.

But, if a morally sick man is unaware of his illness, or does not seek a remedy after becoming aware of it, his end will be like that of a person who disregards a physical ailment and continues to indulge himself—he meets with an untimely death because of self-neglect.

Goodness keeps to a middle path which lies between two equally bad extremes, the *too much* and the *too little*. Liberality is the middle course between miserliness and extravagance; courage, between recklessness and cowardice; humility, between arrogance and self-abasement; contentedness, between avarice and slothful indifference. The whole intention of the noble man is to be good to others through personal service, money or advice, but without bringing suffering or disgrace on himself by it. His is the middle road of conduct.

The mean-minded person does not want others to succeed in anything, even though their success may not bring him any hardship, loss, or injury. His behavior is the one extreme.

The exceedingly generous man, on the other hand, is one who performs deeds of kindness willingly in spite of bringing on himself great injury or disgrace, hardship or considerable loss. His behavior is the other extreme.

Sometimes the extreme of *too much* is considered noble, as when those who risk their lives are hailed as heroes. When people see a man reckless beyond reason—running deliberately into danger and courting death, escaping only by a slim margin—they call him a hero. At other times, the extreme of *too little* is thought good, as when the do-nothing is considered to be a man contented with his share of things. What is really praiseworthy is the middle course of action. Everyone should strive for it, weighing and studying his conduct carefully.

The Torah leads us to the path of moderation. If we examine the commandments, we will find that they are designed for the discipline and guidance of the soul. The commandments which prohibit revenge and the bearing of a grudge, for example, are intended to soften the fury of a person's anger.

If a man carefully keeps to the middle course of action, he will reach the highest degree of perfection possible to a human being. This conduct is the most acceptable way of serving God.

A man must keep his mind constantly on one goal—attainment of the knowledge of God. It is the greatest achievement possible for mortal man. All of his actions, and in fact his whole conduct, must be directed toward this goal. His purpose in eating or drinking, in sleeping, waking or resting should be to preserve his bodily health, and thus secure his mental well-being, so that he can readily acquire wisdom and eventually reach the highest goal—knowledge of God.

Accordingly, he should not choose only what is agreeable in food and drink—but should select what is most healthful, whether or not it tastes good. There are indeed times when agreeable things may be chosen, with a cure in view; for example, when a man is downhearted and wishes to cheer himself by listening to music or by strolling through lovely gardens and splendid buildings, or gazing at beautiful pictures. These things serve to keep the body healthy; but the real purpose in maintaining good health should be to acquire wisdom. Likewise, in the pursuit of wealth one's main purpose should be to spend it for those things in life which lead to attainment of the knowledge of God.

The man who insists on indulging in savory food, even though it may lead to serious illness, should be classed with the lower animals. A man acts like a man only when he eats that which is wholesome and does not satisfy his desires without first considering their good or ill effects.

It is possible to shape one's conduct with no aim beyond that of maintaining one's health or guarding against disease. A person's real duty is to do whatever he can to maintain a perfect condition of the body, so that he may be in position to acquire the ethical and mental virtues. To live according to this standard is to arrive at a very high degree of perfection, which only a few have succeeded in attaining. The man who directs all the faculties of his soul toward the one greatest ideal of comprehending God should be ranked with the prophets.

It is impossible for man to be innately good or bad, just as it is impossible for him to be born skilled in a particular art. It is possible, however, for him to be susceptible from his very birth to the acquisition of good or bad characteristics. If one who has a good mind is left without instruction, he will without doubt remain ignorant. But on the other hand, if a dull, phlegmatic person is given instruction, he will gradually succeed in acquiring knowledge and understanding.

So too, the man who is more hot-tempered than the average is likely to become brave after a little training. A man with a colder than average temperament is predisposed by nature toward cowardice. But he too, under intensive training, can become a brave man.

One should not believe the absurd statements of astrologers, who falsely assert that the constellation occurring at a child's birth determines the child's future character, good or bad. This would be tantamount to saying that the individual is compelled by fate to follow a certain line of conduct. According to the Torah, man's conduct is entirely in his own hands, and no external influence can force him to be good or bad. If he were compelled to act according to the decree of fate, he would have no freedom of choice and the commands of the Torah would thus become null and void. It would also be useless for him to study or attempt to learn an art, since external forces would restrain him from attaining knowledge or skill; and his reward and punishment alike would be pure injustice. Building houses, working for a living and running away from danger would be absolutely useless under these circumstances.

The truth of the matter is that man has full command over all his actions. For this reason, God tells him: "I have set before you this day life and death, good and evil . . . choose life!" Since man is free to act either morally or immorally, it is necessary to teach, command and exhort him, to punish or reward him. He does what is right or wrong by his own determination, without the control of fate. Hence, the divine command; hence, the teaching, the explaining, the reward and the punishment. Of this truth there is absolutely no doubt.

Thirteen Principles of Faith

In the *Thirteen Principles of Faith,* Maimonides sums up his Jewish philosophy, namely: (1) There is a Creator. (2) He is One. (3) He is incorporeal. (4) He is eternal. (5) He alone must be worshiped. (6) The prophets are true. (7) Moses was the greatest of all prophets. (8) The entire Torah was divinely given to Moses. (9) The Torah is immutable. (10) God knows all the acts and thoughts of men. (11) He rewards and he punishes. (12) The Messiah will come. (13) There will be resurrection.

1. I firmly believe that the Creator, blessed be his name, is the Creator and Ruler of all created beings, and that he alone has made, does make, and ever will make all things.

2. I firmly believe that the Creator, blessed be his name, is One; that there is no oneness in any form like his; and that he alone was, is, and ever will be our God.

3. I firmly believe that the Creator, blessed be his name, is not corporeal; that no bodily accidents apply to him; and that there exists nothing whatever that resembles him.

4. I firmly believe that the Creator, blessed be his name, was the first and will be the last.

5. I firmly believe that the Creator, blessed be his name, is the only one to whom it is proper to address our prayers, and that we must not pray to anyone else.

6. I firmly believe that all the words of the Prophets are true.

336

7. I firmly believe that the prophecy of Moses our teacher, may he rest in peace, was true; and that he was the chief of the prophets, both of those who preceded and of those that followed him.

8. I firmly believe that the whole Torah which we now possess is the same which was given to Moses our teacher, may he rest in peace.

9. I firmly believe that this Torah will not be changed, and that there will be no other Torah given by the Creator, blessed be his name.

10. I firmly believe that the Creator, blessed be his name, knows all the actions and thoughts of human beings, as it is written: "It is he who fashions the hearts of them all, he who notes all their deeds."

11. I firmly believe that the Creator, blessed be his name, rewards those who keep his commands, and punishes those who transgress his commands.

12. I firmly believe in the coming of Messiah; and although he may tarry, I daily wait for his coming.

13. I firmly believe that there will be a revival of the dead at a time which will please the Creator, blessed and exalted be his name forever and ever.

Letter to Yemen

My fellow Jews, it is essential for all of you to consider what I am about to point out. You should impress it upon the minds of your women and children, so that their faith may be strengthened. May the Lord keep us from religious doubt.

Remember that our religion is true and authentic. By it God has distinguished us from the rest of mankind. This did not happen because we had merit, but rather as an act of divine grace, and for the sake of our forefathers. God has made us a unique prople through his laws and precepts. Because of this, all the nations, instigated by envy and impiety, rose up against us; all the kings of the earth, motivated by injustice and enmity, set themselves to persecute us. They wanted to thwart God—but God cannot be thwarted!

Ever since the revelation at Mount Sinai, every despot has made it his first aim and his final purpose to destroy our Torah by violence and brute force. Despots are the first of two classes which attempt to foil the divine will. The second class consists of the most intelligent and educated among the nations. These, also, attempt to demolish our Torah through argument and controversy. They seek to wipe out every trace of it by means of their polemical writings, just as despots plan to do with the sword. But neither of them shall succeed. The God of truth mocks and derides them, because they endeavor to achieve a goal that is beyond the power of mortal men.

Our religion differs as much from other religions as a living person differs from a lifeless statue, which is ever so well carved out of marble, wood, bronze, or silver. When an ignorant person sees a statue that superficially resembles man in contour, form, features, and color, he thinks that the structure of its parts is similar to that of a human being. But the informed person, who knows the interior of both, is aware of the fact that the internal structure of the statue shows no skillful workmanship at all, whereas the inner parts of man are truly marvellously made.

So too, a person ignorant of the secret meaning of the Bible, and of the deeper significance of the Torah, would be led to believe that our religion has something in common with another, if he makes a comparison between the two. True, both contain a system of religious observances, sanctioned by reward and punishment. But the tenets of other religions, although they resemble those of the Bible, have no deeper meaning, but are merely superficial imitations. People have modeled their religions after ours in order to glorify themselves.

My brethren, you all know that in the time of Nebuchadnezzar the Jews were compelled to worship idols. Ultimately, God destroyed Nebuchadnezzar and put an end to his laws, and the religion of truth came back into its own.

During the period of the Second Temple, wicked Greek rulers instituted severe persecutions against Israel in order to abolish the Torah. Every Jew was forced to write on his garment the words: "No longer have I anything to do with the Lord God of Israel." This state of affairs lasted about fifty-two years. Finally, God brought to an end their empire and their laws.

Divine assurance was given to Jacob that his descendants would survive those who degraded them, for it is written: "Your descendants shall be like the dust of the earth." That is to say, although his descendants will be abased like dust trodden under foot, they will ultimately emerge triumphant and victorious; and, just as dust settles finally on the man who stamps on it, and remains after he is gone, so shall Israel outlive its persecutors. We possess the divine assurance that Israel is indestructible and imperishable, and that it will always continue to be a preeminent community. Just as it is impossible for God to cease to exist, so is it unthinkable that Israel should disappear from the earth, for it is written: "For I the Lord do not change; and you, O sons of Jacob, will not be consumed."

Do not be dismayed at the persecutions of our people, for these trials are designed only to test and purify us. You should take it upon yourselves to hearten one another. Let your elders guide the youth and let your leaders direct the masses. Accept these principles of a religion that shall never fail:

God is One, and Moses is his prophet and spokesman. The entire Torah was divinely revealed to Moses. It shall neither be repealed nor superseded, supplemented nor abridged. It shall never be supplanted by another divine revelation.

Keep well in mind the revelation at Sinai, and impress it on the minds of our children, for this event is the pivot of our religion. Never before or since has a whole nation witnessed a revelation from God, or beheld his splendor. The purpose of all this was to establish our faith so that nothing can change it. God revealed himself to you in this manner in order to give you strength to withstand all future trials. Now, do not slip or err; be steadfast in your religion and persevere in your faith and in its duties.

I notice that you are inclined to believe in astrology and

in the influence of planets on human affairs. You should dismiss such notions from your thoughts. Cleanse your minds as one cleanses dirty clothes. At the time when Moses rose to leadership, astrologers unanimously predicted that our nation would never be freed from bondage, but they were wrong! Fortune smiled on Israel! Egypt was smitten with plagues at the very time for which the astrologers forecast a wholesome climate, an abundance of good things and prosperity for its inhabitants.

They are also wrong in their predictions concerning the era of the Messiah (may it speedily come). God will prove false their views and beliefs, and will send the Messiah in his own good time.

Remember that it is because of the vast number of our sins that God has hurled us into the midst of the Arabs, who have persecuted us severely and passed harmful and discriminatory laws against us. Never did a nation molest, degrade, and hate us as much as they! This continual illtreatment nearly crushes us. No matter how much we suffer, no matter how much we try to remain at peace with them, they stir up strife and sedition, as David predicted, saying: "I am for peace; but when I speak, they are for war!" Hence, if we start trouble and try to claim power from them we will only be giving ourselves up to certain destruction.

May God grant us the privilege of beholding the return of the exiles. May he take us out from this darkest of valleys in which he has placed us. May he remove the darkness from our eyes and from our hearts. Peace, peace, much peace! Amen.

Mishneh Torah

The basic principle of all wisdom is to know that there is a First Cause who has brought every existing thing into being. This is God, who controls the universe by his infinite power. When a person contemplates God's great and wondrous works and obtains a glimpse of God's incomparable and infinite wisdom, he will straightway love and glorify him, and long to know his great name, even as David said: "My whole being longs for God, the living God!" He will realize that man is a small creature, lowly and obscure, with but limited intelligence, standing in the presence of him who is perfect in knowledge. David said: "When I look up to the heavens which thy fingers made, the moon and stars that thou hast shaped, I ask: What is man that thou shouldst think of him?"

God inspires men with the gift of prophecy. But the spirit of prophecy rests only upon the wise man who has a strong moral character and who always keeps his passions under control. The prophets are of various degrees. Just as some sages are greater in wisdom than others, so are some prophets greater than others in their gift of prophecy.

The prophets received their revelations in dreams, when a deep sleep had fallen upon them. Their limbs trembled, their physical strength failed them, so that the mind became free to comprehend the vision it beheld. They did not prophesy whenever they pleased; they had to be in a joyous and cheerful mood and in solitude, for the spirit of prophecy does not descend upon one who is melancholy or indolent.

Every Jew is obligated to offer his life for the sanctification of the name of God. This, however, applies only to the three capital crimes of idolatry, adultery, and murder: one must choose death rather than commit any of these crimes. Anyone who has acted accordingly, has in truth sanctified the name of God.

But if a Jew is compelled to commit any other sin on pain of death, he should yield rather than lose his life, because the Torah tells us that man is to *live* by God's commands but not to *die* by them. A Jew who sacrifices his life by refusing to violate a divine command is guilty of suicide.

If a person is critically ill, we are permitted to do everything possible to restore him to health, as long as it does not involve one of the three capital crimes. Where life is in danger, we may apply any remedy prescribed by physicians, though it may be otherwise prohibited in the Torah.

He who commits a sin spitefully is guilty of profaning the name of God. If an eminent Jew does something that provokes criticism, though it is not an actual misdeed, he profanes the divine name. His high position requires him to be meticulous in his conduct. He should receive people graciously, be trustworthy in his dealings, and shun the company of disreputable people. At the same time he should avoid extremes which may make him appear eccentric. His conduct should be such as to evoke the love and admiration of his fellow men. A man like this truly sanctifies God's name.

All men vary in their characteristics. Some are hot-tempered and constantly angry, while others are self-possessed and composed. Some are excessively proud, while others are excessively meek. Some are avaricious, while others do not desire even the few vital essentials. Some are so greedy that no money in the world will satisfy them, as it is written: "A lover of money will never be satisfied with his money," while others are content with less than the bare necessities. There are men who starve themselves while hoarding up wealth, and do not enjoy anything for which they have to pay the least amount, while others recklessly squander all they have. And so it is with all human characteristics, such as hilarity and gloom, niggardliness and generosity, cruelty and compassion, cowardice and courage.

A man should be neither easily provoked to anger nor should he be like a corpse that has no feeling. He should not close his hand nor be too lavish; he should give charity according to his means, and extend loans to those who are in need. He should be neither hilarious nor gloomy; he should always be quietly cheerful. He who avoids extremes and follows the middle course in all things is a wise man.

A man should carefully avoid the things that are injurious to the human body, and cultivate habits that will preserve his health. He should not eat except when he is hungry, nor drink except when he is thirsty. He should not gorge himself, but leave the table before his appetite is fully appeased. During a meal he should drink only a little water mixed with wine. One should not eat before taking exercise, such as walking a certain distance to stimulate the body. After a hot bath it is good to wait a little and then eat. One should be seated while eating, and not walk about until after the food is digested. Whoever exerts himself right after a meal may bring serious illness upon himself.

Eight hours of sleep, being one-third of the twenty-four hour day, is sufficient. One should not go to bed immediately after a meal but wait three or four hours. The lighter food should always be eaten first and then the heavier. If poultry and meat are served at the same meal, the poultry should be eaten first. Certain foods are extremely harmful, like stale fish, stale meat or cheese, mushrooms, and wine fresh from the press.

Unripe fruits are to be avoided, for they are like daggers to the body. Sour fruits are bad; they are to be eaten sparingly in the summer or in hot climates. Figs, grapes and almonds are always healthful, whether fresh or dried. Honey and wine are bad for the young but good for the old, especially in the winter. During the summer a man should eat only two-thirds of what he eats in the winter.

Another rule has been laid down regarding the healthy condition of the body: As long as a person takes plenty of exercise, does not eat to excess, and keeps his bowels regulated, he will contract no illness. But whoever sits idle and takes no exercise, even though he eats wholesome food, will suffer all his life and his strength will decline. Excessive eating is like deadly poison to the human body, and is the root of all diseases. Most illnesses which befall man arise either from bad food or from excessive eating.

A man should not take a bath immediately after a meal,

nor when he is hungry, but when the food begins to digest. When he leaves the bath, he should dress and cover his head, so as not to catch cold; even in the summer he must be careful. After the bath, he should wait a while until his body has relaxed and cooled off. If he can sleep a little after the bath, before he takes his meal, it is very healthful. A person should not drink cold water when coming out of the bath, and certainly not while in the bath. However, if he is very thirsty, he should mix the water with wine or honey.

Whoever conducts himself according to these rules will not suffer from illness until he reaches an advanced age.

A wise man does not shout when he speaks, but talks gently with all people. He gives everyone a friendly greeting, judges all men favorably, loves peace and pursues it. If he finds that his words are helpful and heeded, he speaks; otherwise, he keeps quiet.

A wise man does not attempt to pacify an angry person before the latter has calmed down. When his neighbor is in disgrace, he looks away and does not show himself to him. He never misrepresents; he neither makes overstatements nor understatements unless a matter of peace is involved.

A wise man does not walk proudly, with head held high; nor does he step mincingly; nor does he run about in the street like a madman; nor does he stoop like a hunchback. The manner of a man's walking shows whether he is wise and sensible or foolish and ignorant.

A wise man should dress neatly, and should not wear clothes stained with grease and dirt. He should not dress flashily to attract attention, nor shabbily so as to suffer disrespect. His garments should be modest and appropriate.

A wise man manages his affairs judiciously. He eats, drinks and supports his family according to his means. The Talmud recommends that one should spend less than his means on food, within his means on clothes, and more than his means on his wife and children.

Men of intelligence first acquire a livelihood, then a home, and then they marry. Fools, on the other hand, marry first, acquire a home if they can afford it, and, then, seek a trade or else they appeal to charity.

344

A wise man is honest in all his transactions. When he says "no" he means no, and when he says "yes" he means yes. He does not encroach on another man's occupation, and never mistreats anyone. In short, he prefers rather to be among the offended than among the offenders.

It is in the nature of a man to follow the ideas and practices of his friends and colleagues. He should therefore associate with good and wise men, that he may learn their ways. Solomon said: "He who walks with wise men will be wise, but the companion of fools will come to grief."

Love your neighbor as yourself means that you should honor him as you would like to be honored yourself. Whoever glories in the humiliation of others has no share in the world to come.

You shall not hate your brother in your heart means that you must not bear silent hatred for the wrongdoer; ask him frankly: "Why have you done this to me? Why have you wronged me?" If he is sorry and asks your forgiveness, do not be relentless but forgive him.

You shall reason with your neighbor means that if you see him commit misdeeds, you must convince him of his faults. This should be done privately and gently, for "he who puts anyone to shame in public has no share in the world to come." You should never call him by an insulting name, or say anything that is likely to embarrass him.

You shall not afflict a widow or orphan means that, since they are dejected and crushed in spirit even though they may possess wealth and power, you must treat them with respect and refrain from causing them physical pain or mental suffering. A child bereft by death of his father or mother is called an orphan until he can take care of himself.

He who slanders his fellow man violates the law which reads: *You shall not go about spreading slander among your people.* This grievous sin has caused the slaughter of many Jews, and for this reason it immediately precedes the command *You shall not stand forth against the life of your neighbor.*

A talebearer is one who carries gossip from person to person, even though what he says is the truth. If he tells

lies, he is referred to as one who spreads evil reports about
his neighbor in order to injure his reputation. According
to the sages of the Talmud, evil gossip is worse than
idolatry and adultery; the malicious slanderer is compared
to one who denies God. Evil gossip kills three persons: the
one who circulates it, the one who listens to it, and the one
of whom it is spoken.

He who takes vengeance on his fellow man transgresses
the command *You shall take no revenge.* One should be
forbearing in all worldly matters. Intelligent people realize
that worldly matters are vain and void and not worthy of
vengeance.

Every Jew must study the Torah, whether poor or rich,
healthy or ailing, young or old. Even a beggar who goes
from door to door, and a man who has a wife and children
to support, must devote time to Torah, for it is written:
"You shall study it day and night."

None of the divine precepts equals the study of the
Torah in importance; Torah excels all of them, because
it leads to practice. Anyone who aspires to carry out this
precept adequately should not divert his attention to other
objects. Knowledge of the Torah cannot be attained by the
indolent nor by those who study amidst luxury and revelry;
it demands self-sacrifice, painstaking effort, and sleepless
nights.

A teacher should not be angry or excited when his pupils
fail to understand a subject; he should review it with them
many times until they finally grasp it. Neither should a
pupil hesitate to ask questions. If his teacher loses patience,
the pupil may say to him: "Master, this is the Torah! I
must learn it even though my capacity is limited."

Just as it is required that pupils respect their teacher,
so it is the duty of a teacher to be courteous and friendly to
his pupils. The sages said: "Let the honor of your student
be as dear to you as your own." Students increase the
knowledge of a teacher and broaden his mind. One of the
sages said: "I have learned much from my teachers, more
from my colleagues, but most of all from my pupils." Just
as a small burning tree may set a bigger tree on fire, so too

may a young pupil sharpen the mind of a teacher and, by means of questions, stimulate him toward glorious wisdom.

Free will is granted to every man. If he desires to lean toward the good course and be righteous, he is at liberty to do so; if, on the other hand, he desires to follow the evil course and be wicked, he is likewise free to do so.

Pay no attention to the view held by the ignorant, whether non-Jews or Jews, that at man's birth God decrees whether he shall be righteous or wicked. That is not so! Every person has the power of becoming as righteous as Moses or as wicked as Jeroboam—wise or stupid, tender or cruel, miserly or generous. The same applies to all other qualities. Of his own will, one consciously tends toward whatever course he pleases. Jeremiah expressed this thought when he said: "Good and evil do not come by the decree of the Most High," that is, the Creator does not decree whether a man is to be good or bad. Hence, it is the sinner who causes his own ruin. He ought therefore to bewail his faults and lament the harm he has done to his soul.

Do not be perplexed nor ask: "How can man do as he likes? How can he control his own actions? Is there a thing in the world that can be done without the consent and will of the Creator?" Know, indeed, everything is done according to the will of God, though we do have control over our actions. God desired man to possess free will, and granted him the power over his own actions. Therefore man is judged according to his deeds. If he has done well, he is treated well; if he has done wrong, he is punished.

The *Shema* is recited in the evening and in the morning, because it is written in the Torah *You shall speak of them when you lie down and when you rise up*. The non-biblical verse *Blessed be the name of his glorious majesty forever and ever* is inserted because, tradition has it, that when Jacob gathered his sons about him in his dying hour, he asked whether any of them failed to share his belief in the One Creator of the universe, and they unanimously responded: "Hear us, O Israel, our father, the Lord is our

347

God, the Lord is One." Thereupon the patriarch gratefully exclaimed: "Blessed be the name of his glorious
majesty forever and ever." The people of Israel, therefore,
recite the words originally uttered by Israel, the patriarch.

One is to recite the *Shema* audibly, and should enunciate
the letters distinctly. One may recite the *Shema* in any
language that he understands, being careful to avoid grammatical errors and wrong enunciation in the language he
uses, just as he would in the Sacred Tongue.

When the people of Israel had been exiled by Nebuchadnezzar, they mingled with Persians and Greeks and other
nationalities. The speech of their children was a mixture
of many tongues, so that none was able to express his
thoughts adequately in any one language. When Ezra and
his council saw that the descendants of the exiles could not
pray in pure Hebrew, they composed the *Shemoneh Esreh*
and other prayers to enable even the unlearned to pray
in pure and eloquent Hebrew.

Congregational prayer is always heeded by God. One
should, under all circumstances, attend synagogue, morning and evening, since man's prayers are accepted at all
times if they are recited in a synagogue.

When the reader recites the prayers aloud and the worshipers respond *Amen* after each benediction, it is just as
though they were praying in unison. This applies only to
those who are not familiar with the prayers. However, a
person who does know how to pray fulfills his duty only
when he recites the prayers by himself.

Only one who is reputed for his knowledge and exemplary conduct should be appointed as reader to the congregation. If he is an elderly man, all the better. An effort
should be made to obtain one who has a pleasant voice and
can enunciate the words distinctly.

A place of worship should be built wherever there are
ten residents. The inhabitants may compel one another to
contribute toward the building of a synagogue and the pur-
chase of a Torah scroll.

The highest part of the town should be selected for the
site of a synagogue. The shrine, containing the Torah

scrolls, is built on the side towards which the people of the town turn when praying. The elders sit facing the congregation with their backs to the shrine. The people are seated, in rows, facing the shrine and the lectern, on which the scroll is placed.

There must be no frivolous behavior, no mockery or idle talk, in synagogues and houses of learning. If a person has occasion to go into a synagogue to call a child or a friend, he should recite some biblical verse so that his entry may not be entirely for his private interest.

A synagogue may be turned into a house of learning, but a house of learning may not be turned into a synagogue, because the sanctity of a house of learning exceeds that of a synagogue; objects may be raised to a holier use but not degraded to a less holy use.

Moses ordained that the Torah should be read publicly during the morning service on Sabbaths and on Mondays and Thursdays, so that the people would not spend three days without hearing the Torah. Ezra established the rule that the Torah should be read during the afternoon service of every Sabbath for the benefit of those who would otherwise spend the day in frivolity.

The reader must not begin to read in the Torah before the congregation responds *Amen*. If he makes a mistake in the pronunciation of a single letter, he must go back and read the word correctly. All must listen silently and give heed to what is being read. Since the time of Ezra it was customary for an interpreter to translate to the people what was being read from the Torah. The reader read only one verse, waited until it was translated, and then proceeded with the next verse.

The sanctity of *Tefillin* or phylacteries, which are worn by men during the daily morning prayer, is very great. As long as phylacteries are on a man's head and arm, he is humble and respectful; he is not inclined to frivolity and idle talk or evil thoughts, but fills his mind with matters of truth and uprightness. Whoever wears phylacteries regularly is blessed with longevity, for it is written: "The Lord is upon them, they shall live."

The formulae of all benedictions have come down from Ezra and his council. It is improper to change them, to add to or subtract from anything in the phrasing of one of them. Whoever deviates from the form which the sages have given to the benedictions falls into error. A benediction in which the name and the kingship of God are not mentioned is not considered valid unless it immediately follows one in which they are mentioned.

Anyone who can afford it must give charity to the poor according to their needs, for it is written: "You must open your hand to him . . . You shall maintain him and enable him to live beside you . . . Let your brother live with you."

You must provide the poor person with whatever he lacks; if he needs clothes or household goods, he should be supplied with them. If he declines to accept charity, it should be given to him subtly in the form of a loan. However, a rich miser who starves himself rather than spend some of his money on food deserves no help.

It is forbidden to collect charity from a person who deprives himself in order to contribute far more than he can afford. One's first duty lies toward his poor relatives, then toward the needy of his town, and finally toward those of other towns.

We have never seen or heard of a Jewish community without some communal charity fund. Anyone who stays in a town for thirty days should be compelled to contribute to public charity. No one ever becomes impoverished by giving charity.

The quality of mercy is characteristic of the Jewish people. They are like brothers, for it is written: "You are the children of the Lord your God." And if a brother shows no mercy to a brother, who will? On whom then should the poor of Israel depend? On those who hate them and persecute them? Alas, their help must come only from their own brethren.

Anyone who gives aid to the poor in a surly manner and with a gloomy face, completely nullifies the merit of his own deed. Charity should be given cheerfully, compassionately, and comfortingly. He who induces others to contribute to charity is more deserving than the contributor himself.

Eight Degrees of Charity

There are eight degrees of charity, each one higher than the other.

The highest degree is to aid a man in want by offering him a gift or a loan, by entering into partnership with him, or by providing work for him, so that he may become self-supporting.

The next highest degree is when he who gives and he who receives are not aware of each other.

The third, lesser degree is when the giver knows the recipient, but the recipient does not know the giver.

The fourth, still lower, degree is when the recipient knows the giver, but the giver does not know the recipient.

The fifth degree is when the giver puts the alms into the hands of the poor without being asked.

The sixth degree is when he puts the money into the hands of the poor after being asked.

The seventh degree is when he gives less than he should, but does so cheerfully.

The eighth degree is when he gives grudgingly.

One should ever strive not to be dependent on other people. The sages said: "Rather make your Sabbath a weekday with regard to festive meals than be dependent on men." If reduced to poverty, even a distinguished scholar must not disdain manual work, no matter how unworthy of him, in order to avoid dependence upon others. Some of the great sages derived their livelihood from chopping wood, carrying lumber, watering gardens, working in iron or making charcoal, and asked no help of the community; neither would they have accepted charity had it been offered them.

The divine precept of honoring and revering father and mother is highly important. The Bible considers this duty just as important as the duty of honoring and revering God.

Revering means that the son must not stand or sit in the place which is reserved for his father; he must not contradict him; he must not call him by his name. When referring to his father, he should say: "My father, my teacher."

Honoring means providing the parents with food and drink and clothing. If the father is poor, the son is compelled to take care of both his parents.

The duty of honoring parents is binding to the extent that even if they were to take the son's purse full of gold coins, and cast it into the sea, he must not rebuke them or even display anger toward them.

The duty of revering them is binding to the extent that even if they were to come and rend his costly garments, strike him on the head and spit in his face while he is presiding over the congregation, he must not insult them. He should remain silent and thus revere the supreme King of kings who has commanded that he should behave in this manner.

On the other hand, a father is forbidden to impose too heavy a burden upon his children, nor should he be too exacting with them regarding their duty to honor him, lest he may cause them to stumble and rebel. He should pardon and overlook many things.

Guide for the Perplexed

Maimonides completed his *Guide for the Perplexed (Moreh Nevukhim)* in 1190 at the age of fifty-five. A few years later it was translated into Hebrew, first by Samuel ibn Tibbon and then by Judah al-Harizi. Translated into Latin in the thirteenth century and then into various other languages, the *Guide* exerted a profound influence on the thought of Jews and non-Jews. The purpose of the *Guide* was to reconcile reason with faith, to harmonize Judaism with philosophy.

Though acknowledged to be one of the greatest philosophical books of the Middle Ages, much of the *Guide* has had little appeal for the average reader. This will explain why so little is known of Maimonides apart from his name. It is hoped that the few selections which follow will help to create a wish for a fuller acquaintance with the outstanding work of Maimonides.

Here are several excerpts from the *Guide* which characterize Maimonides' approach to life and the manner of his thinking:

"When I have a difficult subject before me, when I find the road narrow and can see no other way of teaching a well-established truth except by pleasing one intelligent man and displeasing ten thousand fools, I prefer to address myself to the one man and to take no notice whatever of the condemnation of the multitude.

"Ease destroys bravery, while trouble creates strength.

"We find consolation in our misfortune, when the same misfortune or a greater one has befallen another person.

"When we continually see an object, however sublime it may be, our regard for that object will be lessened and the impression we have received of it will be weakened."

In a letter to Samuel ibn Tibbon, Maimonides describes his busy life as a physician. He writes:

"My duties to the Sultan are very heavy. I am obliged to visit him every day, early in the morning; and when he or any of his children, or any of the inmates of his harem are indisposed, I dare not quit Cairo, but must stay during the greater part of the day in the palace. It also frequently happens that one or two of the royal officers fall sick, and I must attend to their healing. . . . I do not return home until the afternoon. Then I am almost dying with hunger; and I find the waiting-rooms filled with people, both Jews and non-Jews, nobles and common people, judges and bailiffs, friends and foes—a mixed multitude—all waiting for my return.

"I dismount from my animal, wash my hands, go to my patients and entreat them to bear with me while I partake of some slight refreshment, the only meal I have in twenty-four hours. Then I attend to my patients and write prescriptions and directions for their various ailments. Patients go in and out until nightfall. I prescribe for them while lying down out of sheer fatigue, and, when night falls, I am so exhausted that I can scarcely speak.

"As a result, no Jew can have a private interview with me except on the Sabbath. On that day the whole congregation, or at least the majority of the members, come to me after the morning service, when I instruct them as to their proceedings during the whole week. We study together a little until noon, then they leave. Some of them return, and read with me after the afternoon service until evening prayers . . ."

Of Moses Maimonides it is said: "From Moses [the son of Amram] to Moses [the son of Maimun] there arose none like [this] Moses."

God knows that I hesitated very much before writing on the subjects contained in this work, since they are topics which have not been treated by any of our scholars. How then shall I now make a beginning and discuss them? But, in the words of the psalmist, "it is high time to act."

When I have a difficult subject before me, when I find the road narrow and can see no other way of teaching a well-established truth except by pleasing one intelligent man and displeasing ten thousand fools—I prefer to address myself to the one man, and to take no notice whatever of the condemnation of the multitude. I prefer to free that one intelligent man from his perplexity, so that he may attain to perfection and be at peace.

Some years ago, a learned man asked me a very important question. He said: "In reading the Bible it would seem, at first sight, that man was originally intended to be exactly like the rest of the animal world, which is not endowed with intellect or any power of distinguishing between good and evil. But Adam's disobedience to God's command procured for him that great endowment, the power of distinguishing between good and evil, which is unique to the human race. Hence it seems strange that the punishment for his rebellion should prove to be the means of elevating him to such a pinnacle of perfection, and one which he had not attained previously."

My reply was as follows: You have studied the matter only superficially, it seems, and you think that you can understand a book, which has been the guide of many generations, simply by glancing through its contents as if it were an historical book or some poetic composition. Intellect was bestowed on man before his disobedience. Referring to this gift, the Bible says that man was created in

354

the form and likeness of God. Because he did possess this intellect, he was spoken to by God. Commandments are not given to those devoid of understanding.

Through the intellect, man distinguishes between the true and the false. Adam possessed this power completely. The terms *right* and *wrong*, however, are used in the science of conventional truths, not in that of scientific truths. For instance, it is not correct to use the words *right* and *wrong* in reference to the statements that the sky is round and the earth flat; but we say of one, it is true, and of the other, it is false. Thus, it is the function of the intellect to distinguish between true and false.

When Adam was still in a state of innocence, guided solely by reflection and reason, he was not at all able to understand the principles of convention; according to him, nudity was not unbecoming. After his disobedience, however, when he began to give in to his desires, he was punished by the partial loss of his intellectual faculties. The text reads: "The eyes of both were opened, and they knew that they were naked." It does not read: "and they *saw* that they were naked"; what the man had seen previously and what he saw now was precisely the same. Adam merely received a new faculty whereby he sensed that things were wrong which previously he had not considered wrong.

Just as all people must be informed, and even children must be trained in the belief that God is One and that none else is to be worshiped, so must all be taught that God is incorporeal and that there is no similarity whatsoever between him and his creatures. All must understand that our wisdom and his, or our power and his, do not differ quantitatively or qualitatively. Comparison can be made only between two things that belong to the same class. God's existence and that of any other being are totally different from each other.

This is enough for the guidance of children and average people who must believe that God is perfect, incorporeal and without any deficiency. He cannot be compared with his creatures and is not subject to external influence. These are things which must be explained to everyone according to his capacity. When persons have been trained in this belief, the writings of the prophets must be made clear to them by pointing out the figurative use of certain terms. Their belief in the Oneness of God and in the words of the prophets will then be true and perfect.

By *faith* we do not understand that which is uttered by the lips, but that which is apprehended by the soul, the conviction that the object of belief is exactly as it has been apprehended. If, in addition to this, we are convinced that no reasonable argument can be found for the rejection of the belief, then the belief is true.

Man is naturally a social being, and he seeks to form communities. In this he is different from other living creatures, which do not have the urge to gather themselves into communities. The human race, the highest form of creation, contains such a great variety of individuals that we cannot find two persons who are exactly alike morally or physically. While one person is so cruel that he kills his own child in his anger, another is too delicate and faint-hearted to kill even a fly.

The well-being of society demands that there should be a leader able to regulate people's actions, so that the natural variations of behavior should be counterbalanced by the uniformity of legislation. Since it is the will of God for mankind to exist and be permanently established, prophets and lawgivers are inspired with theories of legislation. Others possess power to enforce the laws. These are the rulers who accept the code of lawgivers in full or in part. They accept the teachings of the prophets and pretend to be prophets, for when we wish to possess a certain talent we sometimes try to make others think that we really do possess it. Thus people adorn themselves with the poems of others and publish them as their own productions. It also occurs that an ambitious, lazy person appropriates an opinion expressed by another person, and boasts that he himself originated it.

The appearance or speech of angels mentioned in the Bible took place in a vision or dream; it makes no difference whether or not this is expressly stated. The general statement that the Lord appeared to Abraham beside the oaks of Mamre is followed by a description of that appearance of the Lord, namely: "Abraham raised his eyes, and there stood three men before him!" So too, Jacob's wrestling with a man took place in a prophetic vision, since it is expressly stated in the end that it was an angel. That which happened to Balaam and the speaking of the ass took place in a prophetic vision. Do not imagine that an angel is seen or his word heard otherwise than in a prophetic vision or prophetic dream, according to the principle laid down: "If there is a prophet among you, I the Lord make myself known to him in a vision, I speak with him in a dream."

The prophets frequently use metaphors, describing the ruin of a kingdom or the destruction of a great nation in phrases like these: "The stars have fallen; the heavens are overthrown; the sun is darkened." When Isaiah depicts the fall of Sennacherib and the evils endured by all those who are defeated, he says: "The skies and their great stars now shed no light, the sun shall be dark at its rising, the moon shall never be bright." I do not think that any person is so foolish and blind as to assume that at the fall of the Assyrian kingdom a change took place in the nature of the stars or in the light of the sun and moon. This is merely a description of a country that has been defeated; the inhabitants undoubtedly find all light dark, and all sweet things bitter. When great troubles befall us, our eyes become dim and we cannot see clearly; on the other hand, when we are full of gladness we feel as if the light has increased. Thus, Isaiah concludes the good tidings that the people shall dwell in Zion and shall weep no more, with these words: "The light of the moon shall be like the light of the sun, and the sun shall shine sevenfold strong, when the Lord heals his bruised people and binds up their wounds."

Jeremiah, in describing the destruction of Jerusalem, says: "I looked on the earth, and lo, it was waste and void; I looked at the heavens, and they had no light." Ezekiel foretells the destruction of the kingdom of Egypt and the death of Pharaoh in the following words: "When I extinguish you, I will shroud the sky and darken its stars, I will

357

shroud the sun with clouds, and the moon shall not shine; all the bright lights of the sky I will darken over you, and put darkness upon your land, says the Lord God." Joel describes the multitude of locusts that came in his days as follows: "At their advance the land is quaking, the heavens are shaking, sun and moon are dark, the stars have ceased to shine." Amos, speaking of the destruction of Samaria, says: "I will make the sun go down at noon, I will darken the earth in the clear day." Micah, in recounting the fall of Samaria, makes use of these rhetorical figures of speech: "Behold, the Lord descends from his place, he strides on the heights of the earth! Mountains melt under him, valleys split asunder, like wax before a fire."

The account given of the creation is not intended to be literal in all its parts. We must blame the practice of some ignorant preachers, who think that wisdom consists in knowing the meaning of words, and that perfection is attained by employing more words and longer speech. However, it is part of the divine plan that everyone who has attained some perfection should pass it on to others. A scholar, therefore, cannot possess knowledge of the creation without communicating part of that knowledge to others. But this must not be done in clear words; it must be done sparingly by means of hints.

Every man possesses a certain amount of courage, otherwise he would not make any effort to get rid of things that might injure him. Courage varies, as do all other forces. There are some people who would attack a lion, while others run away at the sight of a mouse. One man attacks and fights a whole army, and another is terrified by a woman's threat.

The same is true of intuition. All possess it, but in varying degrees. A man's intuitive power is especially strong in things with which he is familiar. Some people have so sound an intuition that when they assume a thing exists, it often does exist, as facts later prove. This power enables some individuals to foretell important events.

The prophets must have had these two forces, courage and intuition, in a highly developed state. Their courage was so great that Moses, for example, dared to address a great king and was not frightened. Jeremiah was told: "Be not afraid of them." Ezekiel was exhorted: "Do not fear them; do not fear what they say." All prophets possessed great courage.

Men frequently think that evil things are more numerous than good things. They judge the whole universe on the basis of what happens to some individuals. An ignorant person thinks that the whole world exists for his sake. If anything turns out contrary to his expectations, he concludes at once that the whole universe is bad.

The evils to which the individual is exposed are due to the defects existing in himself. Indulgence in food and drink, for example, brings disease and affliction both to body and soul. Mental suffering often results from desiring things that are not necessary. Men expose themselves to great danger in order to obtain what is non-essential.

The more essential a thing is, the more abundant it is in nature; the less essential it is, the rarer it is. Air, water and food are indispensable to man. Since air is most necessary, it is found most easily. Water, being more necessary than food, is more abundant than food. The same ratio can be noticed between the various kinds of food: that which is more essential exists in larger quantities than that which is less so.

The strange and wonderful book of Job has been designed to explain men's different opinions concerning divine providence. Some of our sages clearly state that Job never existed, and that he is a product of poetic fiction. Those who assume that he did exist, and that the book is historical, are unable to determine when and where Job lived. Some say that he lived in the days of the patriarchs; others maintain that he was a contemporary of Moses; still others place him in the days of David, while there are some who believe that he was one of those who returned from the Babylonian Captivity. This difference of opinion would seem to indicate that Job never really existed.

According to both theories, the introduction to the book of Job is certainly fiction. I mean the dialogue between God and Satan, and the handing over of Job to Satan. This fiction, however, is different from other fictions in that it includes profound ideas, removes great doubts, and reveals most important truths.

It is remarkable that wisdom is not ascribed to Job. The biblical text does not say that he was an intelligent or clever man, but he is described in terms of goodness and uprightness. Had he been wise, he would not have had some doubt about the cause of his suffering.

The misfortunes of Job are enumerated in the same order as they rank in man's estimation. There are some people who are not discouraged by the loss of their property, but who are terrified when they are threatened with the death of their children. There are others who bear without shock even the loss of their children. But no one is able to endure physical pain if he has any feeling. We generally extol God, and praise him as righteous and benevolent, when we prosper and are happy, or when the grief is moderate. It is quite different, however, when we are stricken with such troubles as are described in the book of Job.

Some people deny God even if only their property is lost. Others retain their faith in the existence of justice and order even when they suffer loss of property, but loss of children is too much affliction for them. Still others remain firm in their faith even with the loss of their children. But there is no one who can patiently bear the pain that reaches his own person. He murmurs and complains of injustice, either aloud or to himself.

Let us assume that the first part of the story of Job actually took place. Job and his four friends agreed that his misfortune was known to God and that it was God who caused Job's suffering. They further agreed that God does no wrong, and that no injustice can be ascribed to him. These ideas are frequently repeated in the words of Job. When you consider the words of the five who take part in the discussion, you will notice that the ideas expressed by one are echoed by the rest.

But the object of this chapter is not to describe the things on which they agree, but rather to define the distinguishing characteristic of each of them regarding the question of why the most upright man is afflicted with the greatest pain. According to Job, this proves that the righteous and the wicked are equal before God, who holds mankind in contempt. Job says: "He destroys blameless and evil men alike. When he is scourging us with sudden death, he mocks at the despair of innocent men." Job wonders why God did not abandon the creation of man altogether, and why, after having created man, he takes no notice of him.

Our sages condemned this view of Job, and expressed their feeling in words like these: "Dust should have filled the mouth of Job, who denied the resurrection of the dead and began to blaspheme." However, God said to Eliphaz and his colleagues: "Unlike my servant Job, you have not told the truth about me." Our sages explain this rebuke with the maxim: "No man is punishable for what he says in his distress." God ignored Job's sinful words because they resulted from his suffering.

Job abandoned his first erroneous view, which suggests itself to those who meet trouble. He is represented as holding this view only as long as he was without wisdom and knew God only by tradition. As soon as he acquired a true knowledge of God, he confessed that there was true happiness in it, undisturbed by any earthly trouble. So long as Job's knowledge of God was based on tradition minus research, he imagined that health, riches and children are the utmost that man can attain. It was because of this that he was perplexed.

According to Eliphaz, Job was guilty of sins for which he deserved his fate. Bildad, on the other hand, defends the theory of reward and compensation. He tells Job that if he is innocent, his terrible misfortunes will prove to be a source of great reward. "If you are pure and upright," he says, "God will answer your prayer indeed, and prosper your godly home; small though your beginning may have been, he will enrich you amply in the end." Zofar maintains that the divine will is the source of everything that happens, and that we cannot ask why God has done this and why he has done that. His true essence demands that he does what he wills. We are unable to fathom the depth of his wisdom.

The book of Job discusses a problem which has perplexed many people. The principal object of the whole book of Job is that we should not fall into the error of thinking God's knowledge is like ours, or that his purpose, providence and rule resemble ours. When we realize this, we shall find anything that may befall us easy to bear; misfortune will not raise any doubts in our hearts about whether God knows our affairs or not, or whether he provides for us or abandons us. On the contrary, our experience will only increase our love for God.

The general aim of the Torah is twofold: the welfare of the soul and that of the body. The welfare of the soul is achieved through the correct beliefs which the Torah inculcates in people. That of the body is attained by establishing good mutual relations between men.

The reason for a divine command is clear whenever it directly tends to remove injustice or to teach good conduct that furthers the welfare of society. No one can be in doubt as to why we are forbidden to kill or to steal, or why we are commanded to love one another. There are, however, precepts which do not seem to have any influence upon the state or the family. Yet all these laws do have some bearing either upon the improvement of society or the teaching of good morals.

Intemperance disturbs the social order of the country and the economy of the family. By yielding to lust a man loses his intellectual energy, injures his health, and perishes before his time. God has therefore given us commandments which forbid excessive desire and lust.

Politeness is a fine quality prescribed by the Torah. A man should be considerate, listening to his fellow man and responding to his appeals. Cleanliness in body and dress is included among the various aims of the Torah, but only if it is associated with purity of action. It would be extremely bad for a man to content himself with physical purity while indulging in lustful pursuits. The laws of the Torah, like the laws of nature, are immutable: they do not vary with changed conditions of men and times.

The precepts are divided into two classes: those that concern the relation between man and God, and those that concern the relation between man and man. The laws concerning the relation of man to God tend to improve the moral condition of mankind, though they do not directly prevent man from injuring his fellow man.

The object of the Sabbath requires no explanation. One-seventh of the life of every man passes thus in comfort and rest from trouble and exertion. The Sabbath effects this in addition to perpetuating the great doctrine of the creation. The object of fasting on the Day of Atonement is evident. Fasting creates a sense of repentance. Yom Kippur occurs on the day when Moses came down from Mount Sinai with the second tablets of the commandments and announced to the people the divine pardon of their great sin. This day was therefore designated forever as a day of repentance and true worship.

Other holy days are designated for rejoicing and pleasant gathering. They also promote good public relations. The reason for the Passover is well known. The Feast of Weeks is the anniversary of the revelation on Mount Sinai. In order to emphasize the importance of this day, we count the forty-nine days between Passover and Shavuoth, just as one who expects his most intimate friend on a certain day counts the days and even the hours.

New Year is a day of repentance in preparation for Yom Kippur, the day of the fast. The Feast of Tabernacles, a festival of rejoicing and gladness, is kept for seven days in the autumn after the ingathering of the crops. During this season it is possible to dwell in tents, as there is neither great heat nor troublesome rain.

Passover teaches us to remember the miracles which God performed in Egypt. The Feast of Tabernacles reminds us of the miracles performed in the wilderness. The moral lesson derived from these feasts is this: man ought to remember his bad times in his time of prosperity. This will move him to thank God repeatedly and to lead a modest and humble life.

The four species of plants used during the Feast of Tabernacles are a symbolic expression of our rejoicing that the people of Israel left the wilderness and came to a country rich in fruit trees and rivers. There are three reasons for the use of these four kinds of plants, namely: the branches of palm trees, the citrons, the myrtles and the willows of the brook were plentiful in Palestine and every one could easily obtain them. Second, they are pleasant to look at, and the citron and myrtle are fragrant as well. Third, they keep fresh and green for seven days.

The food which the Torah forbids to eat is unwholesome. The Torah forbids pork principally because the habits and the food of swine are extremely dirty and loathsome. The fat of an animal's intestines impedes one's digestion and makes for thick blood. Blood is indigestible and harmful as food, and so is the meat of an animal that has died a natural death *(nevelah)*. A diseased animal *(trefah)* is close to becoming *nevelah,* hence harmful and forbidden. The best meat comes from animals that are permitted to be used as food. No doctor has any doubts about this.

We offer up prayers to God in order to establish the principle that God observes our ways, and that success or failure do not happen by chance. It is impossible for man to be entirely free from error and sin. If we were convinced that our ways cannot be corrected, we would forever continue in our errors. Our belief in the efficacy of repentance causes us to improve and become even better than we were before we sinned.

When a man is healthy and prosperous, he enjoys the company of his friends; in times of trouble, he needs them; when he grows old and weak, they are a help to him. Perfect love, brotherhood and mutual assistance, is naturally found among those who are related. The members of a family united by common descent have toward one another a certain feeling of love. They are helpful and sympathetic to one another. To effect this is one of the chief purposes of the Torah.

Harlots were not tolerated in Israel because their existence would disturb the relationship between man and man. Their children are strangers to everybody, and this is the greatest misfortune that can befall any child. Another important object in prohibiting prostitution is to restrain excessive and continual lust, for lust increases with the variety of its objects.

Every narrative in the Torah serves a certain purpose. It either helps to establish a principle of faith or to prevent wrong and injustice among men. The accounts of the flood and the destruction of Sodom serve as an illustration of the doctrine that the good do get their due and that God indeed rules on earth. The story of the war among the nine kings illustrates how Abraham exposed himself to danger in order to save his kinsman, and how he disregarded wealth and preferred good deeds. He said to the king of Sodom: "I will not take a thread or string of yours!" In a like manner, there is a good reason for every biblical passage, the purpose of which we cannot see clearly.

The intellect which emanates from God to us is the link that joins us to God. You have it in your power either to strengthen or weaken that bond. It will become strong only when you make use of it in a spirit of love for God; it will be weakened when you direct your thoughts to other things.

The physical forces of man in his youth prevent the development of moral principles. The more the forces of his body are weakened, and the fire of passion quenched, the more his intellect increases in strength and light. His knowledge becomes purer, and he is happy with it. When this perfect man is near death, his knowledge increases mightily, his joy in that knowledge grows greater, and his love for God, the object of his knowledge, is more intense; and it is in this great delight that the soul departs from the body. This is what our sages meant when they said that the death of Moses, Aaron and Miriam, was nothing but a kiss. The other prophets and saintly men are beneath that degree; but their knowledge of God is strengthened when death approaches.

Man can acquire four kinds of perfection. The first and lowest is the possession of money, land, clothes, furniture and so on. No real bond exists between this type of perfection and its possessor, only an external relation. The owner realizes that his house and property are not part of his own being, but they are entirely external and independent of him. A great king may find himself deprived of his possessions some bright morning, and there would be no difference between him and the poorest individual, although no change has taken place in the things he owned. Anyone who devotes all his efforts to the acquisition of this kind of perfection strives for something illusive and transient.

The second type of perfection is closely connected with man's own self, such as his physical appearance and his health. Even this kind of perfection should not be our principal goal, for it is given to man not because he belongs to the human race but rather because he belongs to the animal kingdom. A man cannot be as strong as a lion or an elephant; at the utmost, he can have the strength to carry a heavy burden. The soul derives no profit whatever from this kind of perfection.

The third kind of perfection is the highest degree of excellence in human character. Most of the divine precepts aim at producing this perfection, which is only a preparation for another perfection. All ethical principles concern the mutual relations between man and his neighbor and are given for the benefit of society. Imagine a person who is alone and has no connection whatever with any one else; none of his ethical qualities would be exercised or needed. They are necessary and useful only when a man comes in contact with others.

The fourth, genuine kind of human perfection is the attainment of intellectual faculties and correct ideas about God. Man's ultimate goal, the true knowledge of God gives him immortality. When you consider each of the preceding three kinds of perfection you will find that, if you possess them, they belong to you and others; but this last perfection is exclusively yours, and no one else has any share in it.

The prophets, too, have explained these things and expressed the same opinion. They say distinctly that perfection in property, in health, or in character is not worthy of pride and glory, but that we should seek true wisdom as the only perfection in which we should glorify ourselves. Jeremiah says: "Let not the wise man boast of his wisdom; let not the strong man boast of his strength; let not the rich man boast of his riches; but a man may glory only in this, that he understands and knows me." Having acquired the knowledge of God, and seeing in what manner God provides for his creatures, man will be forever determined to practise kindness, justice and goodness, so as to emulate the ways of God.

Gates of Instruction

ATTRIBUTED TO MAIMONIDES

Gates of Instruction has been attributed to Moses Maimonides, but Israel Abrahams maintains, in his *Hebrew Ethical Wills*, that the text is a product of the early part of the thirteenth century, having been written by an anonymous author soon after Maimonides's death. That the text is not by Maimonides is shown by the fact that the writer addresses his *children* in the plural. "We know of only one child, Abraham, who carried on the reputation of Maimonides into the next generation."

Free choice is given to you: choose life and good; cultivate the habit of goodness, for habit becomes second nature. Perfection of the body is a prerequisite to perfection of the soul.

Always keep the company of the great and the learned; behave modestly in their presence. Try to understand their words; weigh their opinions, and you will be on the right road. Be careful not to weary them with your tongue; the more you talk, the more mistakes you make. Do not be ashamed to ask questions, but see that you do so at the right moment. Ponder every word before you speak, for it cannot be recalled.

Take delight in listening to lectures on science and ethics. Whether you ask a question or answer one, speak gently and without haste. Use refined language; let your speech be clear and to the point. Behave like one who

367

wishes to learn and to discover the truth, not like one whose aim is dispute and verbal victory. Study while you are young, while others provide for your needs, and before your memory fades. The time will come when you will want to learn, but will be unable to do so.

Love truth and justice; hate falsehood and injustice. Stand behind your promises: let them be as binding as a written contract. Disdain mental reservation, trickery and evasion. Live honestly, conscientiously and cleanly. Let your loyalty to truth be your priceless wealth, for there is no heritage equal to honor.

Be compassionate to the poor and the sorrowing: let them share in your joys and attend your feasts. Avoid those who love friction. If your own relatives like to stir up strife, act like a stranger to them. Avoid revenge, for it may come back on your own head. Revenge results only in hatred, confusion and sleeplessness.

Conduct yourself with humility, for this is the ladder to the topmost heights. There is no ornament as beautiful as meekness. Curb your speech, bridle your tongue. God bestowed the faculty of speech on man that he might learn and teach, and it would be ungrateful of man to turn this gift into an instrument for evil.

Shun harmful foods as you would an enemy who seeks to kill you. Do not nibble incessantly like a mouse, but eat at regular hours. A man's good or bad breeding can be ascertained from his manners at a public banquet. I have returned home hungry and thirsty many a time, because I was nauseated by the behavior of some of the other guests.

The High Ways to Perfection

BY ABRAHAM MAIMONIDES

Rabbi Abraham ben Moses ben Maimun, or Maimonides II, succeeded his father as head of the Jewry of Egypt and physician to the Sultan. He was eighteen years old when his father, Moses Maimonides, died in 1204. Rabbi Abraham distinguished himself as biblical commentator, talmudic scholar, and religious philosopher. He is the author of several works in Arabic. His *High Ways to Perfection* was edited and translated into English by Dr. Samuel Rosenblatt in two volumes. What follows is the essence of two of his chapters on humility and faith.

Pride is abhorrent to God; humility is one of the most praiseworthy of all qualities. Now, inner humility consists in an awareness of one's deficiencies in relation to the degrees of perfection available to him. External humility is attained by forsaking envy and strife and by shunning the company of the proud, by restricting one's dress only to what is necessary, and by living modestly.

One should consider the fact that man is akin to animals of the lowest order; for he eats, drinks, cohabits, sleeps, and is sick even as they. Instead of boasting of his health, man should remember that a mere change of climate or in his food can destroy it. Overeating is often the cause of fatal illnesses. Overindulgence in sexual desires causes impotence. The growth of a living thing is at the same time the cause of its degeneration and death. How foolish, then, for man to boast of a condition which causes its own destruction!

There are some pious men who err in that they are conceited about their piety. Their vanity jeopardizes that of which they are vain. When my father and teacher, blessed

369

be his memory, once heard that a religious man had said on the eve of Yom Kippur: "I do not know of what sin I should repent," he declared: "Poor fellow! If he only knew what he ought to know, he would repent of the very thought that he is sinless."

One should not—must not in fact—be so foolish and contemptible as to kiss the hand of an ignoramus, for that is not humility but servility—an act that points to a mental defect, and not to moral conduct.

Faith in God is one of the fundamental principles of the Torah. Now the essence of faith consists in the belief that God is the Creator and the provider, from whom issue life and death, sickness and health, poverty and wealth; he is the cause of all that happens in this world.

God created this world so that it might function by means of cause and effect. He made man dependent on plants and animals for nourishment. Animals in turn depend on plants for food. Plants are nourished by water, air, or moisture. Rain comes from vapors that rise from the earth and mix with elements in the clouds. The rising of the vapors is caused by the blowing winds, directed by the wish of God. In this way, all natural causes finally return to him. Anyone who is ignorant of this can only be compared to a little boy who relies on his mother for his needs, not knowing that his mother provides for him out of his father's wealth, and that his father's wealth comes from God.

Man should be content with whatever he gains of worldly goods. He should avoid pleasures that lead to sin. Contentment is true wealth. Anyone who nurses far-reaching hopes for gaining worldly possessions generally does not realize his ambitions, as Solomon phrased it: "A lover of money will never be satisfied with his money." When a greedy person sees that his hopes have not been fulfilled, he usually attempts to achieve them by means of deceit, theft, and violence.

Letter of Instruction

BY RABBI MOSES BEN NAHMAN

Rabbi Moses ben Nahman, called *Ramban* (from the initials of his name and that of his father), is also known as Nahmanides. He was born in Spain, where he became famous as a great talmudic authority and biblical commentator, and died in the Holy Land at the age of seventy-six (1194–1270).

Nahmanides professed great respect for Maimonides and defended him against the anti-Maimonists. In his opinion, Maimonides' *Guide for the Perplexed* was intended not for those of unshaken belief, but for those who had been led astray by the teachings of the Greek philosophers. It has been said that Nahmanides represented Judaism from the side of emotion and feeling, as Maimonides did from the side of reason and logic.

The following Letter of Instruction (*Iggereth Musar*), addressed to his son Nahman, is included in some editions of the prayerbook.

Hear, my son, your father's instruction; do not reject your mother's teaching.

Learn to speak gently to all persons at all times.

Remove anger from your heart, and you will attain humility which is the most precious of all qualities.

If you will practise humility and modesty, the divine glory will shine upon you and you will attain life eternal.

Regard every person as greater than yourself.

If you are richer or wiser than another, you must know that you are charged with greater responsibility. If another commits a sin, it is from error; if you commit one, you are guilty.

My beloved son, anyone who exalts himself above his fellow men rebels against the kingdom of heaven. God says concerning the haughty man: "I and he cannot dwell together in this world."

On what should a man pride himself? On his wealth and honor? These surely belong to God, who bestows them upon man, for it is written: "Riches and honor come from thee, who reignest over all."

Nor can a man take pride in his wisdom, for it is written: "He renders speechless men of trust, and deprives elders of their judgment."

God brings low the haughty and lifts up the lowly.

Speak with respect and with love. Your eyes should look downwards, and your heart upwards. When you address a man, do not keep staring in his face.

Always consider yourself in the presence of God.

When you pray, remove all worldly interests from your mind and set your heart toward God.

Purify your thoughts, and think before you speak.

Read these instructions once a week, and fulfill them carefully.

Be diligent to study the Torah day and night, so that you may fulfill its commandments. When you have finished the reading of a book, you should try to retain what you have learned.

You should continually examine your deeds, in order to depart from evil and to do good.

Follow the ways of the Lord and you will succeed wherever you turn; and you will attain the happiness which is reserved for the good people.

Sefer Hasidim

BY RABBI JUDAH HE-HASID

Rabbi Judah he-Hasid of Regensburg, who died in 1217, was a philosopher and poet, scholar and mystic. His ethical work, *Sefer Hasidim* (Book of the Saintly), contains a rich variety of precepts and principles of Jewish living, such as the following:

"The unlearned should pray in a language which they understand, instead of honoring God with lip-worship in a language which they do not understand.

"One must deal honestly with all men, Jews and non-Jews, or else the name of God will be profaned.

"No landmark shall be removed in any part of the liturgy."

The *Sefer Hasidim* is not a uniform book nor is it the product of one author. Important additions were made by Rabbi Judah's disciple, Rabbi Elazar Rokeah.

Never shrink from declaring that you are a Jew.

Do not purposely mislead anyone, Jew or non-Jew.

In your business dealings, do not say that a certain price has been offered for your merchandise if that is not true.

Do no injustice to anyone, not even to those of a different faith.

Call the attention of a non-Jew to an error that he has made in overpaying you, for it is better that you live on charity than that you disgrace the Jewish name by cheating.

When a non-Jew comes to you for advice, tell him frankly who is honest and who is dishonest among the people with whom he wishes to deal.

If a murderer seeks refuge with you, give him no quarter even if he is a Jew.

Return to a non-Jew what he has lost. If he observes the laws of civilized men, hold him in higher esteem than a Jew who transgresses the divine commands.

Do not wear an amulet as a charm against evil, but put your implicit trust in God alone.

Accept nothing from others if you can support yourself with the little you have.

It is better to spend money on poor people than to lavish funds on useless trifles and idle luxuries.

Ingratitude is the rankest evil, even with regard to dumb animals.

Anyone who loads excessive burdens on a draft beast, or plunges his spurs too deeply into a horse's flanks, should be punished.

A sick animal is to be treated with tenderness.

Do not listen to slander; instead, try to restrain the person who bitterly complains about the misdeeds of another.

Do not praise a rich man in the presence of another, or an author in the presence of another author, lest you will be the cause of some faultfinding.

But you may freely praise a saintly person in the presence of another who reveres God.

If a rich man and a poor man are sick, and you see everybody going to visit the rich man, you should go to the poor man even though he is ignorant and illiterate.

Be intimate with an uneducated man who has a generous soul rather than with a learned person who is closefisted.

If you are in debt, pay your debts before you contribute to charity.

Expel all envy and hatred from your heart.

When your wife makes life difficult for you, and you come too close to hating her, do not pray to God to give you another wife, but ask him to turn this one's heart to you once more in love.

A young man should not marry a woman forty years old nor should a young girl marry an elderly man or one she cannot love.

It is highly improper for elderly men to dye their hair black in order to deceive young girls concerning their age.

If a man sees that his children or pupils are badly behaved and does not reprimand or punish them, he leads them to ultimate disaster. They will do evil even to their parents, who will soon despise them and curse the day they were born.

Anyone who supplies weapons of destruction to a murderer, or provides him with food, is as guilty as though he were an accomplice.

A favor sometimes turns out to be harmful, as when criminals are permitted to live in a town.

There was a herdsman who was in the habit of saying every day: "Lord of the world, you know well that if you had cattle and gave them to me to tend, I would take no wages from you because I love you."

Once a learned man, who chanced to hear this prayer, said: "Fool, do not pray in this manner!" When the herdsman asked: "How, then, should I pray?" The learned man taught him the traditional blessings, the reading of the *Shema* and the *Amidah*. But, when the learned man had left, the herdsman forgot all that he had been taught and did not pray at all. He was afraid to say his old prayer because the saintly man had warned him against it.

In a dream by night, the learned man heard a voice saying: "If you do not tell him to say what he was accustomed to say before you met him, misfortune shall befall you, since you have deprived God of one who belongs to the future world."

The learned man at once went to the herdsman and told him what he had dreamed, adding: "Continue to say what you used to say." The Merciful One desires sincerity of heart.

Rokeah

BY RABBI ELAZAR ROKEAH

Sefer Harokeah was written by Rabbi Elazar Rokeah of
Worms, Germany, a pupil of Rabbi Judah he-Hasid, principal
author of *Sefer Hasidim*. During the Crusades he went through
great suffering. In 1196, two crusaders entered his house and
killed his wife, his two daughters, and his son. Rabbi Elazar
died in 1238.

No crown signifies as much royalty as does humility; no
monument bestows as much glory as an unsullied name.

A contrite heart is the highest sacrifice.

The highest wisdom is found in the Torah.

Modesty is the noblest ornament.

To forgive is the most beautiful thing a man can do.

A person who is always aware of the presence of his
Creator talks gently to everyone and teaches his children
to lead a worthy life.

He infuses love and kindness into all his actions, and
reveres his wife.

He loves his neighbors and friends, lending to the needy
and giving charity in secret.

Do not inquire too much concerning your Creator; do
not seek to know the origin of things. Instead, see that God
is never far from your thoughts; do not let your sensuous
nature control your life.

Do nothing of which you are likely to be ashamed.

Let no oath pass your lips. Never speak meaningless
words. Do not get into quarrels with anybody.

Do not crave honor and glory; do not envy wrongdoers;
do not be too eager for money.

Make peace among people whenever you can.

376

If you are poor, be thankful for the air you breathe; if you are rich, do not exalt yourself above your poor brother.

Both you and your poor brother came naked into the world and will eventually sleep in the dust together.

My son, shake off haughtiness and cling to humility; let none of your failings seem small to you.

The thoughts of your soul will be pure if the work of your hands is pure.

Guard yourself against the assaults of envy, which kills sooner than any fatal disease.

You may, however, envy the good qualities of upright men and strive to emulate them.

Do not be a slave to hatred, which ruins the taste of food and the pleasure of sleep.

During the dread days of martyrdom, many gave their lives in defense of their faith. Had you lived at that time you would surely have done the same.

But in these better times, you are only urged to battle against evil desire. If you have been defeated in the struggle, return to God and repent.

Right Conduct

BY RABBI ASHER-ROSH

Rabbi Asher ben Yehiel (known as Rosh from the initials of his Hebrew title *Rabbenu Asher*) was born in 1250 and died in 1327. He migrated from Germany to Spain.

His fame rests on his compendium of the talmudic laws, which omits the discussion and concisely states the final decisions. His work became so popular that it has been printed with almost every edition of the Talmud under the title *Rosh*.

Never be quick to quarrel.

Do not hurt people either by causing them to lose money or by saying unkind words to them; do not envy or hate them.

You must not rely on the broken reed of human support nor put your trust in gold.

Give of your wealth lavishly; God will repay you.

Weigh your words on the scale of your intelligence before you speak.

Conceal in your heart whatever is said in your presence, even when you are not pledged to secrecy.

Train yourself to awaken at dawn, and to rise at the twitter of the birds.

Do not cast envious eyes on one who has become richer than you; instead, consider the one who has less than you.

Never do in private what you would be ashamed to do in public.

Do not raise a threatening hand against your neighbor.

Do not circulate false reports; do not slander anyone.

Never make an insolent reply to one who has said unpleasant things to you.

Do not shout in the street, but speak softly.

Do not expose your fellow man to shame in public.

Never weary of making friends; consider a single enemy as one too many.

If you have a faithful friend, do not lose him; he is a precious possession.

You must not fool your friend by false flattery, or by speaking with an insincere heart.

Never stay angry with your friend for a single day, but humble yourself and ask his forgiveness.

Do not say: "I am the injured party, let him come and apologize to me."

Every night before you go to bed, pardon everyone who has offended you. Do not pry into other men's secrets. Serve your fellow men cheerfully.

Menorath Hamaor

BY RABBI ISRAEL AL-NAKAWA

Rabbi Israel al-Nakawa of Toledo, Spain, died a martyr's death during the religious persecutions of 1391. The return to Judaism of forcibly converted Jews was directly responsible for the establishment of the Spanish Inquisition, which endeavored to cope with the problem of these backsliding converts.

All that is known of al-Nakawa, author of *Menorath Hamaor* (The Lamp of Illumination) is that he was a descendant of a prominent family known for its piety, hospitality and support of scholarship. He drew upon the entire range of talmudic literature for his brilliant work, which is a summation of all phases of Jewish life, both ethical and religious. Many chapters of *Menorath Hamaor* have rarely been equalled for depth of penetration into the Jewish soul.

It has been proved that the popular *Menorath Hamaor* by Rabbi Isaac Aboab of the fifteenth century is merely a recasting of Rabbi Israel al-Nakawa's original ethical work *Menorath Hamaor,* which was edited and published by Rabbi Enelow several decades ago. It has also been shown that Rabbi Judah ibn Kalaaz, author of *Sefer ha-Musar,* and Rabbi Elijah di Vidas, author of *Reshith Hokhmah,* helped themselves to large portions of al-Nakawa's *Menorath Hamaor* and incorporated them in their own books.

Whoever sows the seed of charity shall reap a harvest of blessings. Charity is a tree of life; whoever clings to it is saved from death. The world is a revolving wheel: one who is rich today may be poor tomorrow, and one who is poor today may be rich tomorrow. Let a man therefore give charity before the wheel has turned.

Prominent men in France used to make their coffins out of the tables on which they served food to the poor, to show that no matter what heights a man might attain, he can take nothing with him when he dies except the good he has done.

Charity should be given with a generous spirit and a feeling of compassion. If a host happens to be depressed by personal misfortune and anxieties, he should refrain from discussing them in the presence of his guests. He should wait on his guests himself, even though he has many servants.

Everyone should give to charity according to his means. A man who is not willing to give can be forced by the communal authorities. However, if he is unable to support himself and his family he is not obligated.

In the administration of communal charity the poor should be provided with their accustomed needs. There is, for instance, the man who was rich at one time and now is poor and friendless; there is another who has a small and unprofitable business and is constantly in danger of poverty through accident and illness; there is still another who once enjoyed his riches in secret, not letting the world know it, and, having become poor, cannot count on the sympathy of his neighbors; there is yet another who cannot make a living because he lacks the aptitude for work or business, and does not even know how to apply for charity. It is the duty of communal leaders to understand all such differences and know how to cope with them, so as to alleviate or prevent the misfortunes of the poor.

There are several qualities shown by individuals in the giving of charity. There are those who like to give ostentatiously; others who give both for the common good and for the sake of fame; while some contribute to charity secretly and from noble motives only. But, greater than these is the man who contributes to the common fund, so that neither the recipient of the gift nor the donor know each other's identity. Still greater is the man who lends to the poor in time of trouble and assists them to support themselves and become independent.

The humble person is content with his lot; he does not complain, and so enjoys inward peace. He is loved by his fellow men because he is close to them and takes part in their joys and sorrows. He forgives injuries and bears no grudge against those who have wronged him.

Pride assumes various forms. There are those who make themselves conspicuous by wearing gaudy clothes and occupying front seats. Although they do not say to others "We are better than you," their actions stamp them as haughty. There are some who boast of their pedigree or brag about their beauty, their good deeds, their education or their faith. We should refrain at all times from self-praise. Even in the performance of religious duties a man deserves praise only if he acts without display. However, excessive meekness is often a form of vanity.

The Torah is a crown which is not reserved for a chosen few. Any man can earn it for himself if he cares to try. By placing a learned man ahead of others we honor the Torah, which ranks higher than royalty. Nevertheless, one must not fail to learn a trade in order to be self-supporting instead of becoming a burden on others. Many of the most eminent teachers of the past engaged in humble occupations, though some of them were at the same time heads of academies. To be without an occupation is a sin in itself and leads to sinful consequences.

Yet, a man should not allow his occupation to crowd the Torah out of his life, but he should make definite provision for study. He should find a teacher as well as a companion who might be an incentive toward further study. When one studies alone, a subject is not as pleasant as when it is studied in company. Readiness to undergo all manner of privation in the pursuit of learning has always been a characteristic of Jewish students. Even a learned scholar must not think that he has reached his goal; he can always add to his knowledge.

Next to the duty of personal study comes that of teaching others. This duty rests upon every one who is competent to teach. He who teaches the Torah to another is like a father. Before accepting a pupil one should test his mental and moral character. There is no use trying to teach an inept person, especially one who is unethical. Try to improve his conduct first, and then instruct him. The teacher, too, must be a moral person, or else all of his learning is of little value; people will not and need not listen to him.

Religious observances are the practical aspect of the Torah; they are conducive to the heightening and preserving of the ethical tone of life. They help to sanctify Israel as a people, as well as the life of the individual Jew and Jewess.

As for mourning, one must beware of grieving too much. Unseemly as it is to be callous and indifferent to tragedy, it is just as bad to carry grief to extremes by constantly weeping and sighing. That is a sign of arrogance and reminds one of those haughty people who, when overtaken by misfortune, act as if the sun, moon and stars should cease shining out of sympathy with them. If one is in trouble, let him think of the many noble and illustrious men who had to endure the greatest of hardships.

Kindliness is greater than charity. Visiting the sick is a particular form of human love. It is the duty of the physician to try to cure a sick man even though another physician is handling the case. He should be careful to avoid mishaps just as a judge is expected to beware of errors in cases involving capital punishment.

Attending to the burial of the dead, and thus showing them honor, is another form of kindness. So is rejoicing with one's fellow men on occasions of gladness and good fortune. The true descendants of Abraham are recognized by these qualities—compassion, modesty, and kindliness.

One should try to make the Sabbath a day of joy as well as rest. The same applies to the festivals. An appropriate way of celebrating the Sabbath and festivals is to visit one's parents, relatives and teachers. One should also visit the sick on such days. A man should bear in mind that Sabbaths and festivals are also meant for study, for there is no pleasure greater than the study of the Torah. Every one who rejoices on festive days and brings joy to the members of his household is assured of a great reward.

Honoring one's father and mother is equal to honoring God, since the parents are partners with God in the creation of the child. One should provide them with food and drink if they are poor, as well as with suitable clothing and shelter. They should be cheerfully welcomed when they come for a visit. The happiness of parents depends a great deal on their son's attitude toward them and on his spirit of gentleness and love in which he acts. One may give his father pheasant to eat and yet make him tired of living, while another may give his father hard work to do and yet make life pleasant for him. However, only the parent who leads an exemplary life and gives proper training to his child is entitled to respect and obedience.

When parents are upright, there is no limit to the reverence they deserve. The more careful one is in showing them honor and consideration, the greater one's merit. One should continue to honor his parents after they have passed away, that he may have his own life prolonged and obtain infinite peace.

If a man is fortunate enough to have found a good wife, he will never miss anything. Though he may be poor, he may consider himself rich. According to a biblical proverb, it is easier to obtain precious stones than to find a good wife. Where there is love and trust between husband and wife, there will be riches and contentment. If their hearts are divided, they will miss everything.

A good wife is one who manages her husband's affairs correctly, helps him to the best of her ability, gives him her honest advice, and does not urge him to spend more than is necessary. She intelligently supervises the needs of their home, and the education of their children. She tries to understand his moods and takes delight in serving him because she loves him. She does not act snobbish toward her husband's family even if she happens to come from a more refined environment.

Marriage is not a onesided affair. The man has obligations as well as the woman. First, he must have as high a regard for his wife as he has for himself. He must be particularly careful to provide for the needs of the home, the lack of which is often the cause of quarrels. A man should sacrifice his personal needs in order to provide more abundantly for his wife and children. Above all, he should treat his wife with love and sympathy, for she is part of him and depends on him. He must never abuse her or deceive her.

A woman's supreme beauty is not in her face but in her fair and pure deeds. If a man marries for money, misery is likely to follow. Children of a loveless marriage are likely to be of inferior quality. Many a wealthy home has been ruined by folly, but a good and intelligent wife enriches a house. Faithfulness is one of the essential conditions of marriage. One of the merits of a happy marriage is that it prevents the formation of unclean and corrupt habits.

If you train your child when he is young, you will enjoy rest and peace later on. You will not have to worry about his going astray and forming habits which are hostile to the well-being of society. Do not be discouraged if you find that your child is dull; do not give up training and correcting him. Though he may not master all you try to teach him, he will learn a little. Nothing worse can happen to a man than bringing up a wicked child. If done in a spirit of love and affection, correction is pleasant in the end. Try to induce the child to like the process of education. At first, you may have to coax him with sweets and toys; then you may have to lure him with the prospects of a higher reward; but, in the end, he will come to love education for its own sake.

One should make every effort to provide a religious and ethical education for his child, regardless of cost. The education of the young is a communal obligation. Every community must provide teachers for the children. A city without pupils is doomed. If there are many children, several teachers must be engaged; for no teacher can properly instruct too large a number of pupils. After the children have grown used to one teacher, they should not be taken away from him and sent to another teacher, provided the first is conscientious in the discharge of his duties.

A man should not make a big display of his love for his children, lest they become spoiled. He should treat all his children equally in matters of food, clothes, and presents, so as not to create envy among them. He should be very careful about the example he sets to his children both in speech and action. He should be especially careful not to use unclean language. As the child grows older, his father must be extremely careful not to treat him harshly or over-discipline him. He must learn to treat him with gentleness and refrain from rudeness or violence in addressing him.

The ethical person is content with what he has; the unethical one is never satisfied. If a man is satisfied with his lot, he is likely to live a happy life. For one thing, he will not be too dependent on others. None is so rich as one who is content with little. There is no wealth like generosity; no treasure like wisdom; no glory like self-mastery; no sin like pride; no poverty like the love of money; no ornament like health.

In order to have contentment one must have faith. If a man has no faith he is likely to worry constantly. He will be afraid to spend even a little of what he has lest he lose everything and become poor. But the man of faith is confident that God will supply his needs at all times and so he is always cheerful. He will not be tempted to steal from others and will enjoy a peaceful life. Happy indeed is he who has learned to rely upon God rather than upon man.

Contentment frees a man from greed and envy. Greed leads to many evils; envy and contentment can never be found together. If you are envious, you court all kinds of trouble and ailments. Be generous toward your neighbor; be as concerned about his welfare and reputation as you are about your own.

He who controls his anger shows that he is intelligent and follows the example of the great men of Jewish history. One saintly man, for example, used to say every evening before retiring: "I forgive all those who have offended me." Thus he never passed a night in hatred of any man.

According to an old tradition, he who refrains from anger is beloved of God and his prayers are accepted. Impatience and anger bring on suffering and disease. If a man becomes angry, his wisdom deserts him, as happened even to Moses on three occasions. A quick-tempered person is not fit to be a leader. That is why Eliab, the eldest son of Jesse, was rejected as potential king of Israel. That he was hot-tempered is clearly seen in the story about Goliath, where he became angry with David. This trait was enough to put his selection as the future king of Israel out of the question.

A flatterer is worse than a thief: the thief steals money, but the flatterer steals the mind of the people whom he deceives. Some people flatter in order to please; others flatter in order to obtain position and authority in the community; but the worst are those who are guilty of pretence in religious matters. These pose as being devout and thus strive to be elected leaders of the community.

There is the habitual flatterer who knows that his neighbor is doing wrong, yet speaks approvingly of his actions with a smooth tongue. "You are doing the right thing," he assures him, and so pushes him along on his downward path. Again, there is the one who inwardly begrudges the well-being of the very person he flatters, and rejoices at his misfortune. There is another who hates his fellow men and avoids them until they are in trouble, when he begins to visit them. He says: "Now you can see who is your true friend," and all the while he takes delight in listening to their troubles.

Scoffing, too, is a very bad habit. There are those who despise and poke fun at people who do not happen to be rich or learned or prominent. Then, there are those who are always ready for idle chatter, behaving like clowns and wasting their time in merrymaking.

The common descent of man, taught by the Torah, implies the obligation of mutual friendship. One should try to choose companions from among those who live a good life. Even the best of men have been unable to escape from the contagion of bad companionship. If you want to find out about a man, inquire as to who his associates are. Association with good people is useful in itself, even though one may never receive a favor from them.

There are fifteen things you must do to show that you are truly a person's friend: Be first to greet him; invite him to your joyful occasions; call him by complimentary names; do not give away his secrets; help him when he is in trouble; visit him when he is sick and take care of his affairs; attend to his burial if he dies; look after his inter-

387

ests when he is away; overlook his shortcomings and forgive him promptly; reprove him when he has done wrong; respect him always; do not deceive him in business transactions; fulfill your promises to him; do not lie to him; pray for him and wish him happiness. True friendship means judging your neighbor kindly and favorably even when circumstances seem to point against him.

Life and death often depend upon the use of the tongue. Evil speech not only harms the individual, but undermines the welfare of society. It is just as bad to listen to evil talk as to spread it. Woe to him who makes public the faults of his fellow man but hides his own! If a man is in the habit of talking too much, he is sure to fall into evil chatter and so cause ultimate unhappiness to himself, to the victims of his tongue, and to society in general.

Obscene speech must be avoided. It is particularly offensive among Jewish people, who have always been noted for modesty and decency. It is most reprehensible for one to use the power of speech, by which man is distinguished from beasts, for contemptible purposes. The quarrelsome person who constantly complains about others, claiming that he is being persecuted and wronged, cannot hope to keep his friends. It is good to cultivate the habit of silence. Economy of speech is a sign of wisdom. Many of the things we talk about are of no value either to ourselves or to others.

Even if you are engaged in a lawsuit, confine yourself to the subject of your dispute and do not reveal secrets in order to frighten your opponent or to obscure the issue. To publish the secrets of your fellow man is like killing him, for a man's life is actually endangered sometimes by the disclosure of a secret. A sage was once asked what he did about secrets. He replied: "When anyone entrusts me with a secret, I dig a grave in my heart and bury it there."

It is bad enough to disclose a secret; but to mix lies with it is immeasurably worse. There are seven types of liars: the man who misrepresents things in order to take advantage of his partners or employees; the man who deceitfully ingratiates himself with another in order to take advantage of him later on; the man who shrewdly manages to divert to himself what is intended for another; the man who relates things he has heard but alters them somewhat; the man who promises favors and gifts to another without intending to keep his promise; the man who boasts of having done favors for another when he has not, or the one who presses invitations on another when he knows that they will surely not be accepted; and the man who boasts of qualities he does not possess.

Book of Instruction

BY RABBI JUDAH IBN KALAAZ

The *Book of Instruction,* widely known as *Sefer ha-Musar,* was written by Rabbi Judah ibn Kalaaz, who lived in Algeria at the beginning of the sixteenth century. He frequently quotes kabbalistic works, which he held in great esteem, and leans heavily on the *Menorath Hamaor,* the work of law and ethics by Rabbi Israel al-Nakawa of the fourteenth century.

Reverence for God is the thread upon which the various good qualities of men are strung like pearls. When this string is severed, the pearls scatter in all directions and are lost one by one.

The finest qualities in a person may go down to ruin because of a single failing, as when a man constantly points to his own merits by emphasizing the faults of another. The best wine may escape from a jar through one little hole that has been overlooked.

The habit of cleanliness should be cultivated meticulously. Man who is made in the image of God should keep his body immaculately clean.

He who always prefers his own ideas to those of others cannot make progress.

Be reasonable and modest in your dealings with men; treat everyone with scrupulous fairness.

Practise humility even among your subordinates. Never be ashamed to learn even from those who seem less important than you.

Be on your guard against putting others to shame by revealing their faults or by giving them humiliating nicknames.

You are indebted to God for your sound health. Always be grateful for being spared suffering and distress.

Be open-eyed before the great wonders of nature. Men marvel at the sun's eclipse while failing to notice the daily sunrise.

Do not be content with what you learned in your youth; study the truth when you are mature, and your insight will gain in strength and depth.

One human being is often worth more than a hundred others because of his spiritual and moral standard. So build ever higher and higher the edifice of your soul.

Injure the feelings of no one. If you sit next to a person who has a physical defect, refrain from making reference to it.

If someone tells you something you already know, keep quiet until he has finished. Even though he is telling you nothing new, he is pleased if he thinks he is.

Do not broach the subject of a quarrel that is ended, lest you stir up its smoldering embers.

Do not abuse the hospitality of poor people.

Do not rejoice at someone's disgrace.

It is difficult to get rid of the following five habits: gossip, slander, worry, suspicion, and keeping bad company.

The aim of all thought, the highest of all merits, is love and reverence for God.

The soul is made holy by yearning for the source from which it sprang and to which it is destined to return.

Shulhan Arukh

BY RABBI JOSEPH KARO

Rabbi Joseph Karo, whose *Shulhan Arukh* serves as a practical guide in the observance of traditional Judaism, was the last great codifier of rabbinic law and the greatest talmudic authority of the sixteenth century. He went from Spain to Safed, Palestine, where he was greatly influenced by the mystic teachings of the period. He died in 1575.

Rabbi Abraham Danzig of Wilna (1748–1820) summarized the subjects of two sections of the *Shulhan Arukh* in his work *Hayye Adam* (The Life of Man). Rabbi Solomon Ganzfried of Ungvar (1804–1886) is best known as the compiler of an abridgment of the *Shulhan Arukh*, which became very popular and has been reprinted many times under the title of *Kitzur Shulhan Arukh*. Both authors, Rabbi Danzig and Rabbi Ganzfried use the following statement as an introduction to their respective works:

"The psalmist says: *I keep the Lord always before me.* This verse conveys a high religious-ethical principle. Indeed, when a man is alone in the house he fails to act as if he were in the presence of a great king. His manner of speech among his own relatives and friends is not what it might be in the company of a king. Hence, when a man realizes that the supreme King, whose glory fills the whole world, is always near him marking all his actions, he is bound to be inspired with reverence and humility in the presence of the Holy One, blessed be he."

Tzedakah (righteousness) is the Hebrew equivalent of charity. The Torah frequently emphasizes that men of means are obligated to provide for those in want. Relief is not a matter of philanthropic sentiment, but of legal rightness. It is expected of all men toward all men.

Everyone should give to charity. Even a poor man who is supported by charity should donate a portion of what he receives.

The court used to punish the man who gave less than his due; they would even seize some of his possessions in order to obtain his share.

A generous person who gives more than his share, or one who deprives himself and donates to charity so as not to be embarrassed, should not be approached for money. Whoever humiliates him by insisting that he should contribute, will be punished by God.

A man who wishes to become worthy of divine grace should curb his selfish impulses and contribute generously.

Whatever is given for a noble purpose must be the finest. If a man builds a house of worship, it should be more beautiful than his own home; if he provides food for the hungry, it ought to be the best on his table; if he gives clothing to the naked, it should come from among the finest of his clothes.

If a man and a woman ask for food or clothing, the woman must be attended to first. Whoever comes and asks for food should be given it at once, without investigation as to whether or not he is dishonest.

A man should always avoid accepting charity; he should endure misery rather than be dependent on his fellow men. The sages commanded: "Rather make your Sabbath a week-day, with regard to festive meals, than be dependent on men."

Whoever deceives the public and takes charity without needing it will be in actual need before his days are over. Whoever is so much in need of charity that he cannot live without it, and yet is too proud to accept it, is guilty of bloodshed and suicide.

On Gambling

BY LEON OF MODENA

Leon da Modena (1571–1648) was one of the most versatile Italian rabbis and scholars of his generation. He lacked, however, a stable character and developed a passion for various types of gambling. All of his income from preaching and teaching, proof-reading and bookselling, was swallowed up in gambling, despite the fact that he had written, in his early youth, a special pamphlet against this particular vice. Amidst many trials and tribulations, and the loss of four children, he continued to study and write. Owing to the spirit of tolerance which prevailed in the seventeenth century community of Venice, Leon da Modena remained in the rabbinate until the day of his death.

A gambler violates all the Ten Commandments. To begin with, he breaks the first four commandments which warn one against the sin of idolatry. As soon as his star becomes unlucky he gets furious, and the Talmud says that a man who gives way to anger is like an idolator.

A man will tell one lie after another during play; he will utter thousands of vain oaths. And how easily the Sabbath Commandment might be broken! Imagine two men gambling on Friday near dusk, the loser hoping to win back what he has lost and the winner hoping to get more. Suddenly they find that the Sabbath has overtaken them; they have infringed on the sanctity of the day.

The duty of honoring father and mother is equally threatened by gambling. For it is the obligation of parents to reprove and punish a son who is addicted to gambling; but the son who is steeped in this vice will answer them harshly and refuse to obey them. It will be a source of bitterness in their lives that he has disregarded the fifth commandment.

Furthermore, when a man realizes that he has lost money, envy and hatred flare up in him; he will hunt for an excuse to quarrel with his partner, accusing him of dishonesty and calling him a wicked scoundrel. The other will answer him sharply, and the ensuing argument may result in murder and the breaking of the sixth commandment.

A gambler will mix with loose women, using obscene words which lead to sinful action. And thus he transgresses the commandment: "You shall not commit adultery."

When a gambler is out of money, he will steal, rejecting the commandment: "You shall not steal."

It may happen, too, that during a game a third party will be called on to settle a question of honesty. He may give a wrong decision, so that the commandment "You shall not bear false witness" is broken.

It goes without saying that if a man has no respect for the property of others, he will pay no attention to the commandment "You shall not covet." Whatever he sees he wants, with a longing that knows no bounds.

Memoirs

BY GLUECKEL OF HAMELN

Glueckel of Hameln (1646–1724), a mother of twelve children, wrote seven books of memoirs which have been recognized as a primary source for the history of the Jews in the seventeenth century. At the outset, she addresses her children in the following terms: "I began writing it, dear children, upon the death of your good father, in the hope of distracting my soul from the burdens laid upon it, and the bitter thought that we have lost our faithful shepherd. In this way I have managed to live through many sleepless nights."

My children, be patient. When the Lord sends you a punishment, accept it of him and do not cease to pray. Dear children, bear patiently the loss of your earthly possessions, for nothing is your own anyway. Whatever we have is only a loan.

The gist of the Torah is this: "You shall love your neighbor as yourself." But these days we find only a few who love their fellow men wholeheartedly. The best thing you can do, my children, is to serve God without deception, without pretending to be one thing while in your heart you are really another. Recite your prayers with awe and devotion, and do not stand around talking about other things. It is a great sin to carry on conversation while prayers are being offered to the Creator of the world. Shall God Almighty be kept waiting until you have finished your business?

Make your study of the Torah a regular habit. Be diligent in your business too, for God has commanded you to provide a decent living for your wives and children. We should put ourselves to great pains for our children, since they are the foundation of the world. Children would quickly tire of doing as much for their parents.

A father bird once set out to cross a windy sea with his three fledglings. The sea was so wide, and the wind so strong, that the father bird was forced to carry his young, one by one, in his claws. When he was half-way across the sea with his first fledgling, the wind turned to a gale, and he said: "My child, look how I am struggling; I am risking my life for you. When you are grown up, will you do as much for me and take care of me when I am old?" "Oh, yes! I shall do everything you ask of me," the little bird replied; "only bring me to safety." Whereupon the father bird promptly dropped his offspring into the sea, and as it drowned he said: "So shall it be done to all liars like you."

The father bird then returned to the shore, set forth with his second fledgling, and asked it the same question. Receiving the same answer, he drowned the second also, crying: "You, too, are a liar!"

Finally he set out with the third one, and when he had asked it the same question as he had the other two, the little bird replied: "My dear father, it is true that you are struggling mightily, and risking your life for me, and I would be wrong not to repay you when you are old, but I cannot commit myself. This much, though, I can promise: when I am grown up and have children of my own, I shall do as much for them as you have done for me." Then the father bird said: "Well spoken, little one, I will spare your life and carry you ashore safely."

Above all, my children, be honest in money matters with Jews and non-Jews alike. If you have money or possessions belonging to other people, take better care of them than you would if they were your own. The first question that is put to a man on entering the next world is whether or not he was faithful in his business dealings. A man may work ever so hard to amass money dishonestly; he may, during his lifetime, provide his children with rich dowries and leave them a generous inheritance at his death; and yet, I say, woe shall it be to that wicked man who, because he tried to enrich his children with dishonest money, has

397

forfeited his share in the world to come! In one fleeting moment he has lost eternity!

When God sends evil days upon us, we shall do well to remember the remedy thought of by the physician in the following story: A great king once imprisoned his physician and had him bound hand and foot with chains, and fed only a small portion of barley bread and water. After months of this treatment, the king sent some relatives of the physician to visit him in prison and find out what the unhappy man had to say. To their astonishment, he looked as hale and hearty as when he had entered the cell. He told his relatives that he owed his strength and well-being to a beverage of seven herbs which he had prepared before he went to prison, and of which he drank a few drops every day.

"What magic herbs are these?" they asked, and he answered: "The first is trust in God; the second is hope; and the others are patience, a recognition of my sins, joy in the knowledge that through my present suffering I shall be spared future suffering, contentment because my punishment is not worse, and the realization that God can set me free at any moment."

Mesillath Yesharim

BY RABBI MOSES HAYYIM LUZZATTO

Rabbi Moses Hayyim Luzzatto (1707–1747) began his prolific literary activity at an early age. He is best known today for his ethical work *Mesillath Yesharim* (Path of the Upright), which is a classic in contemporary Hebrew literature. A thorough master of biblical Hebrew, and an ardent believer in the mystic teachings of the Kabbalah, Rabbi Moses Hayyim Luzzatto migrated from Italy to the Holy Land in order to be free to pursue his kabbalistic studies. When he came to Amsterdam, he was warmly welcomed and accorded great respect by the entire Jewish community. One of the wealthy members offered him the hospitality of his home, but Luzzatto preferred to support himself as a lensgrinder. In his leisure hours he wrote on the Talmud and the fundamentals of Judaism. He wrote his *Mesillath Yesharim* at that period. Shortly after arriving in Palestine, he died at the age of forty, and was buried in Tiberias near the tomb of Rabbi Akiba.

In the middle of the nineteenth century, the *Mesillath Yesharim* was adopted as the ethical text of the moralist movement which was founded by Rabbi Israel Salanter.

The quality of cleanliness finds expression in many ways, since to be clean means clean of transgression in all forms.

Let us now consider the common sins that we commit in our social life, as when we taunt, insult, mislead, slander or hate our neighbor; or when we nurse a grudge, swear, lie, or commit sacrilege. No one can say: "I am free from such sins; I am clear of all such guilt." These are sins that take on so many various and subtle forms that only by great effort can we be on our guard against them.

Do not taunt your neighbor means that you must neither do nor say to him that which might shame him, even in private. "If a man has repented of his sins," says the Talmud, "no one should say to him: Remember your former doings." To insult one's neighbor in the presence of others is an even graver sin. We are expressly taught: "He that insults his neighbor in public has no share in the world to come."

If your neighbor seeks advice, do not give him advice that may cause him harm. Do not advise him to sell his field if your object is to get possession of it. You may say: "I have given him good advice." Yet in your heart you know whether or not you are sincere. The Torah says clearly: "Cursed be he who misleads the blind." The upright man should give the kind of counsel that he would take himself if he were placed in a similar position. Under no circumstances should he offer advice with any other object in mind than that of benefiting the one who seeks his aid, unless the advice sought is for the purpose of carrying out some evil design. It is, indeed, a duty to mislead one who seeks advice for an evil purpose.

The human heart finds it hard to escape hatred and revenge. A man is very sensitive to disgrace, and suffers keenly when subjected to it. Revenge is sweeter to him than honey; he cannot rest until he has taken his revenge. If, therefore, he has the power to forgive, to refrain from hating those who provoke him to hatred, if he can forget a wrong done him as though it had never been committed, he is indeed a strong and mighty man. The Torah declares it with the utmost clearness: "You shall not hate your brother in your heart. You shall not take vengeance nor bear any grudge against the children of your people."

The difference between taking revenge and bearing a grudge is well known. To take revenge is to return evil for evil. To bear a grudge is to remind a man of the evil he has done to you though you repay him with good. The Torah lays down a general rule: "You shall love your neighbor as yourself"—*as yourself*, without difference or distinction, without subterfuge and mental reservation, literally *as yourself*.

Lying is a most prevalent disease. It exists in various degrees. There are those who actually make it their business to tell lies. They go about inventing stories without any foundation in truth, in order to have material for gossip or because they wish to be considered clever. There are others less corrupt, who are in the habit of introducing some element of untruth into everything they say. Such liars are never believed. In the words of our sages: "The liar is punished by not being believed even when he speaks the truth." This practice has become so much a part of their characters that they can utter nothing that is free from falsehood.

Truth is one of the pillars upon which the world rests. He who utters a falsehood is like one who removes the foundation of the world. On the other hand, he who is careful to speak the truth is like one who builds the foundation of the world. Our sages tell a story of a city where the inhabitants were so scrupulous about speaking the truth that the angel of death had no control over them.

Pride is an exaggerated sense of our own importance and an inward belief that we deserve praise. Whenever a man believes he is gifted in any way, he is in danger of falling a victim to pride. There is the vain man who, because he considers himself unique and distinguished, deems it proper to assume a dignified bearing when he walks, when he sits, when he stands up, whenever he speaks and whatever he does. He walks leisurely, with measured step; he sits upright; he rises slowly; he speaks only with those of high rank, and even among them he utters only short sentences in an oracular fashion. In all his behavior he displays solemn pomp, as though his flesh were made of lead and his bones of stone.

There is the proud man who thinks that because he possesses some superiority, everyone should tremble before him. How dare an ordinary man speak to him, or ask anything of him! He overawes with his voice those who dare approach him. He overwhelms people with his arrogant replies, and he scowls all the time.

Another behaves as though he were humble and goes to extremes to display modesty and infinite humility, saying to himself: "I am so exalted and so deserving of honor, that I need not have anyone do me honor. I can well afford to forego visible marks of respect."

401

Another is not satisfied with having every one praise him for his superior traits; he wants them also to include in their praises the fact that he is the most humble of men. He takes pride in his humility, and wishes to be honored because he pretends to flee from honor. Such a prig usually goes so far as to put himself below those who are much inferior to him, thinking that in this way he displays the utmost humility. He refuses all titles of greatness and declines promotion in rank, but in his heart he thinks: "There is no one in all the world as wise and as humble as I."

Conceited people of this type, though they strive mightily to look humble, cannot escape some mishap that will cause their pride to burst forth. The humility of such behavior is soon recognized as insincere, hypocritical and nothing but pretense.

Finally, there are the proud who consider themselves great sages, and think they know the truth about everything. They consider very few people their equals in wisdom, and disregard what others have to say. They imagine that whatever they find difficult to understand cannot possibly be intelligible to any one else. They rely so much upon their own understanding they ignore all who disagree with them, whether ancient or recent authorities.

Whoever would attain the trait of cleanness must be free from the taint of pride. He must realize that pride is a form of blindness which prevents even a man of understanding from seeing his own shortcomings.

Let us now speak of anger. There is first the irascible person who usually flares up whenever anyone crosses him. He becomes so enraged that he loses all control of himself. He would destroy the entire world if he had the power. For the moment he is actually deprived of his reason, so that he acts like a wild beast. Being at the mercy of his anger, he is liable to commit any conceivable transgression.

There is another type of choleric person, whose anger is not roused by mere trifles. Yet, when he is angered, he is implacable. He is described in the Mishnah as one whom it is hard to provoke and hard to pacify. To have such a disposition is surely an evil, for in a fit of anger he is liable to commit some rash deed which he can never undo.

Then there is one who is not easily provoked, but his anger lasts a long time. He is less likely to do harm than those already mentioned. Nevertheless, he is far from being spiritually clean, since he has not learned to control himself.

Least obnoxious is the one whom it is hard to provoke and whose anger, when aroused, is too weak to be destructive and soon passes away. Such a man is indeed fortunate. The Rabbis laud the man who can keep silent in the midst of a quarrel.

Yet, desirable above all is the character of Hillel. Nothing could provoke him. Our sages have warned us against anger even for a worthy cause. Not even a teacher should display anger toward his pupil, nor a father toward his son. This does not mean that they should never reprove, but that when they have to reprove they should do so without anger, and only with a view to correction. The anger which they display should be more assumed than real.

He who is envious neither benefits himself nor injures the one he envies. He injures only himself. There are people so foolish that when they see a neighbor in luck, they begin to brood and are so upset and distressed that even the good which they possess no longer affords them pleasure. Of them the wise Solomon said: "Envy makes the bones rot."

Akin to envy is greed, which wears out the heart of man until the day of his death. Even worse than greed is the lust for honor. A man may control his craving for wealth and for pleasure, but the craving for honor is irresistible because it is almost impossible for a man to endure being inferior to his fellows. Were it not for this lust, a man would willingly eat whatever he could get, wear whatever might cover his nakedness, and dwell under whatever roof might protect him from inclement weather. Yet a man assumes tremendous burdens because he does not want to be regarded as inferior to his fellows.

How many are there who would rather starve than engage in work which they consider beneath their dignity, for fear that their honor might be compromised? They submit to idleness which leads to melancholy, lascivious-

403

ness, theft, and all the cardinal sins, in order not to lower their dignity nor spoil what they regard as their reputation.

Granted that, in order to possess the trait of cleanness, a man must exert himself a great deal, yet it does not require as much effort as appears on the surface. It is more difficult in the planning than in the execution. When a man makes up his mind and is persistent in his effort to master this desirable trait, he will find that, with little practice, it is acquired much more easily than he has ever imagined.

Eretz Yisrael

BY RABBI JACOB EMDEN

Rabbi Jacob Emden (1697–1776), who was reluctant to accept the office of rabbi, was finally persuaded to become the rabbi of Emden, Prussia, whence he took his name. He was a prolific writer, and he possessed critical powers rarely found among his contemporaries.

One of his many works is an edition of the daily prayerbook in three parts with a commentary, grammatical notes, and ritual laws. He was severely criticized for his publication of the prayerbook *Ammude Shamayim*, being accused of having dealt arbitrarily with the text. The following excerpt is from his introduction to the daily prayerbook.

Every Jew should steadfastly resolve to go to Eretz Yisrael and remain there. If he cannot go himself, he should support some person in that country.

The mistake our forefathers made was that of ignoring this precious land, and thereby causing much suffering in the generations that succeeded them. The thought of this land has ever been our solace in our bitter exile, where we can find neither peace nor rest. When we forgot our land, we ourselves were forgotten.

Misfortune befell us when Israel enjoyed honors in countries like Spain and assimilated with the people among whom they lived. No one at all yearned for Zion; it was abandoned and forgotten.

Israel and the land of Israel are called God's heritage, and the Torah is connected with both, with the people of God and the heritage of God; whoever abandons the one abandons the other.

A Letter of Advice

BY RABBI ELIJAH WILNA-GAON

Rabbi Elijah Wilna-Gaon (1720–1797) was gifted by nature with such a phenomenal memory that, having read a book once he remembered it for the rest of his life in all its details. At the age of seven he delivered a talmudic lecture in the great synagogue of Wilna which caused a sensation in the community. Before he had reached the age of twenty, he was consulted by celebrated rabbis. He was master of the entire range of rabbinical literature, including Hebrew grammar and biblical exegesis. He was a student of mathematics and other secular sciences, which he regarded as auxiliary branches essential to the proper understanding of the Talmud. The most complicated controversies in the Talmud, which would require other scholars days and weeks to comprehend, Rabbi Elijah Gaon was able to grasp at a glance. Hence the title *Gaon* (Excellence).

Endless goodness and firmness of character were united in his person. Piety, modesty and simplicity were the outstanding features of his character. Although he was the greatest talmudic authority of the period, he refused the office of rabbi; but because of his greatness, his influence on his people continued widespread in spite of his living in retirement.

The Gaon's letter to his family which is here included in condensed form was written when he was on a journey to Palestine. For some reason, he did not proceed farther than Germany but returned home soon afterwards.

This world may be likened to a man who drinks salt water: he seems to quench his thirst, yet actually he only grows more thirsty with each draught. No man dies with even half his desires attained. What does he gain from all his toil? Death is near and inevitable; life is a series of vexations, and sleepless nights are the common lot. Hence, I urge you to get used to solitude, for the sin of the tongue is equivalent to all sins put together. According to our sages, all the pious deeds of a man fail to counterbalance his frivolous speech. Man should often remain silent, tightening his lips like two millstones.

Teach your daughters to avoid oaths, lies and contention. Let their conversation be conducted in peace, love and gentleness. I possess many ethical books with a German translation. Let them read these regularly, but on the Sabbath—exclusively. Punish them for cursing or lying; show no softness in the matter. Parents are punishable for the corruption of their children. Therefore, use the utmost rigor in their moral training. Do not let them gad about in the streets, but see to it that they obey and honor you and all their elders. Urge them to obey all that is written in the moral books.

Bring up your sons in the right way, and with gentleness. You should pay their teachers generously. Pay careful attention to the children's health and diet, so that they shall not lack anything. Do not let the teacher burden them with too much work, for instruction is effective only when it is conveyed easily and agreeably. Give the children small presents to please them; this helps their studies.

The heirs of a wealthy man rejoice at his death, for they inherit his estate. To bring up your sons and daughters well, your words should be tender and kind, winning their hearts' consent. Accustom them to a life of virtue and noble character. Habit is strong, and soon becomes second nature. All beginnings are hard; continuations are easy.

Many a man reads moral words without rousing himself to moral works. This is shown in the parable of one who sows without first plowing the soil: the wind snatches the seed and feeds the birds. Because he cannot control himself, he is like one who sows without first erecting a fence for his field: the animals come trampling and destroying it. Sometimes one sows on stone, the stony heart, into which the seed does not enter at all. It is necessary to strike the stone until it is split and ready to receive the seed. Strike your children if they refuse to obey you. "Train a child in the way he should go, and he will never leave it, even when he grows old" is the great rule. Accustom your children to the study of the *Ethics of the Fathers,* for good manners have precedence over Torah.

Treat all men with respect and amiability. Bring happiness to one another by kindly social relations. In the hour of judgment, each man is asked: "Have you conducted yourself with friendliness toward your fellow man?" Let there be no dissension of any kind, but let love and brotherliness reign. Forgive one another and live in amity for God's sake.

Sefer Ha-Middoth

BY RABBI JACOB KRANZ

Rabbi Jacob Kranz, known as Dubner Maggid (1740–1804), was the most famous Jewish preacher of his time. His sermons were extremely popular, eloquent, and permeated with a rich variety of parables and illustrations taken from human life. His ethical work, *Sefer ha-Middoth,* resembles Rabbi Bahya's *Duties of the Heart* and contains eight sections, each section being divided into several chapters. All his works were published after his death by his son.

Do not displease God by hating him whom he loves. A father's love for his child is only a drop in the ocean compared with God's love for man. How, then, can you slander your neighbor or raise your voice against him?

If your neighbor is guilty of a misdeed, do not hate him for it, since it is quite possible that you in his position would act much worse. Instead, your great love and mercy for him should fill you with sorrow and sympathy because of the misfortune that has befallen him.

If you know in your heart that you are not well disposed toward your neighbor, shut your eyes and do not look at his faults with malicious pleasure in order to shame him with stinging reproof. Close your lips, do not rebuke him, lest you destroy your soul. God's anger turned against tyrants who tormented our souls, even though we deserved to suffer the evil done to us. Those tyrants were punished because of their malicious intent, because they rejoiced in seeing us suffer.

If you have a good heart, you will be sorry for the wrongdoer; you will pray for him and seek to rehabilitate him. If this is not possible, leave him in the care of God who will have mercy on him and direct him in the right path so that he may come to a good end. Seek to love him for the sake of the good he will do in time to come. Enrich your heart with love and friendship. Love your neighbor as yourself and wish him well. Have mercy upon him in his misfortune, and do all you can for him.

Hasidism

Hasidism, as a religious movement, was founded by Rabbi Israel Baal Shem Tov (Besht) in the middle of the eighteenth century. Its emphasis upon cheerfulness and optimism has often dispelled the clouds obscuring the promise of a better tomorrow.

Hasidism has made prayer more meaningful and enriched the liturgy of the synagogue. Despite all persecutions, the followers of Hasidic rabbis have continued to serve God joyously and to hope for the best. Many Hasidic rabbis have proved to be able shepherds of their flock, ever ready to lend courage and wise counsel.

Rabbi Israel Besht (1700–1760) was born of humble parentage somewhere in the Ukraine. Countless legends and myths attest to the profound influence of his luminous personality, striking magnetism, intuitive insight and most sensitive religious temperament. Rabbi Israel settled in the heart of the Carpathian mountains, where he spent his days in praying and teaching. He sought communion with God in the woods and the fields, and taught that life is a divine manifestation; every act performed under that realization is a sanctification of the soul.

In his *Studies in Judaism*, Solomon Schechter writes: The keynote of all Baalshem's teachings is the omnipresence, the immanence of God. The idea of the constant living presence of God in all existence permeates the whole of Baalshem's scheme. It is incumbent upon man to believe that all things are pervaded by the divine life, and when he speaks he should remember that it is this divine life which is speaking through him. There is nothing which is void of God. In every human thought God is present. If the thought is gross or evil, we should seek to raise and ennoble it by carrying it back to its origin.

God the Merciful not only created everything but is embodied in everything. Since God is present in all things, there is good, actual or potential, in all things. It is our duty everywhere to seek out and to honor the good, and not to judge that which may seem to be evil. In thinking of a fellow man, we should above all things realize in him the presence of the spirit of good.

Each of us, while thinking humbly of himself, should always be ready to think well of another. The most hardened of sinners are not to be despaired of, but prayed for. None knows the heart of man, and none should judge his neighbor. Let no one think himself better than his neighbor, for all serve God, each according to the measure of understanding which God has given him.

Your prayer should not be taken up with your wishes and needs, but should be the means to bring you nigh to God. In prayer man must lay aside his own individuality, and not even be conscious of his existence. The test of the real service to God is that it leaves behind it the feeling of humility. If a man after prayer is conscious of the least pride or self-satisfaction, let him know that he has prayed not to God but to himself. Before you can find God you must lose yourself.

He who loves the father will also love his children. The true lover of God is also a lover of man. It is ignorance of one's errors that makes one ready to see the errors of others. Every penitent thought is a voice of God. Every religious action must be done with enthusiasm. A mere mechanical and lifeless performance of a *mitzvah* is valueless.

In his ethical will, Rabbi Israel Baal Shem Tov taught:

He who serves the Creator continually has no time for vainglory. If a man becomes aware of a lovely thing, he should ask himself: Where is this beauty coming from if not from the divine power which permeates the world? Hence, the origin of this beauty is divine. Why, then, should I be attracted by the fragment? It is far better for me to be fascinated by the Source of all beauty.

If a man tastes something good and sweet, let him realize that the sweet quality is derived from the heavenly sweetness. A perception of this kind is indeed equivalent to seeing the Eternal One, blessed be he. Man should concentrate his thoughts on God at all times, forever yearning for the light of the divine presence.

A man is occasionally misled by his evil nature into believing that he has committed a grievous sin, even though he may

411

have done nothing wrong. The purpose of this nature, known as *Yetser ha-ra*, is to drive him into despair and so render him incapable of serving God. Let man beware of this ugly trick! Let him say: If indeed I have sinned, my Creator will be even more gratified to see that I refuse to let my offense interrupt my joyous service. This is the great principle of serving God: Keep away from sadness as much as possible.

Weeping is exceedingly bad, for man should serve God joyfully. However, tears of joy are very good. But let man not yield to paralyzing grief. Let him repent each misdeed and turn again in joy to the Creator, blessed be he.

Seeing Others

Rabbi Isaac once came to a village where only one Jew lived. During a heavy rain the Rabbi was forced to seek shelter from the downpour at the house of this Jew, who gave him supper and prepared a couch for him.

"You have been sighing all this time," observed the Rabbi, "What is the trouble?"

"I am sighing because I am too poor to do you proper honor," answered his host.

Rabbi Isaac gave him his blessing, calling upon heaven to endow the poor man with riches so that he might be able to care for the needy in a generous fashion.

The Rabbi's blessing proved effective. The poor villager prospered in his business and became the wealthiest man in the entire region. But as his wealth grew, so did his avarice, and with his avarice he developed a new and haughty bearing toward the poor, whom he disdained now as much as he had once loved them. He hired a gate-keeper, giving him strict orders to stand at the door and guard it so that no poor man could go beyond the gate.

When Rabbi Isaac heard of the villager's change of heart, he went to the gate of the main house and asked the warden to say to his master: "The man who brought you riches by his blessing is at the gate." His reception by the wealthy man was by no means friendly. Thereupon, Rabbi Isaac requested him to step to the window and look out.

"What do you see?" asked the Rabbi.

"I see people going about their business," answered the rich man.

412

"Now look into the mirror and tell me what you see," continued the Rabbi.

"I see only myself," said the host.

The Rabbi said: "Both the window and the mirror are squares of glass; yet you see others through the window, and only yourself in the mirror. Do you know why? Because the mirror has a coat of silver behind it. It is time to scrape off that coat."

And with this the Rabbi turned the mirror over as if to scrape off the silver.

"Stop, I beg of you," cried his host. "Leave me my wealth, and I will befriend the poor from now on." His change of heart was sincere, and he became a veritable father to the orphan and the widow.

Sabbath Delight

A famous musician once came to a town and posted announcements for a concert. All the well-to-do folk hurried to buy their tickets. Now in this town there lived a man who was a great lover of music, but both his legs were crippled and he was so poor that he lacked the price of a seat. He had just about enough money for standing room which, of course, was of no use to him. However, he could not bear to miss this event, and for a few pennies he induced a poor porter to carry him, perched on his back, to the concert hall.

Thus seated on the porter's shoulders he listened with unbounded delight; but now and then he was so carried away by the beauty of the music that he forgot where he was sitting; he danced about and clapped his hands until the poor porter began to complain: "You are breaking my neck; stop kicking my sides."

But the cripple soon forgot these complaints until finally the porter said: "I cannot bear you any longer; I am going to set you down." Whereupon the cripple asked the porter to carry him to a nearby wine-shop. There he ordered a large brandy for the porter and they returned to the concert hall. Now the porter, cheered and enlivened by the drink, was himself so touched by the music that he swayed and capered to its rhythms, no longer mindful of the antics of his burden. And thus both enjoyed the concert to its end.

"It is the same with the Sabbath," said Rabbi Sholem; "the important thing on the Sabbath is to praise God with a pure soul; but the soul is unfortunately crippled without the body; lacking the body it can neither praise nor thank God. Now, should the body be dissatisfied, the soul will not achieve its Sabbath delight. Hence we are taught to indulge the body, to cheer it with wine and good food, so that it too may be inclined to join the spirit in praise of the Almighty, and to sustain the soul in joyful contemplation. Then only will the Sabbath be perfect.

Hasidic Sayings

A man must labor hard his entire life to rid himself of pride.

If your intellect is clouded, disperse the clouds through the spirit of fervent prayer.

I love to pray at sunrise, before the world becomes filled with hatred and vanity.

Work for peace within your own household, then in your street, and then in your town.

Do not see evil in another and good in yourself, but see good in another and evil in yourself.

Do not criticize another's conduct but only your own.

Do not brood upon your sin, for this leads to melancholy and prevents sincere service to God.

When you admire beauty in a woman, remember that her beauty is but a reflection of the supreme source of beauty—the Lord.

How can one hope to improve another through angry words when anger is impurity in the highest degree?

Reflections

BY RABBI NAHMAN BRATZLAVER

Rabbi Nahman of Bratzlav (1770–1811) was the great-grandson
of Rabbi Israel Baal Shem Tov, the founder of the Hasidic
movement. In 1798 Rabbi Nahman Bratzlaver made a trip to
the Holy Land, the sight of which filled him with ecstasy and
divine inspiration. An unquestioning faith was the essence
of his teaching. He preached a simple mode of living, avoiding
the pursuit of riches. Among the elements of worship he
suggested were joy, song, ecstasy and dance. Rabbi Nahman
of Bratzlav is regarded as the greatest master of the parable and
the fairy tale in Yiddish literature. Full of rich and wild
imagination, his tales are among the most popular of the kind.

Break your anger by doing a favor for the one with whom
you are angry.

God loves the man who forgives his offenders.

He who does not complain about people is loved by
people.

A mitzvah that costs money is worth more than one
that costs nothing.

One should teach his children good manners from baby-
hood.

Good children are a balm and a healing for their parents.

If husband and wife quarrel they cannot raise good
children.

One who displeases his parents will have disobedient
children.

When a man is able to receive abuse smilingly he is
worthy of becoming a leader.

When God wishes to punish Israel he sends them unworthy leaders.

Holy studies renew the mind and the soul.

Those whom we influence for good become our spiritual children.

When we wish to influence another person we should begin by commending his good traits, and by trying to find excuses for his misdeeds.

Wealth will not remain with him who has no pity on others.

The prayer of another in your behalf aids you more than your own prayer.

If you are not at peace with the world, your prayer will not be heard.

Bind your thoughts to the words of your prayers, and you will gain God's grace.

Forget everybody and everything during your worship; forget yourself and your needs; forget the people of whom you have need.

Make every effort to pray from the heart. Even if you do not succeed, the effort is precious in the eyes of the Lord.

A humble man understands that everything that happens to him happens for good.

One who appears to be humble in order to win praise is guilty of the highest degree of pride.

Sometimes a man pays no attention to his opponent in order to vex him the more by his silence. There is no holiness in this behavior. If you understand that a soft answer will calm your foe, do not withhold it from him.

Bear in mind that life is short, and that with every passing day you are nearer to the end. How then can you waste your time on petty quarrels?

Simple language, easily understood, should be employed in explaining the Torah.

No matter how occupied a man may be, he must snatch at least one hour for daily study.

Truth and faith make for cheerfulness and length of life.

Falsehoods are many, but truth is one. In the unity of truth there is strength; truth is divine and it will surely triumph.

416

Yiddish Maxims

Woe to him whom nobody likes; but beware of him whom everybody likes.

A man should be master of his will and slave of his conscience.

One who looks for a friend without faults will have none.

One who has confidence in himself gains the confidence of others.

The most humble man thinks himself greater than his best friend thinks he is.

One who thinks he can live without others is mistaken. One who thinks others cannot live without him is even more mistaken.

While pursuing happiness we flee from contentment.

For the unlearned, old age is winter; for the learned, it is the season of harvest.

Teach your children in youth, and they will not teach you in your old age.

Fear only two: God, and the man who has no fear of God.

To be contrite means to add no fresh sins to the old.

Fear the one who fears you.

False friends are like migratory birds: they fly away in cold weather.

One who believes that anything can be accomplished by money is likely to do anything for money.

It is easier to abandon evil traits today than tomorrow.

Fear of a misfortune is worse than the misfortune.

Want makes people better; luck makes them worse.

God waits long, but pays with interest.

God strikes with one hand and heals with the other.

The world cannot be changed by either scolding or laughing.

Ten enemies cannot do a man the harm that he can do to himself.

Friends are needed both for joy and for sorrow.

Better a fool who has traveled than a wise man who has remained at home.

Parents may have a dozen children, but each one is the only one for them.

One father supports ten children, but ten children do not support one father.

He who saves is worth more than he who earns.

He who is sated does not believe the hungry.

The angel of death always finds an excuse.

Every man knows that he must die, but no one believes it.

Better a noble death than a wretched life.

Nineteen Letters

BY RABBI SAMSON RAPHAEL HIRSCH

Rabbi Samson Raphael Hirsch (1808–1888) was the champion of Jewish neo-orthodoxy in Germany. He is best remembered for his *Nineteen Letters of Ben Uziel* in which he formulated a cultured orthodoxy. This book, the publication of which has been regarded as epoch-making, was an attempt to show that orthodox Judaism could be warmly upheld by Jews with a scientific turn of mind.

Rabbi Samson Raphael Hirsch occupied various positions until he accepted the call as rabbi of a small group of orthodox Jews who opposed the reform tendencies in the community of Frankfurt. He succeeded in building up a large modern-orthodox congregation in Frankfurt, with schools, charities, and a newspaper. His course of action was followed afterwards by men like Dr. Nathan Birnbaum and Rabbi Isaac Breuer.

The selection "Precepts of Jewish Living" is from *Horeb*, designed by Rabbi Samson Raphael Hirsch as a textbook on Judaism for educated Jewish youth.

What is man in this God-filled world? Is he not a creature of God? Should he not also be a servant of God? Every fiber of his body was created, formed and arranged by God. Your spirit, your personality, weaves and works in this miniature universe, this microcosm. The mysterious spiritual force of man emanates from God. Learn to deem yourself holy, as a creature of God, and proclaim yourself a servant of God. The universe serves God; is it conceivable that man should serve only himself?

Man's earthly existence is full of significance. Everything has a purpose. Man's life should be devoted to the fulfillment of the divine will by making full use of his wealth and his faculties. Man bears his head proudly erect so that his eyes may examine the world in which he moves; his hands are equipped with fingers admirably fitted for art and sculpture; he has sufficient intelligence to recognize those things which will best serve his aims. Beyond that, the path of knowledge is difficult and dangerous, and pursued by few. But the heart, which is the source of all action, is capable of embracing all beings in affection and love.

Israel received the Torah in the wilderness and became a nation without a land. It was called "a kingdom of priests" because it was intended to preserve and practise the holy precepts of God in the midst of mankind. Its national existence, eternal as the spirit of the Eternal One, was not conditioned by transitory things. Israel later received the blessings of a land not as an end in itself but as a means to carry out the teachings of the Torah. But only for a short time was Israel able to come close to its ideal in time of prosperity. It became necessary for God to take away its wealth and its land, and the abundance of earthly good, and nothing was saved of Israel except the Torah, the soul of Israel's existence.

Israel accomplished its task better in exile than it did in full possession of good fortune. Without power, without brilliant show of human grandeur, it preserved its faithfulness amidst suffering and agony, and was enabled to withstand the blows of savage fanaticism. On every side proud and powerful states disappeared from the face of the earth, but Israel successfully maintained its existence and was upheld by its fidelity to God and his Torah. Every Jew should serve as a modest priest of God and humanity.

Prayer in Hebrew is not limited to mere petition for divine aid, but expresses our personality and our attitude toward God, man, and universe. The purpose of divine worship is to acknowledge our duties and to cleanse our minds and hearts. It is indeed for this reason that our houses of worship serve as schools for grown people; hence the name *shul* for synagogue.

Jewish law firmly opposes the glorification of wealth and lust, but at the same time it condemns purposeless self-denial as sinful. The highest type of worship is that of

420

being "joyful before the Lord" and ever conscious of his protection and guidance. God is the loving Father of all creatures, of all humankind.

The Bible terms Israel *God's own people,* but that does not imply Israel's exclusive possession of divine love and favor. On the contrary, it means that God has exclusive claim to Israel's service. The most cherished ideal of Israel is that of universal brotherhood. Our Hebrew prayers frequently contain supplications for the speedy realization of this goal. Good men of all nationalities have taught the dignity of humanity by their example of unselfish uprightness.

Judaism has six hundred and thirteen precepts, and no dogmas. Its basic truths are intelligible to all. The truly saintly person does not withdraw from the world but lives in it and for it. Judaism is opposed to a life of seclusion which is devoted only to meditation. Jewish study and worship should ever lead to a life of activity pervaded by the spirit of God.

Why conceal the fact that you are a Jew? Be a real Jew, obeying the law of justice and love, and you will be respected. Be just, truthful and loving to all, as the Torah teaches you. Give food to the hungry and clothes to the naked; comfort those who mourn and care for the sick; give counsel and help to all in sorrow and need. It is still a long way to the glorious ideal which the Torah desires us to realize in life. Let us therefore strive with all our power to reach the height of perfection!

Let us go back to the sources of Judaism and study them in order to live by them. Let us learn the science of living from the Bible, Talmud and Midrash. The Bible should not be studied on the basis of antiquity but as the foundation of a new science. Nature should be contemplated with the sentiments of the Psalmist, and history—with the perception of an Isaiah. One spirit lives in all, from the construction of the holy tongue to that of the universe—one spirit, the spirit of the Only One!

The results of that science must be carried over into life. The young children should be taught the language of the Bible as well as the language of the land; they should be taught to think in both. They should be made to see the world around them as God's world, and themselves as his servants. The wise precepts of the Torah and the Talmud should be made clear to them, so that they might rejoice in the name *Jew* in spite of all scorn and privation.

Parents should be implored not to destroy the work of the school, not to choke with icy indifference the Jewish sentiments in the hearts of their children. Non-Jewish scholars often see Judaism through a distorting glass, but light and truth will eventually emerge from the chaotic circumstances in which our people seem to be placed at present. Thousands may forsake the cause of Judaism, but Israel's cause is not lost so long as one Jew remains—one Jew with the Torah in his hand and Israel's law in his heart.

Precepts of Jewish Living

To love God means to realize that life has value only through God. We love God by loving his Torah and meeting its demands. There should be nothing dearer to us than the faithfulness which we owe to our God.

Sufferings are meant to educate us. If we know ourselves free from guilt, and yet God burdens us with sorrow, we should try to perfect ourselves. According to our sages, we should examine our life when sufferings are imposed on us. If the examination fails to show our faults, we should probe our knowledge of the Torah to see whether it is sufficient to enable us to measure our life by its demands.

Pride makes a man careless and carefree. We should strive to attain modesty and humility. The humility of Moses made him the greatest man. The fruit of such humility is loving devotion to others, which demands nothing for itself but finds satisfaction in furthering the welfare of men. We were created to help and preserve, to teach and spread happiness.

Compassion reflects the pain suffered by one's fellow man. It is a heavenly voice proclaiming the bond of unity which embraces all men as children of the Only One. The feeling of compassion residing in the human heart is strong enough to enable even a stolid and cold-blooded person to suffer with the flower as it mourns its fading beauty. The very existence of this emotion should serve as a reminder that all creatures are entitled to man's love and help.

We must not suppress this feeling of mercy, especially in regard to our suffering brothers and sisters. We must not silence the admonishing voice of duty within us, or the emotions of mercy and compassion will gradually disappear from our hearts, which will turn into stone, responding no longer to the voice of God. We are not entitled to joy so long as a brother suffers at our side. We must not fight our natural feelings of compassion as possible symptoms of human weakness. When the sufferings of our fellow men cause us to suffer, when their tears bring tears of mercy to our eyes, we are ennobled, we are men! True compassion results in the quiet strength which leads to active help and support.

Let us never listen to slanderous rumors. If people would not listen to evil talk, slander and malicious rumors would cease. By listening we complete the crime of the slanderer. How rashly we judge our fellow men! Without even giving the accused a hearing, we throw stones at him, thus killing within us the respect and love for him to which he is entitled.

Of late, it has become fashionable to discuss the need of making Judaism conform with the times. Let us see whether Judaism was ever "up to date." Was Abraham's Judaism in keeping with the spirit of the age when Nimrod ordered him cast into the flaming furnace for destroying the idols of that period? What of Daniel and his companions? What of the Judaism of the Maccabees? These martyrs, these heroes, calmly looked to the future, beyond the times of persecution and destruction. What would have become of Judaism if our ancestors had striven to

423

shape it in accordance with views and conditions of their times? Judaism has wandered through all ages, all lands. What kind of Judaism would there be if we were permitted to shape and reshape it constantly?

Judaism must shape life. Life must never be permitted to shape Judaism. During long centuries, Judaism was the sole voice of protest against a pagan world. God told Abraham, the first Jew, to defy the world by not being up to date. In the midst of the most cultured nations of his time, among Egyptians and Phoenicians, Abraham walked alone—with God.

Consider Abraham, the first most isolated Jew on earth! Alone with God, alone of all human beings on earth! Alone, in opposition to an entire world—and a heart full of modesty, kindness, all-embracing mercy and love for *all*, for the most degenerate men of his time, the men of Sodom. Ever since, Judaism pursues its lonely course through history.

Even in the darkest periods of his history, the persecuted Jew appeared three times daily before his God and derived infinite comfort from the hope that the Only One would implant the lofty ideals of justice and peace in every human heart.

The Jew will not turn his back on any science, art or culture, that is really ethical and truly contributing to the progress of man. The more firmly he stands on the rock of his Judaism and the more conscious he becomes of his Jewish destiny, the more he will be inclined to absorb all knowledge—wherever he may find it—that truly conforms to Jewish truths. Never, never will he sacrifice his Judaism; at no time will he bring his Judaism up to date.

Rabbi Israel Salanter

Rabbi Israel Salanter exerted a strong influence on the development of many young students of the Talmud in some Russian towns during the nineteenth century. He advocated manual training for Jewish youth, and at the same time taught religious ethics. His followers in the practice of severely strict morality were generally referred to as *Musarnikes* or moralists. Their study of ethical works, such as Luzzato's *Mesillath Yesharim,* assumed the proportions of a regular movement.

The powerful influence of Rabbi Israel Salanter's personality overcame all opposition to his work. He was regarded as the keenest-minded Talmudist of his time, who devoted himself to the spreading of morality and integrity among the masses of his people. He strongly believed that anyone might easily curb his own evil desires by means of studying the works of ethics. Memorizing talmudic proverbial sayings, he said, is a good cure for sin.

Professor Louis Ginzberg, in his essay on Rabbi Israel Salanter, writes:

Rabbi Israel Salanter's life was wholly consecrated to ethics and morality. At the age of twenty-five, he became the leader of a small group of students and business men whom he introduced into the study of ethico-religious books. He was scarcely thirty years old when he was appointed head of a talmudic academy in Wilna. His salary amounted to the equivalent of two dollars a week. One is almost inclined to believe that then, as now, salaries were often in inverse ratio to the merits of the recipients. One takes it for granted that the greater the scholar, the smaller are his demands upon life.

According to Rabbi Israel Salanter, faith in the existence of God is of small value in true religion if it is not supplemented by the belief that God is just, rewarding good deeds and punishing evil ones. True service of God is that which is free from self-seeking. He who does what is pleasing to God simply because he hopes for personal reward serves only himself, not God. Frequent meditation and soulful study of the sayings of

425

our wise men and our moralists help a man to conquer his evil nature.

The sensual desire in man often makes him mistake momentary pleasure for the true happiness which he craves, and he succumbs to the pressure of his passion. Frequent yielding to his sensual desires finally produces in man an impure spirit—the decay of his spiritual energy—with the result that he becomes a slave to his evil habits.

The moral-religious clearsightedness commands man to struggle against the temptation of sensual desires, and to be guided in his actions not by the immediate pleasures which they produce but by their remote consequences. By continually increasing his fund of moral views, the spirit of purity is given to him, so that without struggle and combat he always wills the good and the right.

Sincerity is especially important in self-criticism, since our judgment of good and evil is greatly influenced by emotion and sentiment. Without deep sincerity we would find little to criticize in ourselves; self-love would blind our judgment. We often meet people who are extremely conceited and vain, though we fail to see the slightest reason for their good opinion of themselves. Self-love often excites in man so strong a feeling of self-importance that he is unaware of his shortcomings while he sees those of his neighbor quite clearly. In self-criticism we should try to eliminate, or at least reduce to a minimum, this element of self-love, and scrutinize ourselves in the same way that we would others. In fact, we should criticize ourselves only, not our fellow men. We should never rest on our laurels.

The discovery of our faults will not discourage us if we look to the future instead of to the past. Repentance is not remorse, but a serious attempt to profit from past mistakes. No ailment of the soul is worse than discouragement. Man must again and again renew the idea of courage in his mind. He must not become discouraged if he fails to see any improvement in his moral qualities even after much self-discipline. Water continually dropping on a rock will finally wear it away, though the first drops seem to leave no impression. So too, self-discipline cannot fail to affect our conduct if we practise it continually. We must train ourselves so that we no longer obey the ethical teachings reluctantly, but that we may follow them quite naturally.

Calmness of mind and temper is a great virtue; we must never allow ourselves to be ruffled even when the greatest misfortunes befall us. The religious truths which are indispensable to the ethical education of man, and without which he cannot develop morally, are: belief in God, revelation, and reward and punishment.

Rabbi Israel Salanter felt himself in the presence of the divine whenever he saw suffering and pain that produce a meek and contrite spirit. Once on the eve of Yom Kippur, when the synagogue was filled with devout worshipers awaiting in solemn awe and silence the *Kol Nidre* service, rumors and whispers suddenly arose on all sides, for Rabbi Israel had not yet arrived. The congregation waited an hour, and still there was no trace of him. Messengers were sent to search for him, and all returned unsuccessful. At the end of the service, Rabbi Israel appeared in the synagogue. The joy of the people was great, and equally great was their amazement when they learned the reason for his absence. On his way to the synagogue, Rabbi Israel told them, he had heard a little child crying bitterly. When he had drawn near to investigate, he found that the baby's mother, in order to be at the synagogue in good time had put the baby to bed earlier than usual. The child had soon awakened and began to cry for its mother. Rabbi Israel had stayed beside the baby's cradle until its mother returned, and that was what had made him late.

Once, a poor scholar confided to him that if he were able to preach he might succeed in supporting himself and his family by taking up the profession of an itinerant preacher. So Rabbi Israel Salanter composed a number of sermons, and after spending several weeks teaching the poor scholar how to deliver them, he dismissed him—well prepared for his new calling.

Dr. Menahem G. Glenn, in his book on Rabbi Israel Salanter, speaks at length about his giving the people permission to break the fast of Yom Kippur when a frightful epidemic disease raged in the city of Wilna, where he lived. This event was used by Frishman as the theme of his short story *Three Who Ate*, translated from the Hebrew into English by Helena Frank. The following condensation contains but few minor changes in the style.

It is Yom Kippur afternoon. The Rabbi stands on the platform of the synagogue, and there is a fascination in his noble features. He is old, but tall and straight. His long beard is white, his lips are pale, and only his eyes shine and sparkle like the eyes of a young lion.

The Musaf service is over, and the people are waiting to

hear what the Rabbi will say. When he begins to speak, his weak voice grows stronger every minute. He speaks of the holiness of Yom Kuppur and the Torah, of repentance and prayer, of the living and the dead, and of the pestilence that has broken out and destroys without pity, without rest, without a pause . . . How long? How much longer?

He speaks of cleanliness, of wholesome air, of dirt which is dangerous to man, of hunger and thirst which are man's evil angels when there is a pestilence, devouring without pity. "Man shall live by the observance of God's commands, and not die by them." There are times when we must turn aside from the law, if by so doing a whole community may be saved.

He implores like a child, and his words are soft and gentle; every now and then he weeps so that his voice cannot be heard. "Eat, fellow Jews, eat. Today we must eat! This is a time to turn aside from the law. We are to *live* by the commandments, and not die because of them."

But no one in the synagogue has stirred from his place, and there he stands and begs of them, weeping, and declares that he takes the whole responsibility on himself, so that the people may remain innocent. But no one stirs. Presently he begins again in a changed voice—he does not beg, he commands: "I give you leave to eat . . ."

His words are like arrows shot from a bow. But the people are deaf to him; no one stirs. Then he begins again in his former voice and implores like a child: "What would you have me do? Why will you torment me till my strength fails? Do you think that I have not struggled with myself from early this morning till now?"

The Rabbi grows white as chalk, and lets his head fall on his breast. There is a groan from one end of the synagogue to the other, and then the people are heard to murmur among themselves. The Rabbi, like one speaking to himself, says: "It is God's will. This is also a law, it is a mitzvah. Doubtless, the Almighty wills it so!"

The sexton comes, and the Rabbi whispers a few words into his ear. He also confers with the spiritual leaders, and they nod their heads and agree. The sexton brings cups of wine and little rolls of bread out of the Rabbi's chamber. And though I should live many years and grow very old, I shall never forget what I saw then; and even now, when I shut my eyes, I see the whole thing: three Rabbis standing on the platform in the synagogue and eating before all the people on the Day of Atonement!

Jewish Thought

BY RABBI ABRAHAM ISAAC KOOK

Rabbi Abraham Isaac Kook (1864–1935) was elected chief rabbi of Palestine in 1921 and exerted a great influence as talmudist, philosopher-poet and mystic. After his death, an institution was founded in his memory for the purpose of finding, collecting and publishing the numerous manuscripts which he had left. His *Oroth Hakodesh* (The Holy Lights), in two volumes, is a collection of philosophical, mystical essays on Judaism.

What follows is a collection of excerpts from *Banner of Jerusalem* by Dr. Jacob B. Agus and from "The Teachings of Rav Kook" by Herbert Weiner (Commentary, May, 1954).

Faith is the song of life. Woe to him who wishes to rob life of its splendid poetry. The whole mass of prosaic literature and knowledge is of value only when it is founded on the perception of the poetry of life.

Faith and love are the very essence of life. There would be nothing of value left in the travail of life if these two luminaries, faith and love, were taken from it.

Contemporary civilization throughout the world is founded entirely on unbelief and hate, forces which nullify the essence of life. It is impossible to overcome this disease of modern society unless we discover the good that is contained in faith and love. The Torah and the divine precepts are the channels through which faith and love flow unceasingly.

All the troubles of the world, especially the ills of the soul such as sadness, impatience, disgust with life and despair are due only to the failure of knowing how to face the majesty of God in utter surrender.

Death is an illusion. Fear of death, the universal disease of mankind, stems from sin. All the labors of man center round his desire to escape death, but he cannot achieve his goal without first enriching his soul in the direction of its inner source.

The Torah and all its precepts form a great and mighty divine poem of trust and love. Because of our reverence and affection for the people of Israel, we lovingly observe the customs of Israel, even if they are not wholly based on divine revelation. This affection of ours is sacred, derived from a high and divine source.

The basic principle of the observance of the rules and regulations introduced by our sages is the fact that all Israel has accepted them. The honor of our nation and its historical influence are embodied in them. Hence, whatever is more ancient is more beloved, since the will and the general character of the people are revealed in it.

A wonderful vital force is hidden in the heart of each Jew, which impels him to attach himself to his people, whose life stream flows within him. This subconscious impulse makes him share the powerful yearning for the pure and uplifting light of truth and divine equity, a yearning that is bound to be realized some day in actual life.

The Jewish precepts, practices and customs are the vessels which contain a few sparks from the great light from above. The vital force of the Torah will do its work in the innermost being of him who clings to its precepts, even though that person remains unaware of its operation. The moment a man desires to have a share in the spirit of Israel, the divine spirit enters his aspirations, even in spite of himself. All the possessions of Israel are suffused with the indwelling spirit of God: its land, its language, its history and its customs.

Prayer is an absolute necessity for us and for the whole world; it is also the most sacred kind of joy. The waves of our soul beat ceaselessly on the shores of consciousness. We desire of ourselves and of the whole world the kind of perfection that the limitation of existence renders impossible. In our despair and frustration we are likely to turn against our better judgment and against our Creator. But before this cancer of the spirit has had time enough to grow in our midst, we come to pray. We give utterance to our thoughts and are uplifted to a world of perfect existence. Thus our inner world is rendered perfect in truth, and restful joy fills our consciousness.

Every plant and bush, every grain of sand and clod of earth, everything in which life is revealed or hidden. the smallest and the biggest in creation—all longs and yearns and reaches out toward its celestial source. And at every moment, all these cravings are gathered up and absorbed by man, who is himself lifted up by the longing for holiness within him. It is during prayer that all these pent-up desires and yearning are released. Through his prayer, man unites in himself all being, and lifts all creation up to the fountainhead of blessing and life.

Every sin brings about a particular type of trembling in the soul, which does not cease until repentance has been made. It is possible to detect this trembling in the lines of the face, in gestures, in the voice, in the handwriting or style of language and speech. The defect is to be observed precisely where the sin has walled off the light. When man repents out of love, the cosmic light of the world of unity shines upon him and everything is joined in oneness; evil joins with the good and raises it to even a higher value.

The sage is even more important than the prophet. What prophecy, with all its militant and fiery weapons, failed to do, the sages accomplished by developing many students and by the repeated study of the Torah and all its laws. In time, the efforts of the sages overshadowed the words of the prophets, and prophecy itself disappeared. But it shall come to pass in the latter days that the light of prophecy shall return, as it is written: "I shall pour forth my spirit upon all flesh." Prophecy shall recognize the great accomplishments of the sages and declare: "The sage is greater than the prophet."

431

Festive Joy and Peace

BY HERMANN COHEN

Hermann Cohen (1842–1918) was professor of philosophy at the University of Marburg from 1873 to 1912, where he earned a reputation as a perceptive interpreter of Kant's philosophy. He is considered the founder of the "Marburg School," which made the small German university famous.

His interest in Judaism was reawakened in 1880, when he became intensely concerned with Jewish life and thought. In 1904 he took a leading part in establishing the Society for the Advancement of Jewish Studies in Berlin, where he gathered about him a small circle of disciples. Included among them was Franz Rosenzweig whose own literary works later exercised a great influence on Jewish theology and philosophy.

The following selection is from the conclusion of Cohen's work *The Religion of Reason from the Sources of Judaism* (Die Religion der Vernunft aus den Quellen Judentums), which was published after his death. It is considered the classic work in Jewish religious philosophy of modern times.

It is highly significant that the Jewish festivals, except those connected with repentance and atonement, are chiefly dedicated to the idea of joy. "You shall rejoice at your festival together with your son and daughter, your male and female servants, as well as the stranger, the orphan and the widow" (Deuteronomy 16:14). Joy is the very purpose and goal of the festivals, and it must be shared with the strangers and the poor. You are to be happy with them and they are to be happy with you. This rejoicing is designed to raise man above social afflictions at least during the festival days. Our holidays would indeed lose all meaning and value if they were unable to implant brief joy in the heart of anyone who observes them.

Festive joy symbolizes peace. The road to peace becomes

the path of life. The joy which is experienced during the festival of freedom and deliverance from slavery celebrates the revelation on Mount Sinai, the legislation of a moral code. The Sabbath represents the first step toward the abolition of slavery. It symbolizes the universal joy which is yet to come when all men will be free to work and to search for truth. There is no blessing which excels peace. The Hebrew word for peace, *shalom,* means perfection, the supreme goal of man. Peace is the Messiah who will resolve all strifes and human struggles and will lead man to a reconciliation with God.

Despite all the sufferings the Jew has endured throughout his history, he has miraculously managed to preserve his equanimity and good humor, without which he would never have been able to rise from deep humiliation to lofty heights. The Jewish festivals are largely responsible for this miracle. Festive joy, being a religious duty, has proved a vital force in the consciousness of the Jew. During the Sabbath and the festivals joy prevailed in the ghetto, no matter what sufferings the week had brought.

"Peace, peace to him who is far off, and to him who is near, says the Lord; I will heal him" (Isaiah 57:19). Peace was the healing power of prophecy: peace as opposed to warfare, peace as opposed to human passions. Peace is founded on knowledge, on Torah. Therefore, the study of Torah has always been an essential part of festival rejoicings. Founded on the spirit, this intellectual joy has never degenerated into sensuality.

The Jew could never remain a man of mourning: his festivals and his studies always raised him to the celestial heights of joy. Peace, like all other virtues, came to be his natural way of life. If the Jewish character can be described in one word, it is peace. We should expect hatred and vengeance to rule the Jewish mind, since the Jew has been hated and oppressed by the whole world. But Jewish teachings and Jewish living make this impossible. There is no room for hatred in the heart of one who believes in peace. Messianism is the basic force of Jewish consciousness. Life receives its meaning and purpose through peace.

Saints and Saintliness

BY SOLOMON SCHECHTER

Professor Solomon Schechter (1850–1915) won an international reputation when he discovered countless ancient manuscripts in the *Genizah,* or store-room, of an old Cairo synagogue. The work of sorting as many as one hundred thousand manuscript fragments, amidst the accumulated dust and dirt of centuries, impaired his health considerably.

In 1902, he came to New York from England and was appointed president of the Jewish Theological Seminary of America. He found a much wider field for his activity in the United States. He was the acknowledged leader of Jewish scholarship in America. His writings include *The Wisdom of Ben Sira, Some Aspects of Rabbinic Theology,* and *Studies in Judaism.*

The best Hebrew equivalent for the term saint is *hasid,* commonly used in the sense of pious, devout, and godly. But the noun *hesed* implies the qualities of grace, graciousness, and kindness. When an ancient rabbi wanted to be polite to a newly-married couple, he would compliment the bride with the words *naah wa'hasudah* (beautiful and graceful). Hence, the best equivalent for *hasidim* would be *beautiful souls.*

The saint is described as a regent, having absolute control over all his organs. Of these, the mouth is the most important. A maxim of Judaism is that things which enter the mouth as well as those which proceed from it may be unclean. Accordingly, the Jewish saint must constantly watch the imports and the exports of his mouth. There is a story about a famous Jewish saint who fasted the first six days of the week. When asked how he accomplished this feat, he answered that he never meant to fast: he simply forgot to eat.

Even more strictly would the saint keep watch over the things which proceed from his mouth. "Be careful not to utter an untruth," says an old Jewish saint, "even in the way of a joke, or in the way of over-emphasis, for we are warned in the Torah against the most weighty sins with only one prohibitive command, while the law forbidding the speaking of untruth is ever so many times repeated in the Bible."

Altogether, there is no room in the soul of the saint for those ugly qualities which are bound to impair the proper relations between a man and his fellow. These traits are pride, anger, despair, hatred, jealousy, dissipation, desire for power, and self-assertion. Vanity is the root of all evils —man setting himself up as an idol, and thus bound to come into collision with both God and fellow man.

The best remedy for this ugly disease is love. Hence the warning of the saint: He who hates a man hates the Holy One who created him. We are all children of the Lord our God, all souls having their roots in him. Therefore, let man love all creatures and envy none. Let this be a love which leaves no room for self. Man will not succeed in attaining to this love until he has acquired the virtue of humility.

In matters of philanthropy, the saint would be inclined to extravagance. The rabbis of the Talmud drew the limit when they said: He who wishes to be lavish in his philanthropic work, let him not spend more than twenty percent of his income. The saint transgresses this limit, taking as his norm: "What is mine is thine, and what is thine is thine."

Sympathy and tenderness are not confined by the saint only to the human species. They extend also to dumb creatures. We read the story of a man who was cruel to his dog. The dog sought refuge under the robes of a sage. When the man pursued the dog intent on beating him, the sage protested: "Since this dog sought my protection, you shall not touch it."

Consciousness of sin and assurance of grace are the two great motive powers in the working of religion. Without them, religion sinks to the level of a mere cult in which

there is no room for devotion and submission. Hence the
tendency toward self-accusation so manifest in many a
writing by the Jewish saints. Sometimes it is the sin of his
fellow man for which the saint holds himself responsible.
This is rightly explained on the ground that the sense of
solidarity and responsibility was so keen within the Jewish
saint that he saw nothing incongruous in pleading guilty
to the sum total of iniquities committed by his contemporaries.

The exhortation to feel shame before God, who is present everywhere and witnesses man's deeds, is a favorite
appeal with all the Jewish moralists. The saint, however,
is so strongly overcome with shame before God that he
says: "A sinful thought should bring a blush to man's face
and make him experience the same sensation of confusion
and shame as would the sudden appearance of an intimate
friend just at the moment when he is about to do something disgraceful."

At the Parting of the Ways

BY AHAD HAAM

Ahad Haam (One of the People) is the pseudonym of Asher Ginsberg (1856–1927), whose collected Hebrew essays have been published in four volumes, entitled *Al Prashath Derakhim* (At the Parting of the Ways).

Many attempts have been made to analyze Ahad Haam's teachings; they are subjects of intensive discussion. He has been described as a sublime moralist, a noble personality, a master in the art of essay writing, and an eminent educator of his generation.

Ahad Haam gave a new tone to modern Hebrew literature. He reached the zenith of his career, as a writer on the philosophy of Jewish life, when he left Russia and settled in London. His last years were spent in Tel Aviv, where he was accorded special honors.

Adam became a great philosopher when he first uttered the word "I." Philosophers have never arrived at a full understanding of this little word.

What is the "self"? This question is asked again and again in every age. We may say that the "self" of each individual is a combination of memory and will, uniting the past and the future. When a man says "I" he is not thinking of his hands and feet, or any part of his constantly changing anatomy. He is thinking of that inner spirit or force which, in some hidden manner, unites his impressions and memories of the past with his desires and hopes for the future, making the entire pattern a single entity.

This spiritual entity grows and develops side by side with the physical, external man. But its growth is in reverse, for the spiritual man grows from the future toward the past. The "self" of a young man has few memories, but it is rich in hope and desire. When man reaches middle age and has grown rich in experience and memory, a

437

balance is established between the physical and spiritual "self": the future spurs his will to activity, but this activity is curbed and guided by the past. Finally, when he grows old, he is emptied of desire and hope. There is nothing left for him but to plunge into the sea of the past. Old age in its distress calls faith to its aid, and faith gives to the "self" the future it lacks.

The Hebrew word *nefesh* (soul) includes body and soul and all the life-processes that depend on them. Judaism finds eternal life on earth by strengthening the social feeling in the individual, and by making man look upon himself not as an isolated being with an existence bounded by birth and death but as part of a larger pattern—a limb of the entire social body. Man is one and indivisible. All his limbs, his feelings, his emotions, his thoughts make up a single whole. His life is not wasted, because he is a member of the nation which exists for a lofty end. This philosophy of life raises the individual above self-love and teaches him to find the purpose of his life in the well-being of the community.

The prophet, as represented by Moses, has two fundamental qualities which distinguish him from the rest of mankind. First, he is *a man of truth*. He sees life as it is, with a view unwarped by subjective feelings; and he tells you what he sees just as he sees it, unaffected by irrelevant considerations. The prophet is an *extremist*. He concentrates his entire heart and mind on his ideal. He accepts no excuse, consents to no compromise and never ceases to thunder his denunciations, even when the whole world is against him. As a man of truth he cannot help being just and upright, since uprightness is truth in action. His righteousness is absolute, knowing no restriction. On the one hand, he cannot altogether reform the world in accordance with his desires; on the other, he cannot cheat himself or shut his own eyes to its defects. Hence it is impossible for him ever to be at peace with the actual life in which his days are spent. Yet his vision of what is to come, of "the latter end of days," is his comfort whenever his cup of sorrow overflows and he seems not to have the strength with which to pour out his soul in bitterness against the evil.

When Moses first goes out into the world, he is at once brought face to face with a violation of justice, and he takes the side of the injured. "An Egyptian striking a Hebrew"—the everyday occurrence wherein the strong tramples the weak—is his first experience. The prophet's indignation is aroused and he helps the weaker man. Then "two Hebrews fighting"—two brothers, both weak, both slaves of Pharaoh, and yet fighting each other. Once more the prophet's sense of justice prompts him to meddle in a quarrel which is not his. But this time he discovers that it is no easy matter to fight the battle of justice. The world is stronger than he, and he who stands against the world does so at his peril. Yet his experience does not make him cautious. His zeal for justice drives him from his own country; and, as soon as he reaches another habitation of man—even before he has had time to find shelter—he hears once more the cry of outraged justice, and runs immediately to its aid. The prophet makes no distinction between man and man, only between right and wrong. He sees strong shepherds trampling on the rights of weak women— and he runs to defend the weak.

The prophet teaches, trains, forgives and hopes to see the fruit of his labor. He remains in the wilderness, buries his own generation, and trains a new one. Year after year passes, and he does not weary of repeating to the new generation the laws of righteousness that must guide it in the land of its future. The past and the future are the prophet's whole life, each completing and uniting the other. He sees in the present nothing but a wilderness—a life far removed from his ideal. He lives in the future world of his vision, and seeks strength from the past. Something of Moses has illumined the life of our people in every generation.

Israel has never lived in the present. The present, with its evil and its wickedness, fills us with anguish, indignation and bitterness. Even our Hebrew language, the garment of the Jewish spirit, has no present tense, only a past and a future. The Jew is both optimist and pessimist. His pessimism is for the present, but his optimism is for the future.

The Hebrew Book

BY HAYYIM NAHMAN BIALIK

Hayyim Nahman Bialik (1872–1934), the foremost Hebrew poet of his generation and one of the greatest masters of the Hebrew language, was accorded the highest recognition of any Hebrew writer. He became the poet laureate of the Jewish renaissance, the only Hebrew poet of world fame. He was equally respected by all factions in Jewry; his voice was that of an entire people whose soul was hurt.

While still in Soviet Russia, Bialik championed the cause of the Hebrew language and culture with heroic self-sacrifice. In 1924, he finally settled in Tel Aviv, Israel. Bialik's poetry is distinguished by its prophetical pathos and intense longing for Jewish deliverance.

What follows is a condensation of Bialik's essay, which he delivered in the form of an address at a conference held in 1913. His principal ideas concerning Hebrew revival were included in the plan of the Bialik Institute (*Mosad Bialik*), established in Jerusalem in 1935 to commemorate his name.

Our literature is thousands of years old and comprises tens of thousands of volumes; it represents the creative forces of hundreds of generations and is highly varied in form and content. Yet, for all this wealth, we are hardly in a position to indicate even a limited number of books which could become significant to the contemporary Jew with a taste for literature, books precious enough to turn to for spiritual sustenance.

In all ages our rich literature had a certain number of books of permanent value which deserved to be called *the books of a people,* because they were a source of enjoyment to every class of Jews, the highest as well as the lowest. There has not been a single period which did not make some permanent contribution to posterity. Each era deposited behind it a sort of layer which became the soil for the spiritual crops of the succeeding period. If a literature lacks tradition and continuity, it is deprived of growth and self-renewal. For thousands of years our people thought and felt and expressed itself in various styles and forms. Our modern literature, compared with that which preceded it, is no more than a drop in the sea. The Bible, the Apocrypha, the Talmud, Philosophy, Kabbalah, Poetry, Ethics, Homiletics, Hasidism—each of these represents an entire era with its own atmosphere and special physiognomy.

But now, we have arrived at a period of great spiritual distress. We have difficulty in meeting a request for a book, or set of books, by means of which a young person may familiarize himself with our people's creativity through choice selections from original books. We certainly cannot advise the mere reader to dig for himself in the vast amount of ancient literature. Such labor is for experts and not for casual readers. What are we to do, then, for our contemporary Jew who wants to know the literary activity of the Jewish people through the best illustrations culled from all periods?

We must resort to literary ingathering. In the past, literary works that were considered most important were collected and arranged; the rest automatically remained unknown, destined to *genizah* or concealment from the wide public. This was a great national undertaking, a sacred task. It not only saved the people from confusion, but it also opened up paths leading into a new literary era of different content and form. When a tree has shed its old fruits it begins to bear new ones.

There are those who fear the word *genizah,* because it has caused us great losses. There are also those who will regard this as an imposed censorship, telling the public to read this and not to read that. This is a groundless fear, based upon false reasoning. Are not entire sections of our literature relegated to *genizah,* concealment, even in our own days? People cease to read them, hence *genizah.*

In ancient times, scholars preserved the vital remnants of the past by collecting and arranging the finest pieces of literature which often lay buried in heaps of worthless material. They separated the chaff from the wheat. *Genizah* is good for literature, just as pruning is good for trees. Who is to decide? Who is to select? Why, the spirit of the people! We have no other criterion. Scholars are but spiritual representatives of the people, and must submit to the dictates of reality.

The guardians of freedom among us may well rest at ease. Freedom of choice will not be curtailed. Every revival is nothing more than a rediscovery of the past. The pruning of plants does not mean their ultimate destruction. On the contrary, a large part of the trunk is left, whether for the purpose of having it blossom again or in order to graft onto it new shoots.

If we wish to restore to our literature some of its vital force and influence, we must produce a new collection of the best Hebrew works of all times. We must draw forth the sparks from every nook and corner in which there is concealed a bit of the holy spirit of the people, and combine them into one complete unit. This anthological activity adds rather than detracts. All the old material will of itself be lit up by a new light.

That compilation, or whatever you wish to call it, must include the best. In the bookcase of the literary-minded Jew there will again appear books containing the essence of Jewish thought and feeling throughout the ages. The Hebrew book will regain its pristine glory. It will become a vital necessity to every Jewish home. Who knows? Perhaps even those who have drifted far away will return to the source which fed their forefathers.

A time to gather is the dictate of the hour, and this is all we can afford to do at present. We must not belittle the imporance of a book commonly loved. The land of Israel bequeathed one little book to us. Who knows? Perhaps the book will ultimately restore that land to us. May it not happen, in the history of a nation as well as an individual, that the effect becomes the father of the cause?

The Philosophy of Jewish History

BY SIMON DUBNOW

Simon Dubnow (1860–1941), author of an exhaustive history of the Jews, died a martyr's death during the Nazi massacres in which some six million Jews were killed.

Dubnow's *General History of the Jewish People* was originally written in Russian and published in 1901. It has gone through several editions in German, Hebrew and Yiddish translations.

This selection is from his *Essay in the Philosophy of History,* published by the Jewish Publication Society of America in 1927.

The Jewish people was the contemporary of the earliest civilized nations and, in common with modern nations, it strides forward on the path of progress without interruption. It continues to fill a place in the world of thought as one of the most active and intelligent forces. Like an unbroken thread, the history of the Jewish people runs through the ancient civilizations of Egypt and Mesopotamia down to the present-day Western civilization.

Jewish history falls into two parts, divided by the collapse of the Jewish state in the year 70. The people of Israel have successfully preserved their spiritual unity and originality, even though they have been stripped of all their land and government. We have before us not a simple political or racial entity, but a spiritual people, whose prophets cannot be paralleled in the entire history of the world. Slowly and consistently their ideals penetrated the very pith and marrow of Jewish national consciousness.

Out of Judaism came forth the religion that in a short time transformed barbarians into civilized beings, in fulfillment of the promise that the nations would walk in the

443

light of Israel. The period of Israel's homeless wandering began, however, at the very moment when the strength and fertility of the Jewish mind reached its culmination. *To think and to suffer* became now the watchword of the Jewish people. A thrilling drama of martyrdom is unrolled before our eyes.

If ever the time comes when the prophecies of the Jewish seers are fulfilled, and nation no longer raises the sword against nation, the history of the world will have the character of Jewish history. On its pages will be inscribed the progress of culture and its practical application in real life. Israel made its personality felt among the nations by its theory of life and its literature. The first half of Jewish history contains the account of Israel as a teacher of religion; the second half contains the account of Israel as a thinker and sufferer.

In the days of antiquity, the Jews were welded into a united nation by means of state and religion. Later, in the period of homelessness and dispersion, it was chiefly religious consciousness that cemented Jewry into a whole. In our days, the keystone of our national unity seems to be our historical consciousness. By the common memory of a great past, we Jews are bound to one another. Common sorrow unites men more closely than common joy. A long chain of historical traditions is cast about us all like a strong band.

Israel bestowed upon mankind a religious theory of life; Judah gave it a thrilling example of tenacity, vitality, and the power to resist for the sake of convictions. Zunz (1794–1886) writes: "If there are ranks in suffering, Israel takes precedence of all the nations. If the duration of sorrows and the patience with which they are borne ennoble, the Jews are among the aristocracy of every land. If a literature is called rich in the possession of a few classic tragedies, what shall we say to a national tragedy lasting for fifteen hundred years, in which the poets and the actors were also the heroes?" Perhaps Jewish history will have a considerable share in the spiritual change that is to uproot national intolerance, the modern substitute for the religious bigotry of the Middle Ages.

The Rabbinical Student

BY LOUIS GINZBERG

Louis Ginzberg (1873–1955) was professor of Talmud at the Jewish Theological Seminary of America for 47 years. He published a variety of works dealing with Midrash, Aggadah and liturgy. He is the author of the *Legends of the Jews* in seven volumes and a monumental commentary on the Palestinian Talmud.

His *Students, Scholars and Saints* is a collection of several lectures which Professor Ginzberg delivered at long intervals. This selection is a condensation of his lecture entitled *The Rabbinical Student,* which provides us with some insight into the cultural life of the Jew during the Middle Ages.

The title *People of the Book* characterizes the Jews in many ways. Primarily it indicates their devotion to the Bible, the most precious gift conferred upon mankind by Israel. But the Jews are the people of the book in general. The national heroes of Israel are not heroes of the sword but of the pen. Jewish history is essentially the history of a literature and of a culture.

The rabbi of centuries gone by was neither an official of the synagogue nor its minister. He was master over none but himself; he was servant to none but his God. In the good old times every Jew considered himself at home in the synagogue; every single member of the congregation was an eager participant in the worship service. There was no need of an orator, nor of a specialist who recites the prayers for the rest of the worshipers. In short, the rabbinate as a profession is of comparatively recent growth.

The first and highest communal duty was to provide for the broadest possible dissemination of a knowledge of Jewish literature among the members of the community.

Besides elementary schools, every Jewish community of size and standing had an intermediate school for the advanced study of Bible and Talmud. The principle underlying the study of the Talmud in Poland was not quantity but quality. Whatever was studied was searched out in every detail. The Yeshivah was more than a religious school; it was the institution for general Jewish education.

Errors are transmitted like diseases. The inaccurate rendering of the Hebrew word *Torah* by *law* has all along been a barrier, preventing certain theologians from understanding the ideal which is summed up in the term *Talmud Torah,* the study of the Torah. Torah is not law but Jewish teachings. It comprises every field of culture—morality, justice, education.

Student life began for the Jewish youth when, at the age of seventeen or eighteen, he left home and fared forth, defying hunger and cold, only to drink in the words of a far-famed master. He would wander about for half a year across ditches and mountains for the sake of a Talmudic explanation to be had from an Italian scholar. There were no entrance examinations, no graduating exercises. The schools made demands upon the students without conferring privileges.

The authority of our great teachers radiated from their personality. Life can be enkindled only by life; deeds produce deeds. That personal association with the scholar by far outweighs the effect of his teaching is a principle laid down in the Talmud. The disciple was admonished to observe the teacher as well as heed his instruction. The student observed the master from morning until midnight and was influenced by the daily conduct of his teacher no less than by his formal instruction. The intellectual enthusiasm of the rabbis communicated itself to all who associated with them.

Character and learning are dependent upon each other. Great thoughts do not spring from the head but from the heart. For the Jew, saint and scholar became almost identical concepts. Information may be useful, but knowledge is power—knowledge which permeates the whole man and has become a live and active force. Here, in part, lies the

446

explanation of the remarkable influence which our teachers of medieval days exerted upon their followers. Their knowledge was an integral part of their ego. They mastered it, and it mastered them; therefore they were able to exercise mastery over others. Their knowledge was invested with creative, vitalizing power; their views spread abroad and became the common property of the people as a whole.

The medieval rabbi preserved his independence not only from the congregation, but to a still greater extent, from the individual members composing the congregation. When he delivered an exhortation he could enjoy the pleasant feeling that he was bidding others do what he himself had already illustrated in deeds.

Hafetz Hayyim

BY RABBI ISRAEL MEIR HA-KOHEN

Rabbi Israel Meir Ha-Kohen (1838–1932) is best known by the title of one of his books—*Hafetz Hayyim* (desiring to live). This saintly talmudic author has been described as one of the prime guardians of the moral genius of the Jews in Poland and Russia during many decades. Throughout his long life he taught faith and kindliness by precept and example. What follows is based on *Saint and Sage* by Rabbi Moses M. Yoshor, and an essay by Rabbi Oscar Z. Fasman in *Israel of Tomorrow,* edited by Rabbi Leo Jung.

Those who listen to slanderous gossip are just as guilty as the talebearers. Repeated use of the evil tongue is like a silk thread made strong by hundreds of strands. The foul sin of talebearing often results in a chain of transgressions.

Leprosy was regarded as a punishment for slander, because the two resemble each other: they are both slightly

447

noticeable at the outset, and then develop into a chronic, infectious disease. Furthermore, the slanderer separates husband from wife, brother from brother, and friend from friend; he is therefore afflicted with the disease which separates him from society.

One sinful Jew can do harm to all his people, who are like a single body sensitive to the pain felt by any of its parts. When a group of people are sailing in a boat, none of them has a right to bore a hole under his own seat, for this may cause the sinking of all his companions.

All are equal before the majesty of justice: the weak and the strong, the poor and the rich, the native and the alien. If one of the parties in a lawsuit is poor and the other rich, judges must not favor the poor nor respect the rich. The judge must not say to himself: "This man is poor and must be provided for; I will render judgment in his favor, to enable him to make an honest living." On the other hand, he must not say: "This man is rich and highly respected—why cause him shame and degradation? I will clear him now, and then ask him privately to make good the claim of the poor party." The judge must pass judgment with utmost impartiality and unbiased justice.

The Torah warns us against the postponement of paying a workman's wage. One should never hire a man when he is certain that he cannot pay him on time. According to our sages, the one who withholds the wages of a hired worker violates several commands against cheating and robbing.

The Torah is the most sacred possession of the Jew. The parchment of the *Sefer Torah* is sanctified by what is written on it. How much more sanctified does a man become when his life-blood absorbs the living words of the Torah. Knowledge is the noblest human ideal. There is no joy loftier than an understanding of the principles of Judaism. The ultimate goal of every thoughtful Jew should be to attain a knowledge of the Torah.